THE ART OF
LINUX KERNEL DESIGN

Illustrating the Operating System Design Principle and Implementation

THE **ART** OF LINUX KERNEL DESIGN

Illustrating the Operating System Design Principle and Implementation

**Yang Lixiang • Liang Wenfeng
Chen Dazhao • Liu Tianhou,
Wu Ruobing • Song Qi • Feng Ke**

CRC Press
Taylor & Francis Group
Boca Raton London New York

CRC Press is an imprint of the
Taylor & Francis Group, an **informa** business

Contents

2. Device Initialization and Process 0 Activation 45

3. Creation and Execution of Process 1 85

5. File Operation   231

6. The User Process and Memory Management   283

7. Buffer and Multiprocess File   343

8. Inter-Process Communication   431

9. Operating System's Design Guidelines   481

Preface

During the past several years, we have worked very hard to develop a new operating system that could resist any intrusion attacks of illegal program from outside. We have established two testing sites to welcome all hackers around the world to give it a try. People can access the following website for intrusion testing:

ftp://203.198.128.163 or ftp://114.242.35.6

During the process of developing the new operating system, we realized that the importance of understanding the operating system as a whole is much greater than just focusing on details. The easiest way to understand the operating system is to look into a simple operating system instead of any modern complicated ones nowadays. It is the main reason that we have chosen Linux 0.11 (less than 20,000 lines of source code). After 20 years of development, compared with Linux 0.11, Linux has become very huge, complex, and difficult to learn. But the design concept and main structure have no fundamental changes. Learning Linux 0.11 still has important practical significances.

We have not only analyzed the detail of source code and the execution sequence of the operating system but also focused on the "jobs" the operating system has done, especially the relationship among them, their means, the reason that they are executed, and the design ideas that are hidden behind them. All of these have been analyzed in detail and in depth.

The book is divided into three sections to explain the Linux operating system: the first part (Chapters 1 to 4) analyzes the processes from booting the operating system to the operating system that has been initialized and enters into the idle state; the second part (Chapters 5 to 8) describes the actual operation process and status of the operating system and the user process during the execution of the user program after the idle state; the third part (Chapter 9) describes the entire Linux operating system design guidelines, from microscopic detail up to macroscopic architecture.

In the first section, we explain the powering up and booting BIOS in great detail, the BIOS loading the operating system, the initialization of the host, opening protected mode and paging, calling main function, creating process 0, process 1, process 2, and shell process, and the interactions with peripheral through the file system.

In the second part, we provided some simple but classical application programs and explained the mount file system in detail, file operations, user process and memory management, multiple processes operating files, and IPC among user processes with the background of the implementation of these procedures.

We try to integrate the principle of the operating system into the explanations of the actual operation process of a real operating system. We hope that after reading, the readers may find that the operating system is not a pure theory, or "the liberal arts" concept of computer theory, but systematic and has real, concrete, and actual code and case. Theory and practice are closely combined with each other.

The third section elaborates the "master-and-slave mechanisms" and three key technologies to achieve the mechanisms: protection and paging, privilege level, and interruption. It also analyzes the decisive factor to ensure master-and-slave mechanism—the initiative, furthermore, detailed explains the buffer, shared pages, signals, and pipeline design guidelines. We try to explain the operating system design guidelines from the perspective of the operating system designers. By using the system ideology, we hope to help readers understand and navigate the operating system itself and the design ideas hidden behind.

This book was translated by Dr. Tingshao Zhu, the professor of the Institute of Psychology, Chinese Academy of Sciences. Without his wisdom and hard work, it would have been impossible to bring this book to English readers.

I also want to thank Wen Lifang, who is the vice president of Huazhang Press, China Machine Press, and Yang Fuchuan, the deputy editor of Huazhang Press. They gave a full range of support to the Chinese version of the book. I especially thank Mr. He Ruijun, CRC Press, who handled the publishing to the English version and gave us great help. I would also like to thank Kari Budyk, CRC Press, and the help of Mr. Zhang Guoqiang and Miss Yang Jin.

Yang Lixiang
University of Chinese Academy of Sciences

Author

Lixiang Yang is an associate professor of the University of Chinese Academy of Sciences. His research interests include operating systems, compilers, and programming language. Recently, he and his team successfully developed a new operating system that aims to fundamentally solve the problem concerning the intrusion of illegal programs into computers. They set up two websites for hackers to perform the intrusion attack test. These addresses are ftp://203.198.128.163/ and ftp://114.242.35.6/. Furthermore, the contents in the ftp address, even the address itself will be changed based on the research and developing of our operating system.

1 From Power-Up to the Main Function

There are three steps from power-up to the main function, and they are designated to load the operating system (OS) from a boot disk and prepare for the main function. The first step is to load the BIOS (Basic Input/Output System), build the interrupt vector table, and start interrupt service routines in real address mode. The second step is to load the OS program from the boot disk into the memory using the interrupt service routines. The third step is to complete any other preparation to run the 32-bit main function. This chapter describes how these three steps work in the computer.

Tip:

The real address mode is designed to be compatible with Intel 80286 and 80x86. It has a 20-bit memory address space ($2^{20} = 1,048,576$, which is 1 MB memory to the maximum). It can directly access BIOS and peripheral devices, but it does not provide any hardware support for paging and real-time multitasking. From 80286, the 80x86 central processing unit (CPU) is powered on from the real address mode; earlier CPUs (e.g., 8086) have only one mode of operation, which is similar to the real address mode.

▮ 1.1 Loading BIOS, Constructing Interrupt Vector Table, and Activating Interrupt Service Routines in the Real Mode

As we know, we need to install an OS to operate a computer; otherwise, the computer is useless. People just press the power button to boot up the computer, but they mostly know very little about how the OS interacts with the hardware. Here, we will look into the whole process of running an OS in great detail.

It is impossible to operate a computer without any software. However, at the moment of power-up, the computer's memory (i.e., random access memory [RAM]) is empty, and the OS is on the floppy disk. Since the CPU can only run programs in memory, it cannot run an OS from a floppy disk directly. To run an OS, it should be loaded into the memory from a floppy disk first.

Tip:

RAM: The common memory of personal computers is a kind of RAM. After power-up, it can be read and written directly. But if powered off, the data will be lost.

The question is if the RAM is empty, who would load the OS?
The answer is BIOS.

1.1.1 Procedure for Starting BIOS

Before describing how BIOS loads the OS into memory, we should know the procedure for starting BIOS. As we know, to execute a program, we should double click it or enter the command in a command line interface, in case it actually runs on an existing OS. However, at the moment of powering up, no program is in the memory, not even the OS. Given that BIOS cannot be executed manually, who executes it then?

It is 0xFFFF0!!!

From the perspective of the system, it is quite clear that we cannot start BIOS by any software, but by hardware instead.

An Intel 80×86 series CPU can be worked in 16-bit real address mode and 32-bit protected mode. For the purpose of compatibility, the 80×86 CPU is in real address mode after power-up. The most important thing here is that the CPU forces CS to 0xFFFF and IP to 0x0000; hence, the address of CS:IP is 0xFFFF0, as depicted in Figure 1.1, in which we could find that 0xFFFF0 is actually the address of BIOS.

Tip:

IP/EIP: instruction pointer. In the CPU, IP stores the offset of instructions to be executed in the code segment. Working with CS, they make up the memory address of the instruction to be executed. IP is the offset in the real address mode, and EIP is the offset in the protected mode.

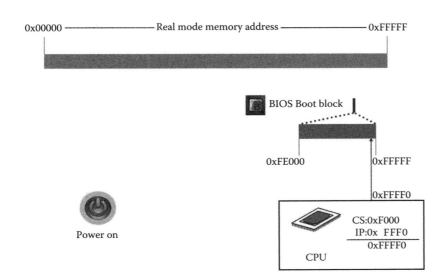

0x00000 ——————— Real mode memory address ——————— 0xFFFFF

BIOS Boot block

0xFE000   0xFFFFF

0xFFFF0

CS:0xF000
IP:0x FFF0
0xFFFF0

CPU

Power on

Figure 1.1 The BIOS state in the memory after power-up.

Tip:

CS: code segment register. In the CPU, it points to the code segment to be executed.

Attention: This action is completed by hardware completely! If there is nothing at 0xFFFF0, the computer crashes. Otherwise, the system will start and run on.

The entry address of the BIOS is 0xFFFF0! That is, the first instruction of BIOS is at this location.

1.1.2 BIOS Loads the Interrupt Vector Table and Interrupt Service Routines into Memory

BIOS is not very big. But to understand it thoroughly, you must be familiar with computer architecture, which is obviously beyond the topic of this book. Since we only focus on the OS here, we only explain the BIOS code that is directly related to the OS.

The BIOS code is stored in a small ROM (read-only memory) chip on the motherboard. Typically, different motherboards have different BIOS, but they follow a similar procedure. To make it easy to walk through, we choose BIOS, which is only 8 KB. The address is 0xFE000–0xFFFFF, as shown in Figure 1.1. The CS:IP points to 0xFFFF0, where BIOS starts. While starting BIOS, some information is printed on the screen, such as graphics, memory, and so on. During this period, the interrupt vectors table and interrupt service routines are built and executed, which are very important to boot the OS.

Tip:

ROM: it is usually made by flash memory now. Although flash memory chips can be written under specific conditions, when used by BIOS, it serves as ROM. ROM is able to keep information even if powered off, which is quite similar to the hard disk.

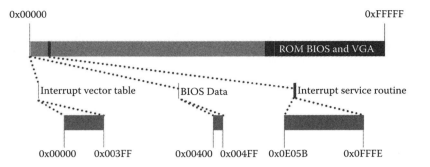

Figure 1.2 Loading the interrupt vector table and interrupt service routine.

The BIOS puts the interrupt vector table at the beginning of the memory, which is 1 KB (0x00000–0x003FF). The BIOS data area is next to it, 256 B (0x00400–0x004FF), and then the interrupt service routine (8 KB), 56 KB, comes after it (0x0E05B). Figure 1.2 shows the exact locations.

Tip:

Note that 0x00100 is 256 bytes and 0x00400 is 4 × 256 bytes = 1024 bytes, or 1 KB. Since it is from 0x00000, the high section of the 1 KB is not 0x00400 but 0x00400-1 instead, which is 0x003FF.

The interrupt vector table has 256 interrupt vectors and 4 bytes for each vector, including 2 bytes for CS and 2 bytes for IP. Each interrupt vector points to a particular interrupt service routine.

We will explain in detail how to use these interrupt service routines to load OS kernel into the memory.

Tip:

INT: interrupt. As its name suggests, INT refers to an interrupt of an ongoing process. An external event interrupts the program that is being executed, to run a specific procedure to handle this event. After the INT procedure is done, the interrupted program will continue. Interrupts are quite similar to the function call in C.

Interrupt means a lot to the OS; we will discuss it further later on.

▌▌ 1.2 Loading the OS Kernel and Preparing for the Protected Mode

From now on, the computer will perform the actual boot operation, loading the OS from the floppy disk to the memory. For Linux 0.11, it tries to load three parts of the OS kernel into the memory step by step. First, BIOS INT 0x 19h loads the first sector Bootsect into the memory. Then, Bootsect loads the second and the third parts into the memory, which are 4 sectors and 240 sectors, respectively.

1.2.1 Loading Bootsect

According to our experience, if you press the Del key immediately after power-up, the computer will display a BIOS screen, which allows you to change the configuration of the boot device. Nowadays, we usually set the hard disk as a boot disk. For Linux 0.11, which was released in 1991, the boot device is a floppy disk. But it does not matter, since booting from either a floppy disk or a hard disk is almost the same.

After running BIOS, the computer finishes self-check (these operations have no direct relationship with starting the OS; thus, we just ignore them). By BIOS, the CPU receives INT 19h and then looks up the INT 19h interrupted vector. We can find the exact location of the INT 19h interrupt vector in Figure 1.3, which is next to 0x00000.

CS:IP points to 0x0E6F2, which is the entry address of the interrupt service program of INT 19h, as shown in Figure 1.3. This interrupt program is designed to load the first sector (512 B) into the memory, regardless of the version of Linux. No matter what the Linux kernel is, the BIOS program just loads the first sector into the memory, nothing else.

Tip:

The interrupt vector table is an important part of the real address mode interrupt mechanism, as it stores the memory address of the interrupt service routine.

Interrupt service routines are indexed by the interrupt vector table that responds to the interrupt, and these routines are special codes with a designated purpose.

According to the "stiff" rule, the interrupt service routine of INT 0x 19h loads the contents of floppy disk No. 0, track 0 of 1 sector into memory at 0x07C00. We can identify the exact location of the first sector on the left in Figure 1.4.

This sector is the boot part of Linux 0.11, that is, the Bootsect, which loads other parts of the OS into the memory. After the first sector loaded, Linux 0.11 is about to be ready to serve as an OS.

This action is very important, since the computer and the OS are linked together from now on. The first sector is bootsect.s (later referred to as Bootsect), which is written in

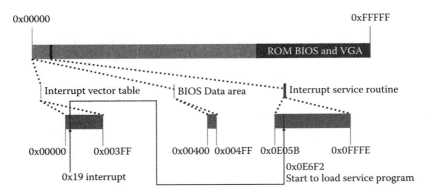

Figure 1.3 Run int 0x 19h.

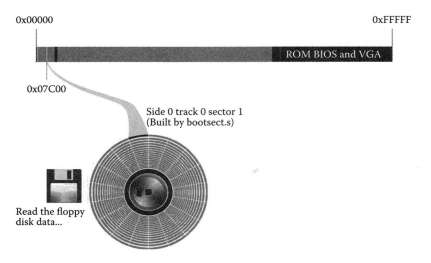

0x00000   0xFFFFF

ROM BIOS and VGA

0x07C00

Side 0 track 0 sector 1
(Built by bootsect.s)

Read the floppy
disk data...

Figure 1.4 Load the program from the first sector to the memory.

assembly language. It is the first system code that was loaded into the memory, although only for booting.

At this stage, Bootsect has been loaded from a floppy disk into the memory, and it then loads the second and third sectors into the memory consequently.

Comment

Note: All BIOSs are stored in the ROM on the mainboard, and they are quite different. The main reason for this is the mainboard; OS has nothing to do with it.

Theoretically, one can install any suitable OS, either Windows or Linux on a computer. It is obvious that each OS has its own boot scheme. The BIOS and the OS are quite different. In order to work together smoothly, they must establish a coordination mechanism to communicate and cooperate.

It is possible to set up a coordination mechanism with an existing OS. The difficulty is in setting up coordination mechanisms compatible with any future OS. The proposed approaches are "two side conventions" and "orientation recognition."

To the OS (Linux 0.11), "conventions" means that the OS designers have to put the starting program in the boot sector (0 side 0, track 1 in the floppy disk sectors); the remaining program can be loaded into memory in order.

To the BIOS, "conventions" means loading the boot sector into 0x07C00, regardless of what this sector really does. If there is an error, it only reports the mistake and does nothing.

The coordination mechanism must be useful, simple, and effective. As long as the manufacturers of the BIOS and OS follow the same mechanisms, they can build systems with their own features.

1.2.2 Loading the Second Part of Code— —Setup

1. Bootsect memory planning

Now, BIOS has loaded Bootsect into the memory. Then, it loads the second and third sectors into the memory. But first of all, the Bootsect would do some memory planning.

In general, we use a high-level language, such as C, to write programs and run these programs on an OS. We just write the code and do not care about its location in the memory. It is because the OS and the compiler have done a great deal of ensuring that it works correctly. Since we are now focusing on the OS itself, we have to better understand the memory arrangement to ensure that no matter how the OS runs, there are no collisions between code and code, between data and data, and between code and data. To do so, we would like to discuss the memory planning of the OS.

In the real address mode, the maximum memory is 1 MB. To arrange the memory, Bootsect has the following code first:

```
SETUPLEN = 4                   ! nr of setup-sectors
BOOTSEG = 0x07c0               ! original address of boot-sector
INITSEG = 0x9000               ! we move boot here - out of the way
SETUPSEG = 0x9020              ! setup starts here
SYSSEG = 0x1000                ! system loaded at 0x10000 (65536).
ENDSEG = SYSSEG + SYSSIZE      ! where to stop loading
```

The code is to set the location of the following variables: the number of setup program sectors (SETUPLEN), the address of the setup (SETUPSEG), the address

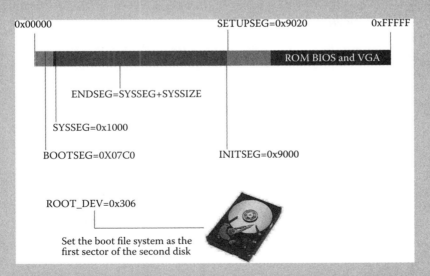

Figure 1.5 Memory arrangement in the real mode.

of Bootsect (BOOTSEG), the new address of Bootsect (INITSEG), the address of the kernel (SYSSEG), the end address of the kernel (SYSEND), and the number of the root file system device (ROOT_DEV). These are shown in Figure 1.5. These addresses are used to make sure that the code and data could be loaded into the correct place. We will find the benefit of memory planning in the following sections.

From now on, we should keep in mind that OS memory planning is very important. With this concept, let us continue to talk about the execution of Bootsect.

2. Copy the Bootsect

Bootsect copies itself (total 512 B) from 0x07C00 to 0x90000, as shown in Figure 1.6. The operation code is as follows:

```
mov      ax,#BOOTSEG
mov      ds,ax
mov      ax,#INITSEG
mov      es,ax
mov      cx,#256
sub      si,si
sub      di,di
rep
movw
```

Please note that DS (0x07C0) and SI (0x0000) constitute the source address 0x07C00; ES and DI constitute the target address 0x90000 (see Figure 1.6), and the line mov CX,#256 provides a "word" number (a word is 2 bytes); 256 words is just 512 bytes, which is the byte number of the first sector.

Also, from the code, we can see that the BOOTSEG and INITSEG mentioned in Figure 1.5 start to work. Note that CS points to 0x07C0 now, which is the address of the original Bootsect.

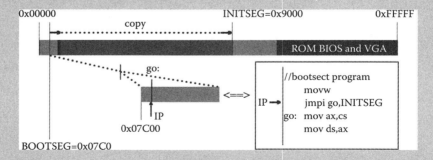

Figure 1.6 Bootsect copies itself.

Because of the "two side conventions" and "orientation recognition," Bootsect is "forced" to load into 0x07C00. Now, it moves itself to 0x90000, which means that the OS starts to arrange memory to meet its own requirements.

After being copied to the new address, Bootsect executes the following:

```
        rep
        movw
        jmpi    go,INITSEG
go:     mov     ax,cs
        mov     ds,ax
```

We already know in Figure 1.6 that the original value of CS is 0x07C0; after executing these codes, CS becomes 0x9000 (INITSEG), and IP is the offset from 0x9000 to "*go:mov* AX,CS *0x9000*." In other words, CS:IP now points to "*go:mov* AX,CS." We can learn it clearly from Figure 1.7.

The previous 0x07C00 was built by "two side conventions" and "orientation recognition." From now on, the OS becomes independent of BIOS, and it can put its own code anywhere.

```
        jmpi    go, INITSEG
go:     mov     ax,cs
```

These two lines of codes are very tricky. After Bootsect copies itself, the contents in 0x07C00 and 0x90000 are the same. Please note that before "*jmpi go, INITSEG*," CS is 0x07C0. After that, CS becomes 0x9000. Then, it executes the next line, "*mov ax,cs*." It is a good way to "jump and continue performing the same codes."

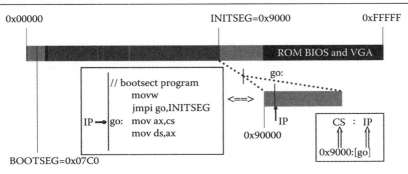

Figure 1.7 Jump to "go" and continue.

After Bootsect copied itself to a new place, and continued to execute, the segment was changed, and then other segments changed accordingly, including DS, ES, SS, and SP. Let us look into the following lines:

```
go:     mov     ax,cs
        mov     ds,ax
        mov     es,ax
! put stack at 0x9ff00.
        mov     ss,ax
        mov     sp,#0xFF00                ! arbitrary value >>512
! load the setup-sectors directly after the bootblock.
! Note that 'es' is already set up.
```

The above lines are to set the data segment registers (DS), additional segment registers (ES), and stack base address registers (SS) into the same value as the code segment register (CS) and set SP to point 0xFF00, as shown in Figure 1.8.

Now, let us focus on the register settings that relate to stack operation. SS and SP constitute the location of stack data in the memory. Setting the value of these two registers is the foundation of stack operations (e.g., push and pop).

Now, we switch to Bootsect. Before setting SS and SP, there is no stack; after that, the stack is available for operation. It is great significance to set SS and SP, which means that OS could execute more complex instructions then.

Each stack operation has a direction, and the direction of push is depicted in Figure 1.8. Note: that is the direction from high to low address.

Tip:

DS/ES/FS/GS/SS: data segment registers in CPU. SS points to the stack segment, which is managed by the stack mechanism.

SP: stack pointer, points to the current top of the stack segment.

Now, the first operation of Bootsect has arranged the memory and copied itself from 0x07C00 to 0x90000.

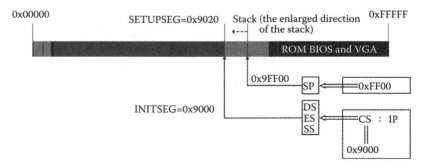

Figure 1.8 Set the value of the segment register.

3. Load the Setup program into memory

Next, Bootsect will execute the second step, to load the setup program into the memory.

Loading the setup program relies on the INT 0x 13h interrupt vector, which refers to the interrupt service routine in BIOS. Figure 1.9 shows the location of the INT 0x 13h interrupt vector and the entry address of the service routine.

The loading service handler pointed by the INT 0x 19h interrupt vector is executed by BIOS, while the INT 0x 13h interrupt service program is executed by Bootsect, which is part of the OS.

The INT 0x 19h interrupt service routine loads the first sector of the floppy disk to 0x7C00, while INT 0x 13h loads the sector to the specific location of memory. Actually, it can load the sector to any designated location.

According to this feature of the service routine, it passes the sector and memory position to the service routine when calling INT 0x 13h.

```
//code path:boot/bootsect.s
Load_setup:
        Mov dx, #0x0000
        Mov cx, #0x0002
        Mov bx, #0x0200
        Mov ax, #0x0200+SETUPLEN
        Int 0x13
        Jnc load_setup
        Ok_load_setup:
```

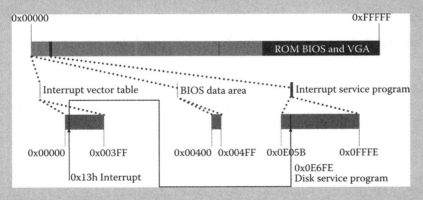

Figure 1.9 Call INT 0x 13h interrupt.

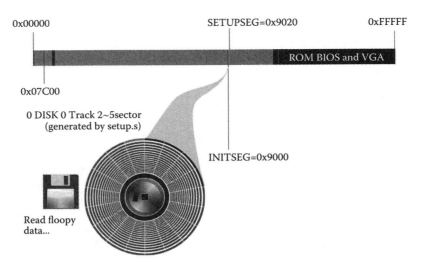

Figure 1.10 Load the setup program.

We can see from the four mov operators that the system passes parameters to the BIOS interrupt service routine by using several general-purpose registers. This is commonly used by the assembly program, which differs from C.

After passing the parameters, BIOS executes INT 0x13, to fire 0x13 interrupt and look up the interrupt service routine in the interrupt vector table. Then, it loads setup.s to SETUPSEG. According to Figure 1.5, Bootsect starts from 0x90000 with a size of 512 bytes. Obviously, 0x90200 is next to the end of Bootsect; thus, they combine each other. Figure 1.10 indicates the locations of sectors, the number of sectors, address, and length, which will be loaded from the floppy disk.

Now, the OS has loaded five sectors from the floppy disk. *Setup* begins to work after the execution of Bootsect.

The address of SS:PP is 0x9FF00. There is abundant space between 0x90200 and the setup program. The system has enough space to execute any operation (e.g., push) after loading setup. During startup, the data pushed are countable, and we will find out that the OS designer has calculated the space precisely.

1.2.3 Load the System Module

The second part of codes has loaded into the memory, followed by the third part. We call the INT 0x 13h interrupt to load the code, as shown in Figure 1.11.

Next, Bootsect will load the system module into the memory. There is no significant difference between this procedure and previous ones. The only difference is that the number of sectors is 240, which is 60 times greater than previous ones and a bit time-consuming. In order to prohibit any improper operation by the user while waiting, Linux printed out a message, "Loading system…," to indicate that the computer is still working. Since the main function of the OS has not started, it is much more difficult than C to do so, as all should be done by the assembly code. From an architectural perspective, the monitor is also a peripheral device, and it can be operated by calling BIOS interrupt. But

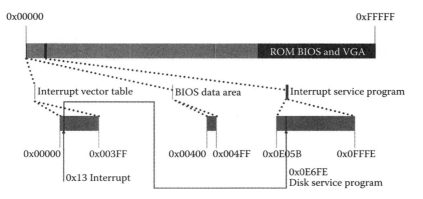

Figure 1.11 Call INT 0x 13h interrupt.

since they are not particularly helpful for us to understand the OS, we will not discuss this further. We should know that Bootsect loads 240 sectors of the system module into the memory after INT 0x 13h. The main function is done by loading the 240 sectors into SYSSEG(0X10000). Figure 1.12 shows the memory space that is occupied by the system module.

Because reading a floppy disk is very time-consuming, it is necessary to monitor the whole process and check the results. Reading consists of many steps, and it can be done by 0x13h interrupt service in the end.

Now, the OS has been loaded into the memory as a whole. Bootsect has almost done all its work except inspecting the root device number, as shown in Figure 1.13.

After inspecting, the root device number is saved in root_dev, which is part of system data.

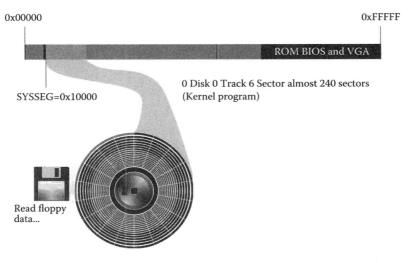

Figure 1.12 Load the system module.

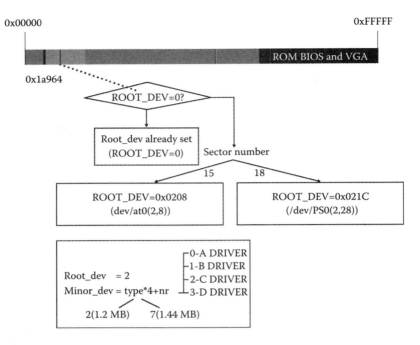

Figure 1.13 Confirm the root device number.

Tip:

Root Device: Linux 0.11 used the file system management which was used by Minix, which requires that the system must have a root file system. Linux 0.11 does not provide tools to build a file system on a device, so it creates a file system and then loads to the machine using tools like FDISK and Format. Linux 0.11 has a system kernel image and root file system.

Here, the file system does not refer to the traditional file system in the OS but the device, for example, a formatted floppy disk.

Now, Bootsect has done all its tasks.

The execution of "*jmpi 0, SETUPSEG*" will jump to 0x90200, which is the location of setup, while CS:IP points to the first instruction of setup. It means that the setup program will do the work after Bootsect. Figure 1.14 describes the initial state right after jumping to the setup program.

```
//code path:boot/bootsect.s
Jmpi 0, SETUPSEG
```

Setup begins to work. The first task is to extract the system data by calling the interrupt service. It will also get the hard disk parameter table 1 and hard disk parameter table 2 from the memory, which is pointed by the 0x41 and 0x46 vectors, and then save them in 0x9000:0x0080 and 0x9000:0x0090.

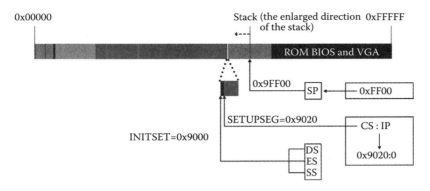

Figure 1.14 Setup begins to execute.

The system data are loaded into 0x90000–0x901FC. Figure 1.15 shows its content and position precisely, and they play an important role in the main function.

```
//code path:boot/setup.s
Mov ax, #INITSEG
Mov ds, ax
Mov ah, #0x03
Xor bh, bh
Int 0x10
Mov [0], dx
! Get memory size (extended mem, KB)
    Mov ah, #0x88
    Int 0x15
        Mov [2], ax
```

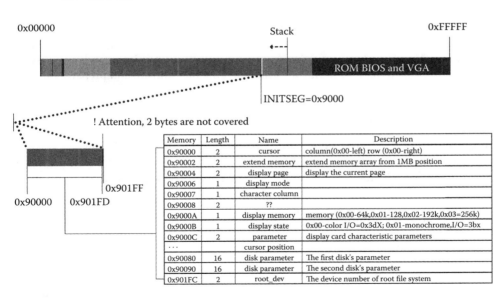

Memory	Length	Name	Description
0x90000	2	cursor	column(0x00-left) row (0x00-right)
0x90002	2	extend memory	extend memory array from 1MB position
0x90004	2	display page	display the current page
0x90006	1	display mode	
0x90007	1	character column	
0x90008	2	??	
0x9000A	1	display memory	memory (0x00-64k,0x01-128,0x02-192k,0x03=256k)
0x9000B	1	display state	0x00-color I/O=0x3dX; 0x01-monochrome,I/O=3bx
0x9000C	2	parameter	display card characteristic parameters
. . .		cursor position	
0x90080	16	disk parameter	The first disk's parameter
0x90090	16	disk parameter	The second disk's parameter
0x901FC	2	root_dev	The device number of root file system

Figure 1.15 Load the machine system data.

```
...
...
Mov cx, #ox10
Mov ax,#0x00
Rep
stosb
```

The system data extracted by BIOS will cover part of Bootsect, and some data cannot be covered since they are still being used.

Review

The system data takes up memory space from 0x90000 to 0x901FD, which is 510 bytes in total. The Bootsect only has 2 bytes left. The OS is strict to using memory, and it uses memory according to its need. The loaded data just take up one sector, and the size of Bootsect is also one sector. The released memory will be used by other routines immediately. After Bootsect has completed its task, the setup puts its data to cover the exact space, and the efficiency of memory usage is very high.

Now, the core part of the OS has been loaded completely. Then, the system will transfer from the real address mode to the protected mode.

∎ 1.3 Transfer to 32-bit Mode and Prepare for the Main Function

The OS will then run in the 32-bit protected mode, in which it completes much reconstruction and continues to prepare for executing the main processes. In this section, the OS executes many operations, including enabling the 32-bit addressing control, opening the protected mode, establishing the interrupt response mechanism, conducting issues about the protected mode, building a memory paging mechanism, and preparing for the main function.

1.3.1 Disable Interrupts and Move System to 0x00000

As shown in Figure 1.16, the preparation will disable the interrupts. It means that no matter what happens, the system will not respond until the interrupt service in the protected mode is enabled. The interrupt service is no longer the service provided by BIOS but by the OS.

```
//code path:boot/setup.s
cli
```

Tip:

EFLAGS is stored in the CPU, including state flags, control flags, and system flags.

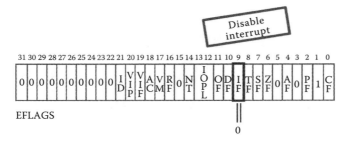

Figure 1.16 Disable interrupt.

Review

The operation of cli and sti frequently appears in the OS. It is easy to find that cli and sti always emerge on the two sides of the operation process in order to disable interrupt during a process. Then, the system will enter the protect mode, and the interrupt vector table in the protect mode takes over the IDT in the real mode.

Next, setup completes a very important operation: copying the core program from the 0x10000 to the 0x00000 position (Figure 1.17).

```
//code path:boot/setup.s
Do_move:
Mov es, ax
Add ax, #0x1000
Cmp ax, #0x9000
Jz end_move
Mov ds, ax
Sub di, di
Sub si, si
Mov cx, #0x8000
Rep
Movsw
Jmp do_move
```

If we look into the content of Figure 1.2, 0x00000 originally stores the interrupt vector table and BIOS data. Copying will cover the interrupt vector table and BIOS data completely. The OS will not have the ability to deal with the interrupt, and this is the real meaning of disabling interrupt.

Tip:

There are several benefits to doing this:

1. Covering BIOS interrupt vector table means disabling the interrupt service provided by BIOS in the real address mode.
2. Collecting the memory space that is used by the program.
3. Putting the core modules at the beginning and at the most advantageous position of physical memory.

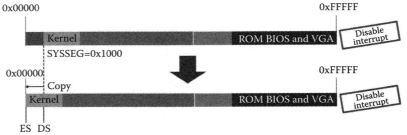

*DS and ES coordinate for the completion of the copy operation of kernel

Figure 1.17 Copy the system module to the beginning of memory.

After the system module is copied to 0x00000, this operation covers the interrupt vector table of BIOS, that is, the abolition of the 16-bit interrupt mechanism. The OS cannot run without interruption, since the peripheral devices, system calls, and process scheduling depends on the interrupt. Linux is a 32-bit OS; thus, the 16-bit interrupt mechanism is obviously not appropriate, which is the main reason for the abolition of the 16-bit interrupt mechanism. Hence, it makes use of the 32-bit interrupt mechanism instead.

1.3.2 Set the Interrupt Descriptor Table and Global Descriptor Table

The setup routine continues to prepare for the protected mode and set the initial value of IDTR and GDTR.

Tip:

GDT: It is the only array that stores segment register values in the system and cooperates with the program during the protected mode. It also plays an important role while switching OSs. It can be regarded as the total list of all processes, storing every task LDT (local descriptor table) address and TSS (task structure segment) address to complete segment addressing, site protection, and recovery.

GDTR: GDT can be stored at any position in the memory. A program needs the entrance of GDT when using the segment descriptor through the segment register. It can use the LGDT (load GDT) operator to load the GDT base address into GDTR after the initialization of GDT.

IDT: The entrance of all interrupt services in the protected mode.

IDTR: The IDT register stores the beginning address of IDT.

```
//code path:boot/setup.s
    Lidt idt_48
    Lgdt gdt_48
Gdt :
.word 0, 0, 0, 0
.word 0x07FF
.word 0x0000
.word 0x9A00
.word 0x00C0
.word 0x07FF
```

```
.word 0x0000
.word 0x9200
.word 0x00C0
Igt_48 :
    .word 0
    .word 0, 0
Gdt_48 :
    .word 0X800
    .word 512+gdt, 0x9
```

Tip:

The 32-bit interrupt mechanism differs from the 16-bit interrupt mechanism in principle. The most significant difference is that the 16-bit interrupt mechanism uses the interrupt vector table, while the 32-bit interrupt mechanism uses the interrupt descriptor table. The beginning position of the interrupt vector table is 0x00000 and fixed all the time, while the beginning position of the interrupt descriptor table is not fixed, and it can be changed accordingly.

The GDT table is a data structure that manages the segment descriptor in the protected mode. It is important to the OS and for process scheduling.

Now, the kernel does not really run, and there is no process either. Thus, the first item of the GDT table is empty, the second is the kernel code segment descriptor, the third is the kernel data segment descriptor, while others are null.

Although the IDT table has been set, it is empty because of the cli.

The whole procedure of creating the two tables can be divided into two steps:

1. The two tables and the data have been hard-coded when implementing the kernel.
2. IDTR and GDTR tables.

The data are set and compiled in the kernel code and load into the memory while running. The register is operated by the lidt and lgdt operator in the program, as shown in Figure 1.18.

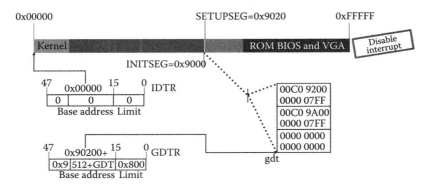

Figure 1.18 Set GDTR and IDTR.

There are two methods to put data in memory:

1. Allocate a memory district and initialize it by the data.
2. The code generates data, such as push into the stack.

1.3.3 Open A20 and Achieve 32-bit Addressing

The next action is to open A20 (Figure 1.19).

Opening A20 means that the CPU can be 32-bit addressing, and the maximum addressable space is 4 GB.

Linux can only support 16 MB of physical memory, but the linear address space is already 4 GB.

```
//code path:boot/setup.s
Call empty_8042
Mov al, #0xD1
Out #0x64, al
Call empty_8042
Mov al, #0xDF
Out #0x60, al
Call empty_8042
```

Tip:

A CPU has 1 MB space ranging from 0 to 0xfffff and needs 20 address lines in the real mode. A CPU will use the 32-bit address in the real mode.

Addressing in memory after opening A20

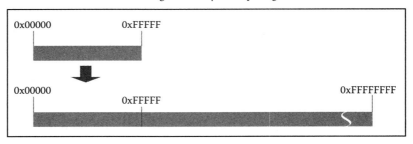

Addressing in physical memory after opening A20

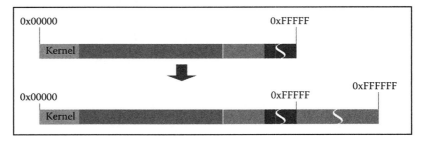

Figure 1.19 Open A20.

In the real address mode, if the program address is more than 0xFFFFF, the CPU will roll back to the beginning of the memory for addressing. For example, every segment register cannot exceed 0xFFFF, the same as IP. They both can address to 0x10FFFE at the most, which means that the program can address more than 0xFFFFF in the real address mode. Because of this, enabling the A20 address line means disabling the "rollback" addressing mechanism of the CPU in the real mode.

1.3.4 Prepare for the Implementation of head.s in the Protected Mode

To establish the interrupt mechanism, setup.s will have to reprogram the PIC 8259A (Figure 1.20).

Tip:

8259A: 8259A is a chip designed for 8085A and 8086/8088 to control interrupt. One piece of 8259A can manage eight priority interrupt levels. 8259A can cascade to a system that can manage up to 64 priority interrupt levels in the case of no circuit adding.

Codes as follows:

```
mov     $0x11,%al         # initialization sequence(ICW1)
                          #ICW4needed(1),CASCADEmode,Level-triggered
out     %al, $0x20        # send it to 8259A-1
.word   0x00eb,0x00eb     # jmp $+2, jmp $+2
out     %al, $0xA0        # and to 8259A-2
.word   0x00eb,0x00eb
```

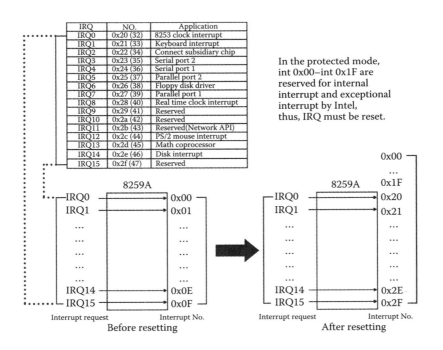

IRQ	NO.	Application
IRQ0	0x20 (32)	8253 clock interrupt
IRQ1	0x21 (33)	Keyboard interrupt
IRQ2	0x22 (34)	Connect subsidiary chip
IRQ3	0x23 (35)	Serial port 2
IRQ4	0x24 (36)	Serial port 1
IRQ5	0x25 (37)	Parallel port 2
IRQ6	0x26 (38)	Floppy disk driver
IRQ7	0x27 (39)	Parallel port 1
IRQ8	0x28 (40)	Real time clock interrupt
IRQ9	0x29 (41)	Reserved
IRQ10	0x2a (42)	Reserved
IRQ11	0x2b (43)	Reserved(Network API)
IRQ12	0x2c (44)	PS/2 mouse interrupt
IRQ13	0x2d (45)	Math coprocessor
IRQ14	0x2e (46)	Disk interrupt
IRQ15	0x2f (47)	Reserved

In the protected mode, int 0x00–int 0x1F are reserved for internal interrupt and exceptional interrupt by Intel, thus, IRQ must be reset.

Figure 1.20 Resetting 8259A.

```
mov     $0x20,%al               # start of hardware int's (0x20)(ICW2)
out     %al, $0x21              # from 0x20-0x27
.word   0x00eb,0x00eb
mov     $0x28,%al               # start of hardware int's 2 (0x28)
out     %al, $0xA1              # from 0x28-0x2F
.word   0x00eb,0x00eb           #      IR 7654 3210
mov     $0x04,%al               # 8259-1 is master(0000 0100)─  \
out     %al, $0x21              #                               |
.word   0x00eb,0x00eb           #                      INT      /
mov     $0x02,%al               # 8259-2 is slave( 010─  > 2)
out     %al, $0xA1
.word   0x00eb,0x00eb
mov     $0x01,%al               # 8086 mode for both
out     %al, $0x21
.word   0x00eb,0x00eb
out     %al, $0xA1
.word   0x00eb,0x00eb
mov     $0xFF,%al               # mask off all interrupts for now
out     %al, $0x21
.word   0x00eb,0x00eb
out     %al, $0xA1
```

In the protected mode, INT 0x00–int 0x1F is reserved for internal and exception interrupt by Intel. If we do not reprogram 8259A, INT 0x00–int 0x1F will be overlapped. For example, IRQ0 (timer interrupt) is the eighth interrupt (INT 0x08), but this interrupt is reserved as "Double Fault" in the protected mode. Hence, we must reprogram 8259A to respond to IQR0x00–IQX0x0F; in other words, IQR0x00–IQR0x0F corresponds with INT 0x20–int 0x2F in the protected mode (Figure 1.21).

Setup.s enables the CPU in the protected mode by the first two lines as follows, setting the PE bit of the CR0 Register.

```
//code path:boot/setup.s
mov ax,#0x0001 ! protected mode (PE) bit
lmsw ax ! This is it! !
jmpi 0,8 ! jmp offset 0 of segment 8 (cs) !
```

Tip:

CR0 Register: No. 0 32-bit control register is used to store systemic control flags. No. 0 bit is PE (protected mode enable) flag. If set, the CPU will work in the protected mode; otherwise, in the real mode.

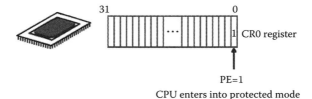

Figure 1.21 Open the protected mode.

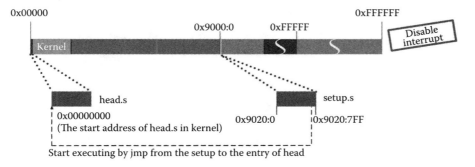

Figure 1.22 Jump from setup.s to head.s.

The key character of the CPU in the protected mode is that it executes a program according to GDT.

Note that the value of GDT in Figure 1.18 is the default setting. The way from setup.s to head.s is described in Figure 1.22.

In this code, "0" is offset address and "8" is segment selector, which is used to select GDT (global descriptor table), the No. of GDT, and the descriptor privilege level. Here, "8" should be "1000" in binary. To understand this code, we should refer to Figure 1.23 and know that every bit of "1000" has a designated purpose.

The last two bits of "1000" means kernel privilege level, in which "11" means user privilege level. No. 3 bit of "1000" means selecting GDT; accordingly, "1" means LDT. No. 4 bit of "1000" means No. 1 of GDT. We know that the CPU executes the program where the segment base address is 0x00000000 and the offset address is 0, which is the starting location of head.s, and which means the CPU will execute head.s.

Setup.s finishes here, and the following preparation will be done by head.s.

1.3.5 CPU Starts to Execute head.s

Before introducing head.s, let us look into the whole process from Bootsect to main.

Before executing main, the CPU must execute three routines: bootsect.s, setup.s, and head.s.

First, bootsect.s is loaded to 0x07C00, which will then be copied to 0x90000. Second, setup.s is loaded to 0x90200. They both are loaded and executed, respectively, but head.s is different.

The main process is described as follows. First, head.s should be compiled into object code and then linked into the system module. That means that the system module has both kernel program and head.s. It is important that head.s is loaded before the kernel. The size of head.s is 25 KB + 184 B in memory. As mentioned above, setup.s copies the system module to 0x00000; because head.s is loaded in front of the kernel in the system module, 0x00000 is the start address of head.s as shown in Figure 1.24.

In addition to the preparation for main, head.s manages the layout of the kernel program in memory and the normal operation of kernel program by creating the kernel paging system in the memory space of head.s. That means that head.s creates the page table directory, page table, buffer, GDT, and IDT at 0x00000 in memory where head.s will be covered.

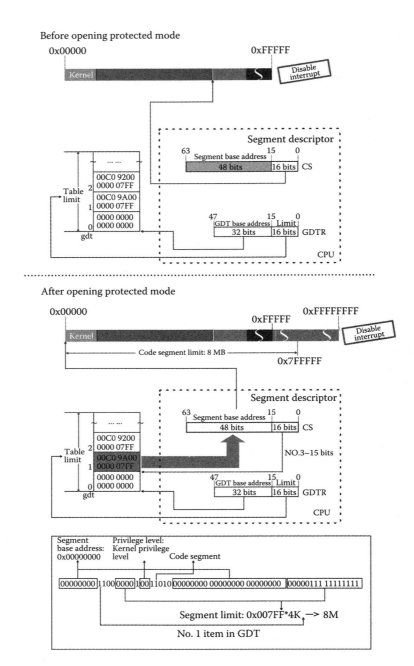

Figure 1.23 Addressing in different modes.

Figure 1.24 The address of the system in memory.

The main procedure of head.s has been described briefly, and we will look into head.s in detail below.

Before introducing head.s, let us take a look at a marknumber: _pg_dir.

```
//code path:boot/head.s
_pg_dir:
startup_32:
movl $0x10,%eax
mov%ax,%ds
mov%ax,%es
mov%ax,%fs
mov%ax,%gs
```

_pg_dir is used to mark the starting address of the kernel after the kernel paging system has been established. The starting address is 0x00000. Head.s will create the page table directory here to prepare for the kernel paging system, as described in Figure 1.25.

Now, head.s starts working. In the real address mode, CS is the segment base address but the segment selector in the protected mode. jmpi 0,8 attaches CS to No. 1 item of GDT, which means the code segment base address is 0x00000000.

From now on, DS, ES, FS, and GS will work in the protected mode (Figure 1.26).

After executing, the values of DS, ES, FS, and GS are all 0x10 (in binary, "00010000"). The last two bits of "00010000" means kernel privilege level; accordingly, "11" means user privilege level. The No. 3 bit of "00010000" means selecting GDT; accordingly, "1" means LDT. The No. 4 and No. 5 bit of "00010000" mean selecting the No. 2 item of GDT, that is, the third item of GDT. DS, ES, FS, and GS all use the same global descriptor. It should be noted that the segment limit is 0x07ff, which means that the limit of the segment is 8M.

Specific settings are similar to Figure 1.23. They both refer to GDT. In *movl $0x10,%eax*, 0x10 is the offset value in GDT, which means the CPU uses the No. 2 item of GDT to set the segment, and it is the kernel data segment descriptor.

SS is changed to stack segment selector now, SP becomes 32-bit esp, as the following describes.

```
Lss _stack_start,%esp
```

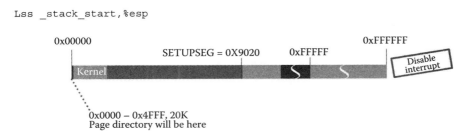

Figure 1.25 Prepare for the kernel paging system.

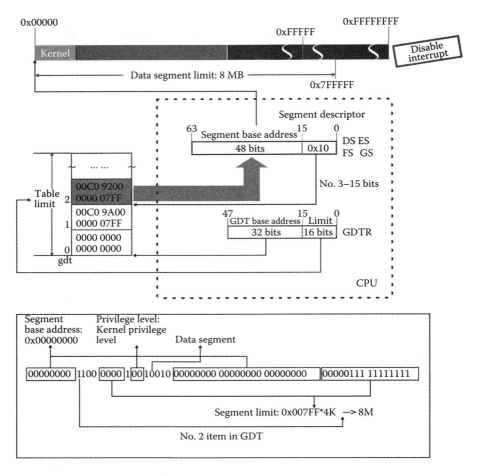

Figure 1.26 Set DS, ES, FS, and GS.

In kernel/sched.c, stack_start = {&user_stack[PAGE_SIZE>>2],0x10}; this code makes SP point to the last position of the user_stack data structure. This structure is defined in kernel/sched.c as the following:

```
long user_stack [PAGE_SIZE>>2]
```

We find that the start address of this structure is 0x1E25C.

Tip:

Load segment instruction: the function of this instruction is to load a "low word" in the memory to the 16-bit segment specified by this instruction and then load a "high word" to the corresponding segment (DS, ES, FS, or GS). The form of this instruction looks like the following:

```
LDS/LES/LFS/LGS/LSS Reg, Mem
```

LDS (load data segment register) and LES (load extra segment register) are subsistent in an 8086 CPU, but LFS, LGS, or LSS does not appear until 80386. If Reg is a 16-bit register, Mem must be a 32-bit pointer. If Reg is a 32-bit register, Mem must be a 48-bit pointer; the low 32 bits are loaded to the 32-bit register, while the high 16 bits are loaded to the segment register in this instruction.

The CPU sets SS with the value 0x10, which is the same value as the four-segment register selector mentioned above. Thus, for SS, the segment base address is 0x000000, and the segment limit is 8M in kernel privilege level.

Please note that the segment base address in the real mode is very different from that in the protected mode. In the protected mode, the segment base address is generated by GDT. These instructions setting the segment selector can be located by GDT. Now, we know that if setup.s does not create GDT in the real mode, these instructions cannot be executed.

Note that SP increases from a high address to a low address in memory, as shown in Figure 1.27.

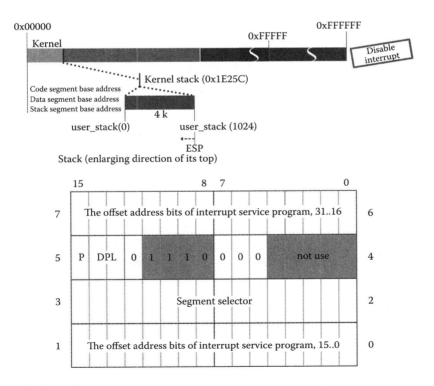

Figure 1.27 Set stack.

In Figure 1.8, when setting the stack pointer register, we set sp, but here we set esp instead to adapt to the protected mode. The code is as follows.

```
//code path:Boot/head.s
Lss _stack_start,%esp
```

The following codes are used to set IDT:

```
//code path:boot/head.s
Call setup_idt
......
setup_idt:
lea ignore_int,%edx
movl $0x00080000,%eax
movw%dx,%ax/* selector = 0x0008 = cs */
movw $0x8E00,%dx/* interrupt gate - dpl = 0, present */
lea _idt,%edi
mov $256,%ecx
rp_sidt:
movl%eax,(%edi)
movl%edx,4(%edi)
addl $8,%edi
dec%ecx
jne rp_sidt
lidt idt_descr
ret
```

Tip:

The structure of the interrupt descriptor is introduced as follows.

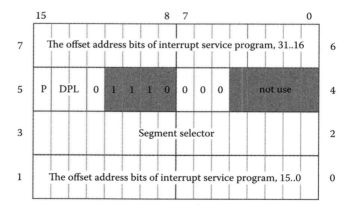

The interrupt descriptor has 64 bits including OFFSET, SELECTOR, DPL, P, TYPE, and so on. The No. 0–No. 15 bits and the No. 48–No. 63 bits are combined as the 32-bit offset address of the interrupt service routine. The No. 16–No. 31 bits are the SELECTOR, which is used to fix the segment including the interrupt service routine. The No. 47 bit is P, which is used to identify whether the segment is in memory or not. The No. 45–No. 46 bits are DPL. The No. 40–No. 43 bits are TPYE, and the TPYE of the interrupt descriptor is 1110(0xE), which tags this segment descriptor with "386."

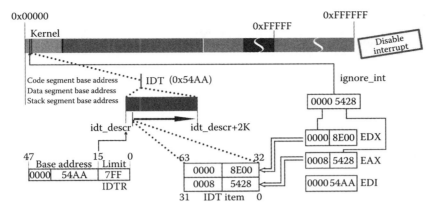

Figure 1.28 Set IDT.

This is the start point for rebuilding the interrupt service system. It makes all interrupt descriptors point to ignore_int and then sets the value of IDTR. Figure 1.28 shows the whole process.

Comment

By creating IDT and pointing the interrupt descriptor to ignore_int, it is possible to build an interrupt mechanism framework and prevent a dangling pointer.

Now, head.s abolishes the existing GDT and creates a new GDT in the new position in the kernel, as shown in Figure 1.29. The second and third items of the GDT are the kernel

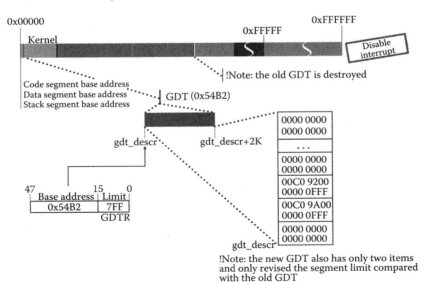

Figure 1.29 Rebuild GDT.

code segment descriptor and the kernel data segment descriptor, respectively. The segment limit is set to 16M, and the value of GDTR is set.

```
//code path:boot/head.s
setup_gdt
......
setup_gdt:
lgdt gdt_descr
Ret
_gdt:.quad 0x0000000000000000/* NULL descriptor */
.quad 0x00c09a0000000fff/* 16Mb */
.quad 0x00c0920000000fff/* 16Mb */
.quad 0x0000000000000000/* TEMPORARY - don't use */
.fill 252,8,0
```

Comment

Why does head.s abolish the existing GDT and create a new one?

The original GDT location is assigned in setup.s; this setup module's location in the memory will be covered by buffer in the future. If the location does not change, the contents of GDT will certainly be covered by buffer and thus influence system operation. Thus, the only safe place in the memory is within the location of head.s.

Hence, is it possible to directly copy GDT to the location of head.s when setup.s is being executed? The answer is no. If you copy the contents of the GDT first and then move the system module, the GDT will be covered by the system module. If you move the system module first and then copy the contents of the GDT, head.s will be covered before executing.

The location and content of the GDT might change. The last 3 bits become FFF, which means the segment limit is not 8M, but 16M. Thus, we need to reset some segment selectors, including DS, ES, FS, GS, and SS, as shown in Figure 1.30.

The routine to set DS and ES is as follows:

```
//code path:boot/head.s
movl $0x10,%eax # reload all the segment registers
mov%ax,%ds # after changing gdt. CS was already
mov%ax,%es # reloaded in 'setup_gdt'
mov%ax,%fs
mov%ax,%gs
```

Through testing, we found that if we set the segment limit with 16M in setup.s, we do not need to reset these segment selectors.

The starting location of the user_stack data structure is the bottom of the kernel stack; esp points to the outer edge of the user_stack data structure, which is the top of the kernel stack. Thus, when the latter program needs to be pushed, it can maximize the use of stack space. The top of the stack growth direction is from high to low, as shown in Figure 1.31.

The routine that sets esp is as follows.

```
//code path:boot/head.s
Lss _stack_start,%esp
```

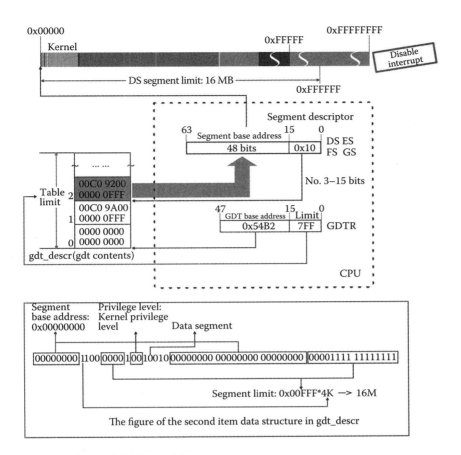

Figure 1.30 Readjust DS, ES, FS, and GS.

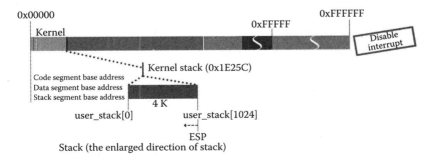

Figure 1.31 Set the kernel stack.

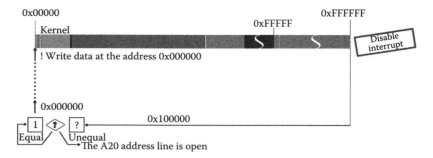

Figure 1.32 Inspect the opening of A20.

The fundamental difference between the protected mode and the real mode is that whether the address line A20 is open or not, we need to check that the address line is really open. In Figure 1.32, there is a visual representation of the inspection.

The code we use to check whether the address line is opened or not is as follows:

```
//code path: boot/head.s
xorl%eax,%eax
1: incl%eax
movl%eax, 0x000000
cmpl%eax,0x100000
je 1b
```

Comment

If the address line A20 is not opened, then the computer is in the real mode. In that condition, when the addressing is beyond the limit of 0xFFFFF, the rollback will happen. For example, when the address 0x100000 rolls back to the address 0x000000, the value stored in the address 0x100000 is the same as that stored in the address 0x000000 (find the description in Figure 1.30). The solution is to write data in the address 0x000000 of the memory and then compare the consistency between the data and data stored in the address 0x100000 (1 Mb; notice that it is beyond the limit of the real mode).

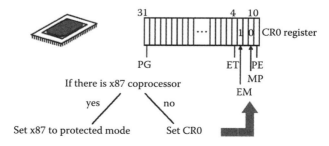

Figure 1.33 Inspect the maths coprocessor.

After checking whether the address wire named A20 is open or not, the code head.s will set the math coprocessor in the protected mode if it detects the existence of the math coprocessor, as shown in Figure 1.33.

Tip:

x87 coprocessor: in order to meet the requirement of x86 in the floating point arithmetic, Intel designed the math coprocessor in the x87 series, which was an external and optional chip in 1980. In 1989, Intel released the 486 processor. After that, there is an internal coprocessor in the CPU. Thus, it is necessary that the OS is able to detect the existence of the math coprocessor for computers earlier than the series 486.

The code we use to inspect the math coprocessor is as follows:

```
//code path:boot/head.s
movl%cr0,%eax
......
call check_x87
check_x87:
......
ret
```

The code head.s is the last preparation for calling the main function. The stage is the last stage of the execution of the program head.s and is also the last stage before the main function.

The execution code is as follows:

```
//code path:boot/head.s
jmp after_page_tables
after_page_tables;
pushl $0
pushl $0
pushl $0
```

Figure 1.34 shows the whole process.

The code head.s pushes the flag L6 and the entrance address of the main function into the stack. The top of the stack is the address of the main function, in order to execute the main function directly with the instruction "ret" after executing the code head.s, as shown in Figure 1.35.

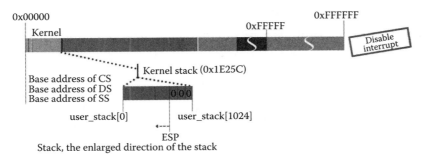

Figure 1.34 Push evnp, argv, and argc.

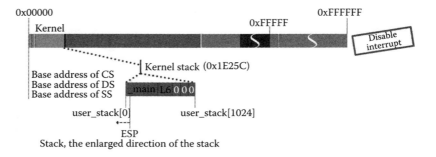

Figure 1.35 Push the entry address of the main function and the L6 symbol.

If the main function exits, the program returns to the flag L6 and continues to run, which means it is actually an infinite loop.

The execution code is as follows:

```
//code path:boot/head.s
pushl $L6
pushl $_main
```

After pushing, head.s jumps to "setup_paging:" to start building the paging mechanism.

At first, the program places the page directory tables and four page tables at the starting position of the physical memory. The memory space amounting to five pages from the starting position is clear. It is noticed that the space that the program head.s shares is covered by one page directory table and four page tables, as shown in Figure 1.36.

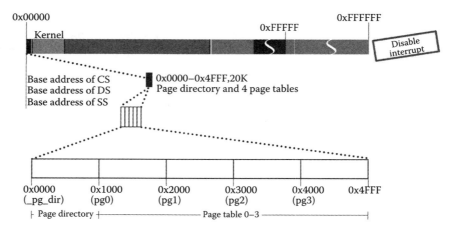

Figure 1.36 Place the page directory tables and page tables at the beginning of memory.

The execution code is as follows:

```
//code path:boot/head.s
jmp setup_paging
setup_paging:
movl $1204*5,%ecx
xorl%eax,%eax
xorl%edi,%edi
cld;rep;stosl
```

Comment

It is important that the program places the page directory tables and four page tables at the starting position of the physical memory. It is the basis of the OS to control overall and master the process safely in the memory. We will talk about fundamental effects later.

The head.s clears the space the page directory table and four page tables share and then sets the first four entries of the page content table in order to make them point to four page tables, as shown in Figure 1.37.

The execution code is as follows:

```
//code path:boot/head.s
movl $pg0+7,_pg_dir /* set present bit/user r/w */
movl $pg1+7,_pg_dir+4 /*— — — — — —  \'''— — — — — —  - */
movl $pg2+7,_pg_dir+8 /*— — — — — —  \'''— — — — — —  - */
movl $pg3+7,_pg_dir+12 /*— — — — — —  \'''— — — — — —  - */
movl $pg3+4092,%edi
movl $0xfff007,%eax /* 16Mb-4096+7(r/w user,p) */
```

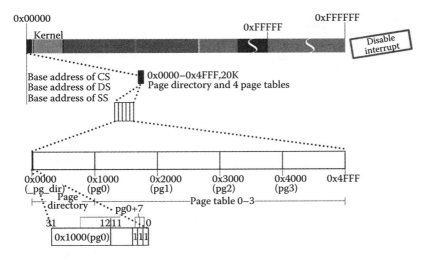

Figure 1.37 Make the entries of page directory table point to four page tables.

After setting the page directory table, the range of addressing based on Linux in the protected mode expands to 0xFFFFFF (16 MB). The last item where the pg3 + 4902 points refers to the last page in the range. It is about the size of 4 KB starting from the address 0xFFF000, as shown in Figure 1.38.

Then, all four page tables are cleared from the high address to the low address and successively point to the pages of the memory from the high address to the low address. In Figure 1.38, the process of setting the page tables for the first time is shown.

Continually, the last second item (pg3−4 + 4902 points to the item) of the fourth page table (pg3 points to the table) is set to point to the last second page. It is about the size of 4 KB starting from the address 0xFFF000−0x1000. It is obvious that there are differences between Figures 1.38 and 1.39.

In the end, all four page tables have been cleared from the high address to the low address, and every entry of the page tables points to each page in the same direction correspondingly. In Figure 1.39, there is a visual representation of the process.

All these four page tables belong to the kernel privately. Similarly, every user process has its private page tables. In the next chapter, we will discuss the difference between the kernel and the user process in the range of addressing.

The execution code executed in Figures 1.38 through 1.40 is as follows:

```
//code path:boot/head.s
movl $pg3+4092,%edi
movl $0xfff007,%eax      /* 16Mb-4096+7(r/w user,p) */
std
1: stosl                 /* fill pages backwards-more efficient θ */
        subl $0x1000,%eax
        jpe 1b
```

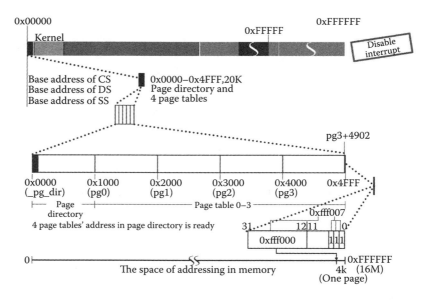

Figure 1.38 Status of page content tables after being set.

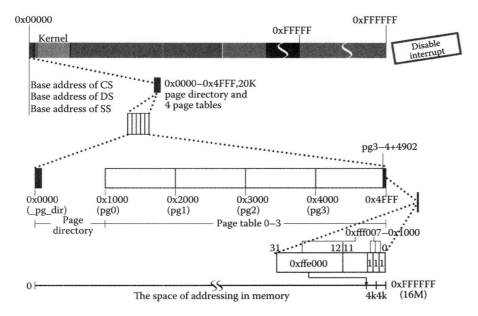

Figure 1.39 Set the page tables.

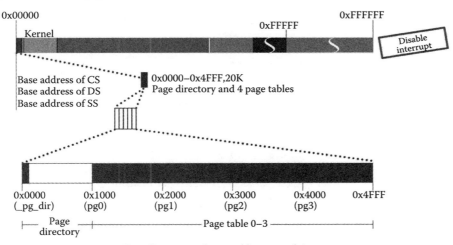

Page directory and page tables are ready!

Figure 1.40 Status of page content tables and page tables after being set.

The overall arrangement of the memory is shown in Figure 1.41, after executing the previous code. There is only 184 bytes left in the memory for the kernel. Thus, the planning is accurate when the program head.s and the system module are designed.

The program head.s has set the page tables; however, the paging mechanism has not been finished. The process that creates the paging mechanism is as follows: the page content register named CR3 is set to point to page content tables and then the highest position of the register CR0 is set as 1, as shown in Figure 1.42.

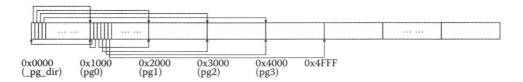

0x0000   0x1000   0x2000   0x3000   0x4000   0x4FFF
(_pg_dir)   (pg0)   (pg1)   (pg2)   (pg3)

Figure 1.41 The overall arrangement of the memory.

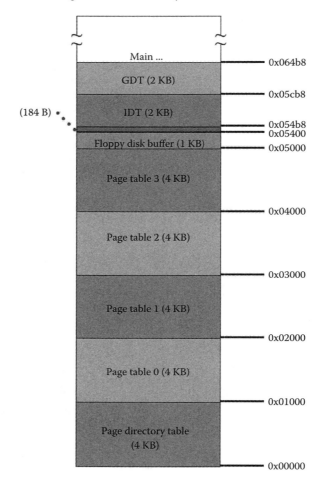

Figure 1.42 Structure of the memory.

Tip:

PG (paging) mark: the 32nd bit of the register CR0 controls the paging mechanism. When the first bit PE of CR0 is set to 1, the bit PG can be set as open status. In this status, the address mapping mode is the paging mechanism. When PE is 0, PG cannot be set; otherwise, CPU will be illegal.

Register CR3: a 32-bit control register, the first 20 bits stores the base address of the page content. When PG is set, the CPU maps the virtual address to the physical address with the page content and the page tables that CR3 points to.

The execution code is as follows:

```
//code path:boot/head.s
xorl%eax,%eax /* pg_dir is at 0x000 */
movl%eax,%cr3 /*cr3-page directory start */
movl%cr0,%eax
orl $0x80000000,%eax
movl%eax,%cr0 /* set paging (PG) bit */
```

The first two lines make CR3 point to the page content tables. The OS treats 0x0000 as the start of the page content tables. The next three lines start the paging mechanism by switching PG bit to enter the paging address mode. Until now, the kernel's paging mechanism has been set up (Figure 1.43).

The following code is more important:

```
xorl%eax,%eax /* pg_dir is at 0x000 */
```

In Figure 1.17, we move the system module to the address 0x0000. In Figure 1.25, we create the paging mechanism for the kernel. Lastly, the page content tables are at the start of the memory because of the above code. Based on those, the kernel can control user programs. The address 0x0000 is the only starting one that can guarantee that the linear address is the same as the physical one. We will talk about it in detail later.

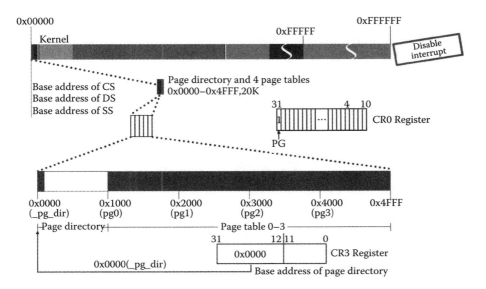

Figure 1.43 Global status after setting the paging mechanism.

The last step in executing the program head.s is "ret." Then, jump to the main function.

In Figure 1.35, the entrance address of the main function is pushed at the top of the stack. When executing the instruction "ret," the pushed entrance address is popped to EIP. Figure 1.44 describes the whole process of popping the address.

There is a trick usually used in the bottom code. We talk about it in detail in Figure 1.45.

Let us consider the call and return method for the common function first. Because Linux 0.11 calls the main function by way of returning, the position returned and the entrance of the main function are in the same stack. In part I of Figure 1.45, the process of calling and returning in the same stack is shown.

The instruction CALL pushes the value of EIP automatically, protects the returning, and executes the program of the function called. Until the execution reaches the instruction "ret," it pops the value to EIP and returns to the origin, and then continues to execute the next instruction of the program CALL. That is the common way to call a function. But for the main function of the OS, it does not work. If the main function of OS is called by CALL, what should be returned when "ret" is to be executed? Is there another host to catch the returning of OS? Obviously, it is incorrect, since OS is the basis. People may wonder how to call the main function of OS without returning? Linus presents us with an ingenious method in part II of Figure 1.45.

The designer calls the main function of OS achieved by "ret." Because it is called by "ret," there is no need for returning. However, the process of pushing and jumping can be achieved only through CALL. The designer copies the process manually. The code used for pushing and jumping is to call setup_paging. Please note that the pushed value of EIP is the executing entrance address "_main" to the main function of the OS. In this way, when the setup_paging function reaches the instruction "ret," the entrance address is popped to EIP from the stack. EIP points to the entrance address to the main function. Hence, we can call the main function with the returning instruction.

In Figure 1.45, the pushed executing entrance address to the main function is popped to CS:EIP. From now on, the CPU starts to execute the program "main." There is a description of this status in Figure 1.46.

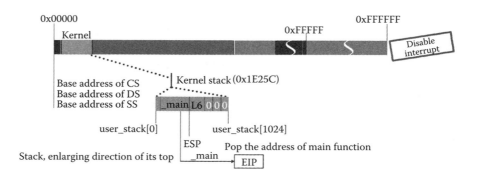

Figure 1.44 Execute ret, pop address to EIP.

Call and return of CALL

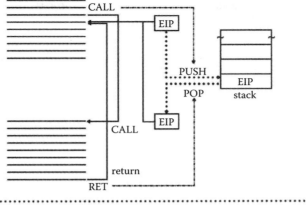

Call and return of "copy CALL"

after_page_tables

setup_paging

_main

Figure 1.45 Description of "copy CALL."

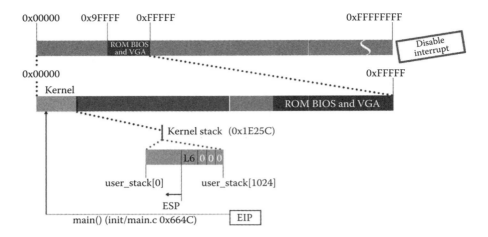

Figure 1.46 Begin to execute the main function.

Comment

Why is the main function called at first?

In the program written in C, there is a main function as well. The execution starts from the main function. Linux 0.11 is coded in C. It is strange why three programs written in compilation language are executed first before the main function when the OS starts.

Usually, the programs written in C are user applications. One important characteristic of these programs is that they must be executed on the fundamentals of the OS. That is to say, the OS creates a process for programs and loads the executable code from the hard disk to the memory. When talking about the OS, the question what loads the executable code of the OS exists.

We know from previous sections that when loading the OS, the computer is just powered. At that time, only the BIOS is executed and the computer is in the 16-bit real mode status. The code on the first sector of the floppy disk (512 bytes) is loaded into the memory according to the addresses kept in 16-bit interrupt vector tables, and 16-bit interrupt service routine is created by the program BIOS. There BIOS ends. Exactly, it is an appointment that loading the code of the first sector is the same for any OS. The code on rest sectors is loaded based on the former.

So why not execute the main function right now after loading the code of OS?

As we know, Linux 0.11 is a 32-bit, real-time, and multitasking OS. Hence, the main function must execute a 32-bit code. When compiling the code of the OS, there are 16-bit and 32-bit compiler options. In the 16-bit condition, the compiled code is 16 bits. It may be because a variable of type int only has 2 bytes. However, Linux 0.11 wants the compiled code of 32 bits. Only in this way will the code of the OS be 32 bits. The 32-bit code can use a 32-bit bus, protected mode, and paging. It is thus a modern OS with real-time and multitasking characteristics. The 16-bit real mode is completely different from the 32-bit protected mode. So what can change the real mode to the protected mode? The answer is "head.s." The program head.s opens the address line A20, opens pe and pg, abandons the old 16-bit interrupt response mechanism, and builds up the new 32-bit IDT. After these preparations, the computer is in a 32-bit protected mode. It is ready to call the 32-bit main function. Then, all operations can be finished by the 32-bit compiled main function.

From here on, one important stage of starting the kernel has been finished, and it will be followed by the main function. It is noticed that the system is in the closed interrupt status.

■ 1.4 Summary

This chapter has two parts: part I, loading the OS; part II, preparation for executing the main function in the 32-bit protected mode and paging mode.

Beginning with loading "bootsect.s" into the memory with BIOS, the files "setup.s" and "system" are executed to load the OS. Then, it is followed by the preparation for executing the main function in the 32-bit protected mode and paging mode. During this period, IDT, GDT, page content tables, page tables, and machine statistics are set.

After all these, the system jumps from the execution entrance to the main function and starts executing it.

2 Device Initialization and Process 0 Activation

From now on, the main function begins!

Before the operating system (OS) enters the idle state, the core purpose of all the preparatory work is to allow user applications to run normally in the "process" way. There are three aspects involved: the user application can run computing on the host, interaction with peripherals, and human–computer interaction. This chapter explains the content to achieve this goal, including device initialization and activation of the first process—process 0.

Linux 0.11 is a modern OS supporting multi-processes, which means to ensure normal host operation, user processes cannot interfere with each other while processing. However, the process does not have a natural "boundary" to protect itself, which relies on the boundary, that is, the process management information data structure. Process management information data structure consists of the following: task_struct, task[64], and GDT, et al. Task_struct is a unique structure for the process, which identifies each attribute value of a process, including the remaining time slice, execution state, local descriptor table LDT, and task status descriptor table TSS. Task[64] and GDT are data structures for the management of multi-processes, and the task[64] structure stores all the task_struct pointers of the process. If the OS needs to compare and choose from multiple processes, it can traverse through the task[64] structure to meet the requirement. GDT keeps a set of index structure for all the processes; thus, the OS can locate each process indirectly by the LDT and TSS through index.

This section will also explain how the OS sets the memory, central processing unit (CPU), serial port, monitor, keyboard, hard disk, floppy disk, and other hardware, and how the OS attaches the interrupt service routine of the corresponding hardware with the interrupt descriptor table and sets up the environment for process 0, as well as the subsequent process created directly or indirectly by process 0, to communicate with peripherals.

■ 2.1 Set Root Device 2 and Hard Disk

The kernel initializes the root device and the hard disk first, using the information of the machine system data in 0x901FC written by bootsect.s (refer to Section 1.2.3) to set the floppy disk as the root device. The hard disk parameter table, namely, the 32 bytes starting from the location 0x90080, is used to set drive_info.

The code is as follows:

```
//Code path:init/main.c:
......
#define DRIVE_INFO (*(struct drive_info *)0x90080)//Disk parameter
                                                  //table, see
                                                  //system data
#define ORIG_ROOT_DEV (*(unsigned short *)0x901FC)//root device id


    ......
struct drive_info {char dummy[32];} drive_info; //The structure stores
                                                //disk parameter table
void main(void)
{
        ROOT_DEV = ORIG_ROOT_DEV;//According to the system data written
                        //by bootsect
        drive_info = DRIVE_INFO;//the root device is floppy disk
        ......
}
```

The location of setting the root device and the hard disk in the memory is shown in Figure 2.1.

■ 2.2 Set Up Physical Memory Layout, Buffer Memory, Ramdisk, and Main Memory

Second, the kernel begins to set buffer memory, ramdisk, and main memory. The CPU and the memory need to work together to execute computation. As memory is an important component in computing, the layout of the buffer and the main memory fundamentally determines the amount of memory and mode used by all processes, which will surely affect the computing speed of the process.

The layout is as follows: except for memory space occupied by the kernel code and data, the rest of the physical memory is divided into three main parts: main memory,

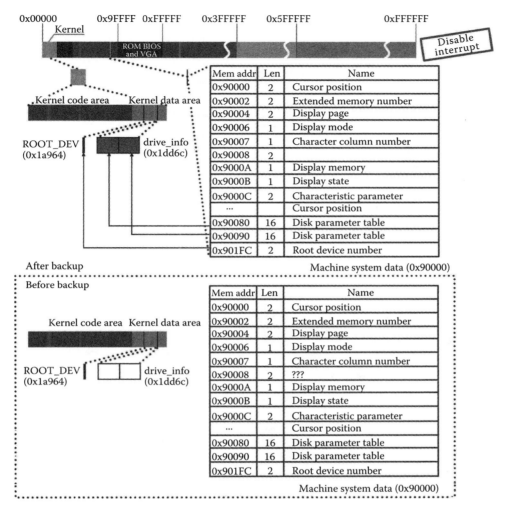

Figure 2.1 Copy root device number and disk parameter table.

buffer memory, and the ramdisk. The main memory is the place where the process code resides, and it also contains the data structure that the kernel uses to arrange the process; the buffer memory is mainly used as the data transfer station between the host and peripherals; the ramdisk is optional. If the ramdisk is to be used, the data in peripherals should be copied to the ramdisk at first. Since data operating speed in memory is higher than that in peripherals, system performance can be improved in this manner.

As discussed, the OS sets the size, location, and management mode of these three different regions in the memory.

According to the size of the memory, the location and size of the buffer and main memory are initialized first (Figure 2.2).

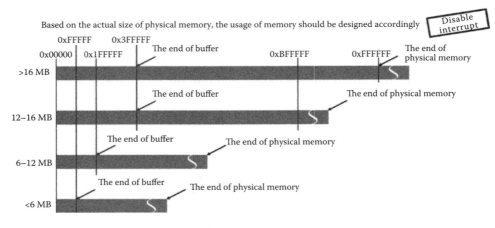

Figure 2.2 The initial setting of the memory.

The execution code is as follows:

```
//Code path:init/main.c:
......
#define EXT_MEM_K (*(unsigned short *)0x90002)//Extended memory(KB)
                                              //starts from 1M


......
void main(void)
{
    ......
    memory_end = (1<<20) + (EXT_MEM_K<<10);//1M+extend memory,i.e. the
                                           //total number of memory

    memory_end & = 0xfffff000;//Get integer multiple of pages, ignore
                    //the part less than one page at the end of memory

    if (memory_end > 16*1024*1024)
            memory_end = 16*1024*1024;
    if (memory_end > 12*1024*1024)
            buffer_memory_end = 4*1024*1024;
    else if (memory_end > 6*1024*1024)
            buffer_memory_end = 2*1024*1024;
    else
            buffer_memory_end = 1*1024*1024;
    main_memory_start = buffer_memory_end;//After the buffer is in
                                          //main memory
```

Memory_end is the end of effective memory; the exceeding part is not visible to the OS. Main_memory_start is the starting position of the main memory. Buffer_memory_end is the end of buffer memory. The starting position of the buffer memory will be introduced in detail in Section 2.1.13.

Tip:

There are several common data relations of left shift and right shift that should be mentioned:

<<20 or >>20 is equivalent to be multiplied or divided by 1M,
<<12 or >>12 is equivalent to be multiplied or divided by 4K (associate with the page)
<<10 or >>10 is equivalent to be multiplied or divided by 1K

Thus, 1 << 20 is 1M; EXT_MEM_K << 10 is the bytes of EXT_MEM_K (kilobytes of extended memory).

2.3 Ramdisk Setup and Initialization

The kernel sets up the ramdisk in the peripheral as follows. First, the kernel checks the "ramdisk label" in makefile to determine whether the system uses the ramdisk. We assume that the computer has a 16 MB physical memory and the ramdisk size is set as 2 MB; thus, the kernel allocates a 2 MB memory space for the ramdisk from the buffer memory end, and the starting position of the main memory is moved 2 MB back to the end of ramdisk space. Figure 2.3 shows the result of the layout in physical memory.

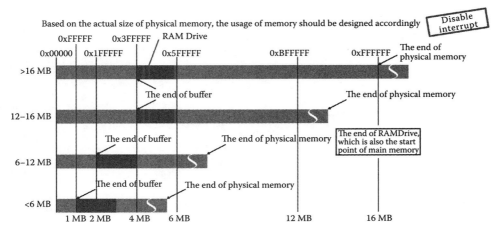

Figure 2.3 Physical memory layout.

The system calls rd_init to start setting the ramdisk, and the code is as follows:

```
//Code path:init/main.c:
void main(void)
{
    ......
#ifdef RAMDISK
    main_memory_start + = rd_init(main_memory_start, RAMDISK*1024);
#endif
    ......
}


//Code path:kernel/blk_drv/blk.h:
    ......
#define NR_BLK_DEV       7
    ......
struct blk_dev_struct {
        void (*request_fn)(void);
        struct request * current_request;
};
    ......
#if (MAJOR_NR == 1)
    ......

#define DEVICE_REQUEST do_rd_request
    ......


//Code path:kernel/blk_drv/ll_rw_blk.c:        //ll means low level
    ......
struct blk_dev_struct blk_dev[NR_BLK_DEV] = {
        {NULL, NULL},            /* no_dev */
        {NULL, NULL},            /* dev mem */
        {NULL, NULL},            /* dev fd */
        {NULL, NULL},            /* dev hd */
        {NULL, NULL},            /* dev ttyx */
        {NULL, NULL},            /* dev tty */
        {NULL, NULL}             /* dev lp */
};
    ......


//Code path:kernel/ramdisk.c:
    ......
#define MAJOR_NR 1
    ......
long rd_init(long mem_start, int length) //hd_init(),floppy_init() are
                                         //similar to this function
{
        int  i;
        char *cp;
```

```
        blk_dev[MAJOR_NR].request_fn = DEVICE_REQUEST;//hang on do_rd_
                                                     //request ()
        rd_start = (char *) mem_start;
        rd_length = length;
        cp = rd_start;
        for (i = 0; i < length; i++)
                *cp++ = '\0';                    //Initialized to 0
        return(length);
}
```

In rd_init, do_rd_request in the ramdisk is attached with the second item of blk_dev[7], which is the control structure, as shown at the left upper part of Figure 2.3. The primary function of blk_dev[7] is to attach the equipment with its corresponding request processing function, and the system that we are discussing can operate six kinds of equipment. The request will be explained in detail in Section 2.1.6. The attachment means that the kernel can operate the ramdisk request by calling do_rd_request. After attachment, all ramdisk space is initialized to 0. Note that the ramdisk is just a piece of "blank disk," which is not yet processed by operations such as "format"; thus, it cannot be used as a block device. The block equipment and "format" of the ramdisk will be introduced in detail as part of the rd_load function. Figure 2.4 shows the execution of the rd_init().

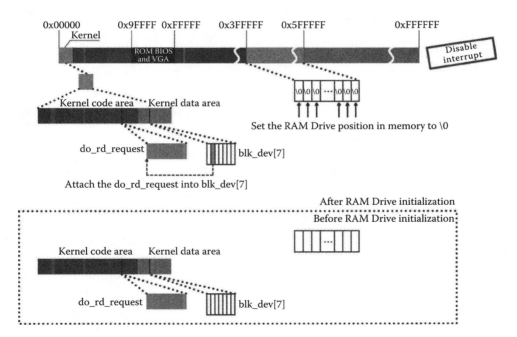

Figure 2.4 Ramdisk setup and initialization.

Then, the length value of the ramdisk is returned, which will be used to reset the starting position of the main memory.

2.4 Initialization of the Memory Management Structure mem_map

As the starting position of the main memory is reset, the location and size of the main memory and buffer memory are both identified. The system calls mem_init. First, the kernel sets the management structure of the main memory; the process is shown in Figure 2.5.

The execution code is as follows:

```
//Code path:init/main.c:
void main(void)
{
        ......
        mem_init(main_memory_start,memory_end);
        ......
}


//Code path:mm/memory.c:
        ......
        #define LOW_MEM 0x100000        //1MB
        #define PAGING_MEMORY (15*1024*1024)
        #define PAGING_PAGES (PAGING_MEMORY>>12)     //Page number of 15M
        #define MAP_NR(addr) (((addr)-LOW_MEM)>>12)
        #define USED 100
        ......
        static long HIGH_MEMORY = 0;
        ......
        static unsigned char mem_map [PAGING_PAGES] = {0,};
        ......
void mem_init(long start_mem, long end_mem)
{
        int i;


        HIGH_MEMORY = end_mem;
        for (i = 0 ; i<PAGING_PAGES ; i++)
              mem_map[i] = USED;
        i = MAP_NR(start_mem);         //The size of start_mem is 6M,
                                       //after virtual disk
        end_mem - = start_mem;
        end_mem >> = 12;                            //Page number of 15M
        while (end_mem--  >0)
              mem_map[i++] = 0;
}
```

By mem_map, the system will manage the memory above 1 MB in paging mode and keep the reference number of each page.

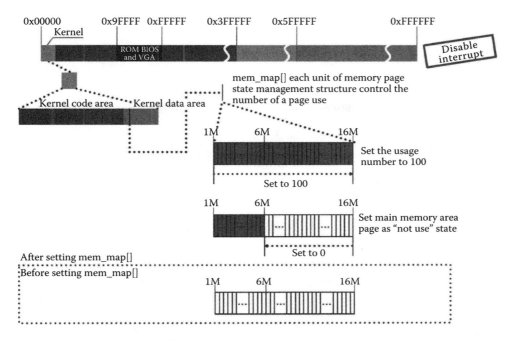

Figure 2.5 The initialization of the memory management structure mem_map.

First, mem_init sets the reference number of all memory pages as USED (100, i.e., being used), and then it initializes all reference numbers in the main memory to 0, after which the system will take the page with reference number 0 as idle page.

Why can't the system use this paging method to manage the memory within 1 MB? The reason is that the designer implemented two different paging management methods for the kernel and the user process. For the kernel, the linear address and physical address are exactly the same and mapped one by one. That means the kernel can access the physical address directly. But for the user mode, the linear address differs from the physical address dramatically, and there is no relationship between them. The aim of the design is that the user process cannot extrapolate the special physical address by the linear address. The kernel can access the user process and the user process cannot access the kernel and other user processes. The memory space within 1 MB is just for the code and data controlled only by the kernel, which the user process cannot access. The memory space beyond 1 MB, especially the main memory, is for the user process. We will talk about memory management in detail in Chapter 6 and the mechanism behind in Chapter 9.

■ 2.5 Binding the Interrupt Service Routine

The user process and the kernel often use interruption and handle many exceptions, such as overflow, boundary checking, page fault exception, and so on. The interruption mechanism is also widely used in system call. These interruptions and exceptions need a special service program to execute. The function trap_init can hook the service program of the interruption and exception to the interruption descriptor table (idt), which also rebuilds the interruption service to support the operation of the kernel and the process in the host.

The process of binding and the space occupied by the interruption service routine are shown in Figure 2.6.

The execution code is as follows:

```
//Code path:init/main.c:
void main(void)
{
    ......
    trap_init();
    ......
}


//Code path:kernel/traps.c:
void trap_init(void)
{
    int i;
    set_trap_gate(0,&divide_error);//Divide by zero error
    set_trap_gate(1,&debug);                    //step-by-step debugging
    set_trap_gate(2,&nmi);                      //Non-maskable interrupt
    set_system_gate(3,&int3);        /* int3-5 can be called from all */
    set_system_gate(4,&overflow);               //overflow
    set_system_gate(5,&bounds);                 //bounds check error
    set_trap_gate(6,&invalid_op);               //Invalid operation
    set_trap_gate(7,&device_not_available);     //Invalid device
    set_trap_gate(8,&double_fault);             //double fault
    set_trap_gate(9,&coprocessor_segment_overrun);//coprocessor segment
                                                   //overrun
    set_trap_gate(10,&invalid_TSS);             //Invalid TSS
    set_trap_gate(11,&segment_not_present);     //Segment does not present
    set_trap_gate(12,&stack_segment);           //stack exception
    set_trap_gate(13,&general_protection);      //general protection exception
    set_trap_gate(14,&page_fault);              //page fault
    set_trap_gate(15,&reserved);                //reserved
    set_trap_gate(16,&coprocessor_error);       //coprocessor error
    for (i = 17;i<48;i++) //they are all binding, the interrupt service routine
                          //name is initialized to reserved
        set_trap_gate(i,&reserved);
    set_trap_gate(45,&irq13);                   //coprocessor
    outb_p(inb_p(0x21)&0xfb,0x21);//Allow IRQ2 interrupt request
    outb(inb_p(0xA1)&0xdf,0xA1);   //Allow IRQ2 interrupt request
    set_trap_gate(39,&parallel_interrupt); //parallel port
}


//Code path:include\asm\system.h:
    ......
#define _set_gate(gate_addr,type,dpl,addr) \
__asm__ ("movw%%dx,%%ax\n\t" \        //The low word of edx is assigned to the low
                                      //word of eax
        "movw%0,%%dx\n\t" \           //% 0 corresponds to "i" at the first line
                                      //after the second colon
        "movl%%eax,%1\n\t" \          //% 1 corresponds to "o" at the second line
                                      //after the second colon
        "movl%%edx,%2" \              //% 0 corresponds to "o" at the third line
                                      //after the second colon
        : \          //After this colon are outputs, After the next colon are
                     //inputs
        : "i" ((short) (0x8000+(dpl<<13)+(type<<8))), \        //Immediate
        "o" (*((char *) (gate_addr))), \   //Address of the former 4 bytes
                                           //of interrupt descriptor
        "o" (*(4+(char *) (gate_addr))),  \//Address of the last 4 bytes
                                           //of interrupt descriptor
```

```
          "d" ((char *) (addr)),"a" (0x00080000))//"d" corresponds to edx,
                                      //"a" corresponds to eax
          ......
#define set_trap_gate(n,addr) \
       _set_gate(&idt[n],15,0,addr)
```

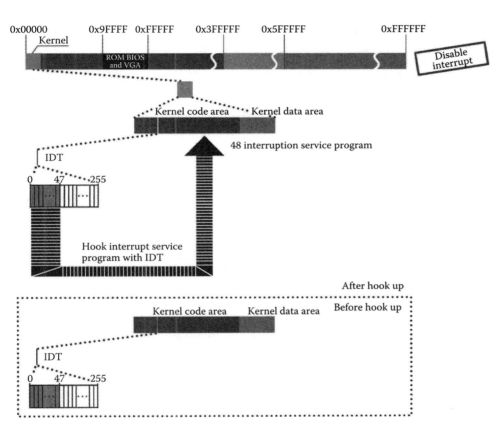

Figure 2.6 Hooking the interrupt service program.

The purpose of the code is to make up the idt descriptors described in Section 1.3.5.
The idt is copied for ease of reading, as shown in the following:

The result of executing the above code is as follows (Figure 2.7):

Comparing:

```
set_trap_gate(0,&divide_error)
set_trap_gate(n,addr)
_set_gate(&idt[n],15,0,addr)
_set_gate(gate_addr,type,dpl,addr)
```

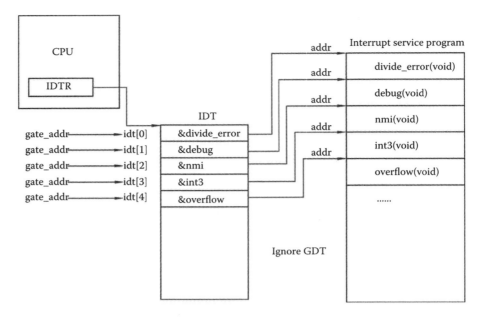

Figure 2.7 An overview of the interrupt handle.

As we can see, n is 0; gate_addr is &idt[0], which is the address of the first content of idt; type is 15; dpl (descriptor privilege level) is 0; and addr is the entrance address of the interrupt service program "divide_error(void) (Figure 2.8)."

The instruction "movw%**0**,%%dx\n\t" means that the low word of edx is assigned to the low word of eax. Then edx is (char *) (addr), as well as &divide_error. The value of eax is 0x0080000, which is mentioned in head.s. Here, 8 is 1000 in binary, of which every bit is meaningful. Thus, the value of eax is 0x0080000 + (the low word of(char *)(addr)). 0x0008 is the segment selector, with the same meaning as the "jmpi 0,8" described in Chapter 1.

The instruction "movw%**0**,%%dx\n\t" means that (short) (0x8000 + (dpl<<13) + (type<<8)) is assigned to dx. Do not forget that, here, edx is (char *) (addr), as well as &divide_error.

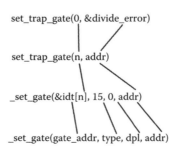

Figure 2.8 Function parameters.

Because data of this part is spliced by bit, we must calculate precisely as follows.

0x8000 is 1000 0000 0000 0000 in binary.

dpl is 00, and dpl<<13 is 000 0000 0000 0000.

type is 15, and type<<8 is 1111 0000 0000.

Adding them up amounts to 1000 1111 0000 0000, which is the value of dx. Calculation result of edx is the high word of (char *) (addr), as well as the high word of &divide_error +1000 1111 0000 0000.

The instruction "movl%%eax,%1\n\t" means that the value of eax is assigned to *((char *) (gate_addr)), also the first 4 bytes of idt[0]. Similarly, "movl%%edx,%2" means that the value of edx is assigned to *(4+(char *) (gate_addr)), also the last 4 bytes of idt[0]. All 8 bytes together is integral **idt**[0]. The result is as follows (Figure 2.9):

The first entry of interrupt descriptor "diving by zero" in the IDT table is initialized completely. Initialization of other interrupt service routine and IDT is quite similar.

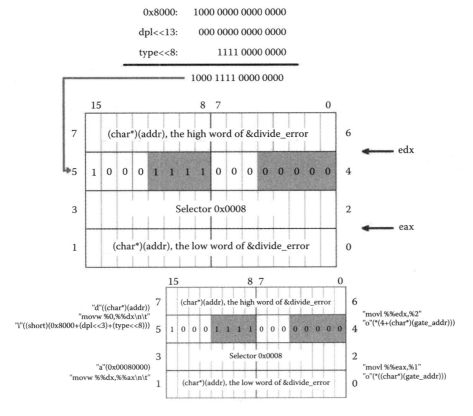

Figure 2.9 How the parameters add into the IDT.

Both set_system_gate(n,addr) and set_trap_gate(n,addr) use the same _set_gate(gate_addr,type,dpl,addr), and the difference is that the dpl of set_trap_gate is 0 while the dpl of set_system_gate is 3. "dpl is 0" means that it can only be handled by the kernel. However, "dpl is 3" means that system can be called from privilege level 3 (also the user privilege level).

Learn more about privilege level in Volume 3.pdf of the Intel IA-32 Architectures Software Developer's Manual.

Next, int 0x11–0x2F of idt are all initialized, and the pointer to interrupt service program in idt is set with the status "reserved."

Set the idt of the co-processor.

Enable the interrupt request from IRQ2 and IRQ3 of the 8259A interrupt controller.

Set the idt of the parallel port (access to printer).

The 32-bit interrupt service system is established to meet the interrupt signal mechanism "passive response," which is described as follows. On one hand, the hardware sends signals to 8259A, and 8259A preliminarily handles signals and transfers interrupt signals to the CPU. On the other hand, if the CPU does not receive signals, it executes the program. Otherwise, the program being executed is interrupted and a specific interrupt service program is located by the idt, which will be executed immediately. After interruption is completed, the CPU will return to the program point where interrupt happens to continue. If interrupt signal is again received, the CPU will repeat the process.

The original design is not like this. Originally, the CPU polls all hardware from time to time to check whether its task has been completed or not. If not, the CPU continues. This method takes time for handling user process and reduces the overall efficiency of the system. We can see that it is not efficient to handle signals by way of "active polling." It is an improvement that the "passive response" mode takes the place of the "active polling" mode in handling the I/O problem between host and peripherals.

▌▌ 2.6 Initialize the Request Structure of the Block Device

In Linux 0.11, peripherals are divided into two categories: block device and character device. The block device divides storage space into little parts with the same size named as a block. Every block has its own block ID and is independent, which can also be read or written randomly. Hard disks and floppy disks are both block devices. Character devices carry out I/O communication by character. Keyboards and command displays are character devices.

Any process communicates with a block device using the buffer in the host's memory. Request management structure "**request[32]**" is a data structure for reading and writing, which is a "bridge" between buffer block in the OS buffer and logical block in a block device.

I/O communication between the process and a block device is shown in Figure 2.10.

The OS executes the reading and writing operation between the buffer and the block device based on their priorities and records the buffer needed to operate on the request.

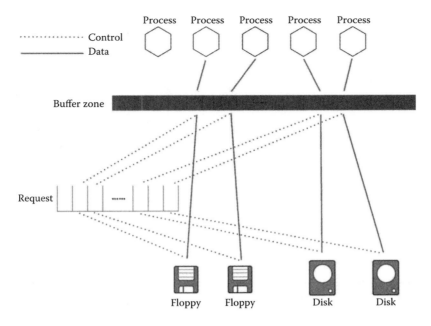

Figure 2.10 An overview of the relationship among block device, buffer, request, and process.

After receiving the operation command, the CPU locates the logical block according to the request.

The code is as follows:

```
//Code path:init/main.c:
void main(void)
{
        ......
        blk_dev_init();
        ......
}


//Code path:kernel/blk_dev/blk.h:
        ......
#define NR_REQUEST      32
struct request {
        int dev;                        /* -1 if no request */
        int cmd;                        /* READ or WRITE */
        int errors;
        unsigned long sector;
        unsigned long nr_sectors;
        char * buffer;
        struct task_struct * waiting;
        struct buffer_head * bh;
        struct request * next;  //This means requests can build a link-list
};
        ......
```

```
//Code path:kernel/blk_dev/ll_rw_block.c:
     ......
struct request request[NR_REQUEST];       //array list
     ......
void blk_dev_init(void)
{
        int i;


        for (i = 0 ; i<NR_REQUEST ; i++) {
                request[i].dev = -1;     //set as idle
                request[i].next = NULL; //break the link
        }
}
```

Notice that **request[32]** is an array link-list. "**request[i].dev** = **–1**" means that this request does not specially correspond to any device. This flag is used to specify whether the current requested device is free or not. "request[i].next = NULL" means that the queue of the request is not built. The process of initialization and the results are shown in Figure 2.11.

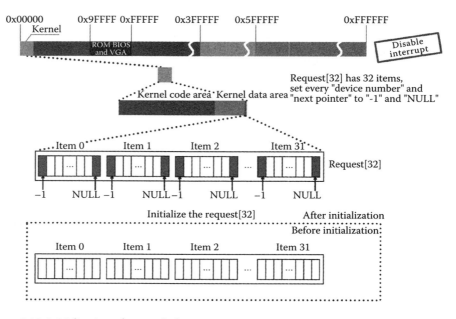

Figure 2.11 Initialization of request[32].

2.7 Binding with the Interrupt Service Routine of Peripherals and Establishing the Human–Computer Interaction Interface

Linus Torvalds originally designed chr_dev_init() in the OS to initialize the character device, but it does nothing. Linus then implemented tty_init() to initialize the character device. Note that people sometimes explain tty as teletype.

Character device initialization builds work environment for process and serial port, which means initializing serial port, display and keyboard, and binding the relevant interrupt service routine with IDT (interrupt descriptor table). In tty_init, it first calls rs_init to set the serial port and then calls con_init to set the display. The specific code is as follows:

```
//Code path:init/main.c:
void main(void)
{
        ......
        tty_init();
        ......
}

//Code path:kernel/chr_dev/tty_io.c:
void tty_init(void)
{
        rs_init();
        con_init()
}
```

2.7.1 Set the Serial Port

The two serial port interrupt service programs and IDT are connected, and two serial ports are initialized based on the content of the tty_table data structure, including the following: setting the line control register DLAB bit, setting the send baud rate factor, and setting the DTR and RTS. Finally, IRQ3 and IRQ4 of 8259A are enabled to send the interrupt request.

The specific process of binding is shown in the upper part of Figure 2.12.

The specific code is as follows:

```
//Code Path:kernel/chr_dev/serial.c:
void rs_init(void)
{
    set_intr_gate(0x24,rs1_interrupt);    //Set interrupt of serial port 1,
                                          //referring 2.5
    set_intr_gate(0x23,rs2_interrupt);    //Set interrupt of serial port 2
    init(tty_table[1].read_q.data);       //initialize serial port 1
    init(tty_table[2].read_q.data);       //initialize serial port 2
    outb(inb_p(0x21)&0xE7,0x21);          //allow IRQ3,IRQ4
}
```

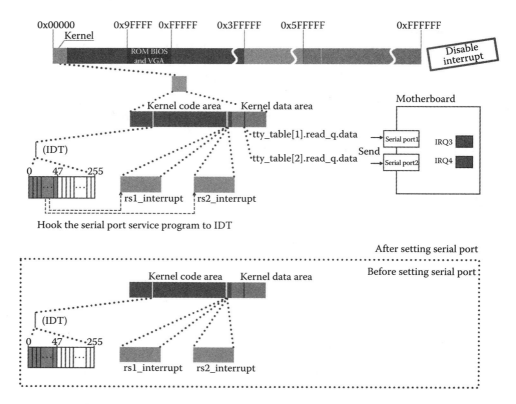

Figure 2.12 Hanging serial port interrupt service routine.

The function set_intr_gate that hooks the two serial port interrupt service programs with IDT is similar to set_trap_gate introduced before. The difference is that the type of set_trap_gate is 15(1111), but it is 14(1110) for set_intr_gate.

2.7.2 Set the Display

As the system provides information to indicate whether the graphics card is "monochrome or color," the OS sets the matching information. At the time of Linux 0.11, most graphics devices are monochrome, so we assume that the attribute of the graphics card is monochromatic EGA, the graphics memory location is 0xb0000–0xb8000, the index register port is set to 0x3b4, the data port is set to 0x3b5, and the graphics card attribute, EGA, is printed on the screen. Furthermore, initialize the variables used for scrolling screen, including the origin, scr_end, top and bottom.

The effect is shown in Figure 2.13.

2.7.3 Set the Keyboard

How is the keyboard set? First, the OS hooks the interrupt service routine with IDT and then removes the keyboard interrupt mask of 8259A, enabling IRQ1 to send an interrupt signal. After disabling the keyboard work, the keyboard is enabled to be ready. The function set_intr_gate() is designed to do so, which is similar with the set_trap_gate() introduced before.

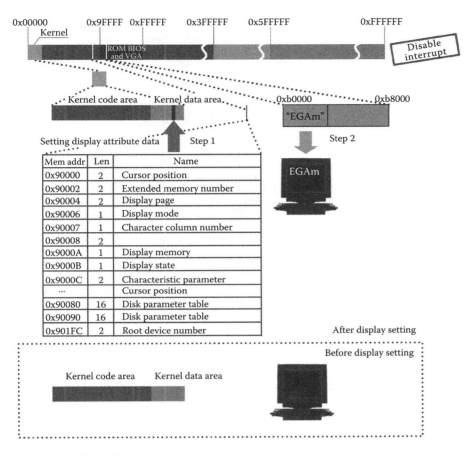

Figure 2.13 Set the display.

The execution process is shown in Figure 2.14.
The specific code is as follows:

```
//Code Patvh:kernel/chr_dev/console.c:
    ......
#define ORIG_X              (*(unsigned char *)0x90000)
#define ORIG_Y              (*(unsigned char *)0x90001)
#define ORIG_VIDEO_PAGE     (*(unsigned short *)0x90004)
#define ORIG_VIDEO_MODE     ((*(unsigned short *)0x90006) & 0xff)
#define ORIG_VIDEO_COLS     (((*(unsigned short *)0x90006) & 0xff00) >> 8)
#define ORIG_VIDEO_LINES    (25)
#define ORIG_VIDEO_EGA_AX   (*(unsigned short *)0x90008)
#define ORIG_VIDEO_EGA_BX   (*(unsigned short *)0x9000a)
#define ORIG_VIDEO_EGA_CX   (*(unsigned short *)0x9000c)


#define VIDEO_TYPE_MDA      0x10     /* Monochrome Text Display   */
#define VIDEO_TYPE_CGA      0x11     /* CGA Display               */
```

```c
#define VIDEO_TYPE_EGAM          0x20    /* EGA/VGA in Monochrome Mode    */
#define VIDEO_TYPE_EGAC          0x21    /* EGA/VGA in Color Mode */


#define NPAR 16
    ......
void con_init(void)
{
        register unsigned char a;
        char *display_desc = "????";
        char *display_ptr;


        video_num_columns = ORIG_VIDEO_COLS;//see the machine system data
        video_size_row = video_num_columns * 2;
        video_num_lines = ORIG_VIDEO_LINES;
        video_page = ORIG_VIDEO_PAGE;//see the machine system data
        video_erase_char = 0x0720;


        if (ORIG_VIDEO_MODE = = 7)  /* Is this a monochrome display? */
        {
          video_mem_start = 0xb0000;
          video_port_reg = 0x3b4;
          video_port_val = 0x3b5;
          if ((ORIG_VIDEO_EGA_BX & 0xff) ! = 0x10)//see the machine system data
          {
                  video_type = VIDEO_TYPE_EGAM;
                  video_mem_end = 0xb8000;
                  display_desc = "EGAm";
          }
          else
          {
                  video_type = VIDEO_TYPE_MDA;
                  video_mem_end     = 0xb2000;
                  display_desc = "*MDA";
          }
        }
        else                                    /* If not, it is color. */
        {
        video_mem_start = 0xb8000;
        video_port_reg    = 0x3d4;
        video_port_val    = 0x3d5;
        if ((ORIG_VIDEO_EGA_BX & 0xff) ! = 0x10)//see the machine system data
        {
                  video_type = VIDEO_TYPE_EGAC;
                  video_mem_end = 0xbc000;
                  display_desc = "EGAc";
          }
          else
          {
                  video_type = VIDEO_TYPE_CGA;
                  video_mem_end = 0xba000;
                  display_desc = "*CGA";
        }
        }

        /* Let the user known what kind of display driver we are using */

        display_ptr = ((char *)video_mem_start) + video_size_row - 8;
        while (*display_desc)
```

```
{
  *display_ptr++ = *display_desc++;
  display_ptr++;
}


/* Initialize the variables used for scrolling (mostly EGA/VGA)        */

origin = video_mem_start;
scr_end = video_mem_start + video_num_lines * video_size_row;
top = 0;
bottom = video_num_lines;

gotoxy(ORIG_X,ORIG_Y);//see the machine system data
set_trap_gate(0x21,&keyboard_interrupt);//set the interrupt of keyboard,
                                        //reference Section 2.5
outb_p(inb_p(0x21)&0xfd,0x21);//Cancel the keyboard  interrupt mask,
                              //allow IRQ1
a = inb_p(0x61);
outb_p(a|0x80,0x61);          //disable the keyboard
outb(a,0x61);                 //allow the keyboard
}
```

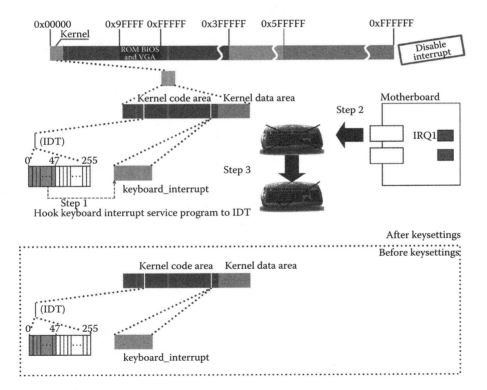

Figure 2.14 Set the keyboard.

▮ 2.8 Time Setting

startup_time is the basis of calculations related to time. In the OS, some operations depend on time information, furthermore, some programs need the time as parameter, for example, the file modification time, file access time, i node modified time, and so on. Other time information can be calculated according to startup_time.

The process is as follows: First, the system collects time data by calling time_init, which is on CMOS, a small memory chip on the main board, to extract different level time factors, for example, second time.tm_sec, minute time.tm_min, year time.tm_year, and so on. Then, integrate these factors to obtain startup_time.

The code is as follows:

```
//Code path:init/main.c:
void main(void)
{
        ......
        time_init();
        ......
}


#define CMOS_READ(addr) ({\          //read time data from COMS
outb_p(0x80|addr,0x70); \            //0x80|addr:read CMOS address,0x70:write port
inb_p(0x71); \                       //0x71 : read port
})


#define BCD_TO_BIN(val) ((val) = ((val)&15) + ((val)>>4)*10)//Change 10 hex to 2
                                                            //hex
static void time_init(void)
{
    struct tm time;


        do {
            time.tm_sec = CMOS_READ(0);//the second value of current time, The
                                       //following analogy
            time.tm_min = CMOS_READ(2);
            time.tm_hour = CMOS_READ(4);
            time.tm_mday = CMOS_READ(7);
            time.tm_mon = CMOS_READ(8);
            time.tm_year = CMOS_READ(9);
        } while (time.tm_sec ! = CMOS_READ(0));
    BCD_TO_BIN(time.tm_sec);
    BCD_TO_BIN(time.tm_min);
    BCD_TO_BIN(time.tm_hour);
    BCD_TO_BIN(time.tm_mday);
    BCD_TO_BIN(time.tm_mon);
    BCD_TO_BIN(time.tm_year);
    time.tm_mon-- ;
    startup_time = kernel_mktime(&time);//boot time, start from 0 clock 1970.1.1}


//Code path:include\asm\io.h:             //Embedded assembler refers to the comments of
                                          //trap_init
#define outb_p(value,port) \              //write value to port
__asm__ ("outb%%al,%%dx\n" \
                "\tjmp 1f\n" \            //jmp to the first next 1:to delay
```

```
                        "1:\tjmp 1f\n" \
                        "1:"::"a" (value),"d" (port))


#define inb_p(port) ({\
unsigned char _v; \
__asm__ volatile ("inb%%dx,%%al\n" \        //disable compiler optimize the
                                            //following codes
                        "\tjmp 1f\n" \      //delay
                        "1:\tjmp 1f\n" \
                        "1:":" = a" (_v):"d" (port)); \
                        _v; \
                        })
```

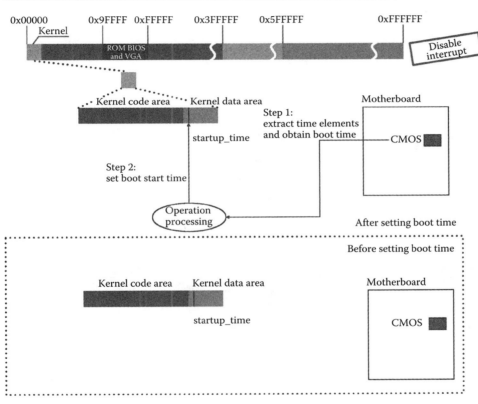

Figure 2.15 Boot time setting.

The calculation process and storage locations of boot time in the memory are as shown in Figure 2.15.

▌ 2.9 Initialize Process 0

Process 0 is the first process on Linux, which is also the first parent process to start the Linux OS. The following contents have the most important and deeply influence on the normally operation of process 0 in the host, mainly including three aspects:

1. Initialize process 0.

   The task_struct (init_task = {INIT_TASK,}) of process 0 has been implemented in the code design stage, but this does not mean that process 0 was available. We need to hook LDT and TSS in the task_struct of process 0 with GDT and initialize GDT, the process tank, and registers related to process scheduling.

2. As a modern OS, the most important indicator of Linux 0.11 is that it supports multiple-process execution, which means that a process is required to have multiple processes' polling capacity. System will set the timer interrupt in order to laying foundations for the schedule of process 0 and other processes, which are directly or indirectly by process 0.

3. Process 0 needs to cope with system calls. Each process in operation may interact with the kernel, by a system call program. The system uses the set_system_gate function to bind system_call with IDT and then process 0 becomes capable of dealing with system calls. System_call is the general entrance of any system call.

Process 0 needs to acquire the above three kinds of ability to ensure that it operates properly in the future and passes on these abilities to its offspring.

The code is as follows:

```
//Code path:init/main.c:
void main(void)
{
        ......
        sched_init();
        ......
}


//Code path:kernel/sched.c:
        ......
#define LATCH (1193180/HZ)      //The vibration frequency of each time slice
        ......
union task_union {              //The union of task_struct and kernel's stack
        struct task_struct task;
        char stack[PAGE_SIZE];         //PAGE_SIZE is 4K
};
static union task_union init_task = {INIT_TASK,};//task_struct of process 0
        ......
//task[0] is used by process 0
struct task_struct * task[NR_TASKS] = {&(init_task.task),};
        ......


void sched_init(void)
{
        int i;
        struct desc_struct * p;

        if (sizeof(struct sigaction) != 16)
                panic("Struct sigaction MUST be 16 bytes");
        set_tss_desc(gdt+FIRST_TSS_ENTRY,&(init_task.task.tss));//set TSS0
        set_ldt_desc(gdt+FIRST_LDT_ENTRY,&(init_task.task.ldt));//set LDT0
        p = gdt+2+FIRST_TSS_ENTRY;      //Set all above of TSS1 to 0 from the sixth of
        for(i = 1;i<NR_TASKS;i++) {     //gdt table and clear the process slot from 1
                task[i] = NULL;
                p->a = p->b = 0;
                p++;
                p->a = p->b = 0;
                p++;
        }
```

```
/* Clear NT, so that we won't have troubles with that later on */
        __asm__("pushfl ; andl $0xffffbfff,(%esp) ; popfl");
        ltr(0);    //Important!Bind tss with TR register
        lldt(0);//Important!Bind ldt with LDTR register
        outb_p(0x36,0x43); /* binary, mode 3, LSB/MSB, ch 0 *///set timer
        outb_p(LATCH & 0xff, 0x40);   /*LSB*///timer interrupt each 10 millisecond
        outb(LATCH >> 8, 0x40);    /* MSB */
        set_intr_gate(0x20,&timer_interrupt);   //Important! Set timer interrupt and
                                        //it's the base of process scheduling
        outb(inb_p(0x21)&~0x01,0x21);           //allow time interrupt
        set_system_gate(0x80,&system_call);//Important! Set the entry of system call
}

//Code path:include\linux\sched.h://    //embedded assembly refer the
                                     //trap_init's comments

#define FIRST_TSS_ENTRY 4           //See the entry of TSS
#define FIRST_LDT_ENTRY (FIRST_TSS_ENTRY+1)
#define _TSS(n) ((((unsigned long) n)<<4)+(FIRST_TSS_ENTRY<<3))
#define _LDT(n) ((((unsigned long) n)<<4)+(FIRST_LDT_ENTRY<<3))
#define ltr(n) __asm__("ltr%%ax"::"a" (_TSS(n)))
#define lldt(n) __asm__("lldt%%ax"::"a" (_LDT(n)))


//Code path:include\asm\system.h:

#define set_intr_gate(n,addr) \
        _set_gate(&idt[n],14,0,addr)

#define set_trap_gate(n,addr) \
        _set_gate(&idt[n],15,0,addr)

#define set_system_gate(n,addr) \
        _set_gate(&idt[n],15,3,addr)

#define _set_tssldt_desc(n,addr,type) \//See the trap_init's comments of
                                    //embedded assembly


__asm__("movw $104,%1\n\t" \//put 104(1101000)in the first word in LDT
        "movw%%ax,%2\n\t" \//put low 16-bit base address of TSS or LDT into
                        //NO.3, 4 bytes of this descriptor
        "rorl $16,%%eax\n\t" \
        "movb%%al,%3\n\t" \   //put NO.3 byte of base address into NO.5 byte
        "movb $" type ",%4\n\t" \//put 0x89 or 0x82 into NO.6 byte
        "movb $0x00,%5\n\t" \//put 0x00 into NO.7 byte
        "movb%%ah,%6\n\t" \//put NO.4 byte of base address into NO.8 byte
        "rorl $16,%%eax" \    //restore eax
        ::"a" (addr), "m" (*(n)), "m" (*(n+2)), "m" (*(n+4)), \
        "m" (*(n+5)), "m" (*(n+6)), "m" (*(n+7)) \
        //"m" (*(n))is a memory cell start from NO.n descriptor of the GDT.
        //"m" (*(n+2)) a memory cell start from NO.3 byte of NO.n descriptor of the GDT.
                //The remaining and so on
                )
#define set_tss_desc(n,addr) _set_tssldt_desc(((char *) (n)),addr,"0x89")
#define set_ldt_desc(n,addr) _set_tssldt_desc(((char *) (n)),addr,"0x82")


//Code path:include/linux/sched.h:

struct tss_struct {
        long        back_link;       /* 16 high bits zero */
        long        esp0;
        long        ss0;             /* 16 high bits zero */
        long        esp1;
        long        ss1;             /* 16 high bits zero */
        long        esp2;
        long        ss2;             /* 16 high bits zero */
        long        cr3;
        long        eip;
        long        eflags;
        long        eax,ecx,edx,ebx;
        long        esp;
        long        ebp;
```

```
        long    esi;
        long    edi;
        long    es;                     /* 16 high bits zero */
        long    cs;                     /* 16 high bits zero */
        long    ss;                     /* 16 high bits zero */
        long    ds;                     /* 16 high bits zero */
        long    fs;                     /* 16 high bits zero */
        long    gs;                     /* 16 high bits zero */
        long    ldt;                    /* 16 high bits zero */
        long    trace_bitmap;           /* bits: trace 0, bitmap 16-31 */
        struct i387_struct i387;
};


struct task_struct {
/* these are hardcoded - don't touch */
        long state;              /* -1 unrunnable, 0 runnable, >0 stopped */
        long counter;
        long priority;
        long signal;
        struct sigaction sigaction[32];
        long blocked;            /* bitmap of masked signals */
/* various fields */
        int exit_code;
        unsigned long start_code,end_code,end_data,brk,start_stack;
        long pid,father,pgrp,session,leader;
        unsigned short uid,euid,suid;
        unsigned short gid,egid,sgid;
        long alarm;
        long utime,stime,cutime,cstime,start_time;
        unsigned short used_math;
/* file system info */
        int tty;                 /* -1 if no tty, so it must be signed */
        unsigned short umask;
        struct m_inode * pwd;
        struct m_inode * root;
        struct m_inode * executable;
        unsigned long close_on_exec;
        struct file * filp[NR_OPEN];
/* ldt for this task 0 - zero 1 - cs 2 - ds&ss */
        struct desc_struct ldt[3];
/* tss for this task */
        struct tss_struct tss;
};


/* task_struct of process 0
 * INIT_TASK is used to set up the first task table, touch at
 * your own risk!. Base = 0, limit = 0x9ffff (= 640kB)
 */
#define INIT_TASK \
/* state etc */      {0,15,15, \              //Ready state,15 time slice
/* signals */        0,{{},},0, \
/* ec,brk... */      0,0,0,0,0,0, \
/* pid etc.. */      0,-1,0,0,0, \            //PID 0
/* uid etc */        0,0,0,0,0,0, \
/* alarm */          0,0,0,0,0,0, \
/* math */           0, \
/* fs info */        -1,0022,NULL,NULL,NULL,0, \
/* filp */           {NULL,}, \
        {\
                        {0,0}, \
/* ldt */ {0x9f,0xc0fa00}, \
                        {0x9f,0xc0f200}, \
        }, \
/*tss*/  {0,PAGE_SIZE+(long)&init_task,0x10,0,0,0,0,(long)&pg_dir,\
         0,0,0,0,0,0,0,0, \  //the value of eflags determines the cli only can be
                                //used in the 0 privileges
         0,0,0x17,0x17,0x17,0x17,0x17, \
         _LDT(0),0x80000000, \
                 {} \
        }, \
}
```

2.9.1　Initialization of Process 0

```
sched_init():
```

The difficulty in understanding the sched_init() function is seen in the following two lines:

```
set_tss_desc(gdt+FIRST_TSS_ENTRY,&(init_task.task.tss));
set_ldt_desc(gdt+FIRST_LDT_ENTRY,&(init_task.task.ldt));
```

The purpose of the two lines is to initialize the 4, 5 items of process 0 in the GDT table. The initialization of TSS0 and LDT0 is shown in Figure 2.16.

Take the TSS0 as an example; based on the comments in the source code, we can draw the picture below (Figures 2.17 and 2.18).

Compared to the source code, comments, and figure, we can find the movw$104,% 1 assign 104 to 15:0 part to segment limit, G is 0, that indicates the segment limit is 104 bytes, and TSS just has 104 bytes except struct i387_struct i387. LDT is 3 × 8 = 24 bytes, 104 bytes limit is long enough. The TSS type is x89, that is the 10001001 binary. We can see that the movb $" type ",% 4 to assign the type 1001. By the way, will assign the value of P DPL, S fields. Similarly, movb $0 x00,%5 assign the part of 0000, at the same time, also conveniently assign G, D/B, preserved, and AVL fields.

The task_struct of process 0 has been hard-coded by the OS designers, which is the INIT_TASK in sched.h (see the source code, the related structure, and comments below), and the INIT_TASK pointer initialized 0 item of task[64] (Figure 2.19).

Sched_init() will clear the task[64] except for the 0 item in process 0 subsequently and, at the same time, will clear all items above TSS1 and LDT1 in GDT. The results are shown below.

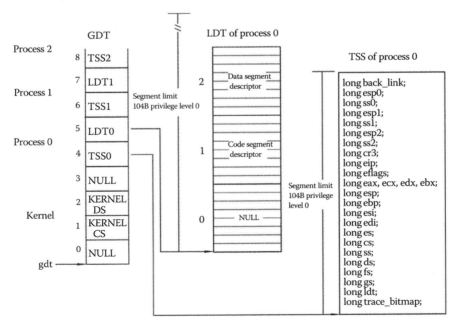

Figure 2.16 The relationship among GDT, LDT, and TSS.

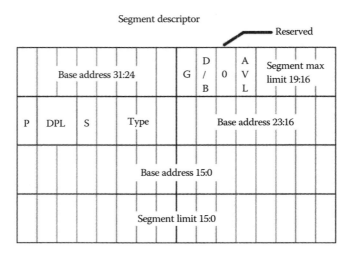

Figure 2.17 The structure of the segment descriptor.

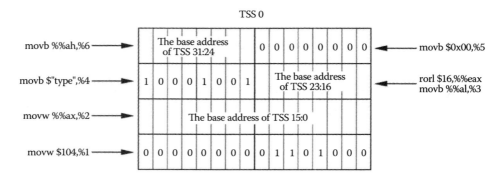

Figure 2.18 The structure of TSS0.

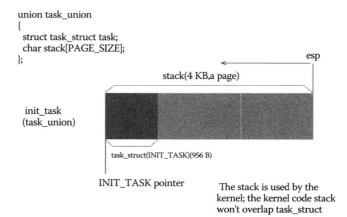

```
union task_union
{
  struct task_struct task;
  char stack[PAGE_SIZE];
};
```

Figure 2.19 The structure of task_union.

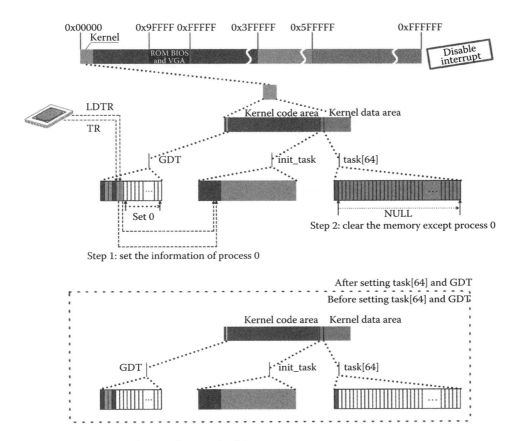

Figure 2.20 Initialize the correlative task of the process.

The final step of initializing the management structure is also very important (Figure 2.20). It puts the TR register point to TSS0 and the LDTR register point to LDT0. The CPU can find the TSS0 LDT0 in process 0 through the TR and LDTR registers, and you can find the related management information of process 0.

2.9.2 Set the Timer Interrupt

The timer interrupt is the basis of schedule of process 0 and other processes created by process 0. The process of setting timer interrupt is divided into the following three steps:

1. Set the 8253 timer that supports polling. This operation is the first step in Figure 2.21, in which the key is LATCH, defined by a macro, and through it define "# define LATCH (1193180/HZ)" in sched.c, namely, the system happens once timer interrupt in every 10 seconds.

2. Set the timer interrupt, which is the second step in Figure 2.21, after the timer_ interrupt function is binded; when timer interrupt occurs, the system can find this service routine through the interrupt descriptor table and perform some specific actions.

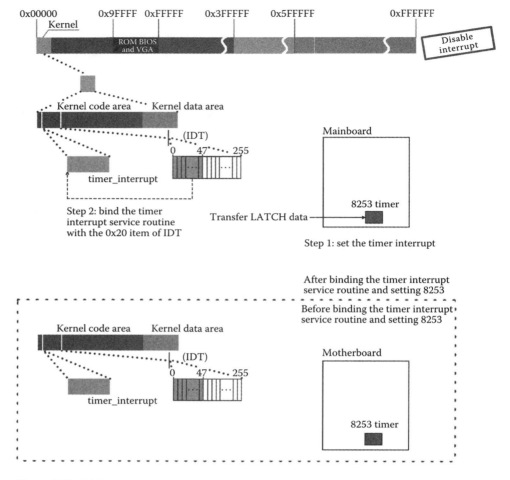

Figure 2.21 Set timer interrupt.

3. Open the maskable bits related with timer interrupt in the 8259A chip. After opening, the timer interrupt produce, from now on, the timer interrupt produce in each 1/100 seconds. Because of the "disable interrupt" state, the CPU does not respond, but process 0 has the potential to be involved in the schedule.

2.9.3 Set the Entrance of System Call

The system call processing function system_call needs to be bound with the int 0x80 interrupt descriptor. System_call is the total entry of system call soft interrupt in the whole OS. All user programs use system call. After producing int 0x80 soft interrupt, OS finds specific system call functions through the total entry. This process is shown in Figure 2.22.

The system call's function is the basic support of the OS to the user program. In the OS, the core is protected by the privilege level that relies on the hardware and does not allow the user process to directly access the kernel code. But there are a lot of processes,

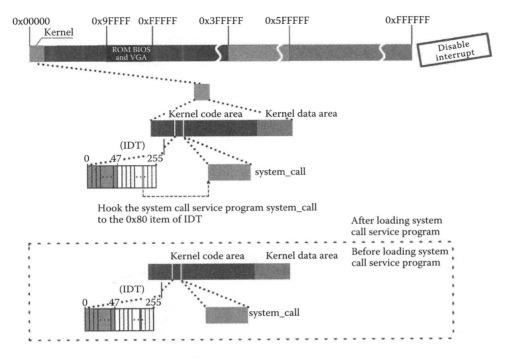

Figure 2.22 Call service program of the system.

such as reading a disk and creating the child process of such specific transaction processing, that need the support of the kernel code. In order to resolve the contradiction, the designer of the OS provides the system call solutions and a set of system service interface. When the user process needs to deal with the kernel, it calls the interface program, which immediately triggers int 0x80 soft interrupt. The following things don't need the user program, but through a different route which the CPU responds to the interrupt signal, change privilege level, from a user process privilege level 3 flip to 0 privilege level, through the interrupt descriptor table find system call port, call specific system function to handle affairs, and then, iret flip back to the 3 privilege level of process, the process continue to execute the original logic, contradiction is solved.

▋ 2.10 Initialize the Buffer Management Structure

The buffer area is the medium through which the memory exchanges data with peripherals. The biggest difference between the memory and the hard drive lies in the fact that the disk saves large amounts of data at a low cost. The disk is not involved in operations (because the CPU cannot address the disk). In addition, the memory not only needs to store data, but the more important thing here is to perform data operation with the CPU and bus. The buffer is in between, and it not only saves the data but also participates in some searching, organization, and indirect, auxiliary operation. After having the buffer medium to the peripherals, it only needs to consider exchanging data with the buffer in accordance with the requirements and does not need to consider how the memory will use these interaction data. As for memory, it also only needs to consider whether the condition of the interaction with the buffer is ready and does not need to care about the interaction between buffer and peripherals. Organization, management, and coordination are operated by the OS.

The OS manages the buffer through the hash_table[NR_HASH] and the buffer_head two-way chain complex hash table.

The OS sets the buffer by calling the buffer_init function; the execute code is as follows:

```
//code path:init/main.c:
void main(void)
{
    ......
    buffer_init(buffer_memory_end);
    ......
}
```

In the buffer_init function, from the kernel end and the terminal of the buffer area beginning at the same time grow in relative direction, pair to make buffer_head, buffer block, until less than a pair of buffer_head, a buffer block, in the second chapter, at the beginning of the memory set pattern, with about 3000 pairs of buffer_head, buffer block, buffer_head in low address, buffer block in the high address (Figure 2.23).

Set the member of device head: device id b_dev, b_count, "update" sign b_uptodate, "dirty" logo sign b_dirt, and "locking" flag b_lock to 0. As shown in the figure, the b_data pointer points to the corresponding buffer block. Using the b_prev_free and b_next_free of the buffer_head, set all the buffer_head into a two-way linked list. The free_list refers to the first buffer_head, and use free_list to set the two-way linked list formed by the buffer_head link into a bidirectional ring chain, as shown in the following illustration (Figure 2.24).

Notice the memory change shown at the top of Figure 2.25. There is a black area of the memory near the system core part that stored the buffer management structure. Because it manages more than 3000 buffer blocks, it takes up the same memory space as the kernel. The figure describes the two-way linked list structure.

Finally, set the hash_table[307] and all the contents of hash_table[307] to NULL. As shown in Figure 2.25, the code is as follows:

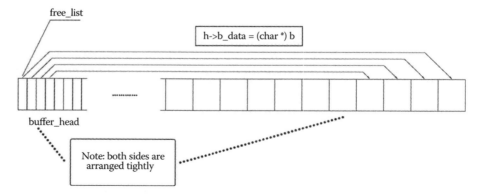

Figure 2.23 An overview of initialization a.

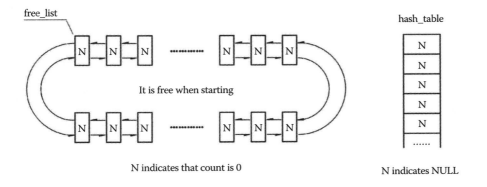

N indicates that count is 0   N indicates NULL

Figure 2.24 An overview of initialization b.

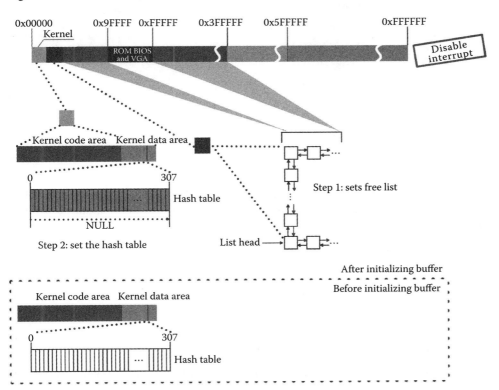

Figure 2.25 Initialize the buffer management structure.

```
//code path:fs/buffer.c:
......
struct buffer_head * start_buffer = (struct buffer_head *) &end;
struct buffer_head * hash_table[NR_HASH];
static struct buffer_head * free_list;
......
```

```
void buffer_init(long buffer_end)
{
        struct buffer_head * h = start_buffer;
        void * b;
        int i;


        if (buffer_end = = 1<<20)
                b = (void *) (640*1024);
        else
                b = (void *) buffer_end;
//Eachtime h and d enter the buffer_head and buffer block one piece from the low and
//high address of buffer. Ignore the remain buffer_head and the space of buffer.
        while ((b - - BLOCK_SIZE) > = ((void *) (h+1))) {
                h->b_dev = 0;
                h->b_dirt = 0;
                h->b_count = 0;
                h->b_lock = 0;
                h->b_uptodate = 0;
                h->b_wait = NULL;
                h->b_next = NULL;               //Initialize the two item empty,
                                                //articulate the subsequent to hash table
                h->b_prev = NULL;
                h->b_data = (char *) b;         //articulate each buffer head to a buffer
                h->b_prev_free = h-1;           //The two items articulate buffer head to front
                h->b_next_free = h+1;//and rear of buffer head, produce a doubly linked list
                h++;
                NR_BUFFERS++;
                if (b = = (void *) 0x100000)  //avoid ROMBIOS&VGA
                        b = (void *) 0xA0000;
        }
        h--;
        free_list = start_buffer;               //free_list points to buffer_head
        free_list->b_prev_free = h;             //let buffer_head doubly linked list
        h->b_next_free = free_list;             //form doubly linked list
        for (i = 0;i<NR_HASH;i++)               //clear hash_table[307]
                hash_table[i] = NULL;
}
```

Look at the code struct buffer_head *h = start_buffer; in this line, start_buffer identifies the starting position of the buffer. This also solves the problem about the starting position of the buffer. It is defined in buffer.c:

```
struct buffer_head * start_buffer = (struct buffer_head *) &end;
```

The end is the end address of the kernel code. In the designing stage, it is difficult to accurately estimate this address. Set the end value during kernel module linking and use it here.

■ 2.11   Initialize the Hard Disk

To build the environment of communications between a process and the hard disk, the OS must initialize the hard disk.

In the function hd_init, the program links the hard disk request service routine do_hd_request and blk_dev control structure; the interact work of the hard disk and the request is handled by the function do_hd_request and then links the hard disk interrupt service routine hd_interrupt and the interrupt descriptor table. Finally, it resets the mask bit of primary 8259A int2 to allow the interrupt request signals sent by the vice-chip; it then resets the hard disk interrupt request mask bit (on-vice-chip), allowing the interrupt request signals sent by the hard disk controller.

The code is as follows:

```
//Code path: init/main.c:
void main(void)
{
......
        hd_init();
......
}


//Code path: kernel/blk_dev/hd.c://Similar with rd_init, see the comment of rd_init
void hd_init(void)
{
        blk_dev[MAJOR_NR].request_fn = DEVICE_REQUEST; //Link do_hd_request()
        set_intr_gate(0x2E,&hd_interrupt); //Set the hard disk interrupt
        outb_p(inb_p(0x21)&0xfb,0x21); //Allow 8259A to send interrupt request
        outb(inb_p(0xA1)&0xbf,0xA1); //Allow hard disk to send interrupt request
}
```

Figure 2.26 shows the process of initialization.

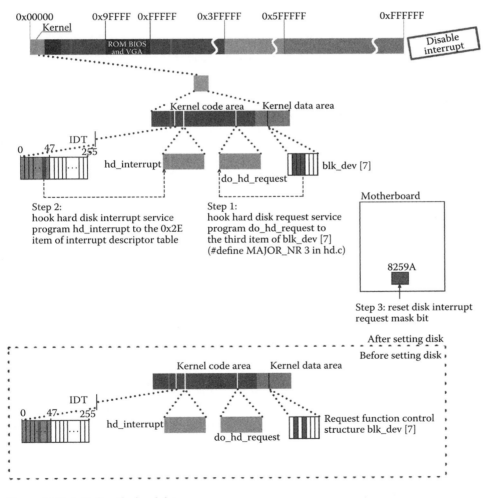

Figure 2.26 Initialize the hard drive.

▐ 2.12 Initialize the Floppy Disk

The floppy disk and floppy disk drives can be detached. In this book, for convenience, floppy disk represents the floppy disk drive and floppy disk as a whole.

Initialization of the floppy disk is similar to hard disk initialization. The difference is the link function do_fd_request(), initializing the interrupt that is associated with the floppy disk. Details can be found in Section 2.11.

The code is as follows:

```
//Code path: init/main.c:
void main(void)
{
        ......
        floppy_init ();//Similar with hd_init()
        ......
}


//Code path: kernel/floppy.c:
......
void floppy_init(void)
{
      blk_dev[MAJOR_NR].request_fn = DEVICE_REQUEST; //Link do_fd_request()
      set_trap_gate(0x26,&floppy_interrupt); //Set the floppy disk interrupt
         outb(inb_p(0x21)&~0x40,0x21); //Allow floppy disk to send a interrupt
}
```

Figure 2.27 gives the main steps to initialize the floppy disk.

▐ 2.13 Enable the Interrupt

Now, all the interrupt service routines and the IDT have been linked; this means that the interrupt service system has been finished. The system can deal with the interrupt in the 32-bit protected mode. Importantly, it means that the system call can be used.

Now we can enable the interrupt!

The code is as follows:

```
//Code path: include/asm/system.h:
#define sti() __asm__ ("sti"::)


//Code path: init/main.c:
void main(void)
{
        ......
        sti();
        ......
}
```

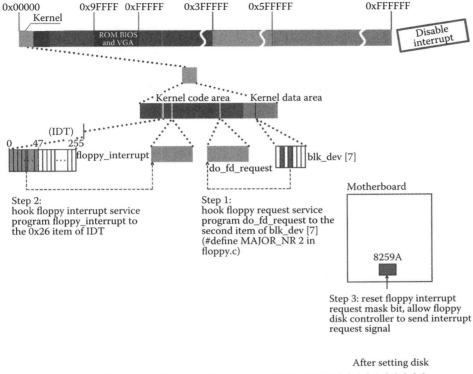

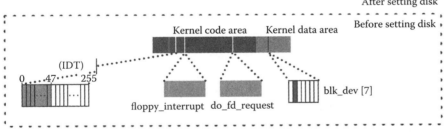

Figure 2.27 Initialize the floppy disk.

Figure 2.28 gives the effect after enabling the interrupt. Be aware of the changes in EFlags.

2.14 Process 0 Moves from Privilege Level 0 to 3 and Becomes a Real Process

Linux OS requires that all processes should be built by an existing process in privilege level 3, with the exception of process 0. In Linux 0.11, the code and data of process 0 are written in the kernel of the OS. It is in privilege level 0; at this time, strictly speaking, the process 0 is not a real process. In order to comply with the rules, before process 0 creates process 1, process 0 must be moved from privilege level 0 to 3. The specific method is to call the function move_to_user_mode, imitating the interrupt return action, to move the privilege level of process 0 from 0 to 3.

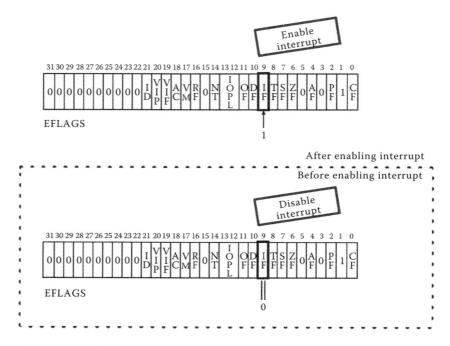

Figure 2.28 Enable the interrupt.

The code is as follows:

```
//Code path: init/main.c:
void main(void)
{
......
        move_to_user_mode();
......
}


//Code path: include/system.h: //See 1.3.4
#define move_to_user_mode() \     //Imitate push, the order is ss, esp, eflags, cs, eip
__asm__("movl%%esp,%%eax\n\t" \
        "pushl $0x17\n\t" \ //Push ss, 0x17 is 10111 in binary system(Privilege
                            //level 3, ldt, data segment)
        "pushl%%eax\n\t" \ //Push esp
        "pushfl\n\t" \ //Push eflags
        "pushl $0x0f\n\t" \ //Push cs, 0x0f is 1111 in binary system(Privilege level
                            //3, ldt, Code segment)
        "pushl $1f\n\t" \ //Push eip
        "iret\n" \ //return, move from the privilege level 0 to 3
        "1:\tmovl $0x17,%%eax\n\t" \   //The following codes make ds, es, fs, gs and ss
                                       //have the same value
                "movw%%ax,%%ds\n\t" \
                "movw%%ax,%%es\n\t" \
                "movw%%ax,%%fs\n\t" \
                "movw%%ax,%%gs" \
                :::"ax")
```

2. Device Initialization and Process 0 Activation

One way to change the privilege level in IA-32 is through interruption, as introduced in Chapter 1. When an interrupt request is received, the CPU can interrupt the current program; cs:eip switches to perform the corresponding interrupt service routine. When finished, perform iret to return to the interrupted program to continue.

During this period, the CPU hardware does two things: to protect and restore the environment and to change the privilege level.

We can see from the code performance that interruption is just like function calls. They can jump from a code that is being executed to another section of the code and then return to the original code to execute after finishing the execution of the new code. In order to make sure that the process could return to the original code accurately, you need to push CS and EIP to save the next line of code (protect environment). When finished executing the called function or interrupt service routine, pop CS and EIP (restore environment). Thus, the CPU can perform the called function or interrupt program accurately. The EFlags and other important registers also need to be protected.

The difference between interruption and function call is that the function call is designed by a programmer; the compiler can compile in advance the protection and the restoration code. While the interruption is unpredictable, they cannot be compiled in advance. Hence, the protection and restoration environment of the interruption have to be performed by the hardware. Therefore, the command int instruction will cause the hardware to complete the push of SS, ESP, EFlags, CS, and EIP. Similarly, when executing the command iret, the hardware will pop them to the corresponding register.

According to the settings of dpl, when the CPU responds to the interruption, it can change the privilege level. In function sched_init(), set_system_gate (0x80,&system_call) is to set the interrupt int 0x80 move from privilege level 3 to 0. When the process of privilege level 3 do the system call int 0x80, CPU will flip to privilege level 0. Similarly, the command iret could change the privilege level from 0 to 3.

The function move_to_user_mode is based on this principle, using iret to change the privilege level from 0 to 3.

So far, process 0 is in privilege level 0; the stack does not have the values of these five registers: ss, esp, eflags, cs and eip. In order to use the command iret, the designer pushes value of these registers manually, which is similar to the command int. When performing the command iret, the CPU automatically pops this 5 value to the register and turns to privilege level 3, executing the code in privilege level 3.

In order to change to privilege level 3, not only should the push order be correct, but the privilege level of SS and CS must also be right. Note that the value of SS in the stack is 0x17, which is 00010111 in the binary system; the last two bits represent 3, the user privilege level. Then, the sixth bit is 1, which means the segment descriptor is obtained from the LDT; the 10 of 4–5 bits means obtaining the stack segment descriptor from the third item of the LDT.

When executing the command iret, the hardware would pop the 5 value from the stack to SS, ESP, EFlags, CS, and EIP in order. The pop order is the same as the usual interruption return; also, the effect of the return is the same.

When the system finished executing the function move_to_user_mode(), equivalent to an interruption return, the privilege level of process 0 changes from 0 to 3, which means process 0 becomes a real process.

3 Creation and Execution of Process 1

▌ 3.1 Creation of Process 1

Now, process 0 is at privilege level 3, which is a process state. As a parent process, its first task is to call fork() to create the first child process—process 1, which is the first implementation of the parent–child process-creating mechanism. On the basis of this mechanism, all processes are created by the parent process later.

3.1.1 Preparation for Creating Process 1

In Linux, any new process is created by calling fork(). The procedure is shown in Figure 3.1.

The code is as follows:

```
//code path:init/main.c:
    ......
static inline _syscall0(int,fork)//correspond to fork
static inline _syscall0(int,pause)
static inline _syscall1(int,setup,void *,BIOS)
    ......
void main(void)
{
        sti();
```

```
        move_to_user_mode();
        if (!fork()) {                /* we count on this going ok */
                init();
        }
/*
* NOTE!! For any other task 'pause()' would mean we have to get a
* signal to awaken, but task0 is the sole exception (see 'schedule()')
* as task 0 gets activated at every idle moment (when no other tasks
* can run). For task0 'pause()' just means we go check if some other
* task can run, and if not we return here.
*/
        for(;;) pause();
}
```

The fork() in main.c indicates that the execution is actually transferred to syscall0 macro in unistd.h. The code is shown as follows:

```
//code path:include/unistd.h:
......
#define __NR_setup   0          /* used only by init, to get system going */
#define __NR_exit    1
#define __NR_fork    2
#define __NR_read    3
#define __NR_write   4
#define __NR_open    5
#define __NR_close   6
......

#define _syscall0(type,name) \
type name(void) \
{\
long __res; \
__asm__ volatile ("int $0x80" \
        : "=a" (__res) \
        : "0" (__NR_##name)); \
if (__res >= 0) \
        return (type) __res; \
errno = -__res; \
return -1; \
}
......
volatile void _exit(int status);
int fcntl(int fildes, int cmd,...);
int fork(void);
int getpid(void);
int getuid(void);
int geteuid(void);
......

//code path:include/linux/sys.h:
extern int sys_setup();
extern int sys_exit();
extern int sys_fork();         //correspond to _sys_fork in system_call.s, there is an
                               //underline"_" in front of
extern int sys_read();         //functions in Assembler corresponding to that in C language.
extern int sys_write();        //such as:_sys_fork is the corresponding function of sys_fork.
extern int sys_open();
......

fn_ptr sys_call_table[] = {sys_setup, sys_exit, sys_fork, sys_read,//sys_fork corresponds to
                                                              //the third item
sys_write, sys_open, sys_close, sys_waitpid, sys_creat, sys_link,  //of _sys_call_table
sys_unlink, sys_execve, sys_chdir, sys_time, sys_mknod, sys_chmod,
......
```

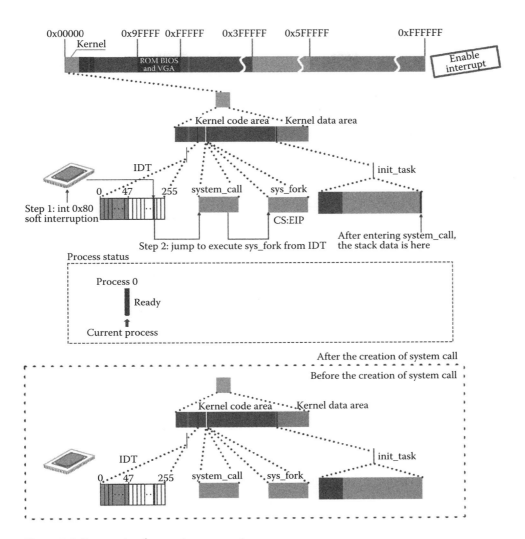

0x00000 0x9FFFF 0xFFFFF 0x3FFFFF 0x5FFFFF 0xFFFFFF

Kernel
ROM BIOS and VGA

Enable interrupt

Kernel code area ···· Kernel data area

IDT

Step 1: int 0x80 soft interruption

0 ··· 47 255 system_call sys_fork init_task

CS:EIP

Step 2: jump to execute sys_fork from IDT

After entering system_call, the stack data is here

Process status

Process 0

Ready

Current process

After the creation of system call

Before the creation of system call

Kernel code area ···· Kernel data area

IDT

init_task

0 ··· 47 255 system_call sys_fork

Figure 3.1 Preparation for creating process 1.

Syscall0 looks like the following after expansion:

```
int fork(void)                  //refer to the code annotation about embedding assemble
{                               //in section 2.5, 2.9, 2.14
long __res;
__asm__ volatile ("int $0x80"   //int 0x80 is the head entry of all system call,one of which
                                //is fork().You can refer to the explanation in section 2.9
    : "=a" (__res)              //output part.The value of __res is assigned to eax.
    : "0" (__NR_fork));         //input part, "0" is eax, NR_fork is 2, which is assigned to eax.
    if (__res >= 0)             //this line will be executed after return from int 0x80
    return (int) __res;
    errno = -__res;
    return -1;
}
//Attentions:Caused by int 0x80, the hardware will automatically push ss, esp, eflags, cs, eip!
//You can refer to the explanation in section 2.14
```

Regarding the long procedure of int 0x80, the general process is illustrated below.
The detailed steps are as follows:

The code "0" (__NR_ fork) is executed first. The value of _NR_fork, which is the corresponding function number of fork in sys_call_table[], is assigned to eax, namely, 2. This number is the offset value of the sys_fork function in sys_call_table.

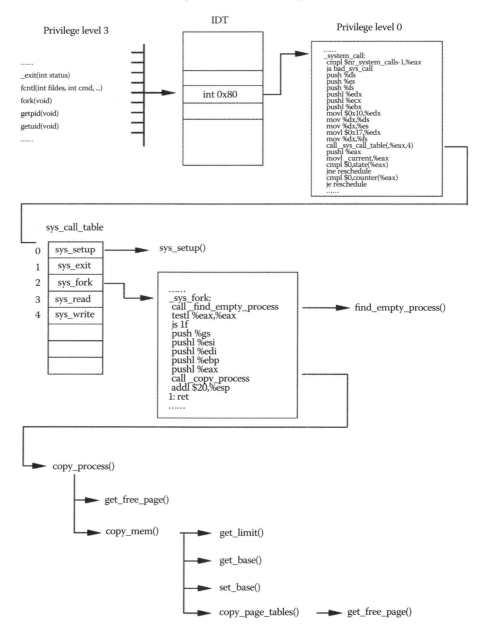

Figure 3.2 The calling path of system call.

After which, "int $ 0x80" is executed. It triggers a soft interrupt and the central processing unit (CPU) starts executing the kernel code in privilege level 0 from the process code in level 3. The hardware automatically pushes ss, esp, eflags, cs, and eip to the kernel stack of process 0 in init_task, which is shown in Figure 3.1. You should pay attention to the red stripe after the init_task structure, which is the value of the five registers. The push action in the move_to_user_mode mentioned before is to imitate hardware push in interruption. The pushed data will be used to initialize the TSS of process 1 in the subsequent copy_process function.

Note that the pushed eip data points to the next line of the instruction "int $ 0x80," which is the line if (__res> = 0). Process 0 will continue to execute this line after being back from interrupt in fork(). In Section 3.3, we will see that this line is also the first instruction that process 1 starts to execute. Keep this point in mind!

According to the settings of set_system_gate (0x80, & system_call) in sched_init() explained in Section 2.9, after pushing automatically, the CPU jumps to _system_call in sytem_call.s and continues to push in ds, es, fs, edx, ecx, and ebx, which is used to prepare for initializing TSS in process 1 when calling copy_process(). Finally, according to the offset value 2, the kernel looks up sys_call_table[] to learn that the corresponding function is sys_fork. The corresponding function name to C language in Assembler has an underscore "_" in front (e.g., _sys_fork in Assembler corresponds to sys_fork in C language); thus, the kernel starts to execute _sys_fork.

Tip:

The function parameters are not defined by the function itself but made out by another procedure through pushing, which is one of the main distinctions between the OS code and the application code. Clearly understanding the compilation and implementation of C language will help one grasp this method. Parameters of C language exist in the stack when operating; hence, system designers can force the value in stacks as parameters of function in sequence. In this way, functions will use the value in stacks as parameters.

The code is as follows:

```
//Code path:kernel/system_call.s:
    ......
_system_call:                    #int 0x80- - head entry of system call
        cmpl $nr_system_calls-1,%eax
        ja bad_sys_call
        push%ds                  #all the 6 pushes are used as the parameters of
                                 #copy_process ().
        push%es                  #remember the order and don't forget int 0x80 in front.
        push%fs                  #5 values are pushed, too.
        pushl%edx
        pushl%ecx                # push%ebx,%ecx,%edx as parameters
        pushl%ebx                # to the system call
        movl $0x10,%edx          # set up ds,es to kernel space
        mov%dx,%ds
        mov%dx,%es
        movl $0x17,%edx          # fs points to local data space
        mov%dx,%fs
        call _sys_call_table(,%eax,4) #eax is 2, this line is equal to call (_sys_call_
                                 table + 2x4),
        pushl%eax                #namely the entry of _sys_fork
        movl _current,%eax
        cmpl $0,state(%eax)      # state
```

```
            jne reschedule
            cmpl $0,counter(%eax)            # counter
            je reschedule
ret_from_sys_call:
            movl _current,%eax              # task[0] cannot have signals
            cmpl _task,%eax
            je 3f
            cmpw $0x0f,CS(%esp)             # was old code segment supervisor ?
            jne 3f
            cmpw $0x17,OLDSS(%esp)          # was stack segment = 0x17 ?
            jne 3f
            movl signal(%eax),%ebx
            movl blocked(%eax),%ecx
            notl%ecx
            andl%ebx,%ecx
            bsfl%ecx,%ecx
            je 3f
            btrl%ecx,%ebx
            movl%ebx,signal(%eax)
            incl%ecx
            pushl%ecx
            call _do_signal
            popl%eax
3:          popl%eax
            popl%ebx
            popl%ecx
            popl%edx
            pop%fs
            pop%es
            pop%ds
            iret
            .....
_sys_fork:                                  #the entry of sys_fork()
            .....
```

In the line call _sys_call_table (,%eax,4), the value of eax is 2. This line can also be seen as call _sys_call_table + 2 × 4, in which the value 4 means 4 bytes in each item of _sys_call_table[]. It is equal to call _sys_call_table[2], namely, sys_fork.

Note: The instruction call _sys_call_table (,% eax, 4) will protect the field by itself, and the sixth parameter in copy_process(), long none, indicates this push action. The execution code is as follows:

```
//Code path:kernel/system_call.s:
            .....
_system_call:
            .....
_sys_fork:
            call _find_empty_process
            testl%eax,%eax          #if the return value is -EAGAIN(11), there have been 64 process
                                    #in execution
            js 1f                   #already.
            push%gs                 #the following values of five registers pushed in the stack
                                    #is set as the initial parameters of copy_process ()
            pushl%esi
            pushl%edi
            pushl%ebp
            pushl%eax
            call _copy_process
            addl $20,%esp
1:          ret
            .....
```

3.1.2 Apply for an Idle Position and a Process Number for Process 1

The sys_fork function begins to work.

As introduced in Section 2.9, all items except for the 0 of task[64] have been cleared by sched_init(). Now, find_empty_process will be called to find an available pid and location in task[64]. The calling effect is shown in Figure 3.3.

In find_empty_process(), the global variable last_pid is used to store all the process numbers after booting, and this variable is also used as the pid of newly created process. After traversing task[64] for the first time, the kernel executes ++last_pid because of the true "&&" condition. On the second time, the kernel will get the first idle i, which is also named as the task number.

After two passes, the new process number of last_pid is 1, occupying the second item of task[64]. The result is shown in the middle right part in Figure 3.3.

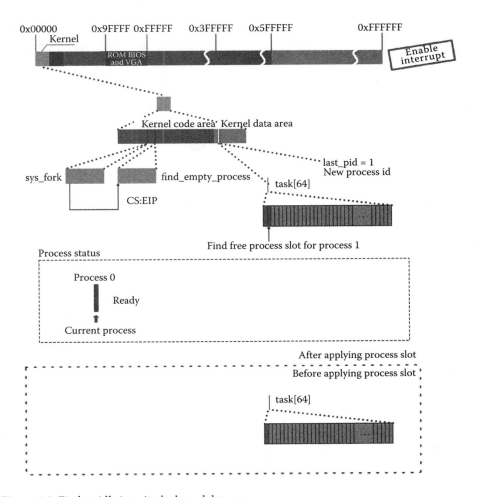

Figure 3.3 Find an idle item in the kernel data area.

Because there are only 64 items in task[64] in Linux 0.11, the maximum number of parallel processes is restricted to 64. If the return value of find_process_number is -EAGAIN, it means that there have been 64 processes currently. By now, this situation will not happen. The execution code is as follows:

```
//code path:kernel/fork.c:
      ......
long last_pid = 0;
      ......
int find_empty_process(void)              //find an idle position for new created
                                          //process, NR_TASKS is 64
{
        int i;

repeat:
        if ((++last_pid)<0) last_pid=1;   //if last_pid overflows after ++, the value
                                          //is set to 1
        for(i=0 ; i<NR_TASKS ; i++)       //find available last_pid,the value is 1
                if (task[i] && task[i]->pid == last_pid) goto repeat;
        for(i=1 ; i<NR_TASKS ; i++)       //return the first idle i
                if (!task[i])
                        return i;
        return -EAGAIN;                   //EAGAIN is 11
}
```

The newly created process 1 gets its ID after confirming the process pid and the location in task[64]. The five registers' value will be pushed into the kernel stacks of process 0, prepared as parameters for calling copy_process() and initializing the TSS of process 1.

Note: *The eax value pushed last is the returned pid of find_empty_process() and is also the first parameter int nr of copy_process().*

3.1.3   Call Copy_process()

Process 0 has become a parent process that can create a child process, and it has management information such as task_struct and page table entry of itself in the kernel. Process 0 will perform some important jobs in calling copy_process(), which reflects the parent–child process-creating mechanism:

1. Creating task_struct. The task_struct of process 0 is copied to process 1.

2. Setting task_struct and TSS for process 1.

3. Creating the first page table. The page items of process 0 are copied to process 1.

4. Sharing the files of process 0.

5. Setting the GDT of process 1.

6. Setting process 1 in ready state. After that, it can participate in process schedule.

Calling copy_process() from now on!

Before explaining copy_process, it is worth reminding that all the parameters are formed through pushing accumulatively by previous codes. The value of the parameters is also related to the pushing state (Figure 3.4). The execution code is as follows:

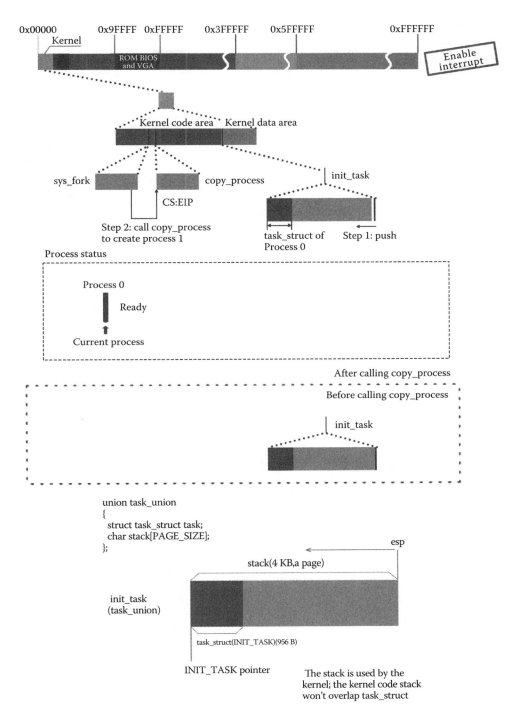

Figure 3.4 Push action before calling copy_process.

```
//code path:kernel/fork.c:
int copy_process(int nr,long ebp,long edi,long esi,long gs,long none,
long ebx,long ecx,long edx,
long fs,long es,long ds,                       //
long eip,long cs,long eflags,long esp,long ss)
//Attention:these parameters are pushed by int 0x80, system_call and sys_fork.
{
        struct task_struct *p;
        int i;
        struct file *f;

        //get one page at the end of 16MB memory.
        p = (struct task_struct *) get_free_page();
        if (!p)
                return -EAGAIN;
        task[nr] = p;        //nr is 1, which means this page is used as task_union. refer
                             //to section 2.9.1.
        ……
}
```

Get_free_page() will be called after entering copy_process(), and the kernel will apply for an idle page. The new cleared page will be used for the task_struct and kernel stack of process 1.

According to the algorithm of get_free_page(), the new page starts from the end of the main memory to the low-address memory progressively. Since it is the first time for the kernel to apply for an idle page in the main memory for process 1 after booting, this new idle page has to be located at the end of the 16 MB main memory.

The code is as follows:

```
//code path:mm/memory.c:
unsigned long get_free_page(void)           //get an idle page,refer to the code annotation about
                                            //embedding assemble.
{
register unsigned long __res asm("ax");

__asm__("std ; repne ; scasb\n\t"          //scan the string reversely, repeat when al(0)is not
                                           //equal to di.
        "jne 1f\n\t"
        "movb $1,1(%%edi)\n\t"             //1 is assigned to edi+1
        "sall $12,%%ecx\n\t"               //ecx arithmetically shifts 12 bits left, namely the
                                           //page address.
        "addl %2,%%ecx\n\t"                //PAGING_PAGES + ecx (page address)
        "movl %%ecx,%%edx\n\t"
        "movl $1024,%%ecx\n\t"
        "leal 4092(%%edx),%%edi\n\t"       //this valid address of edx + 4K is assigned to edi.
        "rep ; stosl\n\t"                  //eax(0) is assigned to the address edi point to, to
                                           //clear the page.
        "movl %%edx,%%eax\n"
        "1:"
        :"=a" (__res)
        :"0" (0),"i" (LOW_MEM),"c" (PAGING_PAGES),
        "D" (mem_map+PAGING_PAGES-1)//edx
        :"di","cx","dx");                  //these values have been changed.
return __res;
}
```

After executing get_free_page, copy_process() converts the pointer of this page to the one pointing to task_struct and assigns it to task[1]; that is, task[nr] = p. nr is the first parameter, which is the returned task number of find_empty_process().

Note that a pointer in C language has both address and types. The conversion deems that the low-address end of this page is the primary address of task_struct, which also

implies that the high-address part belongs to the kernel stack. This helps us understand
p->tss.esp0 = PAGE_SIZE + (long) p later.

Tip:

Task_struct is the most important data structure that the OS uses to identify and
manage processes. Each process must have its own, unique task_struct.

```
//code path:kernel/fork.c:
int copy_process(int nr,long ebp,long edi,long esi,long gs,long none,
long ebx,long ecx,long edx,
long fs,long es,long ds,                    //
long eip,long cs,long eflags,long esp,long ss)
{
        ......
        if (!p)
                return -EAGAIN;
        task[nr] = p;           //nr is 1

/* current points to task_struct of process 0. In next line,task_struct of parent process is
assigned to child process, which is the characteristic of parent-child process creating
mechanism.*/
        *p = *current;          /* NOTE! this doesn't copy the supervisor stack */

        p->state = TASK_UNINTERRUPTIBLE;        //only the process which is set to ready
                                                //state can be waken up.
                                                //there is no other way.
        p->pid = last_pid;                      //initialize the individual settings of
                                                //child process
        p->father = current->pid;
        p->counter = p->priority;
        p->signal = 0;
        p->alarm = 0;
        p->leader = 0;                  /* process leadership doesn't inherit */
        p->utime = p->stime = 0;
        p->cutime = p->cstime = 0;
        p->start_time = jiffies;
        p->tss.back_link = 0;           //set the TSS of child process
        ......
}
```

The effect is shown below (the figure in Section 2.9.1 might be helpful).

```
union task_union
{
    struct task_struct task;
    char stack[PAGE_SIZE];
};
```

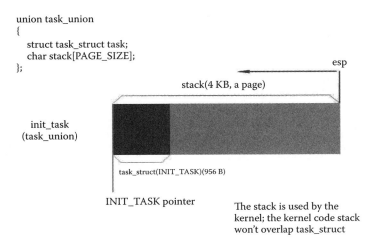

The stack is used by the
kernel; the kernel code stack
won't overlap task_struct

Tip:

Ingenuity lies in the design of task_union. Task_struct is located in front of the page, and the kernel stack is at the end. As the progressive direction is opposite, these two parts occupy just one page, corresponding to the paging mechanism and making it convenient to distribute the memory. The system designer must test the code repeatedly in order to assure that the maximum length of pushing in all possible calling will not overwrite the task_struct in the front part. Since all kernel codes are written by the OS designer, he has an overall arrangement of the page space. On the contrary, there will be a big problem when providing stack space for user processes using this method.

The following code is of great significance:

```
*p = *current;          /* NOTE! this doesn't copy the supervisor stack */
```

Current is the pointer of the current process, and p is the pointer of process 1. The current process is process 0, which is the parent process of process 1. Copying the task_struct of the parent process to the child process means that the most important attribute of the parent process is copied to the child process. Thus, the child process inherits most of the capacity of the parent process, which is one of the characteristics of the parent–child process-creating mechanism.

While the prototype of task_struct in process 1 has been formed, the information of task_struct in process 0 may not be appropriate for process 1; thus, the content of task_struct should be adjusted to specific situations. Codes starting from P-> are used to adjust settings for process 1 individually, and data used to adjust TSS are parameters formed by pushing of previous codes (Figure 3.5).

The execution code is as follows:

```
//code path:kernel/fork.c:
int copy_process(int nr,long ebp,long edi,long esi,long gs,long none,
long ebx,long ecx,long edx,
long fs,long es,long ds,           //
long eip,long cs,long eflags,long esp,long ss)
{
        .....
        p->start_time = jiffies;
        p->tss.back_link = 0;           //start setting TSS of child process
        p->tss.esp0 = PAGE_SIZE + (long) p;     //esp0 is the pointer of kernel stack,
                                        //refer to section 2.9.1
        p->tss.ss0 = 0x10;              //0x10 is equal to 10000, privileged level 0, gdt,
                                        //data segment
        p->tss.eip = eip;              //Note!this eip of parameters is pushed by int 0x80,
                                        //which points to if (__res >= 0)
        p->tss.eflags = eflags;
        p->tss.eax = 0;                 //Note!this line decides the branch of if (!fork())
                                        //in main function.
        p->tss.ecx = ecx;
        p->tss.edx = edx;
        p->tss.ebx = ebx;
        p->tss.esp = esp;
        p->tss.ebp = ebp;
        p->tss.esi = esi;
        p->tss.edi = edi;
        p->tss.es = es & 0xffff;
        p->tss.cs = cs & 0xffff;
        p->tss.ss = ss & 0xffff;
```

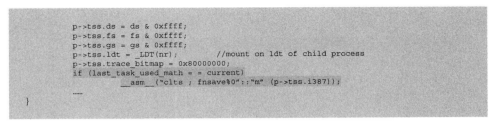

```
p->tss.ds = ds & 0xffff;
p->tss.fs = fs & 0xffff;
p->tss.gs = gs & 0xffff;
p->tss.ldt = _LDT(nr);          //mount on ldt of child process
p->tss.trace_bitmap = 0x80000000;
if (last_task_used_math = = current)
        __asm__("clts ; fnsave%0"::"m" (p->tss.i387));
    ......
}
```

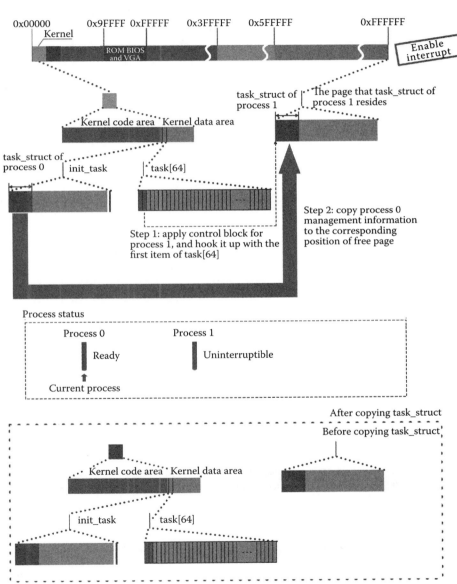

Figure 3.5 Initializing the task structure of process 1.

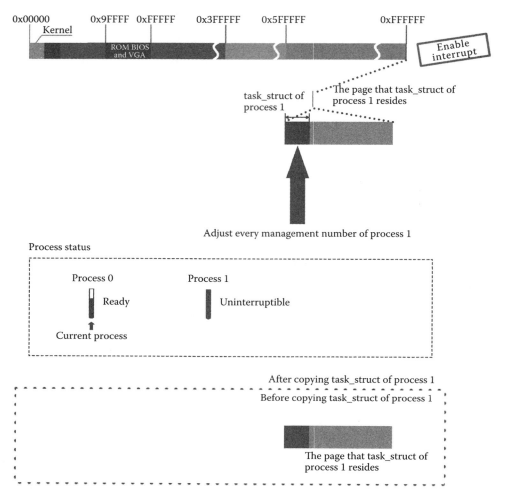

Figure 3.6 Adjusting the task_struct of process 1.

Tip:

```
p->tss.eip = eip;
p->tss.eax = 0;
```

These two lines of code foreshadow executing if (__res> = 0) in fork for the second time. It is not easy to see this foreshadowing, but this should be remembered.

The task_struct of process 1 after adjusting is shown in Figure 3.6.

3.1.4 Set the Page Management of Process 1

The paging mechanism in the architecture of Intel 80x86 is based on the protection mode, which means pe should be opened before opening pg. Since the protection mode is based on segment, setting the segments of process 1 should be done before setting the page management.

Generally speaking, each process has to load its own code and data, of which the addressing mode is the algorithm of segment address plus offset, namely, the logical address. The hardware will automatically convert the logical address to the linear address, which will be converted automatically again to the physical address in pages, according to the settings of the page directory table and page table. Through this technical route, the OS sets the code and data segment in the 64 MB linear address space of process 1 and then in the page directory table and page table.

3.1.4.1 Set the Code Segment and Data Segment in the Linear Address Space of Process 1

By calling copy_mem(), the system sets the segment base address and segment limit length of the segment and data segment of process 1 at first. Extract information on the code segment, data segment, and segment limit length of the current process (process 0); meanwhile, set the base address of the segment and data segment of process 1, which is its process number, nr*64MB, and set the base address in the segment descriptor in the local descriptor tables of the new process. It is shown as the first step in Figure 3.7.

The code is as follows:

```
//Code path:kernel/fork.c:
int copy_process(int nr,long ebp,long edi,long esi,long gs,long none,
long ebx,long ecx,long edx,
long fs,long es,long ds,                    //
long eip,long cs,long eflags,long esp,long ss)
{
    ......
        if (last_task_used_math == current)
            __asm__("clts ; fnsave%0"::"m" (p->tss.i387));
        if (copy_mem(nr,p)) {         //set code segment and data segment of child process,
                                      //create and copy the first page
                                      //table of child process
            task[nr] = NULL;          //now this situation doesn't happen
            free_page((long) p);
            return -EAGAIN;
        }
        for (i = 0; i<NR_OPEN;i++)     //reference count of file corresponding to parent
                                       //process is plused by 1
                                       //showing that parent and child process share the
                                       //same file
    ......
}
```

```
//Code path:include/linux/sched.h:
    ......
#define _set_base(addr,base) \           //set addr by base.Referring to 2.9.1
  __asm__("movw%%dx,%0\n\t" \
                "rorl $16,%%edx\n\t" \
                "movb%%dl,%1\n\t" \
                "movb%%dh,%2" \
          ::"m" (*((addr)+2)), \
                "m" (*((addr)+4)), \
                "m" (*((addr)+7)), \
                "d" (base) \
          :"dx")
    ......
#define set_base(ldt,base) _set_base(((char *)&(ldt)), base)

    ......
#define _get_base(addr) ({\              //obtain base address addr. Referring to _set_base
                                         //and 2.9.1
```

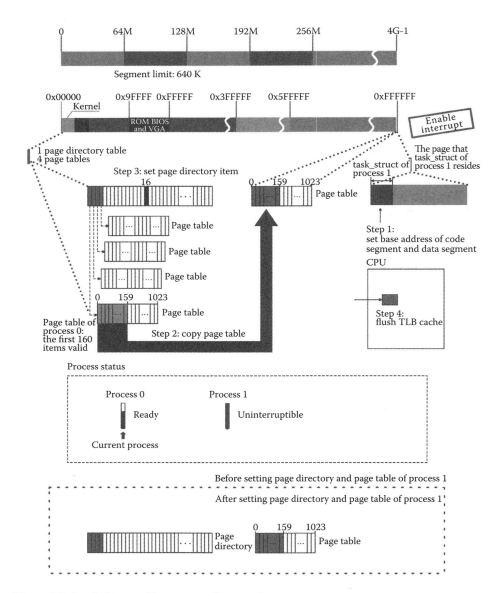

Figure 3.7 Set the linear address space of process 1.

```
unsigned long __base; \
__asm__("movb%3,%%dh\n\t" \
        "movb%2,%%dl\n\t" \
        "shll $16,%%edx\n\t" \
        "movw%1,%%dx" \
        :"=d" (__base) \
        :"m" (*((addr)+2)), \
        "m" (*((addr)+4)), \
        "m" (*((addr)+7))); \
__base;})
```

```
#define get_base(ldt) _get_base(((char *)&(ldt)))
#define get_limit(segment) ({\
unsigned long __limit; \
    __asm__("lsll%1,%0\n\t                      //obtain segment limit length and pass it to __limit
                incl%0"
        :"=r" (__limit)
        :"r" (segment)); \
__limit;})

//Code path:kernel/fork.c:
int copy_mem(int nr,struct task_struct * p)//set code segment and data segment of child
                                           //process, create and copy the first table of
                                           //child process
{
        unsigned long old_data_base,new_data_base,data_limit;
        unsigned long old_code_base,new_code_base,code_limit;

        //obtain limit length of code and data segment of child process
        code_limit = get_limit(0x0f); //0x0f is 1111:code segment, ldt, 3 privilege level
        data_limit = get_limit(0x17); //0x17 is 10111:data segment, ldt, 3 privilege level

        //obtain base address of code and data segment of parent process(Process 0)
        old_code_base = get_base(current->ldt[1]);
        old_data_base = get_base(current->ldt[2]);
        if (old_data_base ! = old_code_base)
                panic("We don't support separate I&D");
        if (data_limit < code_limit)
                panic("Bad data_limit");
        new_data_base = new_code_base = nr * 0x4000000;      //now nr is 1, 0x4000000 means 64MB
        p->start_code = new_code_base;
        set_base(p->ldt[1],new_code_base);       //set base address of code segment of child
                                                 //process
        set_base(p->ldt[2],new_data_base);       //set base address of data segment of child
                                                 //process
        if (copy_page_tables(old_data_base,new_data_base,data_limit)) {
                free_page_tables(new_data_base,data_limit);
                return -ENOMEM;
        }
        return 0;
}
```

3.1.4.2 Create the First Page Table for Process 1 and Set the Corresponding Page Directory Entry

In Linux 0.11, when the program code of every process is executed, its address needs to be specified based on its linear address and it needs to be mapped to the physical memory. As shown in Figure 3.8, the linear address is 32 bits and the CPU parses this address into

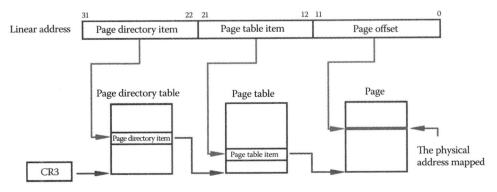

Figure 3.8 Mapping process from linear address to physical address.

three parts: page directory entry, page table entry, and offset within page. The page directory entry is in the page directory table and is used to manage the page table. The page table entry is in the page table and is used to manage the page and ultimately find the specified address in the physical memory. There is only one page directory table in Linux 0.11. We can find the corresponding page directory entry in the page directory table based on the data "page directory entry" provided by the linear address. Then, find the corresponding page table entry in the page table according to the data "page table entry" provided by the linear address. Then, find the corresponding physical page according to this page table item. Finally, find the actual value of the physical address based on the data "offset within page" provided by the linear address.

Calling the function copy_page_tables, setting the page directory table, and copying the page table are as shown in the second and third steps in Figure 3.7. The position where the page directory entry lies should be noticed.

The code is as follows:

```
//Code path:kernel/fork.c:
int copy_mem(int nr,struct task_struct * p)
{
        .....
        set_base(p->ldt[1],new_code_base);      //set base address of code segment of child
                                                //process
        set_base(p->ldt[2],new_data_base);      //set base address of data segment of child
                                                //process

//create first page table and copy page table of Process 0 for Process 1. Set page
//directory entry of Process 1
        if (copy_page_tables(old_data_base,new_data_base,data_limit)) {
                free_page_tables(new_data_base,data_limit);
                return -ENOMEM;
        }
        return 0;
}
```

Entering the function copy_page_tables, apply a free page for the new page table at first and copy the first 160 page table items in the first page table of process 0 to this page (1 page table entry manages a memory space of about 4 KB of a page, and 160 page table items manage a memory space of about 640 KB). Then, both process 0 and process 1 point to the same page, meaning that process 1 can manage the page of process 0. After that, set the page directory table of process 1. Last, refresh page transforming cache by resetting CR3. The setting of the page table and page directory table of process 1 is completed.

The code is as follows:

```
//Code path:mm/memory.c:
    .....
#define invalidate() \
__asm__("movl%%eax,%%cr3"::"a" (0))       //reset CR3 as 0
    .....

int copy_page_tables(unsigned long from,unsigned long to,long size)
{

    unsigned long * from_page_table;
    unsigned long * to_page_table;
    unsigned long this_page;
```

```
        unsigned long * from_dir, * to_dir;
        unsigned long nr;

/* 0x3fffff is 4M, managing range of a page table. In binary there is 22 ones.Both sides of
11 must be 0. So,last 22 bits of from and to must be 0. In this way, a page table corresponds
to contiguous linear address space about 4MB. Paging requests the linear address about
integer multiple of 4M starting from 0x000000.*/
        if ((from&0x3fffff) || (to&0x3fffff))
                panic("copy_page_tables called with wrong alignment");

/*A page directory entry managed space of 4MB, and an item is 4 bytes, so the address of item
is item number *4 which is M number of the starting of linear address managed by item.>> 22 is
MB number of address, and &0xffc is &111111111100b in binary, which is address of page
directory entry.*/
        from_dir = (unsigned long *) ((from>>20) & 0xffc);      /* _pg_dir = 0 */
        to_dir = (unsigned long *) ((to>>20) & 0xffc);
        size = ((unsigned) (size+0x3fffff)) >> 22;              //>> 22 is 4MB number
        for(; size-->0 ; from_dir++,to_dir++) {
            if (1 & *to_dir)
                panic("copy_page_tables: already exist");
            if (!(1 & *from_dir))
                continue;

//*from_dir is address in page directory entry, 0xfffff000& means clear low 12 bits, and high
20 bits is the address//of page table.
            from_page_table = (unsigned long *) (0xfffff000 & *from_dir);
            if (!(to_page_table = (unsigned long *) get_free_page()))
                    return -1; /* Out of memory, see freeing */
            *to_dir = ((unsigned long) to_page_table)|7;        //7 is 111, referring to 1.3.5
            nr = (from = =0)?0xA0:1024;                         //0xA0 is 160, directory number of
                                                                //copied page tables
            for (; nr--> 0 ; from_page_table++,to_page_table++) {    //copy page tables of
                                                                     //parent process
                this_page = *from_page_table;
                if (!(1 & this_page))
                    continue;
                this_page & = ~2;                               //set property of page table
                                                                //item.2 is010.~2 is 101 meaning
                                                                //user, reading only and exitance

                *to_page_table = this_page;
                if (this_page > LOW_MEM) {                      //kernel area within 1MB doesn't
                                                                //manage user paging
                    *from_page_table = this_page;
                    this_page - = LOW_MEM;
                    this_page >> = 12;
                    mem_map[this_page]++;                       //add up reference count.
                                                                //Referring to mem_init
                }
            }
        }
        invalidate();           //reset CR3 as 0. Refresh TLB.
        return 0;
}
```

Now, process 1 is empty, and its page tables are copied from process 0. Hence, they have the same page and share the same managing structure of memory page temporarily, as shown in Figure 3.9.

When process 1 has its programs, the relation will be ceased and process 1 organizes its managing structure of memory.

3.1.5 Process 1 Shares Files of Process 0

At copy_process, the system sets members corresponding to files in task_struct, including p->filp[20], the structure of the currently working directory i node, the structure of the root directory i node, and the structure of the execution file i node. Although these values

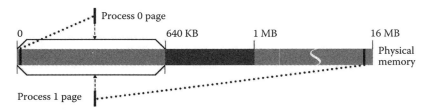

Figure 3.9 Process 0 and process 1 share the same page.

in process 0 are null and process 0 is only operated in the host without any interaction with peripherals, the sharing is meaningful, because the parent–child process-creating mechanism passes down the ability to the child process.

The code is as follows:

```
//Code path:kernel/fork.c:
int copy_process(int nr,long ebp,long edi,long esi,long gs,long none,
                 long ebx,long ecx,long edx,
                 long fs,long es,long ds,
                 long eip,long cs,long eflags,long esp,long ss)
{
    ......
                return -EAGAIN;
}
    for (i = 0; i<NR_OPEN;i++)          //add 1 to reference count of property of files
                                        //corresponding to parent process
            if (f = p->filp[i])
                        f->f_count++;
    if (current->pwd)
                current->pwd->i_count++;
    if (current->root)
                current->root->i_count++;
    if (current->executable)
                current->executable->i_count++;
    set_tss_desc(gdt+(nr<<1)+FIRST_TSS_ENTRY,&(p->tss));   //set items in gdt, referring to
                                                           //sched.c
    ......
}
```

3.1.6 Set the Table Item in the GDT of Process 1

Next, bind the TSS and the LDT of process 1 with the global descriptor table (refer to Section 2.9). It is shown in Figure 3.10. Note the position that process 1 occupies in GDT.

The code is as follows:

```
//Code path:kernel/fork.c:
int copy_process(int nr,long ebp,long edi,long esi,long gs,long none,
            long ebx,long ecx,long edx,
            long fs,long es,long ds,
            long eip,long cs,long eflags,long esp,long ss)
{
    ......
```

3. Creation and Execution of Process 1

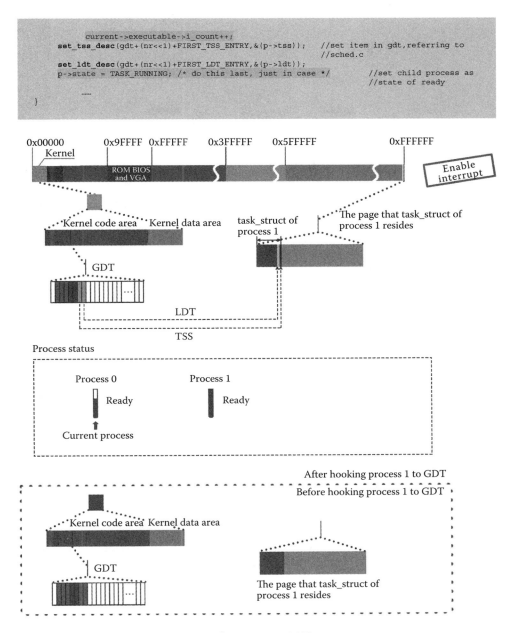

```
        current->executable->i_count++;
    set_tss_desc(gdt+(nr<<1)+FIRST_TSS_ENTRY,&(p->tss));    //set item in gdt,referring to
                                                            //sched.c
    set_ldt_desc(gdt+(nr<<1)+FIRST_LDT_ENTRY,&(p->ldt));
    p->state = TASK_RUNNING; /* do this last, just in case */    //set child process as
                                                                 //state of ready

    ......

}
```

Figure 3.10 Hook managing structure of process 1 to GDT.

3.1.7 Process 1 Is in Ready State to Complete the Creation of Process 1

When process 1 is set as ready, it participates in process scheduling and returns pid 1. Please notice the progress bar representing the process in the middle of Figure 3.10. Process 1 is in ready state. The code is as follows:

```
//Code path:kernel/fork.c:
int copy_process(int nr,long ebp,long edi,long esi,long gs,long none,
        long ebx,long ecx,long edx,
        long fs,long es,long ds,
        long eip,long cs,long eflags,long esp,long ss)
{
        ......
        p->state = TASK_RUNNING;    /* do this last, just in case */ //set child process as
                                                                     //ready state
        return last_pid;
}
```

Now, we have completed the creation of process 1, and process 1 now has all the abilities of process 0.

After creating process 1, the function copy_process has been executed. Then, return to the line next to call_copy_process in sys_fork. The code is as follows:

```
//Code path:kernel/system_call.s:
        ......
_sys_fork:
        call _find_empty_process
        testl %eax,%eax
        js 1f
        push %gs
        pushl %esi
        pushl %edi
        pushl %ebp
        pushl %eax
call _copy_process
        addl $20,%esp      //copy_process returns to this line,and esp+ = 20 means clear
                           //20-byte stack
                           //that is the value of gs, esi, edi, ebp and eax pushed before
1:      ret                //Notice that there remains data in kernel
                           //stack, and return
                           //to pushl%eax in _system_call to execute
        ......
```

We need to clear the values of five registers pushed in sys_fork, that is, the first five parameters of copy_process(): gs, esi, edi, ebp, and eax. Note that eax corresponds to the first parameter nr of copy_process(), which is the return value last_pid of copy_process() and pid of process 1. Then, return to the line pushl%eax next to call _sys_call_table(,%eax,4) in _system_call to execute.

First, inspect whether the current process is process 0 or not. Notice that the line pushl%eax pushes the pid of process 1 and executes at the line _ret_from_sys_call:.

The code is as follows:

```
//Code path:kernel/system_call.s:
        ......
_system_call:
        ......
        call _sys_call_table(,%eax,4)
        pushl %eax             #sys_fork returns here. eax is return value last_pid
                               #of copy_process()
        movl _current,%eax     #current process is Process 0
        cmpl $0,state(%eax)    # state
        jne reschedule         #if Process is not in ready state, schedule process
        cmpl $0,counter(%eax)  # counter
```

```
        je reschedule                    #if Process has no time slice, schedule process
        ret_from_sys_call:
        movl _current,%eax               # task[0] cannot have signals
        cmpl _task,%eax
        je 3f                            #if Process 0 is current process, jump to 3: below
        cmpw $0x0f,CS(%esp)              # was old code segment supervisor ?
        jne 3f
        cmpw $0x17,OLDSS(%esp)           # was stack segment = 0x17 ?
        jne 3f
        movl signal(%eax),%ebx
        movl blocked(%eax),%ecx
        notl%ecx
        andl%ebx,%ecx
        bsfl%ecx,%ecx
        je 3f
        btrl%ecx,%ebx
        movl%ebx,signal(%eax)
        incl%ecx
        pushl%ecx
        call _do_signal
        popl%eax
3:      popl%eax                         #pop values of 7 registers to CPU
        popl%ebx
        popl%ecx
        popl%edx
        pop%fs
        pop%es
        pop%ds
        iret                             #CPU hardware pops values of ss,esp,eflags,cs and eip pushed
                                         #when int 0x80 happens to
                                         #corresponding registers in CPU
        ......                           # cs:eip points to the line if(_res> = 0) next to line int 0x80
                                         #in fork() to execute
```

Because process 0 is the current process, jump to label 3 to revert the values of all registers pushed before. The process of clearing stack in init_task is shown in the first step of Figure 3.11. Note that the line popl%eax means reverting the pid of process 1 mentioned before to the value of eax, which is 1, in the CPU.

Next, the interruption iret returns. The CPU hardware automatically popped values of ss, esp, eflags, cs, and eip pushed when int 0x80 happens to the corresponding registers in the CPU. The execution changes from kernel code in privilege level 0 to process 0 code in privilege level 3. cs:eip points to the line if(_res> = 0) next to line int 0x80 in fork() to execute.

The code is as follows:

```
//Code path:include/unistd.h:
int fork(void)
{
        long __res;
__asm__ volatile ("int $0x80"
        : " = a" (__res)              //value of __res is eax and returning value last_
                                      //pid(1) of copy_process()

        : "0" (__NR_fork));
        if (__res > = 0)              //execute here after iret. _res is eax and the value
                                      //is 1
        return (int) __res;           //return to 1
        errno = - __res;
        return -1;
}
```

Before analyzing how to execute if(_res> = 0), let us look at " = a" (__res), which assigns the value of _res to eax. The line if(_res> = 0) is used to judge the value of eax. As introduced recently, the value of eax is pid 1 of process 1 and return(type)_res returns as 1.

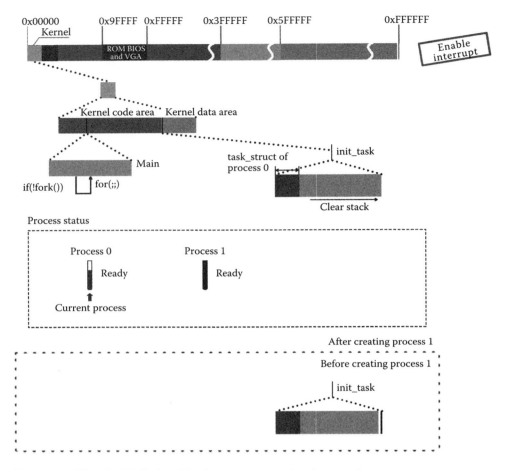

Figure 3.11 How the OS distinguishes between process 0 and process 1.

Process 0 returns to call site if(!fork()) of the function fork to execute, because !1 is false. Then, process 0 continues to execute and comes to the line for(;;)pause().

The code is as follows:

```
//Code path:init/main.c:
    ......
void main(void)
{
        sti();
        move_to_user_mode();
        if (!fork()) {              //the returning value of fork is 1,so if(!1) is
                                    //false/* we count on this going ok */
                init();             //this line isn't executed
        }
        ......
        for(;;) pause();            //execute this line
}
```

The above process is shown in the second step of Figure 3.11.

■ 3.2 Kernel Schedules a Process for the First Time

Now, the code of process 0 is executed. From this time, process 0 prepares to switch to process 1 to execute.

In the process-scheduling mechanism of Linux 0.11, there are two situations when process switch happens.

First, the time allows running processes to end.

When created, a process is assigned with limited time slice to ensure that any process runs in limited time every time. When time slice reduces to 0, it means that this process used up the time and switches to another process to execute. This, in turn, is the implementation of multiprocesses.

Second, a process stops running.

In those situations where a process waits for data applied by peripherals or the results of other programs or a process is finished, even if there is time slice left, a process does not have the logical conditions to continue to run. If it remains waiting for the time interruption to switch to another process, time is wasted and switching to another process should be done immediately.

Either of the above situations happening leads to process switch.

The role of process 0 is special. Now, switching from process 0 to process 1 meets the second situation and also means idling process. We will talk about the idling process in Section 3.3.1.

Process 0 executes the line for(;;) pause() and finally switches to process 1 by executing the function schedule. The process is shown in Figure 3.12.

The code of the function pause() is as follows:

```
//Code path:init/main.c:
    ......
static inline _syscall0(int,fork)
static inline _syscall0(int,pause)
    ......
void main(void)
{
        ......
        move_to_user_mode();
        if (!fork()) {          /* we count on this going ok */
                init();
        }
        for(;;) pause();
}
```

The way of calling pause() is similar to that of fork(). When it comes to syscall0 in unistd.h, according to interruption int 0x80, map call _sys_call_table(,%eax,4) in system_call.s to the system calling function in sys_pause() to execute. The procedure in detail refers to calling the function fork() in Section 3.1.1. There is little difference that the function fork() is written in assembly language and the function sys_pause() is in C language.

In sys_pause(), it sets process 0 as in an interruptible state, just as the first step in Figure 3.12. Then, call the function schedule() to switch process. The code is as follows:

```
//Code path:kernel/sched.c:
int sys_pause(void)
{
//set Process 0 as interruptible state. When interruption happens or
//other process transfers special
//signals to this process, this process is possibly set as ready
//state.
        current->state = TASK_INTERRUPTIBLE;
        schedule();
        return 0;
}
```

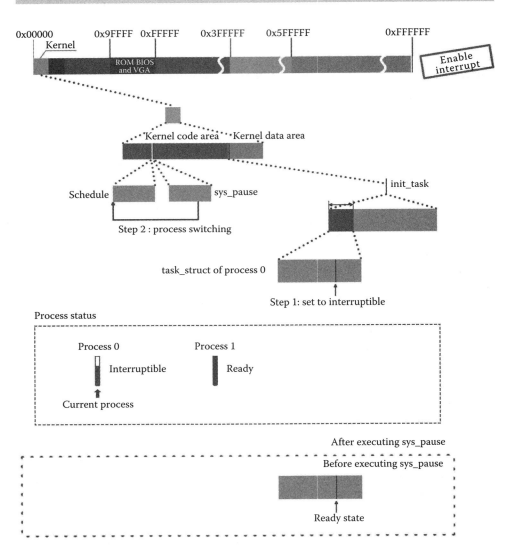

Figure 3.12 Process 0 hangs and executes scheduling programs.

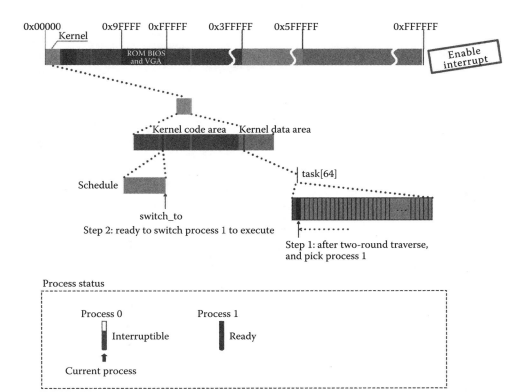

Figure 3.13 Execute scheduling process 1.

In the function schedule, the system first checks the necessity of switching the process. If necessary, it will switch.

First, on the basis of the structure task[64], traverse all the processes for the first time. As long as the address pointer is not null, deal with alarm timer value "alarm" and signal bitmap "signal." Currently, these handles will not take effect, especially since process 0 does not receive any signal and, thus, is in an interruptible state, and impossible to revert to a ready state.

We need to traverse all the processes for the second time and compare the state and time slice of processes to find the process in ready state and with the maximum counter. Now, there are only process 0 and process 1. Process 0 is in an interruptible state, and not in a ready state. Only process 1 is in a ready state. Hence, execute switch_to(next), and switch to process 1 to run. It is shown in the first step of Figure 3.13.

The code is as follows:

```
//Code path:kernel/sched.c:
void schedule(void)
{
    int i,next,c;
    struct task_struct ** p;

/* check alarm, wake up any interruptible tasks that have got a signal */

    for(p = &LAST_TASK ; p > &FIRST_TASK ;--p)
```

```
            if (*p) {
                if ((*p)->alarm && (*p)->alarm < jiffies) {  //set timing or timer
                                                             //has expired
                    (*p)->signal | = (1<<(SIGALRM-1));  //set SIGALRM
                    (*p)->alarm = 0;                    //clear alarm
                }
                if (((*p)->signal & ~(_BLOCKABLE & (*p)->blocked)) &&
                (*p)->state = =TASK_INTERRUPTIBLE)
                    (*p)->state = TASK_RUNNING;
            }

/* this is the scheduler proper: */
    while (1) {
        c = -1;
        next = 0;
        i = NR_TASKS;
        p = &task[NR_TASKS];
        while (--i) {
            if (!*--p)
                continue;
    if ((*p)->state = = TASK_RUNNING && (*p)->counter > c)//find process in ready state with
                                                         //maximum counter
                c = (*p)->counter, next = i;
        }
        if (c) break;
        for(p = &LAST_TASK ; p > &FIRST_TASK ;--p)
            if (*p)
                (*p)->counter = ((*p)->counter >> 1) +
                        (*p)->priority;      //counter = counter/2 + priority
    }
    switch_to(next);
}
```

The code is as follows:

```
//Code path:include/sched.h:
——
//FIRST_TSS_ENTRY<<3 is 100000, ((unsigned long) n)<<4, it is 1000 for Process 1
//_TSS(1) is 110000.Last 2 bit is privilege level.Third bit on the left is gdt. 110 is
//subscript of tts0
#define _TSS(n) ((((unsigned long) n)<<4)+(FIRST_TSS_ENTRY<<3))
——
#define switch_to(n) {\                          //refer to 2.9.1
struct {long a,b;} __tmp; \                       //prepare data structure for cs and eip of
                                                  //ljmp
__asm__ ("cmpl%%ecx,_current\n\t" \
        "je 1f\n\t" \                            //if Process n is current process, exit
                                                  //without switching
        "movw%%dx,%1\n\t" \                      //low word of edx is assigned to *&__tmp.b
        "xchgl%%ecx,_current\n\t" \              //task[n] switch with task[current]
        "ljmp%0\n\t" \                           //ignore the offset
        "cmpl%%ecx,_last_task_used_math\n\t" \   //whether using coprocessor or not last time
        "jne 1f\n\t" \
        "clts\n" \                               //clear the switch task flag in CR0
    "1:" \
        ::"m" (*&__tmp.a),"m" (*&__tmp.b), \     //.a corresponds to eip..b corresponds to cs
        "d" (_TSS(n)),"c" ((long) task[n]));\    //edx is index number of tss n. Ecx is task[n]
}
```

In "ljmp%0\n\t," through the task-gate mechanism of the CPU, ljmp saves the values of each register of the CPU into the TSS of process 0 and also reverts the TSS data of process 1 and the descriptor data of the code/data segment of LDT to each register of the

CPU. Hence, it is a switch from a kernel code with privilege level 0 to a process 1 code with privilege level 3. It is shown in the second step of Figure 3.13.

Next, it is process 1's turn. It will further build the environment, so that the process in the form of a file can interact with the peripherals.

Please note that the procedures of calling pause() involves switching from code of process 0 with privilege level 3 to the kernel code with privilege level 0 by int 0x80 interrupt, and then calling switch() in schdule() in sys_pause(), where the code switch to process 1 by ljmp instruction is executed. However, now, the code after ljmp and call _sys_call_table(,%eax,4) is not executed and int 0x80 does not return as well.

∎ 3.3 Turn to Process 1 to Execute

Before analyzing process 1, let us review the process of creating process 1 based on process 0.

When analyzing the calling of the function copy_process() in Section 3.1.3, we know that the tss.eip set for process 1 is the eip value of ss, esp, eflags, cs, and eip popped automatically by the CPU hardware. Pushing is caused by the interruption int 0x80 when process 0 creates process 1 by calling fork(). This value points to the position of the code next to the line int 0x80, that is, if(_res> = 0).

As ljmp reverts the value of TSS in process 1 automatically to the CPU according to the CPU's task-gate mechanism, tss.eip is also reverted to the CPU. Now, eip in the CPU points to the line "if(_res> = 0)." Thus, process 1 starts to execute here.

The code is as follows:

```
//Code path:include/unistd.h:
#define _syscall0(type,name) \
int fork(void)
{
long __res;
__asm__ volatile ("int $0x80"
        : "=a" (__res)
        : "0" (__NR_fork));
        if (__res > = 0)        //from now on,tss.eip designed for Process
                                //1 by copy_process points to this line
        return (int) __res;
        errno = -__res;
        return -1;
}
```

It is shown in the first step of Figure 3.14.

According to the introduction in Section 3.1.3, __res is the value of eax in the TSS of process 1, and the value is written as 0 in Section 3.1.3 by p->tss.eax = 0; therefore, when return(type) __res was being executed, the return value is 0.

After returning, if(!Fork()) in the main function is executed, !0 is "true," call the init function!

The specific code is as follows:

```
//Code path:init/main.c:
void main(void)
{
        if (!fork()) {          //!0 is true,
              init();
        }
}
```

After entering the init function, first call the setup function. The specific code is as follows:

```
//Code path:init/main.c:
void init(void)
{
        ......
        setup((void *) &drive_info);
        ......
}
```

The way to call this function is similar to the way to call the fork() and pause() functions, but slightly different with the way to call the setup() function, which is completed not through

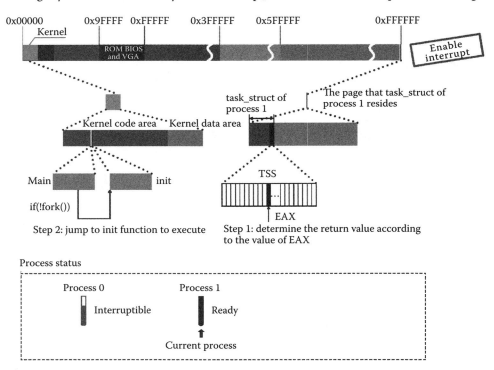

Figure 3.14 State of process 1 when it starts to execute.

_syscall0() but through _syscall1(). The specific implementation processes are similar, that is, also through the int0x80, _system_call, _sys_call_table (call,%eax,4), and sys_setup().

Reminder: *The int 0x80 interrupt in the pause() function is still not returned; now, setup() creates another interruption.*

3.3.1 Preparing to Install the Hard Disk File System by Process 1

In this section, although it introduces a bunch of code, it only has a sole purpose: to prepare to install the hard disk file system, which will be introduced in Chapter 5.

This process probably has three steps:

1. According to the machine system data, set the hard disk parameters.

2. Read the hard disk boot block.

3. Get information from the boot block.

3.3.1.1 Process 1 Set hd_info of Hard Disk

According to the machine data in the drive_info, such as the hard disk cylinder number, head number, and sector number, set the hd_info of the kernel (Figure 3.15).

The code is as follows:

```
//Code path:kernel/blk_dev/hd.c:
      ......
struct hd_i_struct {
     int head,sect,cyl,wpcom,lzone,ctl;
     };
      ......
struct hd_i_struct hd_info[] = {{0,0,0,0,0,0},{0,0,0,0,0,0}};

static struct hd_struct {
     long start_sect;                    //Starting sector number
     long nr_sects;                      //Total number of sectors
} hd[5*MAX_HD] = {{0,0},};
      ......

/* This may be used only once, enforced by 'static int callable' */
int sys_setup(void * BIOS)                    //BIOS is drive_info, refer to 2.1
{
     static int callable = 1;
     int i,drive;
     unsigned char cmos_disks;
     struct partition *p;
     struct buffer_head * bh;
     if (!callable)               //only call one time
          return -1;
     callable = 0;
#ifndef HD_TYPE
     for (drive = 0 ; drive<2 ; drive++) {                      //read drive_info to
                                                               //set hd_info
          hd_info[drive].cyl = *(unsigned short *) BIOS;        //Number of cylinders
          hd_info[drive].head = *(unsigned char *) (2+BIOS);    //Number of Heads
          hd_info[drive].wpcom = *(unsigned short *) (5+BIOS);
          hd_info[drive].ctl = *(unsigned char *) (8+BIOS);
          hd_info[drive].lzone = *(unsigned short *) (12+BIOS);
          hd_info[drive].sect = *(unsigned char *) (14+BIOS);   //the number of sectors
                                                               //per track
```

```
            BIOS + = 16;
    }
    if (hd_info[1].cyl)                  //Judge the number of hard drives
        NR_HD = 2;
    else
        NR_HD = 1;
#endif

    for (i = 0 ; i<NR_HD ; i++) {//one physical hard disk can have four logical disk at most,
                                 //0 is the physical disk, 1-4 is logical disk, in sum, 5; the
                                 //first physical disk is 0*5, the second physical disk is 1*5
        hd[i*5].start_sect = 0;
        hd[i*5].nr_sects = hd_info[i].head*
                hd_info[i].sect*hd_info[i].cyl;
    }

    if ((cmos_disks = CMOS_READ(0x12)) & 0xf0)
        if (cmos_disks & 0x0f)
                    NR_HD = 2;
        else
                    NR_HD = 1;
    else
                    NR_HD = 0;
    for (i = NR_HD ; i < 2 ; i++) {
                hd[i*5].start_sect = 0;
                hd[i*5].nr_sects = 0;
    }

    for (drive = 0 ; drive<NR_HD ; drive++) {//the device id of the first physical disk
                                             //is 0x300, the second is 0x305,
                                             //read the block 0, namely boot block,
                                             //of every physical disk,
                                             //which has the partition information
        if (!(bh = bread(0x300 + drive*5,0))) {
                printk("Unable to read partition table of drive%d\n\r",
                        drive);
                panic("");
        }
        ......
    }
}
```

3.3.1.2 Read the Hard Disk Boot Blocks to the Buffer

In Linux 0.11, the partition table is the most basic information of the hard disk. Other information can be obtained from this information, which is stored in the boot block. A hard disk has only one boot block, that is, No. 0 logic block, and the boot block has two sectors, the first sector of which is useful. Our computer has only one hard disk. The hard disk boot block is read into the buffer, which can be used by follow-up procedures. This work is completed through calling the bread() function (bread is short for block read).

The code is as follows:

```
//Code path:kernel/blk_dev/hd.c:
    ......
//First physical disk device number is 0x300, second is 0x305, read the block 0,
//namely boot block, of every physical disk, which has the partition information
    for (drive = 0 ; drive<NR_HD ; drive++) {
        if (!(bh = bread(0x300 + drive*5,0))) {
            printk("Unable to read partition table of drive%d\n\r",
                drive);
                    panic("");
        }
        ......
    }
}
```

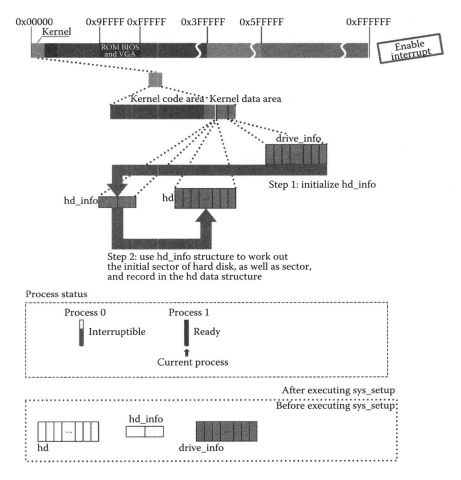

Figure 3.15 Initialize hard drive control data structure.

After entering the bread function, first call the getblk() function to apply for a free buffer block.

The code is as follows:

```
//Code path:fs/buffer.c:
struct buffer_head * bread(int dev,int block)
{//read specific dev, block, dev of the first hard disk is 0x300,
//block is 0
    struct buffer_head * bh;

    if (!(bh = getblk(dev,block))) //get a buffer block corresponding
                                   //to the specific dev and block or
                                   //get a free buffer block in buffer
            panic("bread: getblk returned NULL\n");//it's the first
                                   //time to use buffer, thus, it's
                                   //impossible to have no free buffer
```

```
        if (bh->b_uptodate) //now, it's the first use, the free buffer which
                            //we get is surely not used by other process
                return bh;
        ll_rw_block(READ,bh);
        wait_on_buffer(bh);
        if (bh->b_uptodate)
                return bh;
        brelse(bh);
        return NULL;
}
```

Figure 3.16 describes in detail the procedures when applying for a free buffer block.

In the getblk() function, first call get_hash_table to search hash table, which search the hard disk that will be read (with the same device id and block id) has been read into the buffer by other processes. If it has been read into the buffer, it can be used directly. The purpose of using hash tables for queries is to improve query speed. It is the first step shown in Figure 3.16.

The code is as follows:

```
//Code path:fs/buffer.c:
    ......
//find the corresponding buffer block with the same dev, block or free
//buffer block in the buffer: dev:0x300, block:0
struct buffer_head * getblk(int dev,int block)
{
        struct buffer_head * tmp, * bh;

repeat:
        if (bh = get_hash_table(dev,block))
            return bh;
        tmp = free_list;
        do {
            if (tmp->b_count)
                continue;
            if (!bh || BADNESS(tmp)<BADNESS(bh)) {
                bh = tmp;
                if (!BADNESS(tmp))
                    break;
            }
    ......
}
```

Once inside the get_hash_table function, call the find_buffer() function to search the buffer block whose device number and block number are appointed in the buffer; if it can be found, it can be used directly.

The code is as follows:

```
//Code path:fs/buffer.c:
    ......
//find the corresponding buffer block with the same dev, block or free
//buffer block in the buffer: dev:0x300, block:0
struct buffer_head * get_hash_table(int dev, int block)
```

```
{
        struct buffer_head * bh;

        for (;;) {
                if (!(bh = find_buffer(dev,block)))
                        return NULL; //now, it's the first use, thus, it's
                                     //impossible to find the block has
                                     //been read into buffer
                bh->b_count++;
                wait_on_buffer(bh);
                if (bh->b_dev = = dev && bh->b_blocknr = = block)
                        return bh;
                bh->b_count--;
        }
}
```

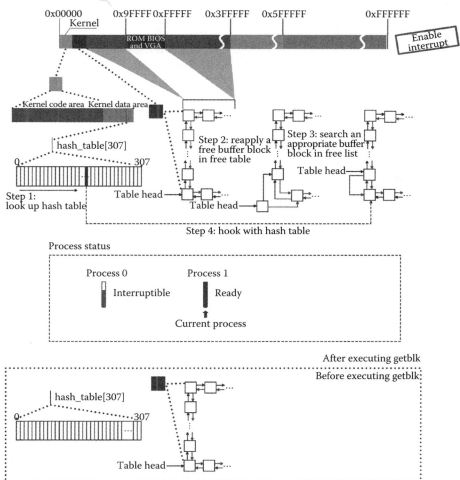

Figure 3.16 Find the buffer block.

Now, this is the first time to use the buffer. Thus, there are no buffer blocks read into the buffer; that is, hash_table does not hook any nodes and find_buffer() returns NULL.

The code is as follows:

```
//Code psth:fs/buffer.c:
    ......
//NR_HASH is 307, for dev:0x300, block:0, _hashfn(dev,block) is 154
#define _hashfn(dev,block)  (((unsigned)(dev^block))%NR_HASH)
#define hash(dev,block)  hash_table[_hashfn(dev,block)]
    ......
//find the buffer block with specific dev, block in the buffer
static struct buffer_head * find_buffer(int dev, int block)
{
    struct buffer_head * tmp;

    for (tmp = hash(dev,block) ; tmp != NULL ; tmp = tmp->b_next)   //now, the tmp->b_next
                                                                    //is NULL
        if (tmp->b_dev == dev && tmp->b_blocknr == block)
            return tmp;
    return NULL;
}
```

The function find_buffer(), get_hash_table(), exit to the getblk() function, and apply for a new free buffer block in the free form. All buffer blocks are now bound in the free table, so apply for a new buffer block in the free table, as shown in the second step in Figure 3.16.

The code is as follows:

```
//Code path:fs/buffer.c:
#define BADNESS(bh) (((bh)->b_dirt<<1)+(bh)->b_lock)//b_dirt, b_lock are 0, BADNESS(bh) is 00
struct buffer_head * getblk(int dev,int block)
{
        struct buffer_head * tmp, * bh;

repeat:
        if (bh = get_hash_table(dev,block))
                return bh;
        tmp = free_list;
        do {
                if (tmp->b_count)                                //tmp-> b_count is 0
                        continue;
                if (!bh || BADNESS(tmp)<BADNESS(bh)) {           //bh is 0
                        bh = tmp;
                        if (!BADNESS(tmp))  //BADNESS(tmp) is 00, get the free buffer!
                                break;
                }
/* and repeat until we find something good */
        } while ((tmp = tmp->b_next_free) != free_list);
        if (!bh) {//in this case, it's impossible to cannot find free buffer
                sleep_on(&buffer_wait);
                goto repeat;
        }
        wait_on_buffer(bh);//buffer block is unlock
        if (bh->b_count)//the buffer block is not in use
                goto repeat;
        while (bh->b_dirt) {//the content of buffer block is not revised
                sync_dev(bh->b_dev);
                wait_on_buffer(bh);
                if (bh->b_count)
                        goto repeat;
        }

        if (find_buffer(dev,block))//now, find the free buffer, but it does not link to the
                                   //hash table
        goto repeat          ;
        ......
```

After getting a buffer block, initialize it, and attach it to the hash_table.

The code is as follows:

```
//Code path:fs/buffer.c:
struct buffer_head * getblk(int dev,int block)
{
        ......
        if (find_buffer(dev,block))
                goto repeat;
        bh->b_count = 1;//be used
        bh->b_dirt = 0;
        bh->b_uptodate = 0;
        remove_from_queues(bh);
        bh->b_dev = dev;
        bh->b_blocknr = block;
        insert_into_queues(bh);
        return bh;
}
```

```
//Code path:fs/buffer.c:
        ......
static inline void remove_from_queues(struct buffer_head * bh)
{
/* remove from hash-queue */
        if (bh->b_next)                          //bh->b_next is NULL
                bh->b_next->b_prev = bh->b_prev;
        if (bh->b_prev)                          //bh->b_prev is NULL
                bh->b_prev->b_next = bh->b_next;
        if (hash(bh->b_dev,bh->b_blocknr) == bh)//in this case, it
                                                 //will never appear
                hash(bh->b_dev,bh->b_blocknr) = bh->b_next;
/* remove from free list */
        if (!(bh->b_prev_free) || !(bh->b_next_free))//never appear in
                                                 //the normal
                                                 //condition
                panic("Free block list corrupted");
        bh->b_prev_free->b_next_free = bh->b_next_free;
        bh->b_next_free->b_prev_free = bh->b_prev_free;
        if (free_list == bh)
                free_list = bh->b_next_free;
}
        ......
```

In order to make it easier to understand the code, we will step out of this process (Figures 3.17 through 3.19).

The code binding hash_ table is as follows (Figures 3.20 through 3.22):

```
//Code path:fs/buffer.c:
    ......
static inline void insert_into_queues(struct buffer_head * bh)
{
/* put at end of free list */
        bh->b_next_free = free_list;
        bh->b_prev_free = free_list->b_prev_free;
        free_list->b_prev_free->b_next_free = bh;
        free_list->b_prev_free = bh;
/* put the buffer in new hash-queue if it has a device */
        bh->b_prev = NULL;
        bh->b_next = NULL;
        if (!bh->b_dev)
                return;
        bh->b_next = hash(bh->b_dev,bh->b_blocknr);
        hash(bh->b_dev,bh->b_blocknr) = bh;
        bh->b_next->b_prev = bh;
}
    ......
```

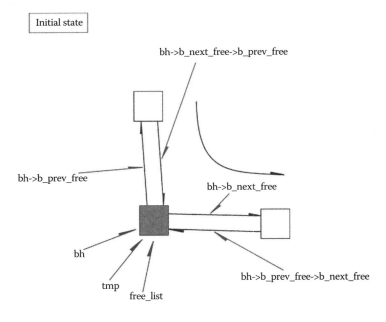

Figure 3.17 Step 1.

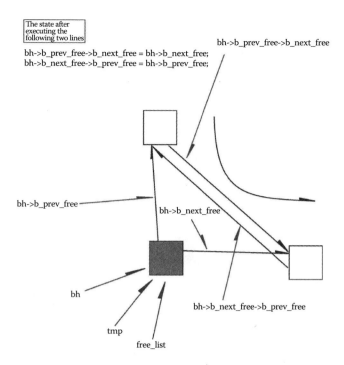

The state after
executing the
following two lines

bh->b_prev_free->b_next_free = bh->b_next_free;
bh->b_next_free->b_prev_free = bh->b_prev_free;

bh->b_prev_free->b_next_free

bh->b_prev_free

bh->b_next_free

bh

bh->b_next_free->b_prev_free

tmp

free_list

Figure 3.18 Step 2.

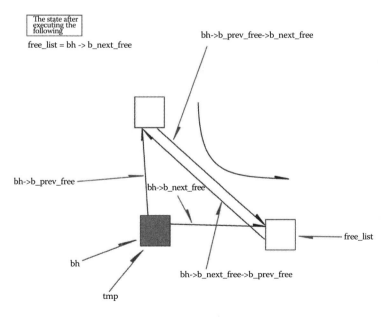

The state after
executing the
following

free_list = bh -> b_next_free

bh->b_prev_free->b_next_free

bh->b_prev_free

bh->b_next_free

free_list

bh

bh->b_next_free->b_prev_free

tmp

Figure 3.19 Step 3.

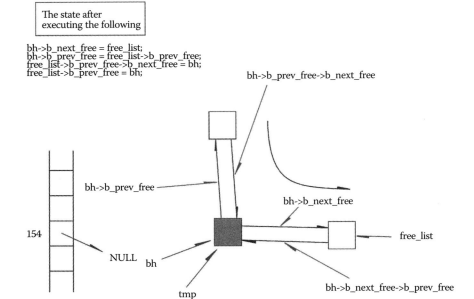

The state after
executing the following

```
bh->b_next_free = free_list;
bh->b_prev_free = free_list->b_prev_free;
free_list->b_prev_free->b_next_free = bh;
free_list->b_prev_free = bh;
```

bh->b_prev_free->b_next_free

bh->b_prev_free

bh->b_next_free

154

NULL bh

free_list

tmp

bh->b_next_free->b_prev_free

Figure 3.20 Step 4.

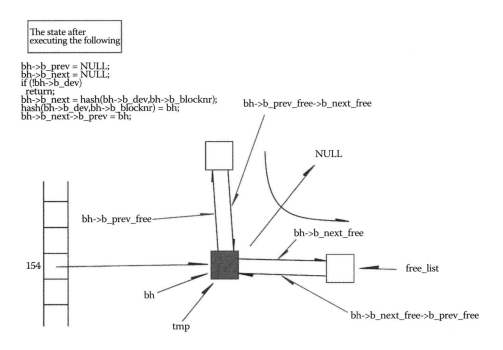

The state after
executing the following

```
bh->b_prev = NULL;
bh->b_next = NULL;
if (!bh->b_dev)
  return;
bh->b_next = hash(bh->b_dev,bh->b_blocknr);
hash(bh->b_dev,bh->b_blocknr) = bh;
bh->b_next->b_prev = bh;
```

bh->b_prev_free->b_next_free

NULL

bh->b_prev_free

bh->b_next_free

154

free_list

bh

bh->b_next_free->b_prev_free

tmp

Figure 3.21 Step 5.

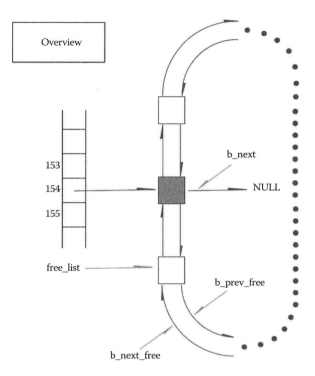

Figure 3.22 Step 6.

After executing getblk(), return to bread().

3.3.1.3 Bind the Buffer Block with Request

After returning to the bread function, call ll_rw_block() to bind the buffer block with request, as shown in Figure 3.23.

The code is as follows:

```
//Code path:fs/buffer.c:
struct buffer_head * bread(int dev,int block)
{
        struct buffer_head * bh;

        if (!(bh = getblk(dev,block)))
                panic("bread: getblk returned NULL\n");
        if (bh->b_uptodate)//the applied buffer block has not been update
                return bh;
        ll_rw_block(READ,bh);
        wait_on_buffer(bh);
        if (bh->b_uptodate)
                return bh;
        brelse(bh);
        return NULL;
}
```

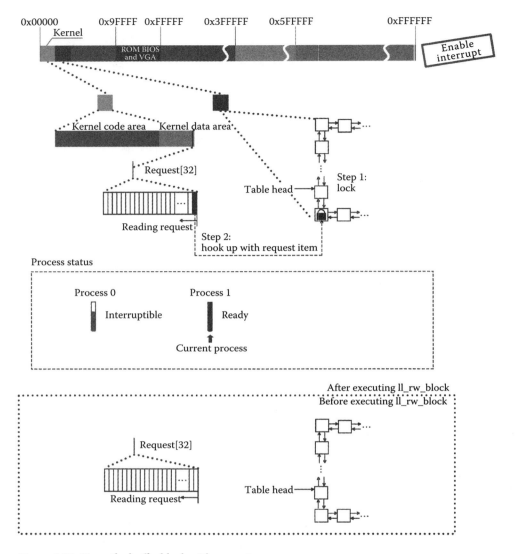

Figure 3.23 Hang the buffer block with request.

Once inside the ll_rw_block function, first determine whether the device corresponding to the buffer block exists or the request function of this device is normal; if it is present and normal, the block buffer can be used. Call the make_request function and prepare to bind the buffer block with request. The code is as follows:

```
//Code path:kernel/blk_dev/ll_rw_block.c:
void ll_rw_block(int rw, struct buffer_head * bh)
{
    unsigned int major;

    if ((major = MAJOR(bh->b_dev)) > = NR_BLK_DEV ||      //NR_BLK_DEV is 7, Major device
                                                          //number0-6,> = 7 means not exists
    !(blk_dev[major].request_fn)) {
        printk("Trying to read nonexistent block-device\n\r");
        return;
    }
    make_request(major,rw,bh);
}
```

Process 1 continues to execute; after entering the make_request function, first lock the buffer block to protect the buffer block from being used by other processes. As shown in the right side of Figure 3.23, the management structure that corresponds to the selected buffer block has been locked.

Then, apply for a free request and bind it with the selected buffer block. If the request is read, the entire request items can be used; if the request is written, only the first two-thirds of the request items can be used. Because user hope reading data faster. As shown in Figure 3.23, the last item of request[32] has been selected. Later, bind the buffer block with the request item and initialize every number of the request item.

The code is as follows:

```
//Code path:kernel/blk_dev/ll_rw_block.c:
static inline void lock_buffer(struct buffer_head * bh)
{
    cli();
    while (bh->b_lock)                        //now, it's unlock
            sleep_on(&bh->b_wait);
    bh->b_lock = 1;                           //lock the buffer block
    sti();
}
    ......
static void make_request(int major,int rw, struct buffer_head * bh)//
{
    struct request * req;
    int rw_ahead;

/* WRITEA/READA is special case - it is not really needed, so if the */
/* buffer is locked, we just forget about it, else it's a normal read */
    if (rw_ahead = (rw == READA || rw == WRITEA)) {
            if (bh->b_lock)//now, it's unlock
                    return;
        if (rw == READA)//abandon pre-read, replaced by normal read/write
            rw = READ;
        else
            rw = WRITE;
    }
    if (rw! = READ && rw! = WRITE)
            panic("Bad block dev command, must be R/W/RA/WA");
    lock_buffer(bh);                          //lock
    if ((rw == WRITE && !bh->b_dirt) || (rw == READ && bh->b_uptodate)) {    //now, it's unused
            unlock_buffer(bh);
            return;
    }
repeat:
/* we don't allow the write-requests to fill up the queue completely:
* we want some room for reads: they take precedence. The last third
* of the requests are only for reads.
*/
```

```
        if (rw == READ)                //read request is from the end of request[32], write request
                                       //is from the 2/3 of request[32]
                req = request+NR_REQUEST;
        else
                req = request+((NR_REQUEST*2)/3);
/* find an empty request */
        while (--req > = request)       //find the free request item from end, dev was
                                       //initialized to -1 in blk_dev_init, namely, free
                if (req->dev<0)         //find the free request item
                        break;
/* if none found, sleep on new requests: check for rw_ahead */
        if (req < request) {
                if (rw_ahead) {
                        unlock_buffer(bh);
                        return;
                }
                sleep_on(&wait_for_request);
                goto repeat;
        }
/* fill up the request-info, and add it to the queue */
        req->dev = bh->b_dev;          //set the request item
        req->cmd = rw;
        req->errors = 0;
        req->sector = bh->b_blocknr<<1;
        req->nr_sectors = 2;
        req->buffer = bh->b_data;
        req->waiting = NULL;
        req->bh = bh;
        req->next = NULL;
        add_request(major+blk_dev,req);
}
```

Call the add_request function to add this request item to the request item queue; after entering add_request, first analyze the work situation of the hard disk and then set this request item as the current request item and call (dev->request_fn)(); that is, the do_hd_request function sent a read command to the hard disk. The corresponding relation between the request item management structure and the do_hd_ request function is as shown in Figure 3.24.

The code is as follows:

```
//Code path:kernel/blk_dev/ll_rw_block.c:
static void add_request(struct blk_dev_struct * dev, struct request * req)
{
        struct request * tmp;

        req->next = NULL;
        cli();
        if (req->bh)
                req->bh->b_dirt = 0;
        if (!(tmp = dev->current_request)) {
                dev->current_request = req;
                sti();
                (dev->request_fn)();                                    //do_hd_request()
                return;
        }
        for (; tmp->next ; tmp = tmp->next)          //the effect of elevator algorithm is
                                                     //making the moving distance of magnetic
                                                     //head of disk is minimum
                if ((IN_ORDER(tmp,req) ||
                !IN_ORDER(tmp,tmp->next)) &&
                IN_ORDER(req,tmp->next))
                        break;
        req->next = tmp->next; //bind the request item queue
        tmp->next = req;
        sti();
}
```

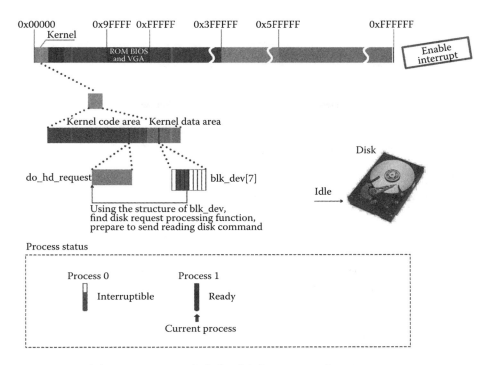

Figure 3.24 Bind the request item with the hard disk processing function.

3.3.1.4 Read the Hard Disk

Execute the do_hd_request function to prepare for reading the hard disk, as shown in Figure 3.25.

First, analyze the members of the request item to get the head, sector, cylinder, and the number of sectors needed to operate. Then, establish the necessary hard drive read parameters and move the head to 0 cylinder. Then, send operation command(read/wrote) to the hard disk; now that the command is read, read boot block of the hard drive and call the hd_out function to send operation command to the hard disk. Take note of the last two real parameters: WIN_READ means read operation and read_intr is an interrupt service program corresponding to read operation, as shown in the third step in Figure 3.25.

The code is as follows:

```
//Code path:kernel/blk_dev/hd.c:
void do_hd_request(void)
{
        int i,r;
        unsigned int block,dev;
        unsigned int sec,head,cyl;
        unsigned int nsect;

        INIT_REQUEST;
        dev = MINOR(CURRENT->dev);
        block = CURRENT->sector;
        if (dev >= 5*NR_HD || block+2 > hd[dev].nr_sects) {
                end_request(0);
                goto repeat;
```

```
        }
        block + = hd[dev].start_sect;
        dev/= 5;
        __asm__("divl%4":" = a" (block)," = d" (sec):"0" (block),"1" (0),
                "r" (hd_info[dev].sect));
        __asm__("divl%4":" = a" (cyl)," = d" (head):"0" (block),"1" (0),
                "r" (hd_info[dev].head));
        sec++;
        nsect = CURRENT->nr_sectors;
        if (reset) {
                reset = 0;                       //set, prevent mutiply execute if (reset)
                recalibrate = 1;                 //set, assure executing if(recalibrate)
                reset_hd(CURRENT_DEV);           //send the command "WIN_SPECIFY" to hard
                                                 //disk by calling hd_out, and establish the
                                                 //necessary parameter for reading hard disk
                return;
        }
        if (recalibrate) {
                recalibrate = 0;                 //set, prevent mutiply execute if
                                                 //(recalibrate)
                hd_out(dev,hd_info[CURRENT_DEV].sect,0,0,0,
                        WIN_RESTORE,&recal_intr); //send the command "WIN_RESTORE" to
                                                  //hard disk, and move the magnetic
                                                  //head to cycle 0 for reading data
                                                  //from hard disk
                return;
        }
        if (CURRENT->cmd == WRITE) {
                hd_out(dev,nsect,sec,head,cyl,WIN_WRITE,&write_intr);
                for(i = 0 ; i<3000 && !(r = inb_p(HD_STATUS)&DRQ_STAT) ; i++)
                        /* nothing */;
                if (!r) {
                        bad_rw_intr();
                        goto repeat;
                }
                port_write(HD_DATA,CURRENT->buffer,256);
        } else if (CURRENT->cmd == READ) {
                hd_out(dev,nsect,sec,head,cyl,WIN_READ,&read_intr);   //Note two parameters!
        } else
                panic("unknown hd-command");
}
```

Send read hard disk command as shown in the first step in Figure 3.26.
The specific code is as follows:

```
//Code path:kernel/blk_dev/hd.c:
static void hd_out(unsigned int drive,unsigned int nsect,unsigned int sect,
                unsigned int head,unsigned int cyl,unsigned int cmd,
                void (*intr_addr)(void))//the parameter is WIN_READ,&read_intr
{
        register int port asm("dx");

        if (drive>1 || head>15)
                panic("Trying to write bad sector");
        if (!controller_ready())
                panic("HD controller not ready");
        do_hd = intr_addr;                  //determine it's read_intr or
                                            //write_intr according to the parameter,
                                            //in this case, it's read_intr
        outb_p(hd_info[drive].ctl,HD_CMD);
        port = HD_DATA;
        outb_p(hd_info[drive].wpcom>>2,++port);
        outb_p(nsect,++port);
        outb_p(sect,++port);
        outb_p(cyl,++port);
        outb_p(cyl>>8,++port);
```

```
             outb_p(0xA0|(drive<<4)|head,++port);
             outb(cmd,++port);
}

//Code path:kernel/system_call.s:
_hd_interrupt:
       ......
       1:        jmp 1f
       1:        xorl%edx,%edx
       xchgl  _do_hd,%edx
       testl%edx,%edx
       jne 1f
       movl $_unexpected_hd_interrupt,%edx
       ......
```

do_hd = intr_addr binds the reading disk service routine with the hard disk interrupt service routine; here the do_hd is the content of "xchgl _do_hd,%edx" in _hd_interrupt function (system_call.s).

In this case, the operation is read disk, so attach to the read_intr(), if in the case of write disk, attach to the write_intr() functions.

Do read disk order!

The hard disk reads the data of the boot block into its cache; at the same time, the program also returns and will call hd_out(), do_hd_request(), add_request(), make_request(), and ll_rw_block() in the opposite direction until it returns to the bread() function.

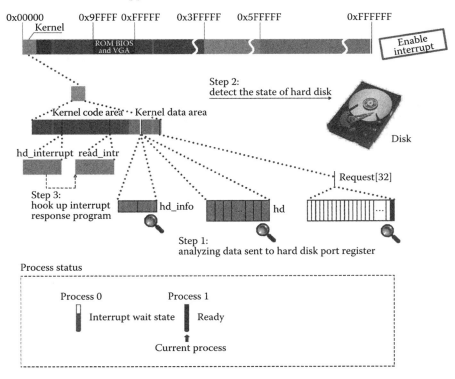

Figure 3.25 Prepare for reading the hard disk.

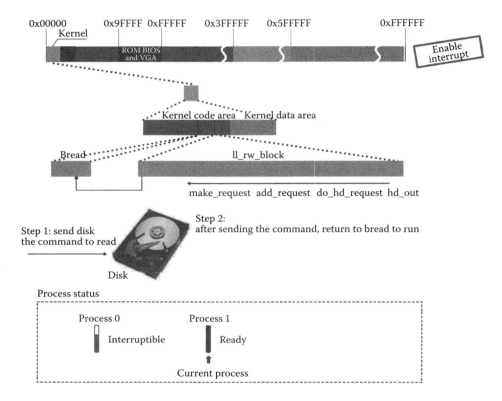

Figure 3.26 Send parameters to hard drive port registers and suspend the current process.

Now, the hard disk continues to read the boot block; if the program continues to execute, it needs to manipulate the data in the boot block, but these data are not read from the hard drive, so call the wait_on_buffer function and suspend the process!

The execution code is as follows:

```
//code path:fs/buffer.c:
struct buffer_head * bread(int dev,int block)
{
        struct buffer_head * bh;

        if (!(bh = getblk(dev,block)))
                panic("bread: getblk returned NULL\n");
        if (bh->b_uptodate)
                return bh;
        ll_rw_block(READ,bh);
        wait_on_buffer(bh);                  //suspend the process waiting
                                             //for unlock buffer

        if (bh->b_uptodate)
                return bh;
        brelse(bh);
        return NULL;
}
```

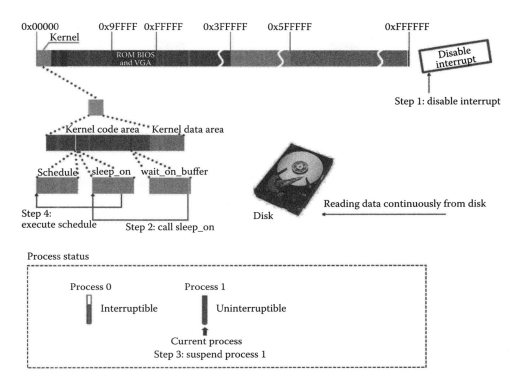

Figure 3.27 Process 1 suspends and executes schedule.

After entering the wait_on_buffer, it checks whether the buffer block is locked or not. If the buffer block is locked, it calls the sleep_on. The code is as follows:

```
//code path:fs/buffer.c:
static inline void wait_on_buffer(struct buffer_head * bh)
{
        cli();
        while (bh->b_lock)                      //has been lock before
                sleep_on(&bh->b_wait);
        sti();
}
```

Enter the sleep_on function and set process 1 to uninterruptible state, as shown in step 3 in Figure 3.27. Process 1 suspends then call the schedule function and be ready to switch processes. The execution code is as follows:

```
//code path:kernel/sched.c:
void sleep_on(struct task_struct **p)
{
        struct task_struct *tmp;

        if (!p)
                return;
        if (current == &(init_task.task))
                panic("task[0] trying to sleep");
        tmp = *p;
        *p = current;
        current->state = TASK_UNINTERRUPTIBLE;
        schedule();
        if (tmp)
                tmp->state = 0;

}
```

3.3.1.5 Wait for Hard Disk Reading Data, Process Scheduling, and Switch to Process 0 to Execute

After entering the schedule functions, it switches to process 0. Figure 3.28 gives the main steps.

Specific implementation steps have been illustrated in Section 3.2. The results are not similar to the execution results in Section 3.2 when traversing task[64] the second time. At this time, only two processes, the state of process 0 is interruptible state, the state of process 1 is set to uninterruptible state, the conventional process switching condition is that has the most of rest time piece and must be ready state. Like the code "if ((*p)-> state == TASK_RUNNING & & (* p)-> counter > c)" give conditions. Now the two processes are not ready condition, according to the conventional conditions, it cannot be the switching process and no process can be executed.

This is a very embarrassing state!

To solve this problem, the designers of the OS are forced to switch to process 0!

Note: The value of c will continue to be -1; hence, the next will still be 0, next is the process ID which switch to. If there is no suitable process, the value of next will always be 0, and the process will switch to process 0 to execute.

The execution code is as follows:

```
//code path:kernel/sched.c:
void schedule(void)
{
     ......
     while (1) {
           c = -1;
           next = 0;
           i = NR_TASKS;
```

```
        p = &task[NR_TASKS];
        while (--i) {
                if (!*--p)
                        continue;
                if ((*p)->state == TASK_RUNNING && (*p)->counter > c)
                        c = (*p)->counter, next = i;
        }
        if (c) break;
        for(p = &LAST_TASK ; p > &FIRST_TASK ;--p)
                if (*p)
                        (*p)->counter = ((*p)->counter >> 1) +
                                        (*p)->priority;
        }
        switch_to(next);//next is 0!
}
```

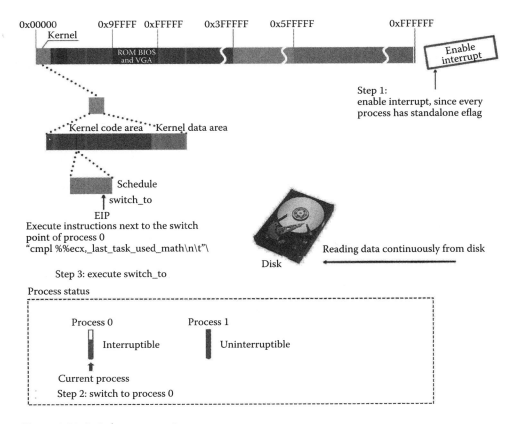

Figure 3.28 Switch to process 0 to execute.

Call switch_to(0). The execution code is as follows:

```
//code path:kernel/sched.h:
#define switch_to(n) {\
struct {long a,b;} __tmp; \
__asm__("cmpl%%ecx,_current\n\t" \
        "je 1f\n\t" \
        "movw%%dx,%1\n\t" \
        "xchgl%%ecx,_current\n\t" \
        "ljmp%0\n\t" \        //jump to process 0, reference the
                              //introduction of switch_to in Section 3.2
        "cmpl%%ecx,_last_task_used_math\n\t" \
        "jne 1f\n\t" \
        "clts\n" \
        "1:" \
        ::"m" (*&__tmp.a),"m" (*&__tmp.b), \
        "d" (_TSS(n)),"c" ((long) task[n])); \
}
```

After executing switch_to(0), it has switched to process 0. As illustrated in Section 3.2, when the process 0 switch to the process 1, it begin with the line "ljmp% 0\n\t" of the switch_to(1) switch to, TSS save all the value of CPU registers, cs,eip points to the next line, so the process 0 begin to execute from the cmpl%% ecx _last_task_used_math \n\t. It is shown as the third step in Figure 3.28.

Execute code as follows:

```
//code path:kernel/sched.h:
#define switch_to(n) {\
struct {long a,b;} __tmp; \
__asm__("cmpl%%ecx,_current\n\t" \
        "je 1f\n\t" \
        "movw%%dx,%1\n\t" \
        "xchgl%%ecx,_current\n\t" \
        "ljmp%0\n\t" \
        "cmpl%%ecx,_last_task_used_math\n\t" \   //from this line to
                                                  //execute, in this case,
                                                  //it's process 0 with
                                                  //privilege level 0

        "jne 1f\n\t" \
        "clts\n" \
        "1:" \
        ::"m" (*&__tmp.a),"m" (*&__tmp.b), \
        "d" (_TSS(n)),"c" ((long) task[n])); \
}
```

In Section 3.2, process 0 switching to process 1 is caused by pause(), sys_pause(), schedule(), and switch_to(1). Now, the latter part of switch_to(1) has been implemented; it will return to sys_pause(), for (;;) the pause() to execute.

Pause() will be called repeatedly in the for (;;) cycle; thus, it will continue to call schedule() to switch process. When switching again, the two processes are not in the ready status, all processes suspend, and the kernel performs switch_to and is forced to switch to process 0.

Now, the condition that switch_to need to deal with has some changes, the meaning of "cmpl%% ecx, _current \n\t" "je, 1f\n\t," is: if the process to switch to is the current process, jump to the following "1:" directly return. The current process is the process 0 and also the process to switch to, just meet this condition.

The execution code is as follows:

```
//code path:init/main.c:
void main(void)
{
......
for(;;) pause();
}
//code path:kernel/sched.h:
#define switch_to(n) {\
struct {long a,b;} __tmp; \
__asm__("cmpl%%ecx,_current\n\t" \
        "je 1f\n\t" \
        "movw%%dx,%1\n\t" \
        "xchgl%%ecx,_current\n\t" \
        "ljmp%0\n\t" \
        "cmpl%%ecx,_last_task_used_math\n\t" \
        "jne 1f\n\t" \
        "clts\n" \
        "1:" \
        ::"m" (*&__tmp.a),"m" (*&__tmp.b), \
        "d" (_TSS(n)),"c" ((long) task[n])); \
}
```

Hence, return to process 0 (Note: it's not switch to process 0).

Repeatedly execute this operation.

From here, the reader can see the special functions of process 0 that are designed by OS designers: when all processes suspend or do not have any process to execute, process 0 emerges to maintain the basic OS functions, waiting other suspended processes meet the ready condition to continue execute (Figure 3.29).

Note: *The read and write speed of the hard disk are much lower than the speed of the CPU in executing instructions (about two to three orders of magnitude). Now, the drive is still busy reading the specified data into its cache.*

3.3.1.6 Hard Disk Interruption Occurs During the Execution of Process 0

After executing repeatedly, the hard drive reads out the data of one sector at some point, resulting in hard disk interruption. After the CPU receives the interrupt instruction, it terminates the program being executed. The position of termination is certainly in the following line instruction: pause(), sys_pause(), schedule(), switch_to (n). This is shown as the first step in Figure 3.30.

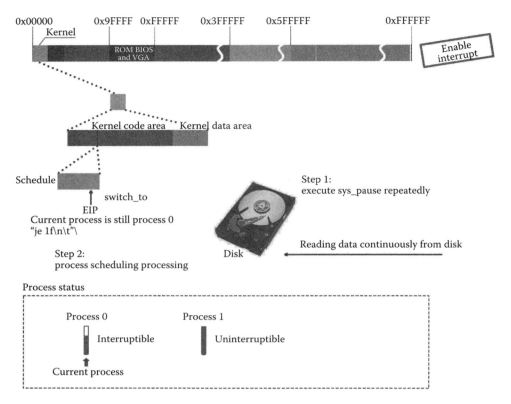

Figure 3.29 The repeatedly executing process of process 0.

Then, change to execute the disk interrupt service program. The execution code is as follows:

```
//code path:kernel/system_call.s:
      ......
_hd_interrupt:
      pushl%eax                      //save the state of CPU
      pushl%ecx
      pushl%edx
      push%ds
      push%es
      push%fs
      movl $0x10,%eax
      mov%ax,%ds
      mov%ax,%es
      movl $0x17,%eax
      mov%ax,%fs
      movb $0x20,%al
      outb%al,$0xA0
      jmp 1f
```

```
1:        jmp 1f
1:        xorl%edx,%edx
          xchgl _do_hd,%edx
          testl%edx,%edx
          jne 1f
          movl $_unexpected_hd_interrupt,%edx
1:        outb%al,$0x20
          call *%edx
          ......
```

Do not forget that the interrupt can automatically push ss, esp, eflags, cs, and eip, and the hard interrupt service program code continues to push register data to save the program interrupt site. Then, execute the reading disk interrupt program of _do_hd. The corresponding code is the line of "call *% edx"; the edx is the address of the reading disk interrupt program read_intr; see the explanation and code comments of the hd_out() function.

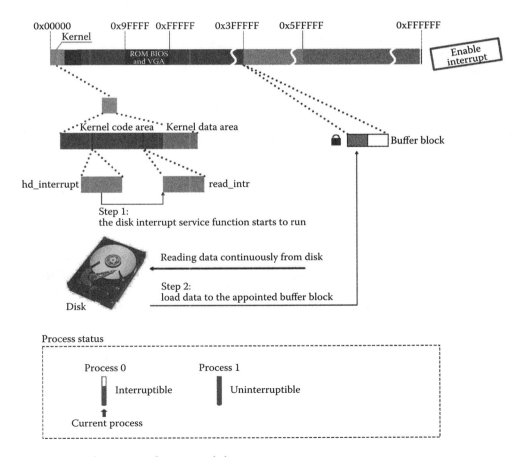

Figure 3.30 The process of executing disk interrupt.

The read_intr() function will copy the data that have already been read into the hard disk cache to the locked buffer block (note: the lock is to stop the operation of the process but does not prevent the operation of the peripherals); then, the data of one sector and 256 words (512 bytes) are read into the buffer block which was applied before. This is shown as the second step in Figure 3.30. The execution code is as follows:

```
//code path:kernel/blk_dev/hd.c:
static void read_intr(void)
{
        if (win_result()) {
                bad_rw_intr();
                do_hd_request();
                return;
        }
        port_read(HD_DATA,CURRENT->buffer,256);
        CURRENT->errors = 0;
        CURRENT->buffer + = 512;
        CURRENT->sector++;
        if (--CURRENT->nr_sectors) {
                do_hd = &read_intr;
                return;
        }
        end_request(1);
        do_hd_request();
}
```

However, the boot block data is 1024 bytes, request requirement is 1024 bytes. Now, half of it has been read, the hard drive will continue to read disk. At the same time, learned that the request corresponding to the buffer block of data is not fully read, the kernel will again binding read_intr() with the hard disk interrupt service routine in order to the next use, then the interrupt service routine return.

Process 1 is still in a suspended state; the pause(), sys_pause(), schedule(), switch_to (0) cycle continues to repeat from the site interrupted by the hard disk, and the hard drive continues to read the disk.

This process is shown in Figure 3.31.

After a period of time, another half data of the hard disk has been read. The hard disk generates an interrupt, and the read disk interrupt service program again responds to the interrupt and enters the read_intr function. It still will determine whether the request corresponding to the buffer data finished reading. The corresponding code is as follows:

```
//code path:kernel/blk_dev/hd.c:
static void read_intr(void)
{
        ......
        if (--CURRENT->nr_sectors)
        ......
        end_request(1);
        ......
}
```

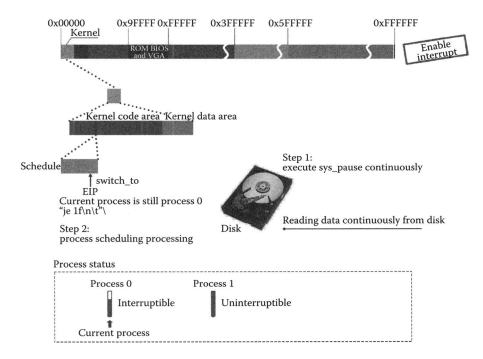

Figure 3.31 Process 0 continued to repeatedly execute.

The data that request requires has been read. After confirmation is complete, do not execute the inside content of if and skip to the end_request function to performing, as shown in Figure 3.32.

After entering end_request and the content of the buffer block has been read, it sets the buffer update flag b_uptodate to 1. The execution code is as follows:

```
//code path:kernel/blk_dev/blk.h:
extern inline void end_request(int uptodate)
{
        DEVICE_OFF(CURRENT->dev);
        if (CURRENT->bh) {
                CURRENT->bh->b_uptodate = uptodate; //uptodate is
                                                    //parameter, its
                                                    //value is 1
                unlock_buffer(CURRENT->bh);
        }
        if (!uptodate) {
                printk(DEVICE_NAME " I/O error\n\r");
                printk("dev%04x, block%d\n\r",CURRENT->dev,
                        CURRENT->bh->b_blocknr);
        }
        wake_up(&CURRENT->waiting);
        wake_up(&wait_for_request);
        CURRENT->dev = -1;
        CURRENT = CURRENT->next;
}
```

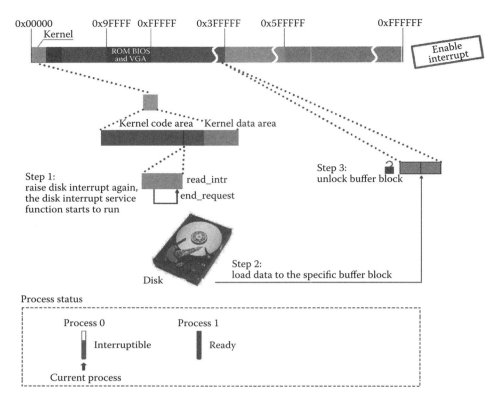

Figure 3.32 Respond to disk interrupt again and wake up process 1.

Then, unlock_buffer() is called to unlock the buffer block. Call the wake_up() function in the unlock_buffer() function, set process 1 to ready state, and operate the request, for example, set its corresponding request to free....

The code is as follows:

```
//code path:kernel/blk_dev/blk.h:
extern inline void unlock_buffer(struct buffer_head * bh)
{
        if (!bh->b_lock)
                printk(DEVICE_NAME ": free buffer being unlocked\n");
        bh->b_lock = 0;
        wake_up(&bh->b_wait);
}

//code path:kernel/sched.c:
void wake_up(struct task_struct **p)
{
        if (p && *p) {
                (**p).state = 0;        //set the ready state
                *p = NULL;
        }
}
```

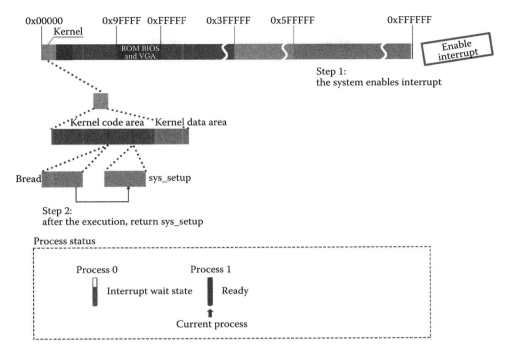

Step 1:
the system enables interrupt

Step 2:
after the execution, return sys_setup

Figure 3.33 Switch to process 1 and then return sys_setup.

After the hard disk interrupt handling ends, which means the end of the loading boot block of hard disk, the computer continues to execute in pause(), sys_pause(), schedule(), and switch_to (0), repeatly, shown as the second step in Figure 3.32.

3.3.1.7 After Reading the Disk, Switch Process Scheduling to Process 1

Now, the two sectors of the boot block have been loaded into the buffer block of the kernel. Process 1 is in a ready state. **Note:** Although process 0 has been involved in the cycle to run, it is in a non-ready state. There are only process 1 and process 0. Thus, when the cycle runs to schedule(), switch to process 1. This process is shown in Figure 3.33.

Switch to process 1. Process 1 then continues to execute from the code of the following function.

```
//code path:kernel/sched.h:
#define switch_to(n) {\
struct {long a,b;} __tmp; \
__asm__ ("cmpl%%ecx,_current\n\t" \
    "je 1f\n\t" \
    "movw%%dx,%1\n\t" \
    "xchgl%%ecx,_current\n\t" \
    "ljmp%0\n\t" \
```

```
        "cmpl%%ecx,_last_task_used_math\n\t" \      //the reason is same to the
                                                    //"switch to" illustrated
                                                    //before

        "jne 1f\n\t" \
        "clts\n" \
        "1:" \
        ::"m" (*&__tmp.a),"m" (*&__tmp.b), \
        "d" (_TSS(n)),"c" ((long) task[n])); \
}
```

This is the model that suits to the switching among all processes.

Process 1 switched from "ljmp%0\n\t"; hence, execute the next line. Now, return to sleep_on(), which is the switch initiator. And eventually return to the bread() function. Judge the field "b_uptodate" of the buffer has been set to 1 in function bread(), then return directly. Function bread run over. The execution code is as follows:

```
//code path:fs/buffer.c:
struct buffer_head * bread(int dev,int block)
{
        struct buffer_head * bh;

        if (!(bh = getblk(dev,block)))
                panic("bread: getblk returned NULL\n");
        if (bh->b_uptodate)
                return bh;
        ll_rw_block(READ,bh);
        wait_on_buffer(bh);
        if (bh->b_uptodate)
                return bh;
        brelse(bh);
        return NULL;
}
```

Continue execution when returning to the function sys_setup(). Perform functions after loading the boot block of the hard disk to the buffer. The buffer is loaded with the contents of the hard disk boot block. Judge the effective sign '55AA' of the hard disk at first. If the last 2 bytes of the first sector is not '55AA', then the data of this sector is invalid. (We assume that the data of the boot block has no problem.) The execution code is as follows:

```
//code path:kernel/blk_dev/hd.c:
int sys_setup(void * BIOS)
{
    ......
    for (drive = 0 ; drive<NR_HD ; drive++) {
        if (!(bh = bread(0x300 + drive*5,0))) {
        printk("Unable to read partition table of drive%d\n\r",
        drive);
        panic("");
        }
    if (bh->b_data[510] ! = 0x55 || (unsigned char)   //We assume that the data of
                                                       //boot block has no problem
```

```
        bh->b_data[511] ! = 0xAA) {
        printk("Bad partition table on drive%d\n\r",drive);
        panic("");
    }
    p = 0x1BE + (void *)bh->b_data;          //set hd[] according to the partition
                                             //information of the boot block.
    for (i = 1;i<5;i++,p++) {
        hd[i+5*drive].start_sect = p->start_sect;
        hd[i+5*drive].nr_sects = p->nr_sects;
    }
    brelse(bh);                              //release buffer block

    }
    if (NR_HD)
        printk("Partition table%s ok.\n\r",(NR_HD>1)?"s":"");
    ......
}
```

Then, use the partition table information collected from the boot block to set hd[], as shown in Figure 3.34.

The buffer of the reading boot block has completed its mission. Then, call the function brelse() for release in order to the program can use it again.

Set hd[] according to the hard disk partition information. The work preparing for the installation of the hard disk file system in Chapter 5 has been completed. Next, we will introduce process 1 using a Ramdisk in place of a floppy disk and make it as the root device in preparation for loading the root file system.

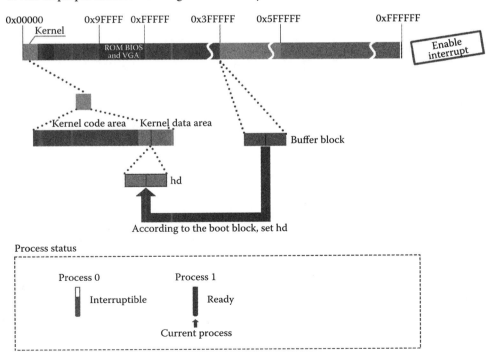

Figure 3.34 Using the boot block to set the hard disk partition management structure.

3.3.2 Process 1 Formats the Ramdisk and Replaces the Root Device as the Ramdisk

In Section 2.3, the Ramdisk space has been set up and initialized. The Ramdisk is still a "blank disk" before a similar deal like "formatting," but it cannot be used as a block device. Information for formatting is in the floppy disk of boot OS. Chapter 1 explains that the first sector is Bootsect, the four sectors behind are setup, and the next 240 sectors are the system module that contains the head, which is a total of 245 sectors. Formatting the Ramdisk information starts from the 256 sectors.

In the following, process 1 calls rd_load() to use the information of the sector in the floppy disk after 256 to format the Ramdisk and make it as a block device.

The execution code is as follows:

```
//code path:kernel/blk_dev/hd.c:
int sys_setup(void * BIOS)
{
    ......
    if (NR_HD)
            printk("Partition table%s ok.\n\r",(NR_HD>1)?"s":"");
    rd_load();
    mount_root();
    return (0);
}
```

After entering rd_load(), call breada() to read-ahead data block from the floppy disk, which are boot block and super block, which are needed for formatting the Ramdisk.

Note: *Now the root device is the floppy disk.*

Breada() and bread() are similar; the difference is that the breada() function can read in a number of consecutive data blocks, a total of three (257, 256, and 258), including guide block 256 (although the guide blocks are not actually used) and super block 257. The principle of reading the data block from a floppy disk is the same as bread reading the hard disk data block (see the explanation in Section 3.3.1). After reading, you can see in Figure 3.35 that three consecutive data blocks are read into the buffer cache block; the super block is marked with a red box.

Then, analyze the super block information, including judging whether the file system is Minix or not, and whether the data blocks of the root file system will be loaded will more than the entire Ramdisk space. These conditions should be satisfied in order to continue to load the root file system. Release the buffer block after analyzing. These are shown as the first, second, and third steps in Figure 3.36.

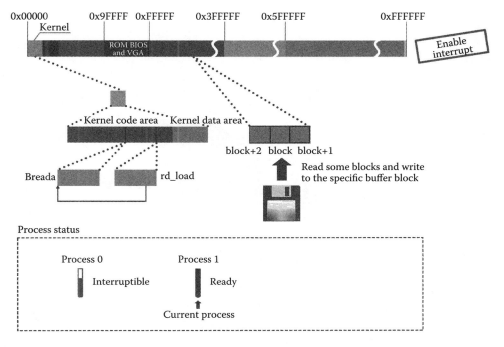

Figure 3.35 Read root file system super block.

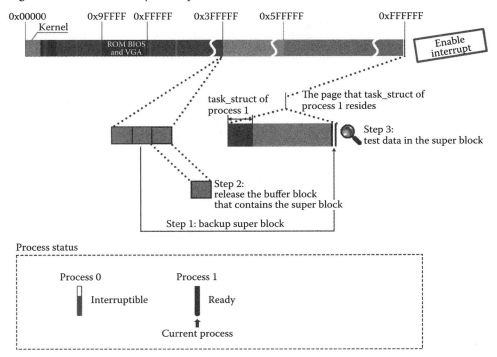

Figure 3.36 Backup super block and test data.

The code is as follows:

```
//code path:kernel/blk_dev/ramdisk.c:
void rd_load(void)
{
        struct buffer_head *bh;
        struct super_block      s;
        int              block = 256;     /* Start at block 256 */
        int              I = 1;
        int              nblocks;
        char             *cp;             /* Move pointer */

        if (!rd_length)
                return;
        printk("Ram disk:%d bytes, starting at 0x%x\n", rd_length,
                (int) rd_start);
        if (MAJOR(ROOT_DEV) ! = 2)        //if the root device is not floppy disk
                return;
        bh = breada(ROOT_DEV,block+1,block,block+2,-1);
        if (!bh) {
                printk("Disk error while looking for ramdisk!\n");
                return;
        }
        *((struct d_super_block *) &s) = *((struct d_super_block *)
bh->b_data);
        brelse(bh);
        if (s.s_magic ! = SUPER_MAGIC) //if unsatisfied, it's not Minix file system
                /* No ram disk image present, assume normal floppy boot */
                return;
        nblocks = s.s_nzones << s.s_log_zone_size; //calculate the block
                                        //numbers in Ramdisk
        if (nblocks > (rd_length >> BLOCK_SIZE_BITS)) {
                printk("Ram disk image too big! (%d blocks,%d avail)\n",
                        nblocks, rd_length >> BLOCK_SIZE_BITS);
                return;
        }
        printk("Loading%d bytes into ram disk... 0000k",
                nblocks << BLOCK_SIZE_BITS);
        ......
}
```

The system then calls breada, copies the file system content from the floppy disk to the Ramdisk and releases the buffer blocks to complete "format," as shown in the first and second steps in Figure 3.37.

After copying, set the Ramdisk as the root device.

```
//The code path:kernel/blk_dev/ramdisk.c:
void rd_load(void)
{
        ......
        printk("Loading%d bytes into ram disk... 0000k",
                nblocks << BLOCK_SIZE_BITS);
        cp = rd_start;
        while (nblocks) {//copy the file system from the floppy disk to the
                        //Ramdisk
                if (nblocks > 2)
                        bh = breada(ROOT_DEV, block, block+1, block+2, -1);
```

```
                else
                        bh = bread(ROOT_DEV, block);
                if (!bh) {
                        printk("I/O error on block%d, aborting load\n",
                                block);
                        return;
                }
                (void) memcpy(cp, bh->b_data, BLOCK_SIZE);
                brelse(bh);
                printk("\010\010\010\010\010%4dk",i);
                cp + = BLOCK_SIZE;
                block++;
                nblocks--;
                i++;
        }
        printk("\010\010\010\010\010done \n");
        ROOT_DEV = 0x0101;          //set the Ramdisk as the root device
}
```

We will introduce the loading of the root file system.

3.3.3 Process 1 Loads the Root File System into the Root Device

The loading of the root file system involves the concept of files, file systems, the root file system, loading file systems, and loading root file systems. In order to make it easier to understand, we will only discuss the block device, which is the floppy disk, the hard disk, and the Ramdisk (for more discussion of the block device, please read Chapters 5 and 7).

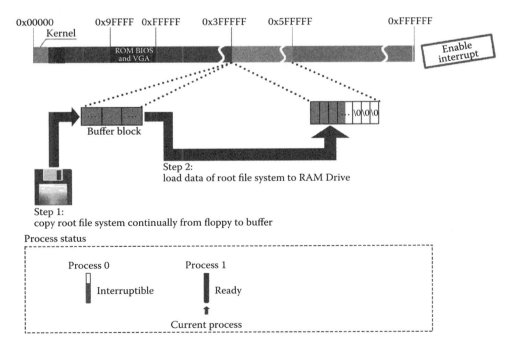

Figure 3.37 Copy the file system content from the floppy disk to the Ramdisk.

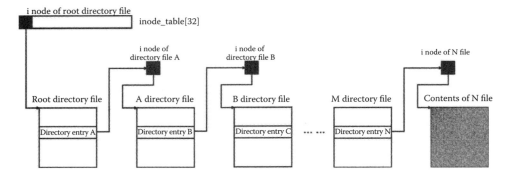

Figure 3.38 The relationship between file path and the i node.

The file system in the OS can be roughly divided into two parts: one is in the OS kernel and the other is in the hard disk, the floppy disk, and the Ramdisk.

The file system is designed to manage the files, and it uses the "i node" to manage files. When there is a file in the OS, there is a corresponding i node. The file path in the OS is managed by the directory entry; a directory entry corresponds to a level of the path, and the directory files are also files that are managed by the i node. A file is mounted on a directory file's directory entry; the directory file may be mounted on another directory according to the different physical path. Hence, a directory file has more than one directory entry to different paths. This is shown in Figure 3.38.

The i node of all files (including the directory files) eventually mounted into a tree-like structure; the root i node is called the file system's root i node. A logical device (a physical device can be divided into multiple logical devices, such as a physical hard disk can be divided into multiple logical hard disks) has only one file system. A file system only contains one tree structure; that is, a logical device only has one root i node.

The most important sign of loading the file system is associating the root i node of a logical device with another file system's i node; which is determined by the user's mount command. This is shown in Figure 3.39.

In other words, a file system must be linked to another file system. According to this policy, there must be a file system to mount any other file systems, and the special file system is called the root file system, and the device is called the root device.

If any other file system can be mounted on the root file system, then where should the root file system be mounted?

The answer? Mount it on the super_block[8].

Linux 0.11 OS has only one super_block[8]. Each element of the array is a super block; a super block manages a logical device, which means that the OS can only manage eight logical devices, and among them, there is only one root device. The most important sign of loading the root file system is that the i node of the root file system is mounted on the corresponding super_block[8].

Generally speaking, the whole process of loading the root file system consists of three main steps:

1. Copying the super block of the root device to the super_block[8] and mounting the i node of the root device to the corresponding super block in super_block[8]

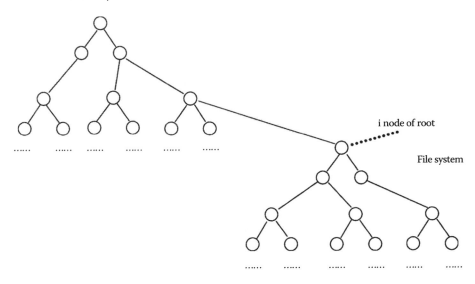

Root file system

i node of root

File system

Figure 3.39 Logical overview of the mount root file system.

2. Mounting the root device logical block bitmap and the i node bitmap to s_zmap[8] and s_imap[8] in super_block[8]

3. Setting the current process's pointers pwd and root pointing to the i node of root device

This is shown in Figure 3.40.

Now, let us switch to the third part of this section: process 1 calls mount_root to mount the root file system on the root device Ramdisk.

The code is as follows:

```
//The code path:kernel/blk_dev/hd.c:
int sys_setup(void * BIOS)
{
......
                brelse(bh);
        }
        if (NR_HD)
                printk("Partition table%s ok.\n\r",(NR_HD>1)?"s":"");
        rd_load();
        mount_root();                   //loading the root file system
        return (0);
}
```

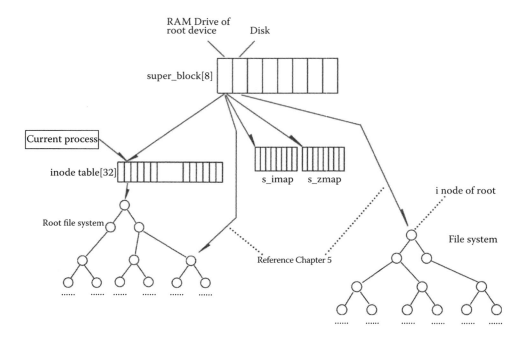

RAM Drive of
root device   Disk

super_block[8]

Current process

inode table[32]   s_imap   s_zmap

Root file system   i node of root

                                                    File system

Reference Chapter 5

Figure 3.40 Overview of the file system.

3.3.3.1 Copying the Super Block of the Root Device to the super_block[8]

In mount_root, the system initializes the super block management structure super_block[8] and then sets the device lock flags and all processes waiting for unlock to 0. Whenever the system wants to exchange data in the form of a file with a device, it must load the super block of the device into the super_block[8]. The system is able to acquire some basic information of the device file system from super_block[8]; also, the super block of the root device works in the same way, as shown in Figure 3.41.

The code is as follows:

```
//the code path:fs/super.c:
void mount_root(void)
{
        int i,free;
        struct super_block * p;
        struct m_inode * mi;



        if (32 ! = sizeof (struct d_inode))
                panic("bad i-node size");
        for(i = 0;i<NR_FILE;i++)                //initialize file_table[32], prepare
                                                //for the following code
                file_table[i].f_count = 0;
```

```
        if (MAJOR(ROOT_DEV) == 2) {//2represents floppy disk, the root device is
                                //Ramdisk, that is 1.
                                //conversely, load the root file system of floppy
                                //disk.
                printk("Insert root floppy and press ENTER");
                wait_for_keypress();
        }

        //initialize super_block[8]
        for(p = &super_block[0] ; p < &super_block[NR_SUPER] ; p++) {
            p->s_dev = 0;
            p->s_lock = 0;
            p->s_wait = NULL;
        }
        if (!(p = read_super(ROOT_DEV)))
            panic("Unable to mount root");
        .....
}
```

rd_load() has "formatted" the Ramdisk and set it as a root device. Then, the system will call the function read_super(), reading the super block of the root device from the Ramdisk and copying it to super_block[8].

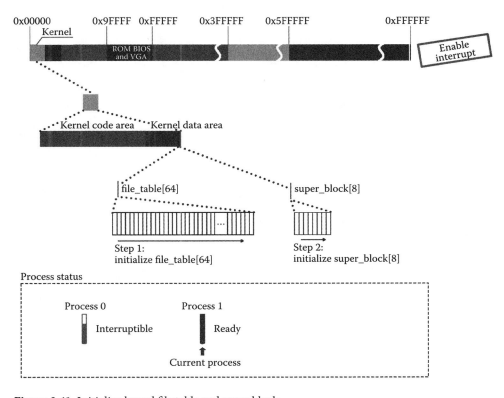

Figure 3.41 Initialize kernel file table and super block.

The code is as follows:

```
//the code path:fs/super.c:
void mount_root(void)
{
......
        if (!(p = read_super(ROOT_DEV)))
                        panic("Unable to mount root");
        ......
}
```

In the function read_super(), it first checks whether the super block has been read into the super_block[8]. If the super_block is there, it will be used directly without loading again.

The code is as follows:

```
//the code path:fs/super.c:
static struct super_block * read_super(int dev)
{
        struct super_block * s;
        struct buffer_head * bh;
        int i,block;

        if (!dev)
                return NULL;
        check_disk_change(dev);         //test whether change the disk
        if (s = get_super(dev))
                return s;
......
}
```

Because the root file system is not loaded, we need to apply a slot in super_block[8], as shown in Figure 3.42. Now, we find the first location of the super_block, initialize and lock it, and prepare for reading the super block of the root device.

The code is as follows:

```
//the code path:fs/super.c:
static struct super_block * read_super(int dev)
{
        ......
        for (s = 0+super_block ;; s++) {
                if (s > = NR_SUPER+super_block)        //NR_SUPER is 8
                        return NULL;
                if (!s->s_dev)
                        break;
        }
        s->s_dev = dev;
```

```
                 s->s_isup = NULL;
                 s->s_imount = NULL;
                 s->s_time = 0;
                 s->s_rd_only = 0;
                 s->s_dirt = 0;
                 lock_super(s);                          //lock the super
                                                         //block
      ......
}
```

The whole process consists of the following steps: calling the function bread, loading the super block from the Ramdisk to the buffer, and copying it from the buffer to the first location of super_block[8]. We have introduced the function bread in Section 3.3.1.2; there is little difference here. As mentioned in Section 3.3.1.5, if we send an order to the hard disk, the system will call the function do_hd_request. Since we operate the Ramdisk now, the system calls the function do_rd_request. It is worth reminding that the Ramdisk is considered as a peripheral, but after all, it is the memory space, not the actual peripheral; thus, calling do_rd_request would not trigger any interrupt, such as hard disk interrupt (Figure 3.43).

After the super block was loaded into the buffer, the system would copy the super block data from the buffer to the first location of super_block[8]. After that, the root device is managed by super_block[8]; then, call the brelse function to free the buffer.

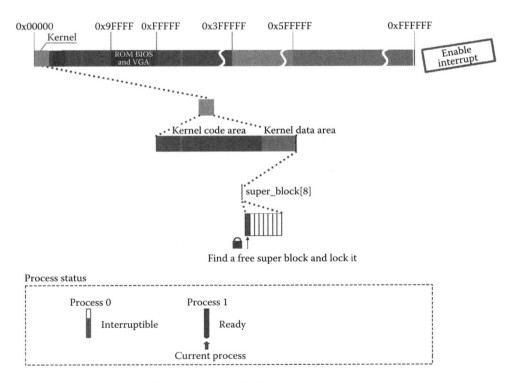

Figure 3.42 Loading root file system's super block.

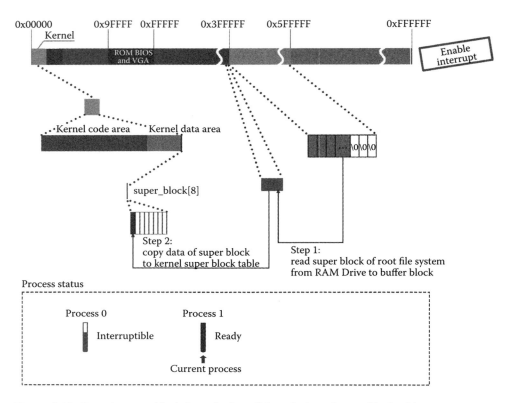

Figure 3.43 Copy the super block from the Ramdisk to the kernel super block table.

The code is as follows:

```
//the code path:fs/super.c:
static struct super_block * read_super(int dev)
{
        ......
        if (!(bh = bread(dev,1))) {          //read the super block of root device to
                                             the buffer
                s->s_dev = 0;
                free_super(s);               //free the super block
                return NULL;
        }
        *((struct d_super_block *) s) =      //copy the super block from the buffer
        *((struct d_super_block *) bh->b_data); //to the first location of super_block[8]
        brelse(bh);                          //free the buffer
        if (s->s_magic != SUPER_MAGIC) {     //test the s_magic
                s->s_dev = 0;
                free_super(s);               //free the super block
                return NULL;
        }
        ......
}
```

The system initializes the i node bitmap management structure s_imap and logical block bitmap management structure s_zmap in super_block[8]; then, load the i node bitmap and logical block bitmap into the buffer and mount them to s_imap[8] and s_zmap[8].

Because we will access them frequently, the system would not release them, and they will be kept in the buffer all the time.

As shown in Figure 3.44, the super block mounts the s_imap and s_zmap.

The code is as follows:

```
//the code path:fs/super.c:
static struct super_block * read_super(int dev)
{
    ......
    for (i = 0;i<I_MAP_SLOTS;i++)                //initialize s_imap[8] and s_zmap[8]
        s->s_imap[i] = NULL;
    for (i = 0;i<Z_MAP_SLOTS;i++)
        s->s_zmap[i] = NULL;
    block = 2;                                   //the 1st block of Ramdisk
                                                 //is super block,
                                                 //the 2nd is I-node bitmap and
                                                 //logical bitmap
    for (i = 0 ; i < s->s_imap_blocks ; i++)     //read all the logical block of
                                                 //I-node bitmap to the buffer
        if (s->s_imap[i] = bread(dev,block))     //mount them to s_imap[8]
            block++;
        else
            break;
    for (i = 0 ; i < s->s_zmap_blocks ; i++)     //read all the logical block of logical
                                                 //bitmap to the buffer
    if (s->s_zmap[i] = bread(dev,block))         //mount them to s_zmap[8]
            block++;
        else
            break;
    if (block != 2+s->s_imap_blocks+s->s_zmap_blocks) { //if the number of blocks is wrong,
            for(i = 0;i<I_MAP_SLOTS;i++)         //that means the system error
                brelse(s->s_imap[i]);            //free them
            for(i = 0;i<Z_MAP_SLOTS;i++)
                brelse(s->s_zmap[i]);
            s->s_dev = 0;
            free_super(s);
            return NULL;
    }s->s_imap[0]->b_data[0] |= 1;               //avoid return 0 and mix up with 0 I-node
        s->s_zmap[0]->b_data[0] |= 1;
        free_super(s);
        return s;
}
```

3.3.3.2 Mount the i node of the Root Device to the Root Device Super Block in super_block[8]

Back to mount_root, it calls iget() to read the root i node from the Ramdisk. The significance of the root i node is as follows: any i node in the system can be located through the root i node, which means we can find any files in the system.

The code is as follows:

```
//the code path:fs/super.c:
void mount_root(void)
{
    ......
    if (!(p = read_super(ROOT_DEV)))
        panic("Unable to mount root");
    if (!(mi = iget(ROOT_DEV,ROOT_INO)))
        panic("Unable to read root i-node");
    ......
}
```

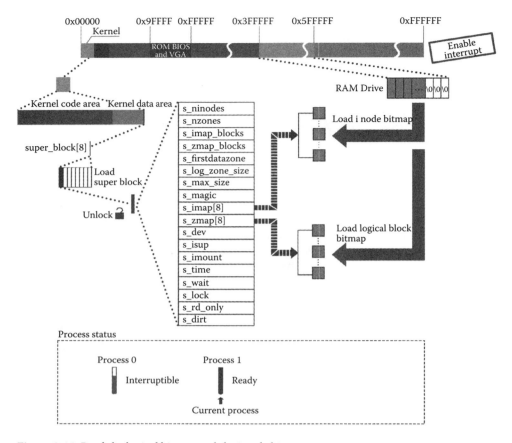

Figure 3.44 Read the logical bitmap and the i node bitmap.

In iget(), the OS would apply for a free i node slot in inode_table[32] (inode_table[32] is used by the OS to control the maximum number of concurrent opening files). At this stage, it should be the first i node; initialize the i node, including the device number of the i node, the node number of the i node. The location of the root i node in the kernel i node table is shown in Figure 3.45.

The code is as follows:

```
//the code path:fs/inode.c:
struct m_inode * iget(int dev,int nr)
{
        struct m_inode * inode, * empty;

        if (!dev)
                    panic("iget with dev ==0");
        empty = get_empty_inode();                      //apply a location for I-node in
                                                        //inode_table[32]

        inode = inode_table;
        while (inode < NR_INODE+inode_table) {          //find the same inode
                if (inode->i_dev ! = dev || inode->i_num ! = nr) {
                        inode++;
                        continue;
```

```
        }
        wait_on_inode(inode);                          //wait for unlocking
        if (inode->i_dev != dev || inode->i_num != nr) {    //if it changes when
                                                              waiting,
                inode = inode_table;                   //go on finding
                continue;
        }
        inode->i_count++;
        if (inode->i_mount) {
                int i;

                for (i = 0 ; i<NR_SUPER ; i++)         //if it is the mount point,
                        if (super_block[i].s_imount = =inode)   //find the super block
                                break;
                if (i > = NR_SUPER) {
                        printk("Mounted inode hasn't got sb\n");
                        if (empty)
                                iput(empty);
                        return inode;
                }
                iput(inode);
                dev = super_block[i].s_dev;            //get the device number in the
                                                       //super block
                nr = ROOT_INO;                         //ROOT_INO is 1,the node number
                                                       //of root I
                inode = inode_table;
                continue;
        }
        if (empty)
                iput(empty);
        return inode;
}
if (!empty)
        return (NULL);
inode = empty;
inode->i_dev = dev;                                    //initialize
inode->i_num = nr;
read_inode(inode);                                     //read the root I-node from the
                                                       //Ramdisk

return inode;
}
```

The function read_inode() first locks the i node in inode_table[32] so that the i node will not be used by another program until it is released. The function then calculates the logical block number of the i node through the super block of the i node and reads in the i node logical block, gets the information of the i node, and loads it to the i node location that has just been locked, as shown in Figure 3.46. Note the change in inode_table. Finally, it will free the buffer and unlock the i node.

The code is as follows:

```
//the code path:fs/inode.c:
static void read_inode(struct m_inode * inode)
{
        ......
        lock_inode(inode);                         //lock the inode
        if (!(sb = get_super(inode->i_dev)))       //get the super block of the I-node
        ......
        block = 2 + sb->s_imap_blocks + sb->s_zmap_blocks +
                (inode->i_num-1)/INODES_PER_BLOCK;
        if (!(bh = bread(inode->i_dev,block)))     //read the logical block of I-node
                panic("unable to read i-node block");
        *(struct d_inode *)inode =                 //copy all
                ((struct d_inode *)bh->b_data)
                        [(inode->i_num-1)%INODES_PER_BLOCK];
        brelse(bh);                                //free the buffer blocks
        unlock_inode(inode);                       //unlock
```

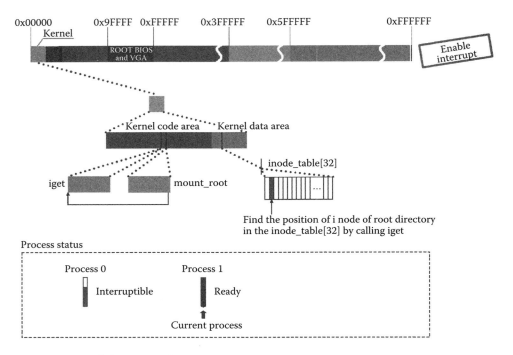

Figure 3.45 Read the root i node.

Back to iGet, it returns the pointer inode to the function mount_root and assigns it to pointer mi.

The following is the process of loading the root file system:

Mount the Ramdisk root i node in inode_table[32] to the s_isup and s_imount in super_block[8]. Hence, the OS could find the files step by step through the relationship established here.

3.3.3.3 Associate the Root File System with Process 1

The system sets the members of task_struct that is related to the file system i node and binds the root i node with the current process (process 1), as shown in Figure 3.47.

The code is as follows:

```
//the code path:fs/super.c:
void mount_root(void)
{
    ......
    if (!(mi = iget(ROOT_DEV,ROOT_INO)))      //the root I-node of root device
            panic("Unable to read root i-node");
    mi->i_count + = 3 ; /* NOTE! it is logically used 4 times, not 1 */
    p->s_isup = p->s_imount = mi;             //The important step
    current->pwd = mi;                        //the current process manage the root
                                              //I-node of root file system
    current->root = mi;                       //The parent-child create mechanism will
                                              //inherit this attribute to child process
    ......
}
```

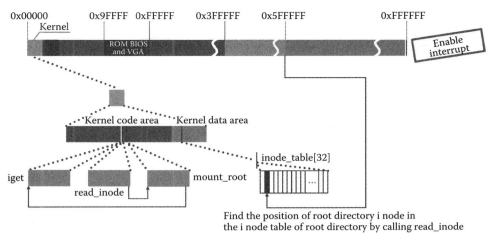

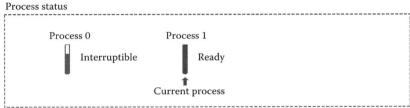

Figure 3.46 Read the i node.

After getting the super block of the root file system, we can identify the status (occupied or free) of the Ramdisk through the information recorded in the super block and record this information in the buffer that was mentioned in Section 3.3.3.1. The code is as follows:

```
//the code path:fs/super.c:
void mount_root(void)
{
    ……
    free = 0;
    i = p->s_nzones;
    while (--i > = 0)              //calculate the number of free logical blocks
        if (!set_bit(i&8191,p->s_zmap[i>>13]->b_data))
            free++;
    printk("%d/%d free blocks\n\r",free,p->s_nzones);
    free = 0;
    i = p->s_ninodes+1;
    while (--i > = 0)              //calculate the number of free I-node in the
                                   //Ramdisk
        if (!set_bit(i&8191,p->s_imap[i>>13]->b_data))
            free++;
    printk("%d/%d free inodes\n\r",free,p->s_ninodes);
}
```

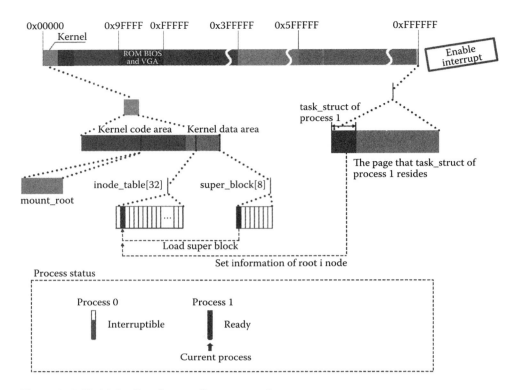

Figure 3.47 Finish loading the root file system and return.

At this stage, the function sys_setup is completed. This function is called by a soft interrupt; hence, return to system_call, and after that, call the function ret_from_sys_call. Now, the current process is process 1; thus, the following will call the function do_signal (as long as the current process is not process 0, it would execute the function do_signal) to detect the bitmap of the current process. The code is as follows:

```
//the code path:kernel/system_call.s:
......
ret_from_sys_call:
        movl    _current,%eax           # task[0] cannot have signals
        cmpl    _task,%eax
        je      3f
        cmpw    $0x0f,CS(%esp)          # was old code segment
                                        supervisor ?
        jne     3f
        cmpw    $0x17,OLDSS(%esp)       # was stack segment = 0x17 ?
        jne     3f
        movl    signal(%eax),%ebx       #the following would get the
                                        #signal bitmap
        movl    blocked(%eax),%ecx
        notl    %ecx
        andl    %ebx,%ecx
        bsfl    %ecx,%ecx
```

```
        je      3f
        btrl    %ecx,%ebx
        movl    %ebx,signal(%eax)
        incl    %ecx
        pushl   %ecx
        call    _do_signal              #call the function do_signal( )
        ......
```

Now, the current process (process 1) does not receive any signal, so there is no need to call do_signal.

At this point, sys_setup has finished and process 1 will return to the calling point mentioned in Section 3.3, preparing the code below.

```
//the code path:init/main.c:
void init(void)
{
        ......
        int pid,i;

        setup((void *) &drive_info);
        (void) open("/dev/tty0",O_RDWR,0);
        (void) dup(0);
        (void) dup(0);
        printf("%d buffers =%d bytes buffer space\n\r",NR_BUFFERS,
                NR_BUFFERS*BLOCK_SIZE);
        ......
}
```

In this chapter, we introduce how the system creates process 1, installs the hard disk file system, "formats" the Ramdisk and makes it as the root device, and loads the root file system into the Ramdisk. After all done, we will explain how process 1 creates process 2 and finish the shell, which is the human–computer interface of the OS.

4 Creation and Execution of Process 2

■ 4.1 Open the Terminal Device File and Copy the File Handle

Shell is a user-interface (UI) process. Through shell, computer users implement human–computer interactions with operating systems by using the monitor and the keyboard (terminal equipment).

4.1.1 Open the Standard Input Device File

Figure 4.1 shows the scene after tty0 file has been loaded.

4.1.1.1 File_table[0] is Mounted to Filp[0] in Process 1

After the root file system is loaded, process 1 opens the standard input device file by calling the open function. The code is as follows:

```
//code path:init/main.c:
void init(void)
{
    int pid,i;

    setup((void *) &drive_info);
```

```
        (void) open("/dev/tty0",O_RDWR,0);//create standard input device,
                                          //the path is /dev/tty0
    (void) dup(0);//create standard output device
    (void) dup(0);//create standard error output device
    printf("%d buffers =%d bytes buffer space\n\r",NR_BUFFERS,//show
//the information with the support of standard output device
        NR_BUFFERS*BLOCK_SIZE);
    printf("Free mem:%d bytes\n\r",memory_end-main_memory_start);
    ......
}
```

The open() function triggers a soft interrupt and the process will be transferred to sys_open(), which is quite similar to fork() in Section 3.1.1.

```
//code path:fs/open.c:
int open(const char * filename, int flag,...)
{
    register int res;
    va_list arg;

    va_start(arg,flag);
    __asm__("int $0x80"//similar to the path from fork() to sys_fork(), refer
                       //the technique route that in Section 3.1.1
        :"=a" (res)
        :"0" (__NR_open),"b" (filename),"c" (flag),
        "d" (va_arg(arg,int)));
    if (res>=0)
        return res;
    errno = -res;
        return -1;
}
```

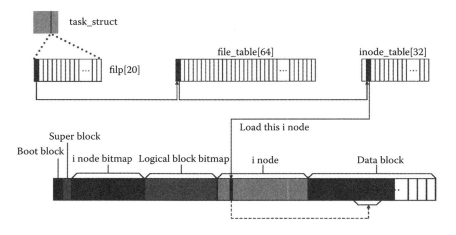

Figure 4.1 The distribution of file information in the memory and process after tty0 is opened.

In sys_open(), the kernel will mount the filp of process 1 to file_table[64] first, and then establish the relationship between process and file_table[64], as shown below:

```
//code path:fs/open.c:
int sys_open(const char * filename,int flag,int mode)
{
    struct m_inode * inode;
    struct file * f;
    int i,fd;

    mode &=0777 & ~current->umask;
    for(fd=0 ; fd<NR_OPEN ; fd++) //parse the filp of process 1
    if (!current->filp[fd])          //get an idle item and fd is the number
                                break;
    if (fd>=NR_OPEN)//return when filp has no more idle item
        return -EINVAL;
    current->close_on_exec &= ~(1<<fd);
    f=0+file_table;//get the initial address of file_table[64]
    for (i=0 ; i<NR_FILE ; i++,f++)  //parse the file_table[64]
        if (!f->f_count) break;      //f is the pointer of the idle item
    if (i>=NR_FILE)//
        return -EINVAL;
    (current->filp[fd]=f)->f_count++;    //mount filp to file_table and
                                         //increase the citation number
    if ((i=open_namei(filename,flag,mode,&inode))<0) {//get the i node
        current->filp[fd]=NULL;
        f->f_count=0;
        return i;
    }
    ......
}
```

The mounting scenario is shown in Figure 4.2.

4.1.1.2 Determine the Starting Point of Absolute Path

The kernel calls open_namei to acquire the i node of the standard input device file as shown below:

```
//code path:fs/open.c:
int sys_open(const char * filename,int flag,int mode)
{
    struct m_inode * inode;
    struct file * f;
    int i,fd;

    mode &=0777 & ~current->umask;
    for(fd=0 ; fd<NR_OPEN ; fd++)
        if (!current->filp[fd])
                        break;
    if (fd>=NR_OPEN)
        return -EINVAL;
```

```
    current->close_on_exec &= ~(1<<fd);
    f=0+file_table;
    for (i=0 ; i<NR_FILE ; i++,f++)
        if (!f->f_count) break;
    if (i> = NR_FILE)
        return -EINVAL;
    (current->filp[fd]=f)->f_count++;
    if ((i = open_namei(filename,flag,mode,&inode))<0) {//filename is
//the pointer of/dev/tty0
        current->filp[fd]=NULL;
        f->f_count=0;
        return i;
    }
    ......
}
```

The object can be satisfied by analyzing the name of the path continuously. The first stage of the analysis is to get the topmost i node by calling dir_namei, that is, the i node of the directory file dev in/dev/tty0. The second stage is to call find_entry to find the tty0 directory item and get the i node of tty0.

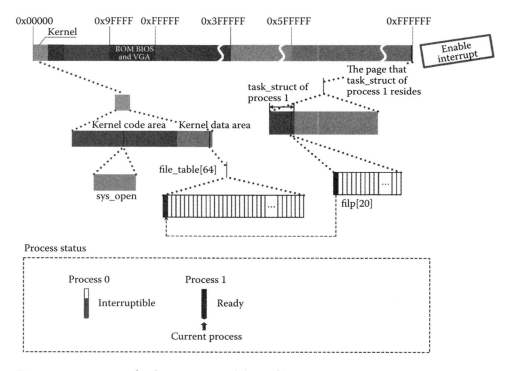

Figure 4.2 Preparation for the open terminal device file.

The code for calling dir_namei is as follows:

```
//code path:fs/namei.c:
int open_namei(const char * pathname, int flag, int mode,
    struct m_inode ** res_inode)//pathname is the pointer of /dev/tty0
{
    const char * basename;//basename records the address of '/' in front
    int inr,dev,namelen;//namelen records the name length
    struct m_inode * dir, *inode;
    struct buffer_head * bh;
    struct dir_entry * de;//de points to the directory content
    if ((flag & O_TRUNC) && !(flag & O_ACCMODE))
        flag | = O_WRONLY;
    mode &= 0777 & ~current->umask;
    mode |= I_REGULAR;
    if (!(dir = dir_namei(pathname,&namelen,&basename)))//get topmost i node
        return -ENOENT;
    if (!namelen) {               /* special case: '/usr/' etc */
        if (!(flag & (O_ACCMODE|O_CREAT|O_TRUNC))) {
            *res_inode=dir;
            return 0;
        }
        iput(dir);
        return -EISDIR;
    }
    bh = find_entry(&dir,basename,namelen,&de);//find the directory through
                                              //topmost i node
    ......
}
```

The function dir_namei() will call get_dir() to get the topmost i node first and then acquires the address of tty0 and the length of the file name by parsing the name of the path. The code for calling get_dir is as follows:

```
//code path:fs/namei.c:
static struct m_inode * dir_namei(const char * pathname,//pathname is the
                                                        //pointer of
                                                        //"/dev/tty0"
int * namelen, const char ** name)
{
    char c;
    const char * basename;
    struct m_inode * dir;

    if (!(dir = get_dir(pathname)))    //execution function of get i node
        return NULL;
    basename = pathname;
    while (c = get_fs_byte(pathname++))
//traverse the characters of/dev/tty0 and copy each one to c till the end
```

```
        if (c=='/')
            basename=pathname;
    *namelen = pathname-basename-1;//determine the name length of tty0
    *name = basename;//get the address of '/' in front of tty0
    return dir;
}
```

It is noteworthy that get_fs_byte is the core function of path resolution, which would extract the string in the path name one by one. This function will be used to analyze the path later. Its internal process is as follows:

```
//code path:include/asm/Segment.h:
extern inline unsigned char get_fs_byte(const char * addr)
{
    unsigned register char _v;

    __asm__ ("movb%%fs:%1,%0"//movb could move 1 byte data to specific
                             //register
        :"=r" (_v)//v is the output character
        :"m" (*addr));//*addr is the memory address to input
    return _v;
}
```

Get_dir() will determine the absolute starting point of the path first, namely, whether the first character of "/dev/tty0" is "/" or not, if yes, it means that it is the absolute path name. Get_dir() starts searching files from the root i node, which is loaded in the kernel when loading root file system in Section 3.3.3 and is determined as the absolute starting point of the path. At the same time, the citation count of the root i node will increase. The code is as follows:

```
//code path:fs/namei.c:
static struct m_inode * get_dir(const char * pathname)//pathname is
                                                      //the pointer
                                                      //of "/dev/tty0"
{
    char c;
    const char * thisname;
    struct m_inode * inode;
    struct buffer_head * bh;
    int namelen,inr,idev;
    struct dir_entry * de;
```

```
    if (!current->root || !current->root->i_count)//root i node of
//current process doesn't exist or citation number is 0, the kernel
//breaks
        panic("No root inode");
    if (!current->pwd || !current->pwd->i_count)
    //root i node of current directory in current process doesn't
//exist or citation number is 0, the kernel breaks.
    panic("No cwd inode");
    if ((c=get_fs_byte(pathname))=='/') {//it identifies that the
//first character of "/dev/tty0" is '/'
        inode = current->root;
        pathname++;
    } else if I
        inode = current->pwd;
    else
        return NULL;     /* empty name is bad */
    inode->i_count++;//the citation count of this i node increases by 1
    ......
}
```

Figure 4.3 shows how to locate the starting point of the path.

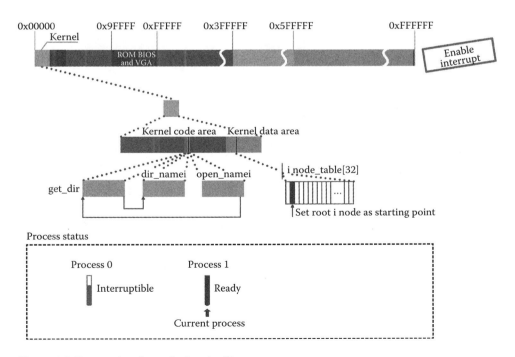

Figure 4.3 Preparation for analyzing the file name.

4.1.1.3 Acquiring the i node of Dev

Starting from the root i node, get_dir() will traverse and parse the pathname "/dev/tty0" to get the directory item dev first. After that, it will find the logical block in Ramdisk and read it into the specific buffer block. The code is as follows:

```
//code path:fs/namei.c:
static struct m_inode * get_dir(const char * pathname)
{
    char c;
    const char * thisname;//thisname records the address of "/", which
                          //is in front of the directory entry name
    struct m_inode * inode;
    struct buffer_head * bh;
    int namelen,inr,idev;//namelen records the name length
    struct dir_entry * de;//de points to the contents of directory entry

    ......
    if ((c=get_fs_byte(pathname))=='/') {
        inode = current->root;
        pathname++;//pathname is the pointer to the first char of "/dev/
//tty0", namely '/', it points to 'd' after ++ operation.
    } else if I
        inode = current->pwd;
    else
        return NULL;    /* empty name is bad */
        inode->i_count++;
while (1) {//loop this process till finding topmost i node
    thisname = pathname;//thisname points to 'd'
    if (!S_ISDIR(inode->i_mode) || !permission(inode,MAY_EXEC)) {
        iput(inode);
        return NULL;
        }
    for(namelen=0;(c=get_fs_byte(pathname++))&&(c!='/');namelen++)
    //the loop breaks when examining '/' or c is '\0'
        /* nothing */;//pay attention to this semicolon
    if (!c)
        return inode;
    if (!(bh = find_entry(&inode,thisname,namelen,&de))) {
    //get directory item through i node and relative information
        iput(inode);
        return NULL;
    }
    inr = de->inode;
    idev = inode->i_dev;
    brelse(bh);
    iput(inode);
    if (!(inode = iget(idev,inr)))
        return NULL;
    }
}
```

Get_fs_byte is used to traverse the path name "dev" from the "d" character in/dev/tty0 again. It will exit the loop when it meets "/" and the value of namelen increases to 3. All this information with the root i node pointer are used as parameters of find_entry, and the logical block, which has the directory will be read into buffer block.

Please note that the last parameter, namely de, of find_entry points to a data structure, which is directory structure. The code is as follows:

```
//code path:/include/linux/fs.h
#define NAME_LEN 14

struct dir_entry {//directory item structure
    unsigned short inode;//i node of corresponding directory file in
                        //device
    char name[NAME_LEN];//directory item name,14 bytes
};
```

After getting the i node id, it can find the inode of directory file corresponding to the "dev" directory entry. Furthermore, the kernel will find the "dev" directory file through this inode. The code is as follows:

```
//code path:fs/namei.c:
static struct m_inode * get_dir(const char * pathname)
{
    ......
    if ((c=get_fs_byte(pathname)) ='/') {
        inode = current->root;
        pathname++;
    } else if I
        inode = current->pwd;
    else
        return NULL;    /* empty name is bad */
    inode->i_count++;
    while (1) {//loop this process till finding topmost i node
        thisname = pathname;
    if (!S_ISDIR(inode->i_mode) || !permission(inode,MAY_EXEC)) {
        iput(inode);
        return NULL;
    }
    for(namelen = 0;(c=get_fs_byte(pathname++))&&(c! = '/');namelen++)
        /* nothing */;
    if (!c)
        return inode;
    if (!(bh = find_entry(&inode,thisname,namelen,&de))) {//de points
                                                          //to dev

        iput(inode);
        return NULL;
    }
    inr = de->inode;//find i node id through directory entry
```

```
        idev = inode->i_dev;//pay attention: this inode is root i node,
                            //which is used to determine device id
            brelse(bh);
            iput(inode);
        if (!(inode = iget(idev,inr)))//store the i node of dev to
                                       //corresponding item in inode_table[32]
                                       //and return the pointer of this item
            return NULL;
        }
}
```

Inode_table is used to manage all the i nodes of opened files and iget would load the i node into the inode_table according to the id of the i node and the id of the device number. Getting the i node of "dev" (directory file) is shown in Figure 4.4.

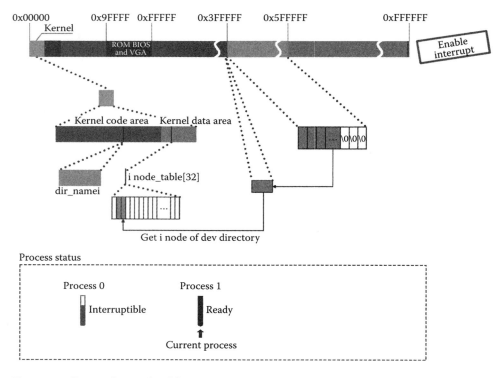

Figure 4.4 Getting the i node of dev.

4.1.1.4 Determine the i node of Dev as the Topmost i node

The execution path of acquiring the topmost i node and target i node is shown in Figure 4.5.

The relationship of directory entry, directory file, and i node has been introduced in Section 3.3.3.

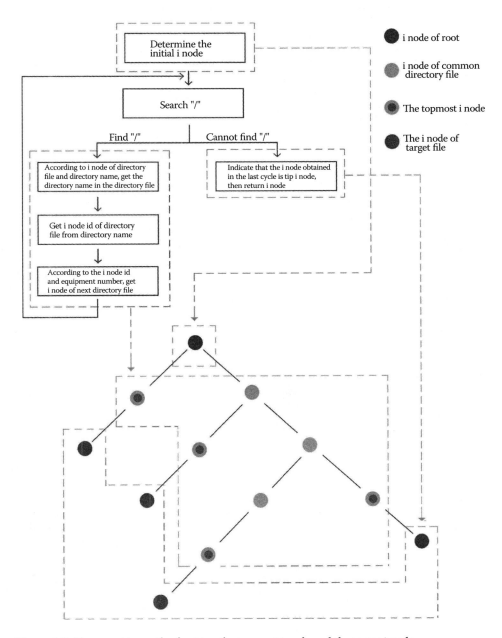

Figure 4.5 The execution path of getting the topmost i node and the target i node.

The process of traversing and parsing the/dev/tty0 continuously is the same as that of parsing dev, although the result is different. The code is as follows:

```
//code path:fs/namei.c:
static struct m_inode * get_dir(const char * pathname)
{
    ......
    if ((c=get_fs_byte(pathname))=='/') {
    inode = current->root;
    pathname++;
    } else if I
        inode = current->pwd;
    else
        return NULL;    /* empty name is bad */
    inode->i_count++;
while (1) {//loop this process till finding topmost i node
        thisname = pathname;//thisname points to first 't' in tty0
        if (!S_ISDIR(inode->i_mode) || !permission(inode,MAY_EXEC)) {
            iput(inode);
            return NULL;
    }
        for(namelen=0;(c=get_fs_byte(pathname++))&&(c!='/');namelen++)
                //continue to search '/' and break loop when c is '\0'
        /* nothing */;
    if (!c)
        return inode;//return the topmost inode
    if (!(bh = find_entry(&inode,thisname,namelen,&de))) {
            iput(inode);
            return NULL;
    }
    inr = de->inode;
    idev = inode->i_dev;
    brelse(bh);
    iput(inode);
    if (!(inode = iget(idev,inr)))
            return NULL;
    }
}
```

C provides "\0" as the end of the character string; thus, the function exits the loop when it meets "\0" because the condition value of c=get_fs_byte (pathname++) is false. This also means that the "/," which is detected at last, is the last character in the string, and the next "tty0" is the file name of the target, which is stored in the directory entry "tty0" of directory file "dev." Through the directory file "dev," the process will find "tty0" finally, and the i node of dev is named as the topmost i node.

After getting the topmost i node, there are two items of information being confirmed, the address of the first character and the name length, which are used to be compared with the directory name in the Ramdisk. The way to get information about the directory name is shown in the code below:

```
//code path:fs/namei.c:
static struct m_inode * dir_namei(const char * pathname,
    int * namelen, const char ** name)
{
char c;
    const char * basename;
    struct m_inode * dir;

    if (!(dir = get_dir(pathname)))        //execution function to
                                           //get i node
    return NULL;
    basename = pathname;
    while (c=get_fs_byte(pathname++))
    //traverse the character string of/dev/tty0 and copy each one
    //to c, until the end of string
        if (c=='/')
                basename=pathname;
    *namelen = pathname-basename-1;//determine name length of tty0
    *name = basename;//get address of first 't' in tty0
    return dir;
}
```

4.1.1.5 Acquire the i node of the tty0 File

In the second stage, the process of acquiring the i node of the target file is the same as that of getting the topmost i node introduced before. First, the kernel loads the directory entry of the target file "tty0" to the buffer by calling find_entry() and gets the i node. It then calls iget() to get the i node of "tty0" in the ramdisk through the i node id and device id, and then return this inode. The code is as follows:

```
//code path:fs/namei.c:
int open_namei(const char * pathname, int flag, int mode,
    struct m_inode ** res_inode)
{
    const char * basename;
    int inr,dev,namelen;
    struct m_inode * dir, *inode;
    struct buffer_head * bh;
    struct dir_entry * de;

    if ((flag & O_TRUNC) && !(flag & O_ACCMODE))
        flag |= O_WRONLY;
    mode &= 0777 & ~current->umask;
    mode |= I_REGULAR;
```

```
    if (!(dir = dir_namei(pathname,&namelen,&basename)))//get topmost
                                                    //i node
        return -ENOENT;
    if (!namelen) {                     /* special case: '/usr/' etc */
        if (!(flag & (O_ACCMODE|O_CREAT|O_TRUNC))) {
            *res_inode=dir;
            return 0;
        }
        iput(dir);
        return -EISDIR;
    }
    bh = find_entry(&dir,basename,namelen,&de);
//load tty0 directory entry to buffer block through topmost i node, de
//points to tty0 directory entry
    if (!bh) {//this if won't be execute cause buffer block is not null
        if (!(flag & O_CREAT)) {
            iput(dir);
            return -ENOENT;
        }
        if (!permission(dir,MAY_WRITE)) {
            iput(dir);
            return -EACCES;
        }
        inode = new_inode(dir->i_dev);
        if (!inode) {
            iput(dir);
            return -ENOSPC;
        }
        inode->i_uid = current->euid;
        inode->i_mode = mode;
        inode->i_dirt = 1;
        bh = add_entry(dir,basename,namelen,&de);
        if (!bh) {
            inode->i_nlinks-- ;
            iput(inode);
            iput(dir);
            return -ENOSPC;
        }
        de->inode = inode->i_num;
        bh->b_dirt = 1;
        brelse(bh);
        iput(dir);
        *res_inode = inode;
        return 0;
    }
    inr = de->inode;//get i node id
    dev = dir->i_dev;//get device id of ramdisk
    brelse(bh);
    iput(dir);
    if (flag & O_EXCL)
        return -EEXIST;
    if (!(inode=iget(dev,inr)))//the i node of tty0 file
        return -EACCES;
```

```
if ((S_ISDIR(inode->i_mode) && (flag & O_ACCMODE)) ||
    !permission(inode,ACC_MODE(flag))) {
    iput(inode);
    return -EPERM;
}
inode->i_atime = CURRENT_TIME;
if (flag & O_TRUNC)
    truncate(inode);
*res_inode = inode;//return this i node to sys_open
return 0;
}
```

Finding out the i node of the tty0 file is shown in Figure 4.6.

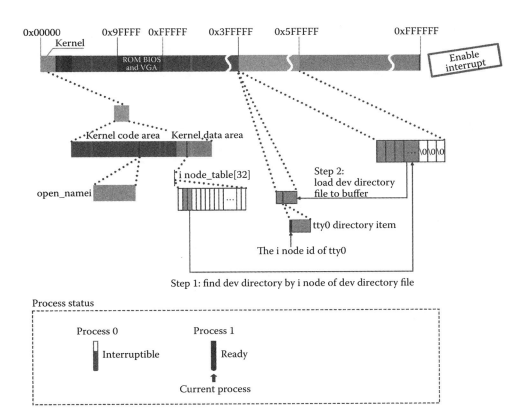

Figure 4.6 Find the i node of tty0.

4.1.1.6 Determine tty0 as the Character Device File

In order to get i_mode, which is the property of the i node of the tty0 file, we will locate the device file and get the id of the device through the i_zone[0] in the i node. The "current->tty" and "tty_table" will be set as well. The code is as follows:

```
//code path:fs/open.c:
int sys_open(const char * filename,int flag,int mode)
{
    ......
    if ((i=open_namei(filename,flag,mode,&inode))<0) {
        current->filp[fd]=NULL;
        f->f_count=0;
        return i;
    }
/* ttys are somewhat special (ttyxx major==4, tty major==5) */
    if (S_ISCHR(inode->i_mode))//examine the i node property of tty0
                              //and confirm it is the device file
        if (MAJOR(inode->i_zone[0])==4) {//device number is 4,
            if (current->leader && current->tty<0) {
                current->tty = MINOR(inode->i_zone[0]);
                //set tty0 number as subset number of this i node
                tty_table[current->tty].pgrp = current->pgrp;
                //set parent process group number of current tty table
                //as the parent process group number of this process
            }
        } else if (MAJOR(inode->i_zone[0])==5)
            if (current->tty<0) {
                iput(inode);
                current->filp[fd]=NULL;
                f->f_count=0;
                return -EPERM;
            }
/* Likewise with block-devices: check for floppy_change */
    if (S_ISBLK(inode->i_mode))
        check_disk_change(inode->i_zone[0]);
    f->f_mode = inode->i_mode;
    f->f_flags = flag;
    f->f_count = 1;
    f->f_inode = inode;
    f->f_pos = 0;
    return (fd);
}
```

Analyzing the properties of the i node and relative settings is shown in Figure 4.7.

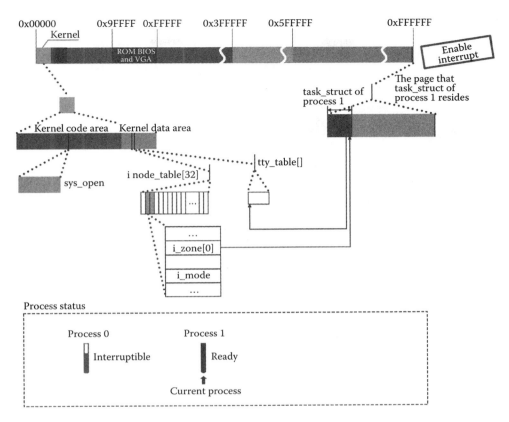

0x00000   0x9FFFF 0xFFFFF   0x3FFFFF   0x5FFFFF   0xFFFFFF

Figure 4.7 Analyzing the tty i node of the current process.

4.1.1.7   Set file_table[0]

At last, sys_open() has to set file_table[0] in file_table[64] correspond to the filp[20] in process 1. In this way, the system establishes the relationship between tty0 (standard input device file) and process 1 by file_table[64]. The specific setup process is shown in the following codes:

```
//code path:fs/open.c:
int sys_open(const char * filename,int flag,int mode)
{
    ......
    if ((i=open_namei(filename,flag,mode,&inode))<0) {
        current->filp[fd]=NULL;
        f->f_count=0;
        return i;
    }
/* ttys are somewhat special (ttyxx major==4, tty major==5) */
    if (S_ISCHR(inode->i_mode))
        if (MAJOR(inode->i_zone[0])==4) {
            if (current->leader && current->tty<0) {
```

```
                              current->tty = MINOR(inode->i_zone[0]);
                              tty_table[current->tty].pgrp = current->pgrp;
                         }
                   } else if (MAJOR(inode->i_zone[0]) = =5)
                         if (current->tty<0) {
                             iput(inode);
                             current->filp[fd] = NULL;
                             f->f_count = 0;
                             return -EPERM;
                         }
/* Likewise with block-devices: check for floppy_change */
      if (S_ISBLK(inode->i_mode))
      check_disk_change(inode->i_zone[0]);
      f->f_mode = inode->i_mode;     //set file attributes based on file i node
                                     //attributes
      f->f_flags = flag;             //set file ID according to parameter flag
      f->f_count = 1;                //the file reference count is incremented
      f->f_inode = inode;            //build relationship between file and
                                     //i-node

      f->f_pos = 0;                  //set file write and read pointer as 0
      return (fd);
}
```

Setting file_table[0] and then return fd is shown in Figure 4.8.

4.1.2 Open the Standard Output and Standard Error Output Device File

In Section 4.1.1, opening the standard input device file using the function open was introduced. We will open the standard output and standard error output device file. The difference here is the method of copying the file handle.

After the function open() returns, process 1 copies the file handle twice according to calling the function dup() based on the condition that the tty0 device file is opened.

The code of the first copy is as follows:

```
//code path:init/main.c:
void init(void)
{
    int pid,i;

    setup((void *) &drive_info);
    (void) open("/dev/tty0",O_RDWR,0);
    (void) dup(0);//copy the handle to build the standard output device
    (void) dup(0);
    printf("%d buffers =%d bytes buffer space\n\r",NR_BUFFERS,
        NR_BUFFERS*BLOCK_SIZE);
    printf("Free mem:%d bytes\n\r",memory_end-main_memory_start);
    if (!(pid=fork())) {//below if is code of process 2
        close(0);
        if (open("/etc/rc",O_RDONLY,0))
```

```
            _exit(1);
        execve("/bin/sh",argv_rc,envp_rc);
        _exit(2);
    }
    if (pid>0)
        while (pid ! = wait(&i))
                /* nothing */;
    ......
}
```

The function dup will eventually be mapped to the system calling function sys_dup()
(this mapping process is broadly consistent with the mapping process from the function
open to the function sys_open) and called the function dupfd() to copy the file handle.
The code is as follows:

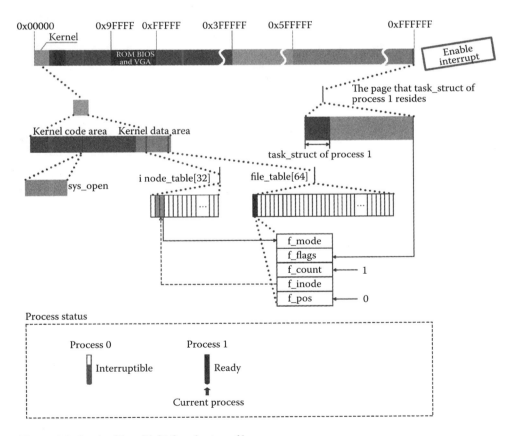

Figure 4.8 Set the file_table[64] and return fd.

```
//code path:fs/fcntl.c:
int sys_dup(unsigned int fildes)//system call function in kernel
                                //corresponding to dup
{
    return dupfd(fildes,0);//copy handle
}
```

After ensuring the copying conditions, we will find free item in the filp[20] of process 1 and then get the second item filp[1]. The system copies the pointer of the tty0 device file stored in filp[0] to filp[1] and increases the reference number of the file f_count in file_table[0] to 2 in order to realize the effect that process 1 opens the standard output device file tty0.

The code is as follows:

```
//code path:fs/fcntl.c:
static int dupfd(unsigned int fd, unsigned int arg)
{
    if (fd >= NR_OPEN || !current->filp[fd])//Detect whether it has the
                                //conditions to copy the file handle
        return -EBADF;
    if (arg >= NR_OPEN)
        return -EINVAL;
    while (arg < NR_OPEN)
        if (current->filp[arg])//find free item in filp[20](it is the
                                //second item) of process 1 to copy
            arg++;
        else
            break;
    if (arg >= NR_OPEN)
        return -EMFILE;
    current->close_on_exec &= ~(1<<arg);
    (current->filp[arg] = current->filp[fd])->f_count++;
        //copy file handle to build standard output device and set
        //f_count as 2
    return arg;
}
```

The situation that opens the standard output device file is shown in Figure 4.9.

When dup returns, process 1 calls it again to copy the file handle for the second time and builds the standard error output device.

The code is as follows:

```
//code path:init/main.c:
void init(void)
{
int pid,i;

    setup((void *) &drive_info);
```

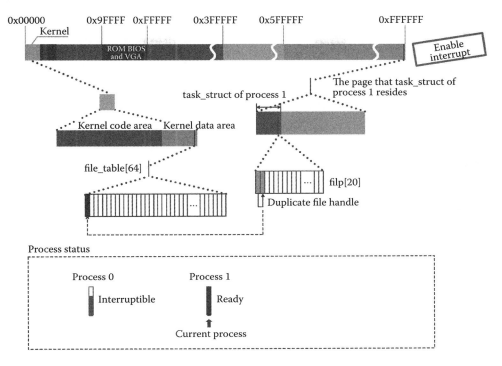

Figure 4.9 Duplicate the filp[fd] and open std output device.

```
(void) open("/dev/tty0",O_RDWR,0);
(void) dup(0);//copy handle to build the standard output device
(void) dup(0);//copy handle again to build the standard error
            //output device
printf("%d buffers =%d bytes buffer space\n\r",NR_BUFFERS,
    NR_BUFFERS*BLOCK_SIZE);
printf("Free mem:%d bytes\n\r",memory_end-main_memory_start);
if (!(pid=fork())) {//below if is code of process 2
    close(0);
    if (open("/etc/rc",O_RDONLY,0))
        _exit(1);
    execve("/bin/sh",argv_rc,envp_rc);
    _exit(2);
}
if (pid>0)
    while (pid !=wait(&i))
        /* nothing */;
    ......
}
```

```c
//code path:fs/fcntl.c:
static int dupfd(unsigned int fd, unsigned int arg)
{
        if (fd >= NR_OPEN || !current->filp[fd])/Detect whether it has
                              //the conditions to copy the file handle
              return -EBADF;
        if (arg >= NR_OPEN)
              return -EINVAL;
        while (arg < NR_OPEN)
              if (current->filp[arg])//find free item in filp[20](it is
                                      //the third item) of process 1
                                      //to copy

                  arg++;
              else
                  break;
        if (arg >= NR_OPEN)
              return -EMFILE;
        current->close_on_exec &= ~(1<<arg);
        (current->filp[arg] = current->filp[fd])->f_count++;
            //copy file handle to build standard output device and set
            //f_count as 3
        return arg;
}
```

```c
//code path:init/main.c:
void init(void)
{
   int pid,i;


        setup((void *) &drive_info);
        (void) open("/dev/tty0",O_RDWR,0);
        (void) dup(0);
        (void) dup(0);
        printf("%d buffers =%d bytes buffer space\n\r",NR_BUFFERS,
             NR_BUFFERS*BLOCK_SIZE);
        printf("Free mem:%d bytes\n\r",memory_end-main_memory_start);
        if (!(pid=fork())) {//process 1 creates process 2
              close(0);
              if (open("/etc/rc",O_RDONLY,0))
                      _exit(1);
              execve("/bin/sh",argv_rc,envp_rc);
              _exit(2);
        }
        if (pid>0)
              while (pid != wait(&i))
                      /* nothing */;
        ......
}
```

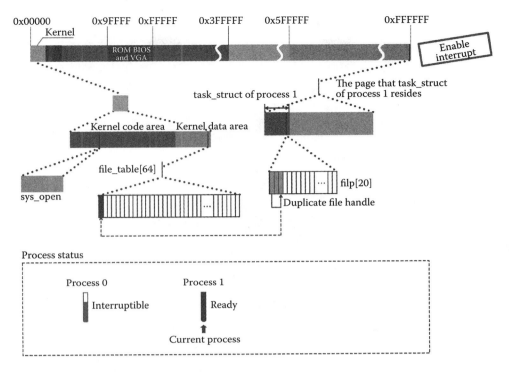

Figure 4.10 Duplicate the filp[fd] and open std output device again.

Let us go back to the function dupfd() again. As the procedure shown before, the kernel finds free item in the filp[20] of process 1. However, this time, it comes to the third item filp[2]. The system copies the pointer of the tty0 device file stored in filp[0] to filp[2] and increases the reference number of the file f_count in file_table[0] to 3 in order to realize the effect that process 1 opens the standard output device file tty0.

The code is as follows:

The situation that opens the standard output device file is shown in Figure 4.10.

At this point, the terminal standard input device file, standard output device file, and standard error output device file have been opened. It means that, in the program, the function printf can be used later (stdio in stdio.h is standard input/output).

4.2 Fork Process 2 and Switch to Process 2 to Execute

Next, process 1 calls the function fork and creates process 2.

The code is as follows:

The process of mapping fork to sys_fork is similar to the procedure introduced in Section 3.1.1, that is, to call the function _find_empty_process to find free task item in task[64] for process 2 and call the function copy_process to copy the process.

The code is as follows:

```
//code path:kernel/system_call.s:
......


.align 2
_sys_execve:
        lea EIP(%esp),%eax
        pushl%eax
        call _do_execve
        addl $4,%esp
        ret
.align 2
_sys_fork:
        call _find_empty_process//find free item in task[64] for
                                //process 2 and set new process pid
        testl%eax,%eax
        js 1f
        push%gs
        pushl%esi
        pushl%edi
        pushl%ebp
        pushl%eax
        call _copy_process//copy process 2
        addl $20,%esp
1:      ret


_hd_interrupt:
        pushl%eax
        pushl%ecx
        pushl%edx
        push%ds
        push%es
        push%fs
        movl $0x10,%eax
        mov%ax,%ds
        mov%ax,%es
        movl $0x17,%eax
        mov%ax,%fs
        movb $0x20,%al
        outb%al,$0xA0            # EOI to interrupt controller #1
        jmp 1f                   # give port chance to breathe
......
```

An instance of finding a new free item for process 2 in task[64] is shown in Figure 4.11.

In copy_process, the kernel applies a free page for task_struct, the kernel stack of process 2, and copies task_struct. The task_struct of process 2 is specifically set, including the settings of every register, management of memory page, shared files, GDT table item, and so on. The process is similar to the process introduced in Section 3.1 where process 0 creates process 1.

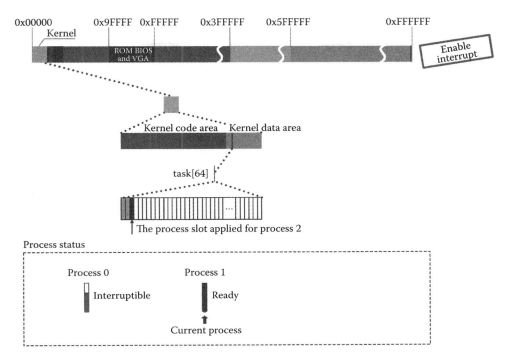

Figure 4.11 Process 1 begins to fork process 2.

The code is as follows:

```
//code path:kernel/system_call.s:
int copy_process(int nr,long ebp,long edi,long esi,long gs,long none,
                 long ebx,long ecx,long edx,
                 long fs,long es,long ds,
                 long eip,long cs,long eflags,long esp,long ss)

{
    struct task_struct *p;
    int i;
    struct file *f;

    p = (struct task_struct *) get_free_page();//apply page for
                                               //process 2
    if (!p)
            return -EAGAIN;
    task[nr] = p;//to ensure address pointer of task_struct of
                 //process 2 is loaded into specified location in
                 //task
```

```c
*p = *current;    /* NOTE! this doesn't copy the supervisor stack
*/                                      //copy task_struct
p->state = TASK_UNINTERRUPTIBLE;//set the process 2 as
                                    //uninterruptible state
p->pid = last_pid; //personalize setting of the process 2
p->father = current->pid;
p->counter = p->priority;
p->signal = 0;
p->alarm = 0;
p->leader = 0;                  /* process leadership doesn't inherit */
p->utime = p->stime = 0;
p->cutime = p->cstime = 0;
p->start_time = jiffies;
p->tss.back_link = 0;
p->tss.esp0 = PAGE_SIZE + (long) p;
p->tss.ss0 = 0x10;
p->tss.eip = eip;
p->tss.eflags = eflags;
p->tss.eax = 0;
p->tss.ecx = ecx;
p->tss.edx = edx;
p->tss.ebx = ebx;
p->tss.esp = esp;
p->tss.ebp = ebp;
p->tss.esi = esi;
p->tss.edi = edi;
p->tss.es = es & 0xffff;
p->tss.cs = cs & 0xffff;
p->tss.ss = ss & 0xffff;
p->tss.ds = ds & 0xffff;
p->tss.fs = fs & 0xffff;
p->tss.gs = gs & 0xffff;
p->tss.ldt = _LDT(nr);
p->tss.trace_bitmap = 0x80000000;
if (last_task_used_math == current)
        __asm__("clts ; fnsave%0"::"m" (p->tss.i387));
if (copy_mem(nr,p)) {//set up paging management of process 2
        task[nr] = NULL;
        free_page((long) p);
        return -EAGAIN;
}
for (i = 0; i<NR_OPEN;i++)//The following is that the process
                        //2 shares files of process 1
        if (f=p->filp[i])
        f->f_count++;
if (current->pwd)
        current->pwd->i_count++;
if (current->root)
        current->root->i_count++;
if (current->executable)
        current->executable->i_count++;
set_tss_desc(gdt+(nr<<1)+FIRST_TSS_ENTRY,&(p->tss));//set entry of
                                        //process 2 in GDT table
```

```
        set_ldt_desc(gdt+(nr<<1)+FIRST_LDT_ENTRY,&(p->ldt));
        p->state = TASK_RUNNING;        /* do this last, just in case */
                                        //set process in ready state
        return last_pid;
}
```

The situation involving copy process and some specific settings is shown in Figure 4.12.

The situation involving copy page tables and setting page directory entry for process 2 is shown in Figure 4.13.

Figure 4.14 shows the situation concerning the adjusting process that process 2 shares files with process 1.

After creating process 2, fork() returns and the return value is 2. Thus, the value of !(pid = fork()) is false (introduced in Section 3.1.7) and the calling wait(). Its function is as follows: if process 1 has a child process in the state of waiting for exit, prepare to exit this process; if process 1 has a child process not in the state of waiting for exit, switch the process; if the process has no child process, the function returns.

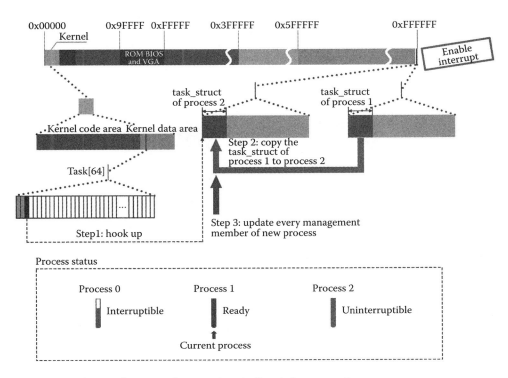

Figure 4.12 Copy task_struct of process 1 and adjust it for process 2.

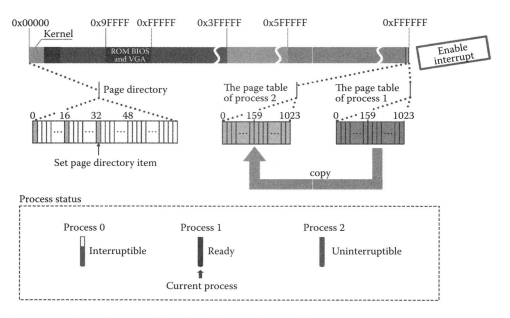

Figure 4.13 Copy the page table and set the page directory for process 2.

The code is as follows:

```
//code path:init/main.c:
void init(void)
{
    int pid,i;


    setup((void *) &drive_info);
    (void) open("/dev/tty0",O_RDWR,0);
    (void) dup(0);
    (void) dup(0);
    printf("%d buffers =%d bytes buffer space\n\r",NR_BUFFERS,
        NR_BUFFERS*BLOCK_SIZE);
    printf("Free mem:%d bytes\n\r",memory_end-main_memory_start);
    if (!(pid = fork())) {            //the following is code of process 2
        close(0);
        if (open("/etc/rc",O_RDONLY,0))
            _exit(1);
        execve("/bin/sh",argv_rc,envp_rc);
        _exit(2);
    }
    if (pid>0)
        while (pid !=wait(&i))         //process 1 waits for exit of child process,
                                       //switch to process 2 finally.
            /* nothing */;
    ......
}
```

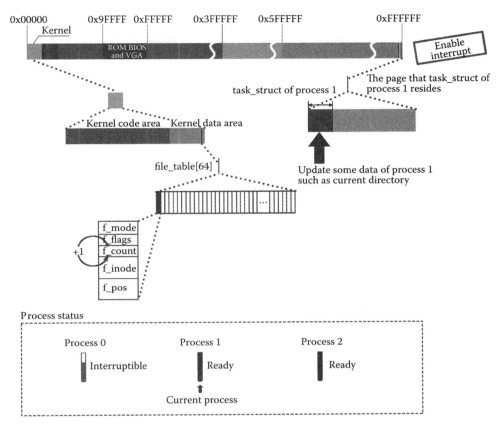

Figure 4.14 Add the count of sharing file in file_table[64].

The function waiting is finally mapped to the system calling function sys_waitpid(). The mapping system is similar to that of the mapping fork() to sys_fork(). The function sys_waitpid() first checks all the processes to find out which process is a child process of process 1. Because process 1 creates a child process only, process 2 is chosen.

The code is as follows:

```
//code path:kernel/exit.c:
int sys_waitpid(pid_t pid,unsigned long * stat_addr, int options)   //wait()
                         //corresponds to system call function sys_waitpid()
{
        int flag, code;
        struct task_struct ** p;


        verify_area(stat_addr,4);
repeat:
        flag = 0;
        for(p = &LAST_TASK ; p > &FIRST_TASK ; --p) {
           if (!*p || *p == current)
                 continue;
```

```
            if ((*p)->father != current->pid)
                continue;
        //select current process, namely the child process of process 1, now,
        //it is process 2
        if (pid>0) {
            if ((*p)->pid != pid)
                continue;
        } else if (!pid) {
            if ((*p)->pgrp != current->pgrp)
                continue;
        } else if (pid != -1) {
            if ((*p)->pgrp != -pid)
                continue;
        }
        switch ((*p)->state) {//judge state of process 2
            case TASK_STOPPED://if process 2 is in stopping state, handle here
                if (!(options & WUNTRACED))
                    continue;
                put_fs_long(0x7f,stat_addr);
                return (*p)->pid;
            case TASK_ZOMBIE://if process is in zombie state, handle here
                current->cutime += (*p)->utime;
                current->cstime += (*p)->stime;
                flag = (*p)->pid;
                code = (*p)->exit_code;
                release(*p);
                put_fs_long(code,stat_addr);
                return flag;
            default://if process 2 is in ready state,handle here and set
                    //flag as 1 to jump out of hoop
                flag=1;
                continue;
        }
    }
    ......
}
```

An instance of searching for a child process of process 1 is shown in Figure 4.15.

Next, the system analyzes process 2 to make sure that process 2 is not prepare to exit, thus setting flag bit as 1. This flag will lead to the process switching.

The code is as follows:

```
//code path:kernel/exit.c:
int sys_waitpid(pid_t pid,unsigned long * stat_addr, int options)
//wait() corresponds to system call function sys_waitpid()
{
        int flag, code;
        struct task_struct ** p;


        verify_area(stat_addr,4);
repeat:
        flag=0;
        for(p = &LAST_TASK ; p > &FIRST_TASK ; --p) {
                if (!*p || *p == current)
```

```
                    continue;
            if ((*p)->father != current->pid)
                    continue;
//select current process, namely, the child process of process 1,
//now, it is process 2
if (pid>0) {
    if ((*p)->pid != pid)
        continue;
} else if (!pid) {
    if ((*p)->pgrp != current->pgrp)
        continue;
} else if (pid != -1) {
    if ((*p)->pgrp != -pid)
        continue;
}
switch ((*p)->state) {//judge state of process 2
    case TASK_STOPPED://if process 2 is in stopping state,
                        //handle here
        if (!(options & WUNTRACED))
            continue;
        put_fs_long(0x7f,stat_addr);
        return (*p)->pid;
    case TASK_ZOMBIE://if process 2 is in zombie state,
                        //handle here
        current->cutime += (*p)->utime;
        current->cstime += (*p)->stime;
        flag = (*p)->pid;
        code = (*p)->exit_code;
        release(*p);
        put_fs_long(code,stat_addr);
        return flag;
    default://if process 2 is in ready state,handle here and
            //set flag as 1 to jump out of hoop
        flag = 1;
        continue;
    }
}
......
}
```

According to the status of process 2, we set the flag, as shown in Figure 4.16.

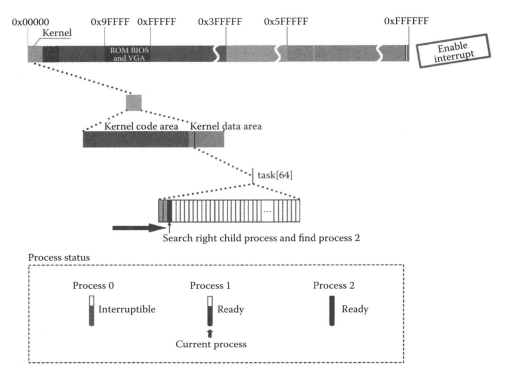

Figure 4.15 Find the child process of process 1.

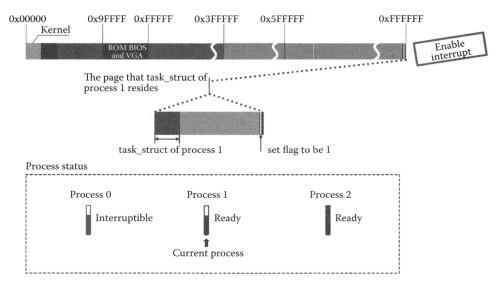

Figure 4.16 Adjust the status of process 2.

Execute if (flag), first, the kernel sets the status of process 1 as interruptible, and then call the schedule function to switch to process 2 because only process 2 is ready, the process of schedule has been introduced in Section 3.2. The code is as follows:

```
//The code path:kernel/exit.c:
int sys_waitpid(pid_t pid,unsigned long * stat_addr, int options) {
    ......
        switch ((*p)->state) {
            case TASK_STOPPED:
                if (!(options & WUNTRACED))
                    continue;
                put_fs_long(0x7f,stat_addr);
                return (*p)->pid;
            case TASK_ZOMBIE:
                current->cutime += (*p)->utime;
                current->cstime += (*p)->stime;
                flag = (*p)->pid;
                code = (*p)->exit_code;
                release(*p);
                put_fs_long(code,stat_addr);
                return flag;
            default:
                flag = 1;
                continue;
        }
    }
    if (flag) {
        if (options & WNOHANG)
            return 0;
        current->state=TASK_INTERRUPTIBLE;//set the state of process 1 as
//interruptible, because there is no child process of process 1 prepare to exit.
        schedule();//switch to process 2
        if (!(current->signal &= ~(1<<(SIGCHLD-1))))
            goto repeat;
        else
            return -EINTR;
    }
    return -ECHILD;
}
```

The procedure on how to switch to process 2 is shown in Figure 4.17.

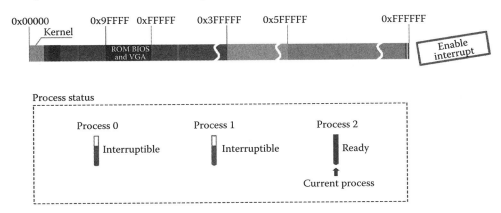

Figure 4.17 Switch to process 2.

∎ 4.3 Load the Shell Program

4.3.1 Close the Standard Input File and Open the rc File

After switching to process 2 and because f (!(pid = fork())) is true, the system calls the close() function to close the standard input file and replaces it by rc file. The code is as follows:

```
//The code path:init/main.c:
void init(void)
{
        int pid,i;


        setup((void *) &drive_info);
        (void) open("/dev/tty0",O_RDWR,0);
        (void) dup(0);
        (void) dup(0);
        printf("%d buffers =%d bytes buffer space\n\r",NR_BUFFERS,
               NR_BUFFERS*BLOCK_SIZE);
        printf("Free mem:%d bytes\n\r",memory_end-main_memory_start);
        if (!(pid = fork())) {
                close(0);//close standard input device file
                if (open("/etc/rc",O_RDONLY,0))//replace it by rc file
                        _exit(1);
                execve("/bin/sh",argv_rc,envp_rc);//load shell program
                _exit(2);
        }
        if (pid>0)
                while (pid != wait(&i))
                        /* nothing */;
        ......
}
```

The close function will be mapped to sys_close function. Because process 2 has received the management information of process 1, the content of the filp file of process 2 is the same as that of process 1; the first item of the filp file should be emptied and decrease the reference number of the f_count in the file_table. Then, it calls the open function, which will select the first item of the filp file to establish the relationship of process 2 and the i node of the rc file, to make "rc" replace "tty0."

The code of the close function is as follows:

```
//The code path:fs/open.c:
int sys_close(unsigned int fd)//corresponding system call function of
                               //close()
{
        struct file * filp;

        if (fd > = NR_OPEN)
                return -EINVAL;
        current->close_on_exec &= ~(1<<fd);
```

```
        if (!(filp = current->filp[fd]))//get the pointer of standard
                                        //input device file of process 2
                return -EINVAL;
        current->filp[fd] = NULL;//release the relationship between
                                //this device file and process 2
        if (filp->f_count == 0)
                panic("Close: file count is 0");
        if (filp->f_count)//decrease the reference count of this
                        //device file
                return (0);
        iput(filp->f_inode);
        return (0);
}
```

The view of closing tty0 file is shown in Figure 4.18.

The procedure of opening rc file is shown in Figure 4.19.

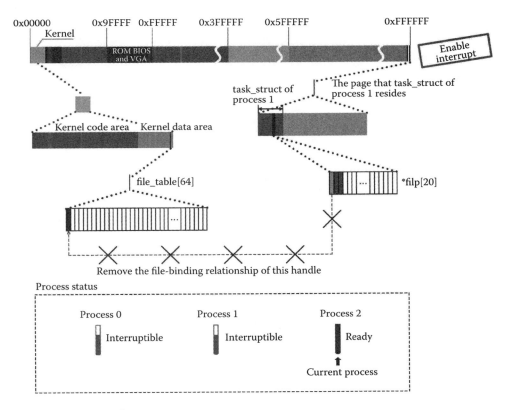

Figure 4.18 Prepare for open/etc/rc.

After opening the rc file, process 2 will call execve to load the shell program. The code is as follows:

```
//The code path:init/main.c:
void init(void)
{
        int pid,i;

        setup((void *) &drive_info);
        (void) open("/dev/tty0",O_RDWR,0);
        (void) dup(0);
        (void) dup(0);
        printf("%d buffers =%d bytes buffer space\n\r",NR_BUFFERS,
                NR_BUFFERS*BLOCK_SIZE);
        printf("Free mem:%d bytes\n\r",memory_end-main_memory_start);
        if (!(pid = fork())) {
                close(0);//close standard input device file
                if (open("/etc/rc",O_RDONLY,0))//replace it by rc file
                        _exit(1);
                execve("/bin/sh",argv_rc,envp_rc);//load shell program,
//"/bin/sh" is the path of shell file, argv_rc and envp_rc is the parameter and
//environment variables respectively

                _exit(2);
        }
        if (pid>0)
                while (pid ! = wait(&i))
                        /* nothing */;
}
```

It is worth mentioning that the arguments and environment variables have been prepared in advance in the kernel code. The code is as follows:

```
//The code path:init/main.c:
...
static char * argv_rc[] = {"/bin/sh", NULL};prepare parameters for
shell process
static char * envp_rc[] = {"HOME =/", NULL, NULL};prepare environment
variables for shell process
...
```

The code of the execve function is as follows:

```
//The code path:kernel/system_call.s:
......
.align 2
_sys_execve:/         //corresponding system call function of execve()
        lea EIP(%esp),%eax
        pushl%eax    //push the address of "eip value in the stack"
        call _do_execve       //do_execve is the main function to
                              //support loading shell program
        addl $4,%esp
        ret
......
```

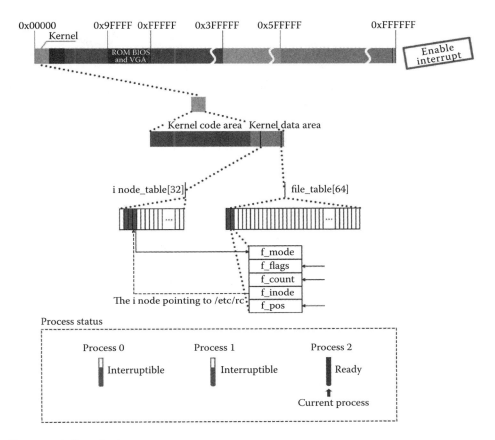

Figure 4.19 Open/etc/rc.

4.3.2 Detect the Shell File

4.3.2.1 Detect the Attribute of the i node

The do_execve() function calls the namei() function to get the i node of the shell first, the procedure of get inode is similar with the process of get inode in Section 4.1.1, and the system checks the attribute of the i node to determine whether the shell program can be loaded. The code is as follows:

```
int do_execve(unsigned long * eip,long tmp,char * filename,
        char ** argv, char ** envp)
{
        struct m_inode * inode;
        struct buffer_head * bh;
        struct exec ex;
        unsigned long page[MAX_ARG_PAGES];
        int i,argc,envc;
        int e_uid, e_gid;
        int retval;
        int sh_bang = 0;
        unsigned long p=PAGE_SIZE*MAX_ARG_PAGES-4;
```

```
        if ((0xffff & eip[1]) !=0x000f //checks whether the kernel calls
//do_execve() by checking privilege level
                panic("execve called from supervisor mode");//if yes, the
//kernel will crash, obviously, it is not true in this case.
        for (i=0 ; i<MAX_ARG_PAGES ; i++)
                page[i]=0; //clear the page pointer management table, which
//used to parameter and environmental variables
if (!(inode = namei(filename)))//get the inode of shell program file
return -ENOENT;
        argc = count(argv);//count the parameters
        envc = count(envp);//count the environment variables


restart_interp:
        if (!S_ISREG(inode->i_mode)) {       /* must be regular file */
                retval = -EACCES;
                goto exec_error2;
        }
        i = inode->i_mode;//check process 2 through checking uid and gid in inode
        e_uid = (i & S_ISUID) ? inode->i_uid : current->euid;//whether has the
                                          //authority to execute shell program
        e_gid = (i & S_ISGID) ? inode->i_gid : current->egid;
        if (current->euid == inode->i_uid)
                i >>= 6;                      //adjust the permission bits in
                                              //inode by analyzing the owner
                                              //relationship between file and
                                              //current process
        else if (current->egid == inode->i_gid)
                i >>= 3;
        if (!(i & 1) &&                  //exit the loading work, if user has no
                                          //permission to execute shell program
           !((inode->i_mode & 0111) && suser())) {
           retval = -ENOEXEC;
           goto exec_error2;
        }
}
......
```

The procedure on how to get the i node is shown in Figure 4.20.

The procedure on how to detect the i node is shown in Figure 4.21.

By detecting the attribute of the i node of the shell file, we know that process 2 can execute the program in this context.

4.3.2.2 Test File Header's Attributes

Through the information of the device id and block id provided by the i node, the system will load the file header to the buffer and get its information. The code is as follows:

```
int do_execve(unsigned long * eip,long tmp,char * filename,
        char ** argv, char ** envp)/*system_call.s*/
{
        ......
        if (!(i & 1) &&//If user don't have permission to perform the
                        //program,the shell will exit the loading work
        !((inode->i_mode & 0111) && suser())) {
        retval = -ENOEXEC;
        goto exec_error2;
    }
        if (!(bh = bread(inode->i_dev,inode->i_zone[0]))) {
```

```
//Through the i_nodes to make sure the device id and block
//id(i_zone[0]) of shell file and get the file header
    retval = -EACCES;
        goto exec_error2;
    }
    ex = *((struct exec *) bh->b_data);//Get the information of file header //
                                        from buffer block
    if ((bh->b_data[0] == '#') && (bh->b_data[1] == '!') && (!sh_bang)) {
    .....
    brelse(bh);
    if (N_MAGIC(ex) != ZMAGIC || ex.a_trsize || ex.a_drsize ||
            ex.a_text+ex.a_data+ex.a_bss>0x3000000 ||
            inode->i_size < ex.a_text+ex.a_data+ex.a_syms+N_TXTOFF(ex)) {
            retval = -ENOEXEC;
            goto exec_error2;
    }
    if (N_TXTOFF(ex) != BLOCK_SIZE) {
            printk("%s: N_TXTOFF != BLOCK_SIZE. See a.out.h.", filename);
            retval = -ENOEXEC;
            goto exec_error2;
    }
    if (!sh_bang) {
            p = copy_strings(envc,envp,page,p,0);
            p = copy_strings(argc,argv,page,p,0);
            if (!p) {
                    retval = -ENOMEM;
                    goto exec_error2;
            }
    }
}
.....
```

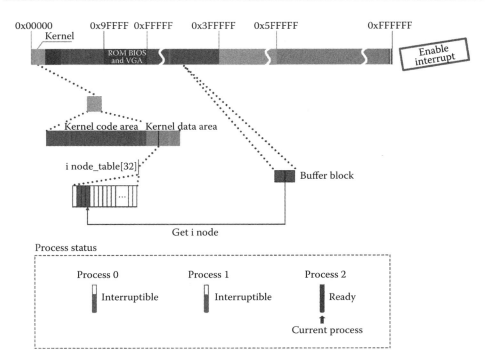

Figure 4.20 Get the i node of shell.

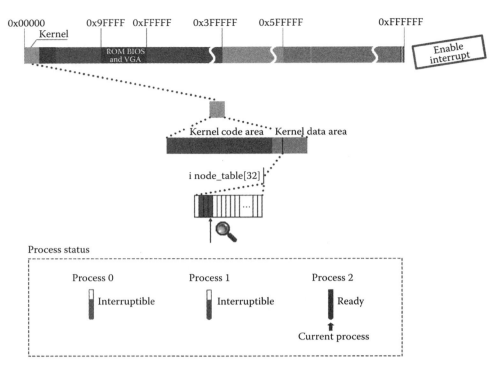

Figure 4.21 Detect the i node of shell.

The procedure of obtaining the file header is shown in Figures 4.22 and 4.23.

The system will check the information of the file header to confirm the content of the shell file and judge whether it is fit for the rule of loading. The code is as follows:

```
int do_execve(unsigned long * eip,long tmp,char * filename,
      char ** argv, char ** envp)/*system_call.s*/
{
      ......
      if (!(i & 1) &&//If user don't have permission to perform the
                    //program,the shell will exit the loading work
      !((inode->i_mode & 0111) && suser())) {
      retval = -ENOEXEC;
      goto exec_error2;
      }
      if (!(bh = bread(inode->i_dev,inode->i_zone[0]))) {
      //Through the i_nodes to make sure the device id and block
      //id(i_zone[0]) of shell file and get the file header
         retval = -EACCES;
         goto exec_error2;
      }
      ex = *((struct exec *) bh->b_data);//Get the information of file header
                                       //from buffer block
      if ((bh->b_data[0] == '#') && (bh->b_data[1] = = '!') && (!sh_bang)) {
      //Test file header, learned that shell file is not script file,so the
      //contents of if don't execute
      ......
      brelse(bh);
```

```
           if (N_MAGIC(ex) ! = ZMAGIC || ex.a_trsize || ex.a_drsize ||
               ex.a_text+ex.a_data+ex.a_bss>0x3000000 ||
               inode->i_size < ex.a_text+ex.a_data+ex.a_syms+N_TXTOFF(ex)) {
           //Test the information of file header to make sure the content of shell
           //file and judge it whether fit for the rule of loading
               retval = -ENOEXEC;
               goto exec_error2;
           }
           if (N_TXTOFF(ex) ! = BLOCK_SIZE) {
           //If the file header size is not equal to 1024, the program might not
           //be executed
               printk("%s: N_TXTOFF ! = BLOCK_SIZE. See a.out.h.", filename);
               retval = -ENOEXEC;
               goto exec_error2;
           }
     }
     if (!sh_bang) {
               p = copy_strings(envc,envp,page,p,0);
               p = copy_strings(argc,argv,page,p,0);
               if (!p) {
                     retval = -ENOMEM;
                     goto exec_error2;
               }
           }
     }
     ......
```

Figure 4.23 shows an incidence of testing the file header.

After checking the header attributes of the shell file, we find that the program in the shell file is ready to run.

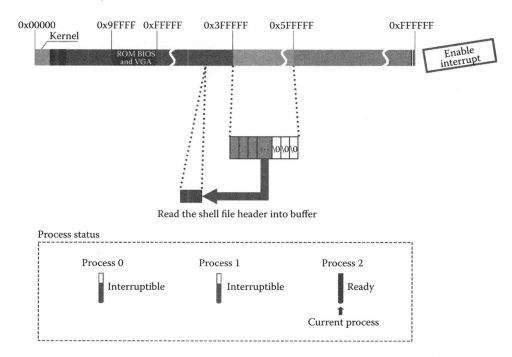

Read the shell file header into buffer

Figure 4.22 Read the shell file header into the buffer.

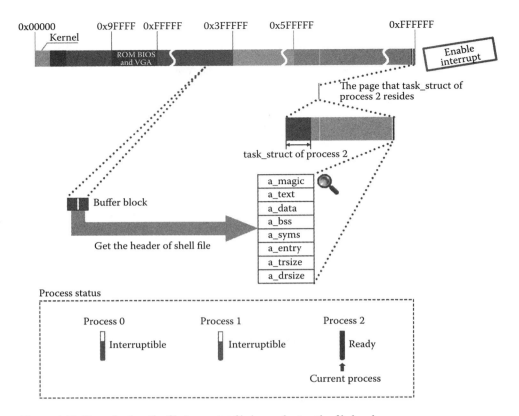

Figure 4.23 Test whether the file is a script file by analyzing the file header.

4.3.3 Prepare to Execute the Shell Program

4.3.3.1 Load Parameters and Environment Variables

The system sets the management point table page of parameters and environment variables, counts the numbers of parameters and environment variables, and copies and maps them to the stack of process 2 eventually.

The code is as follows:

```
int do_execve(unsigned long * eip,long tmp,char * filename,
    char ** argv, char ** envp)/*system_call.s*/
{
        struct m_inode * inode;
        struct buffer_head * bh;
        struct exec ex;
        unsigned long page[MAX_ARG_PAGES];
        int i,argc,envc;
        int e_uid, e_gid;
        int retval;
        int sh_bang = 0;
        unsigned long p=PAGE_SIZE*MAX_ARG_PAGES-4;//Set the parameters and
//environment variables in the process of initial migration space pointer.
        ......
```

```
for (i=0 ; i<MAX_ARG_PAGES ; i++) /* clear page-table */
     page[i]=0;//Set the management point table page of parameters and
              //environment variables to 0
......
argc = count(argv);//statistical the numbers of parameters
envc = count(envp);//statistical the numbers of environment variables
......
if (!sh_bang) {
       p = copy_strings(envc,envp,page,p,0);//Copy environment
                                            //variables to process space
       p = copy_strings(argc,argv,page,p,0);//Copy parameters to
                                            //process space
       if (!p) {
           retval = -ENOMEM;
           goto exec_error2;
       }
}
......
p = (unsigned long) create_tables((char *)p,argc,envc);
//Create the management point table of parameters and environment
//variables in new stack space of process
......
}
```

Examples of loading parameters and environment are shown in Figures 4.25 through 4.28.

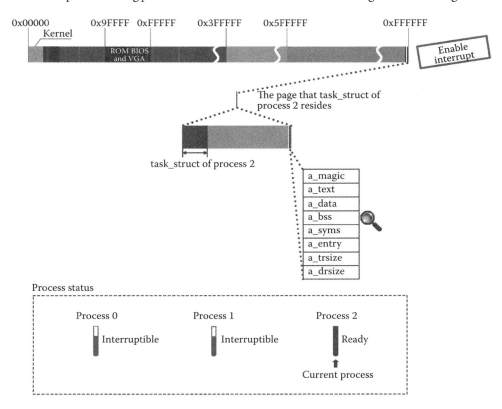

Figure 4.24 Continue to analyze the file header.

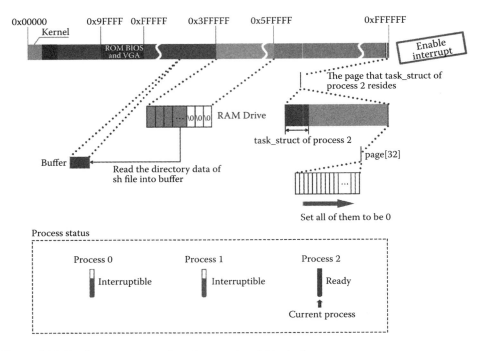

Figure 4.25 Set the parameter and environment variables to 0.

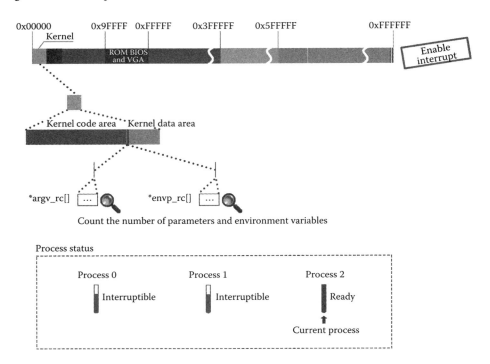

Figure 4.26 Count the number of parameters and environment variables.

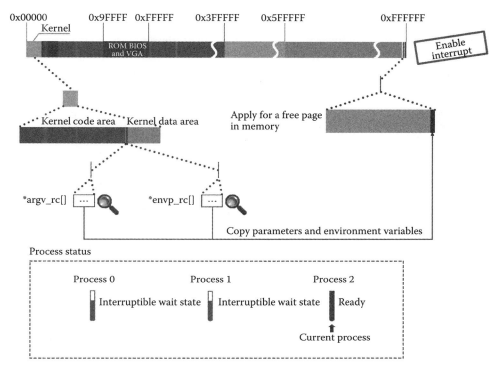

Figure 4.27 Copy the parameters and environment variables.

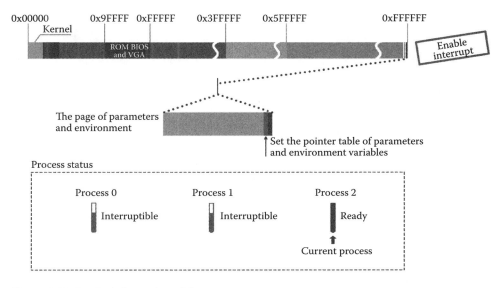

Figure 4.28 Set the information of the segment.

4.3.3.2 Adjust the Management Structure of Process 2

Process 2 has its corresponding shell program; thus, it will adjust its task_struct. For example, it will remove relations with its shared files and memory page with parent process, measure ldt, set code segment, date segment, and stack segment according to the shell program.

The code is as follows:

```
//code path:fs/exec.c:
int do_execve(unsigned long * eip,long tmp,char * filename,
        char ** argv, char ** envp)
{
......
    ...if (!sh_bang) {
        p = copy_strings(envc,envp,page,p,0);
        p = copy_strings(argc,argv,page,p,0);
        if (!p) {
            retval = -ENOMEM;
            goto exec_error2;
        }
    }
/* OK, This is the point of no return */
    if (current->executable)//Test the process whether has its corresponding
                            //executable program
    iput(current->executable);
    current->executable = inode;//Set executable program use the i nodes of
                            //shell program file
    for (i=0 ; i<32 ; i++)
        current->sigaction[i].sa_handler = NULL;//Clear the signal management
                                    //structure of process 2 to NULL
    for (i=0 ; i<NR_OPEN ; i++)
        if ((current->close_on_exec>>i)&1)
                    sys_close(i);//close all files which is labeled by
                                //close_on_exec
        current->close_on_exec = 0;//Clear the close_on_exec to 0
    free_page_tables(get_base(current->ldt[1]),get_limit(0x0f));
    free_page_tables(get_base(current->ldt[2]),get_limit(0x17));
    //Remove the page relation between process 1 and process 2
    if (last_task_used_math == current)
        last_task_used_math = NULL;
    current->used_math = 0;//Clear the sign of math coprocessor in process 2 to 0
    p += change_ldt(ex.a_text,page)-MAX_ARG_PAGES*PAGE_SIZE;//Reset the LDT (local
                                            //descriptor table) in
                                            //process 2
    p = (unsigned long) create_tables((char *)p,argc,envc);
    current->brk = ex.a_bss +
        (current->end_data = ex.a_data +
        (current->end_code = ex.a_text));
    current->start_stack = p & 0xfffff000;
    current->euid = e_uid;
    current->egid = e_gid;
    i = ex.a_text+ex.a_data;
    while (i&0xfff)
        put_fs_byte(0,(char *) (i++));
//Set end_code, end_data, brk, start_stack, ID euid and ID egid. Finally, clear
//a page data of BSS segment in main memory to 0
    eip[0] = ex.a_entry;            /* eip, magic happens :-) */
    eip[3] = p;                 /* stack pointer */
    return 0;
......
}
```

The procedure of adjusting the task_struct of process 2 is shown in Figures 4.29 through 4.33.

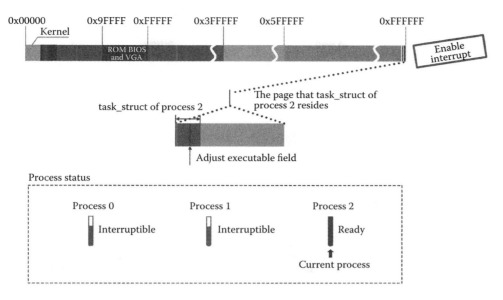

Figure 4.29 Adust the task_struct of Process 2.

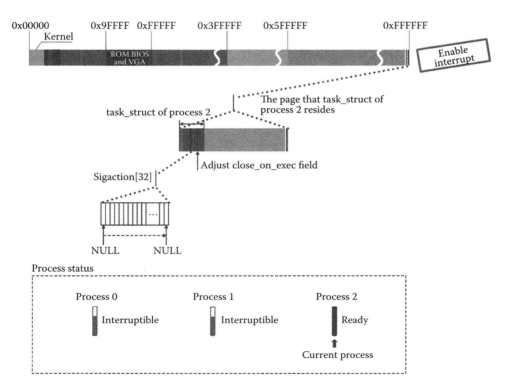

Figure 4.30 Clear the sigaction[32] and filp according to close_on_exec.

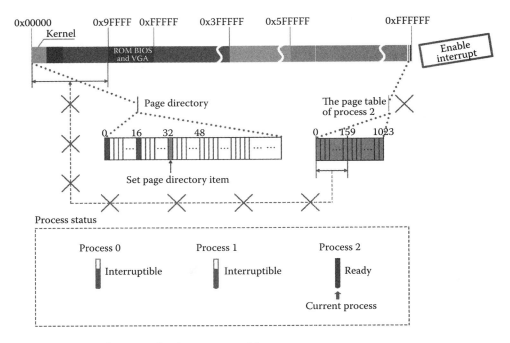

Figure 4.31 Free the pages of code segment and data segment.

4.3.3.3 Adjust EIP and ESP to Execute Shell

The system will set the value in the stack which was pushed by the sys_execve soft interrupt, and set the EIP with the entry address value of the shell program, and set the ESP with the new top stack address value of process 2. The code is as follows:

```
//code path:fs/exec.c:
int do_execve(unsigned long * eip,long tmp,char * filename,
    char ** argv, char ** envp)
{
    ......
eip[0] = ex.a_entry;//Set the entry EIP of process 2
eip[3] = p;          //Set the top stack pointer ESP of process 2
return 0;
...
}
```

After executing the do_execve() function, sys_execve() will return and continue to execute the shell program, the view of adjusting EIP and ESP was shown in Figure 4.34.

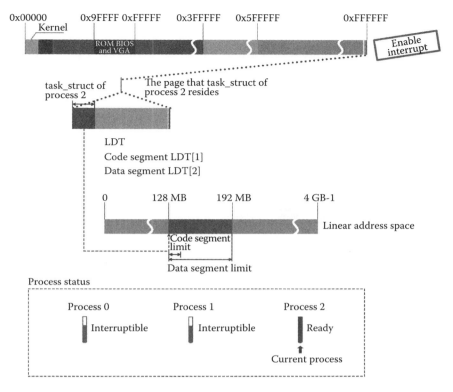

Figure 4.32 Adjust the base of CS and DS.

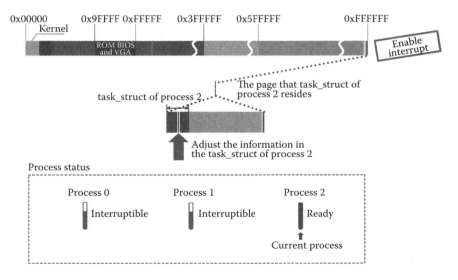

Figure 4.33 Adjust the task_struct of process 2 according to the parameters and environment variables.

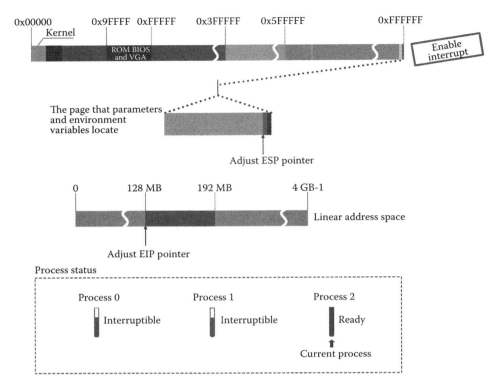

Figure 4.34 Adjust EIP and ESP.

4.3.4 Execute the Shell Program

4.3.4.1 Execute the First Page Program Loading by the Shell

The shell program starts to execute, while its linear address space corresponding program contents are not loading. Thus, do not exit the corresponding page. Then, produce a "page fault" interrupt. The interrupt will distribute the page by calling the "page fault" handler program and loading a page of the shell program.

The code is as follows:

```
//code path:mm/page.s:
_page_fault://page fault handler program entrance
        xchgl%eax,(%esp)
        pushl%ecx
        pushl%edx
        push%ds
        push%es
        push%fs
        movl $0x10,%edx
        mov%dx,%ds
        mov%dx,%es
        mov%dx,%fs
        movl%cr2,%edx
```

```
                pushl %edx
                pushl %eax
                testl $1, %eax
                jne 1f
                call _do_no_page…//Call the do_no_page handler program
```

Figure 4.35 shows how to produce a page fault.

The do_no_page() function starts to execute to identify the reason for the missing page; if it is the need to load program, it will try to share shell with other processes (obviously, there is no process loads shell, thus, cannot share with other process, then) apply for a new page, and read the 4 KB content of the shell program from the ramdisk by calling the bread_page() function and load the memory page. The code is as follows:

```
//code path:mm/memory.c:
void do_no_page(unsigned long error_code,unsigned long address)
{
        …int nr[4];
        unsigned long tmp;
        unsigned long page;
        int block,i;
        address &= 0xfffff000;
        tmp = address - current->start_code;
        if (!current->executable || tmp > = current->end_data) {//If it is not
//loading program, it must be other reason result in page fault
get_empty_page(address); //If there is no space for push in the stack, apply the
//page and then return directly
                return;
        }//Obviously, this is not the case now, really need to load the program
        if (share_page(tmp)) //Try to share the program with other process,but
                                //it's impossible
                return;
        if (!(page = get_free_page()))//Apply a new page for shell program
                oom();
/* remember that 1 block is used for header */
        block = 1 + tmp/BLOCK_SIZE;
        for (i=0 ; i<4 ; block++,i++)
                nr[i] = bmap(current->executable,block);
        bread_page(page,current->executable->i_dev,nr);//Read 4 logical block
                                                //content of shell
                                                //program into memory page
        //After adding a page memory, the part of this page memory may outstrip
        //the end_data position of process
        //The following is handling the beyond part of physical page
        i = tmp + 4096 - current->end_data;
        tmp = page + 4096;
        while (i-- > 0) {
                tmp-- ;
                *(char *)tmp = 0;
        }
        if (put_page(page,address))
                return;
        free_page(page);
        oom();
}
```

Figure 4.36 shows an application of the free page.

Figure 4.37 shows an instance of loading the shell program.

Figure 4.38 shows how the loading content is tested.

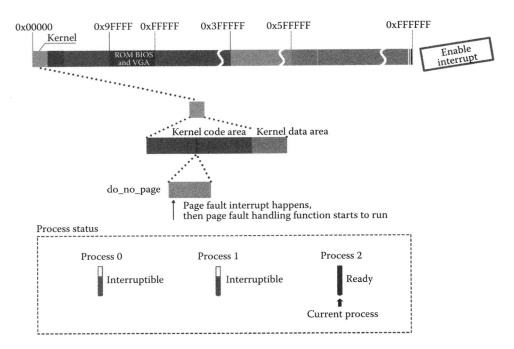

Figure 4.35 Page fault interrupt happens.

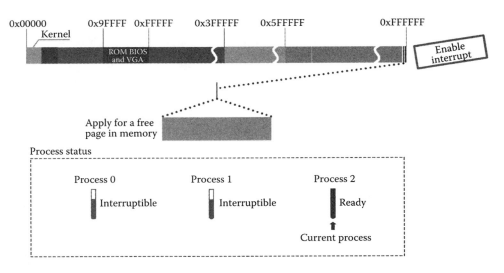

Figure 4.36 Get the free page.

4. Creation and Execution of Process 2

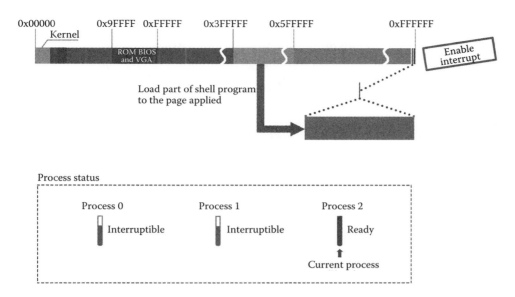

Figure 4.37 Load the shell program.

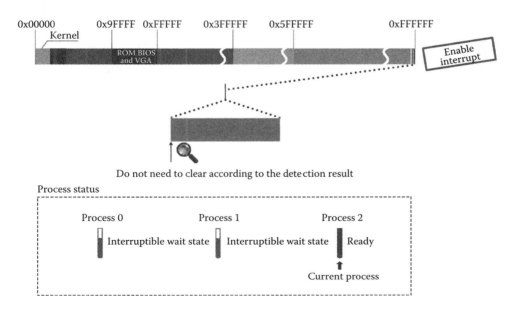

Figure 4.38 Adjust the memory according to the task_struct of process 2.

4.3.4.2 Map the Physical Address and Linear Address of the Loading Page

After loading a page shell program, the kernel will map the content of this page to the linear address space of the shell process and create the mapping management relation in the page directory table, page table, and page. The code is as follows:

```
//code path:mm/memory.c:
void do_no_page(unsigned long error_code,unsigned long address)
{
    ......
    put_page(page,address)//Map the physical address to linear address
    ......
}
```

Mapping of these addresses is shown in Figure 4.39.

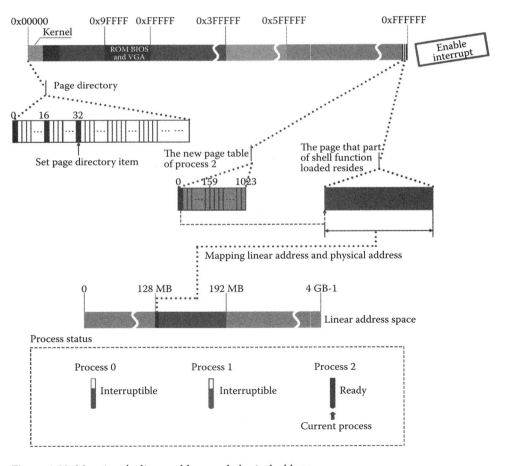

Figure 4.39 Mapping the linear address and physical address.

```
//code path:mm/memory.c:
unsigned long put_page(unsigned long page,unsigned long address)
{
        unsigned long tmp, *page_table;

/* NOTE !!! This uses the fact that _pg_dir = 0 */

        if (page < LOW_MEM || page >= HIGH_MEMORY)
            printk("Trying to put page %p at %p\n",page,address);
        if (mem_map[(page-LOW_MEM)>>12] != 1)
            printk("mem_map disagrees with %p at %p\n",page,address);
        page_table = (unsigned long *) ((address>>20) & 0xffc);//compute the
//corresponding entry of page directory table in address
        if ((*page_table)&1)//If the page directory entry has its corresponding
                        //page table, then get the address of page table
            page_table=(unsigned long *) (0xfffff000 & *page_table);
        else {//If hasn't page table, apply a page for page table
        if (!(tmp = get_free_page()))//The applying page is used to bear the
                                //page information
                return 0;
            *page_table = tmp|7;
            page_table = (unsigned long *) tmp;
        }
        page_table[(address>>12) & 0x3ff] = page | 7;//Create the relation
                                                //between page and page
                                                //table, finally achieve
                                                //mapping

/* no need for invalidate */
        return page;
}
```

■ 4.4 The System Gets to the Idle State

4.4.1 Create the Update Process

During the execution of shell, it would read the information on the standard input file, that is, the file information of the first item in filp[20] in the task_struct. We have introduced it in Section 4.3.1. At the start of the shell process, it replaces the standard device file tty0 by the rc file. Hence, the shell program is reading the information from the rc file.

The specific reading process is shown in Figure 4.40.

Shell reads the commands from the "/etc/rc" script file, which mainly includes the following two commands:

```
......
/etc/update & //create a new process and load the program update
......
echo «/dev/hd1/» >/etc/mtab //write the string «/dev/hd1/» to the file/etc/mtab
......
```

According to the command/etc/update, shell first creates a new process. The new process pid is 3 (the shell process pid is 2; thus, the new process pid is 3). The item in task[64] is also 3; we call it the "process update." Then, it loads the update program, and subsequently suspends itself to switch to the process update. The process of creating, loading,

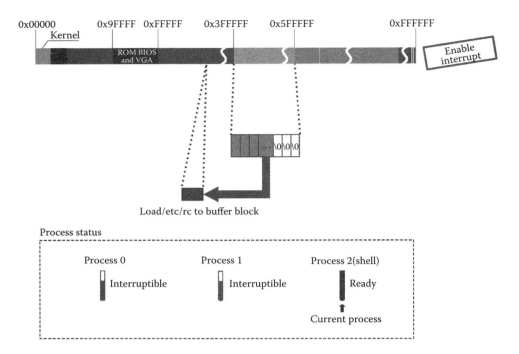

Figure 4.40 Load the "/etc/rc" file into the buffer.

and switching is the same as that when process 1 creates process 2 and switches to process 2, as introduced in Section 4.2.

It is shown in Figure 4.41.

The process update has a very important task: synchronizing the data in the buffer to the peripherals (floppy disk, hard disk, etc.). As the speed of host and peripheral data exchange is much lower than the speed of data exchange in the host, when the kernel needs to write data to the peripherals, it writes the data to the buffer first in order to improve the efficiency and then synchronizes the data to the peripherals from the buffer accordingly.

From time to time, the update process would be woken up, to synchronize the data to the peripherals. Later, the process will suspend and it will wait for the next waking up and continue to execute again and again.

After switching to the update process, there will no synchronization tasks. The process suspends and switches to the shell process to continue.

The procedure is shown in Figure 4.42.

4.4.2 Switch to the Shell Process

As introduced in Section 4.4.1, the shell process has executed the first command in the rc file and created the process update. It will now execute the second command echo "/dev/hd1/" >/etc/mtab and write string "/dev/hd1/" to the "/etc/mtab" file in the Ramdisk. After

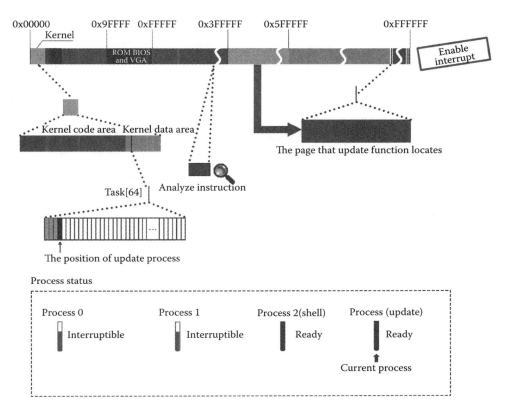

Figure 4.41 The status of the update process.

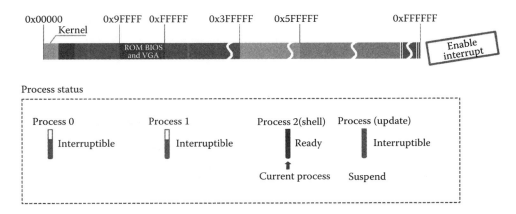

Figure 4.42 Changes in process state.

that, the shell program will continue to read the rc file. The read() function corresponds to the system call sys_read(). The code is as follows:

```
//The code path:fs/read_write.c:
int sys_read(unsigned int fd,char * buf,int count)
{
        ...
        if (inode->i_pipe)//read the pipe file
                return (file->f_mode&1)?read_pipe(inode,buf,count):-EIO;
        if (S_ISCHR(inode->i_mode))//read the character device file
                return rw_char(READ,inode->i_zone[0],buf,count,&file->f_pos);
        if (S_ISBLK(inode->i_mode))//read the block device file
                return block_read(inode->i_zone[0],&file->f_pos,buf,count);
        if (S_ISDIR(inode->i_mode) || S_ISREG(inode->i_mode)) {//read the
                                                       //common file
            if (count+file->f_pos > inode->i_size)
                count=inode->i_size - file->f_pos;
            if (count<=0)
                return 0;
            return file_read(inode,file,buf,count);
        }
        printk(" (Read)inode->i_mode =%06o\n\r",inode->i_mode);
        return -EINVAL;
}
```

As the "/etc/rc" file is a common file, its return value should be -ERROR accordingly (the specific steps of reading a file will be introduced in Chapter 5). This return value will result in the exiting of the shell process, and the corresponding system call function is sys_exit(). The code is as follows:

```
//The code path:kernel/exit.c:
int sys_exit(int error_code)
{
    return do_exit((error_code&0xff)<<8);
}
```

After entering the function do_exit(), it starts to prepare for the exit of the shell process. The code is as follows:
The process of releasing the pages is shown in Figure 4.43.

```
//The code path:kernel/exit.c:
int do_exit(long code)
{
    int i;

    free_page_tables(get_base(current->ldt[1]),get_limit(0x0f));
    free_page_tables(get_base(current->ldt[2]),get_limit(0x17));//free the pages
            //that the code segment and data segment occupied of process shell
    for (i=0 ; i<NR_TASKS ; i++)//detect whether the process shell has a child
                            //process
        if (task[i] && task[i]->father = = current->pid) {
```

```
           task[i]->father = 1;//before the exit of process shell, set the father
                              //process of process update to process 1
           if (task[i]->state = = TASK_ZOMBIE)//if the child process is in the
                                      //zombie state, then send termination signal
                  /* assumption task[1] is always init */
                  (void) send_sig(SIGCHLD, task[1], 1);
           }
       for (i = 0 ; i<NR_OPEN ; i++)//the following is remove the relationship of
                                  //process shell with other process, files,
                                  //terminals, etc.
             if (current->filp[i])
                   sys_close(i);
          iput(current->pwd);
          current->pwd = NULL;
          iput(current->root);
          current->root = NULL;
          iput(current->executable);
          current->executable = NULL;
          if (current->leader && current->tty >=0)
                  tty_table[current->tty].pgrp=0;
          if (last_task_used_math==current)
                  last_task_used_math = NULL;
          if (current->leader)
                  kill_session();
          current->state = TASK_ZOMBIE;//set the current process to zombie state
          current->exit_code = code;
          tell_father(current->father);//send signal to process 1, tell it the
                                      //process shell will exit
          schedule();                 //switch the process
          return (-1);     /* just to suppress warnings */
}
```

The relationship of the shell process and other processes, files, terminals, and so on, as well as sending signal to the father process, is shown in Figure 4.44.

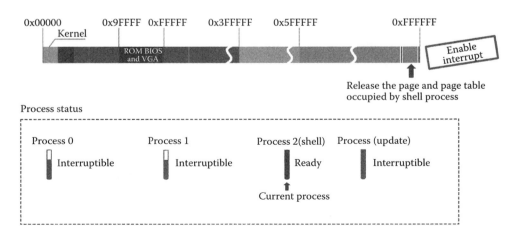

Figure 4.43 Free the page and page table owned by the shell process.

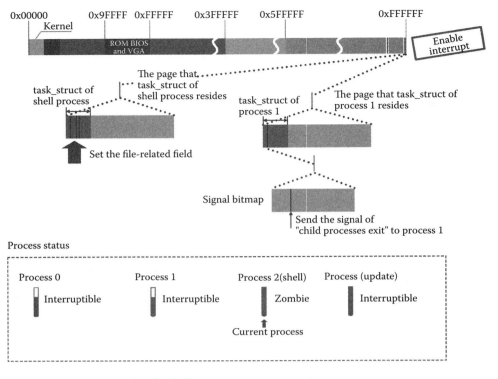

Figure 4.44 Treatment after the shell process exits.

The execution of the function tell_father and schedule is worth noting. In the function tell_father, it will send the SIGCHLD signal to process 1 to notify it that a child process will exit. The code is as follows:

```
//The code path:kernel/exit.c:
static void tell_father(int pid)//notify the father process that the child
                                //process will exit
{
        int i;

        if (pid)
                for (i=0;i<NR_TASKS;i++) {
                        if (!task[i])
                                continue;
                        if (task[i]->pid ! = pid)
                                continue;
                        task[i]->signal | = (1<<(SIGCHLD-1));//send SIGCHLD
                                                             //signal to the
                                                             //father process

                        return;
                }
/* if we don't find any fathers, we just release ourselves */
/* This is not really OK. Must change it to make father 1 */
        printk("BAD BAD - no father found\n\r");
        release(current);
}
```

After the function tell_father(), the system will call the function schedule() to prepare to switch the process; the detection of the signal affects the process switch. The code is as follows:

```
//The code path:kernel/sched.c:
void schedule(void)
{
        int i,next,c;
        struct task_struct ** p;

/* check alarm, wake up any interruptible tasks that have got a signal */

        for(p = &LAST_TASK ; p > &FIRST_TASK ; --p)//traverse all
                                                   //processes
            if (*p) {
                if ((*p)->alarm && (*p)->alarm < jiffies) {
                    (*p)->signal |= (1<<(SIGALRM-1));
                    (*p)->alarm = 0;
                }
                if (((*p)->signal & ~(_BLOCKABLE & (*p)->blocked)) &&
                (*p)->state==TASK_INTERRUPTIBLE)//the process 1 has
                                                //received the signal and
                                                //its state is interruptible
                    (*p)->state=TASK_RUNNING;//set the process 1 to
                                             //ready state

            }

/* this is the scheduler proper: */

        while (1) {
                c = -1;
                next = 0;
                i = NR_TASKS;
                p = &task[NR_TASKS];
                while (-- i) {
                    if (!*-- p)
                        continue;
                    if ((*p)->state==TASK_RUNNING && (*p)->counter > c)
                        c = (*p)->counter, next = i;//find that only
                                                    //process 1 is in the
                                                    //ready state
                }
                if (c) break;
                for(p = &LAST_TASK ; p > &FIRST_TASK ;-- p)
                    if (*p)
                        (*p)->counter = ((*p)->counter >> 1) +
                            (*p)->priority;
        }
        switch_to(next);//decide to switch to the process 1
}
```

As introduced in Section 4.2, when executing the function sys_waitpid(), process 1 calls schedule() and switches to process 2. When it switches to process 1, it will continue to follow the schedule() and eventually return to the function sys_waitpid (for more information, see Section 3.2). The code is as follows:

```
//The code path:kernel/exit.c:
int sys_waitpid(pid_t pid,unsigned long * stat_addr, int options)
//the system call function corresponding to wait()
{
        int flag, code;
        struct task_struct ** p;


        verify_area(stat_addr,4);
repeat:
        flag = 0;
        for(p = &LAST_TASK ; p > &FIRST_TASK ; --p) {
                if (!*p || *p== current)
                        continue;
                if ((*p)->father !=current->pid)
                        continue;
                ......

        }
        if (flag) {
                if (options & WNOHANG)
                        return 0;
                current->state=TASK_INTERRUPTIBLE;
        schedule();//when complete, return to function sys_waitpid
        if (!(current->signal &=~(1<<(SIGCHLD-1))))
                        //receive the SIGCHLD signal, the child process
                        //will exit
                goto repeat;//repeat to deal with the child process exit
        else
                return -EINTR;
        }
        return -ECHILD;
}
```

It is worth noting that the SIGCHLD signal that process 1 received was sent by the function tell_father(). The function sys_waitpid() continues to execute; at this time, there is a child process exit and it needs to be dealt with. The code is as follows:

```
//The code path:kernel/exit.c:
int sys_waitpid(pid_t pid,unsigned long * stat_addr, int options)
{
        ...
        repeat:
        flag = 0;
        for(p = &LAST_TASK ; p > &FIRST_TASK ; --p) {
                if (!*p || *p==current)
                        continue;
                if ((*p)->father != current->pid)
                        continue;
                ......

        ...
```

```
    switch ((*p)->state) {    //continue to prepare for the exit of process shell
    ...
        case TASK_ZOMBIE:                //the process shell is in the zombie state
            current->cutime += (*p)->utime;
            current->cstime += (*p)->stime;
            flag = (*p)->pid;            //record the pid of process 2, that is 2
            code = (*p)->exit_code;
            release(*p);                 //free the page occupied by the
                                         //task_struct of process 2
            put_fs_long(code,stat_addr);
            return flag;                 //return shell's pid, that is 2
    ...
    }
    }
    ...
}
```

Figure 4.45 shows an instance of releasing pages of shell's task_struct.

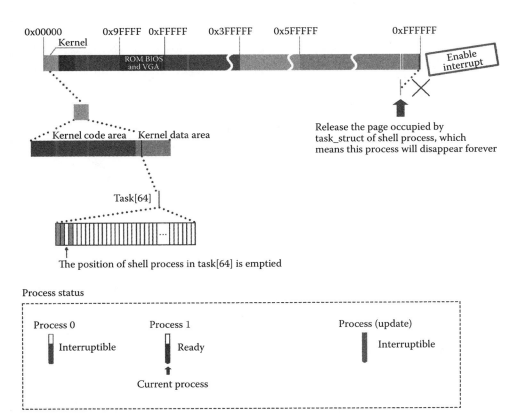

The position of shell process in task[64] is emptied

Release the page occupied by task_struct of shell process, which means this process will disappear forever

Figure 4.45 Process 1 clears the information of the shell process in task[64].

When the function sys_waitpid() is completed, it will return to the function wait() and will ultimately return to the function init(). Process 1 continues to execute. The code is as follows:

```
//The code path:init/main.c:
void init(void)
{
    ......
    if (pid>0)
        while (pid != wait(&i))       //2! = 2 is wrong, jump to
                                      //while(1)
                    /* nothing */;
    while (1) {                        //restart process shell
        if ((pid=fork())<0) {
                printf("Fork failed in init\r\n");
                continue;
        }
        if (!pid) {
                close(0);close(1);close(2);
                setsid();
                (void) open("/dev/tty0",O_RDWR,0);
                    (void) dup(0);
                    (void) dup(0);
                    _exit(execve("/bin/sh",argv,envp));
        }
        while (1)
                if (pid== wait(&i))
                        break;
        printf("\n\rchild%d died with code%04x\n\r",pid,i);
        sync();
    }
    _exit(0);        /* NOTE! _exit, not exit() */
```

What we have introduced in Section 4.2 is worth noting: when process 2 is created, the pid value is 2, and the flag, which is the return value of sys_waitpid(), is also 2. That is, the function wait() returns 2; if the while is false, jump out of the loop.

4.4.3 Reconstruction of the Shell

Process 1 continues to execute and prepares for the reconstruction of the shell. The code is as follows:

```
//The code path:init/main.c:
    void init(void)
{
    ......
    if (pid>0)
        while (pid ! = wait(&i))              //2! = 2 is wrong, jump to while()
                /* nothing */;
    while (1) {                              //restart the process shell
```

```
        if ((pid=fork())<0) {      //the process 1 create process 4, that is, rebuild
                                    //process shell
        printf("Fork failed in init\r\n");
        continue;
            }
        if (!pid) {
                close(0);close(1);close(2);   //new process shell closes all the opened
                                              //file
            setsid();                         //create new session
            (void) open("/dev/tty0",O_RDWR,0);//re-open the standard input device file
                    (void) dup(0);            //re-open the standard input device file
                    (void) dup(0);            //re-open the standard error output
                                              //device file
                           _exit(execve("/bin/sh",argv,envp));//load the process
                                                              //shell
            }
        while (1)
            if (pid = = wait(&i))      //process 1 waits for the exit of child process
                        break;
            printf("\n\rchild%d died with code%04x\n\r",pid,i);
            sync();
        }
        _exit(0);      /* NOTE! _exit, not exit() */
```

Reconstruction of the shell process is shown in Figure 4.46.

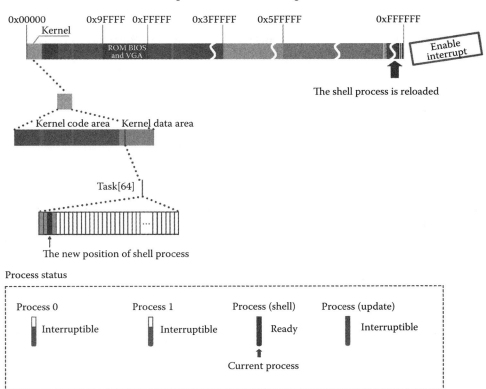

Figure 4.46 Reload the shell process.

Now, we have introduced execution path of the code. The difference that is worth noting is that the pid of the shell process is created by last_pid, so it is 4, but in the task[64], it is still 2, which is the item of shells that exited before. In addition, the shell reopens the standard input device file tty0 instead of the rc file, which prevents the shell from exiting. The code is as follows:

```
//The code path:fs/read_write.c:
int sys_read(unsigned int fd,char * buf,int count)
{
        ......
    if (inode->i_pipe)
            return (file->f_mode&1)?read_pipe(inode,buf,count):-EIO;
    if (S_ISCHR(inode->i_mode))//the shell reads tty0 as the character
                               //device file
            return rw_char(READ,inode->i_zone[0],buf,count,&file->f_pos);
    if (S_ISBLK(inode->i_mode))
            return block_read(inode->i_zone[0],&file->f_pos,buf,count);
    if (S_ISDIR(inode->i_mode) || S_ISREG(inode->i_mode)) {//the rc file is
                                                           //a common file
            if (count+file->f_pos > inode->i_size)
                    count = inode->i_size - file->f_pos;
            if (count<=0)
                    return 0;
            return file_read(inode,file,buf,count);
    }
    printk("(Read)inode->i_mode =%06o\n\r",inode->i_mode);
    return -EINVAL;
}
```

After entering the function rw_char, all processes are in the interruptible state. Now, switching to process 0 again, the system enters the idle state.

After the system enters the idle, users should use the shell process to communicate with the computer. The principle of the shell process is as follows: the users input information through the keyboard and store it in the specified character buffer queue, which is the content of the tty0 terminal device file. The shell process will read the data in the buffer queue again and again. If the user does not give any command, there will be no data in the buffer queue, and the shell process will be set to the interruptible state. If the user types a command on the keyboard, it will trigger a keyboard interrupt. The interrupt service routine will store the information in the buffer queue and will send a signal to the shell process. The signal will wake up the shell process. The shell continues to read data from the buffer queue and deal with it. Upon completion, the shell process will be suspended again and will wait for the next keyboard interrupt.

5 File Operation

▋ 5.1 Install the File System

In Section 3.3.3, the operating system (OS) loads the root file system successfully, so that data can interact with the root device. Installing the file system means that the file system in the hard disk is loaded as the root file system, in order for the OS to interact data with the root device.

There are three steps to install the file system:

1. Read the super block from the hard disk and load it into super_block[8] in the system.

2. Read the specified i node from the Ramdisk and load it into inode_table[32] in the system.

3. Mount the super block of the hard disk into the specified i node of inode_table[32].

The overall structure of the file system of the hard disk, after it is completely installed, is shown in Figure 5.1.

The command "mount/dev/hd1/mnt" can be used to install the file system in shell. This command includes three parameters, that is, mount, /dev/hd1, and /mnt. "mount" is the name of a command with the purpose of installing the file system. "/dev/hd1" and "/mnt" are directory path names, to indicate the mount file system of the device "hd1" to

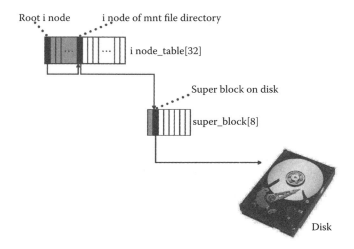

Figure 5.1 Schematic diagram of a successful file system installation.

the directory file "mnt." After shell receives this command, it creates a new process. This process calls mount(), which is eventually mapped into the system function sys_mount(). The task of installing the file system is finished by sys_mount().

5.1.1 Get the Super Block of Peripherals

Tip:

The hard disk can be partitioned. Each partition can be taken as a device. In this and the following chapter, the entire hard disk is a partition by default. hd1 represents the hard disk.

The function sys_mount() first calls the function namei() to get the i node of the device hd1 file based on the directory name "/dev/hd1." It then gets the device id from the i node and reads out the super block of the device based on the device id.

The code is as follows:

```
//code path:fs/super.c:
int sys_mount(char * dev_name, char * dir_name, int rw_flag)
{
  struct m_inode * dev_i, * dir_i;
  struct super_block * sb;
  int dev;


  if (!(dev_i = namei(dev_name)))          //get inode of device hd1 file
    return -ENOENT;
  dev = dev_i->i_zone[0];                  //get device number based on inode
  if (!S_ISBLK(dev_i->i_mode)) {           //if hd1 file is not block device file
    iput(dev_i);                           //free its inode
    return -EPERM;
```

```
       }
       iput(dev_i);//free inode of device hd1 file
       if (!(dir_i = namei(dir_name)))
          return -ENOENT;
       if (dir_i->i_count != 1 || dir_i->i_num == ROOT_INO) {
          iput(dir_i);
          return -EBUSY;
       }
       if (!S_ISDIR(dir_i->i_mode)) {
          iput(dir_i);
          return -EPERM;
       }
       if (!(sb = read_super(dev))) {          //get super block of device from device number
          iput(dir_i);
          return -EBUSY;
       }
       if (sb->s_imount) {
          iput(dir_i);
          return -EBUSY;
       }
       if (dir_i->i_mount) {
          iput(dir_i);
          return -EPERM;
       }
       sb->s_imount = dir_i;
       dir_i->i_mount = 1;
       dir_i->i_dirt = 1;                      /* NOTE! we don't iput(dir_i) */
       return 0;                               /* we do that in umount */
}
```

The process of getting the i node in the function namei() is similar to that in Section 4.1.1.

There are three steps to read the device super block by read_super(). First, it chooses an free slot to store the super block in super_block. Second, it loads the super block into this item. Finally, it loads the i node bitmap and logic block bitmap on the basis of the information from the super block. Besides, before being operated, the super block table item should be locked to avoid interfering with other actions. After the operation is finished, it will be unlocked. The code is as follows:

```
//code path:fs/super.c:
static struct super_block * read_super(int dev)
{
    struct super_block * s;
    struct buffer_head * bh;
    int i,block;


    if (!dev)
       return NULL;
    check_disk_change(dev);
    if (s = get_super(dev))                //if super block of hd1 has been loaded, return
                                           //directly
       return s;
    for (s = 0+super_block ;; s++) {       //find free item for hd1 in super_block
       if (s >= NR_SUPER+super_block)
          return NULL;
       if (!s->s_dev)                //the second item of super_block is free
          break;
    }
    s->s_dev = dev;                        //following s->... is to set parameters in super
                                           //block item
    s->s_isup = NULL;                      //corresponding to memory operation
```

```
        s->s_imount = NULL;
        s->s_time = 0;
        s->s_rd_only = 0;
        s->s_dirt = 0;
        lock_super(s);                          //lock super block item to avoid interfacing
        if (!(bh = bread(dev,1))) {
//read super block according to device number and block number of hd1
//(1 indicates the second block in device,which is the logic block number of super block)
            s->s_dev = 0;
            free_super(s);
            return NULL;
        }
        *((struct d_super_block *) s) =         //load information of super block into item,namely
                                                //the second item
            *((struct d_super_block *) bh->b_data);
        brelse(bh);
        if (s->s_magic ! = SUPER_MAGIC) {       //check super magic number to determine whether
            s->s_dev = 0;                       //the file system of device is available
            free_super(s);
            return NULL;
        }
        for (i = 0;i<I_MAP_SLOTS;i++)
//load inode bitmap and logic block bitmap, and correspond them with s_imap and s_zmap
            s->s_imap[i] = NULL;
        for (i = 0;i<Z_MAP_SLOTS;i++)
            s->s_zmap[i] = NULL;
        block = 2;
        for (i = 0 ; i < s->s_imap_blocks ; i++)
            if (s->s_imap[i] = bread(dev,block))
                block++;
            else
                break;
        for (i = 0 ; i < s->s_zmap_blocks ; i++)
            if (s->s_zmap[i] = bread(dev,block))
                block++;
            else
                break;
        if (block ! = 2+s->s_imap_blocks+s->s_zmap_blocks) {
//check whether logic block amount read form device is equal to that the device should have
            for(i = 0;i<I_MAP_SLOTS;i++)
                brelse(s->s_imap[i]);
            for(i = 0;i<Z_MAP_SLOTS;i++)
                brelse(s->s_zmap[i]);
            s->s_dev = 0;
            free_super(s);
            return NULL;
        }
        s->s_imap[0]->b_data[0] | = 1;
        s->s_zmap[0]->b_data[0] | = 1;
        free_super(s);                          //completing process of setting, unlock super block
                                                //item

        return s;
}
```

5.1.2 Confirm the Mount Point of the Root File System

The system calls namei() to get the i node of the mnt directory file based on the directory name "/mnt." It then analyzes the property of the i node and checks whether the i node is available to mount the file system. The code is as follows:

```
//code path:fs/super.c:
int sys_mount(char * dev_name, char * dir_name, int rw_flag)
{

  struct m_inode * dev_i, * dir_i;
  struct super_block * sb;
  int dev;
```

```
    if (!(dev_i = namei(dev_name)))  //get inode of hd1 device file
        return -ENOENT;
    dev = dev_i->i_zone[0];             //get device id from inode
    if (!S_ISBLK(dev_i->i_mode)) {   //if file hd1 is not block device file
        iput(dev_i);                    //free its inode
        return -EPERM;
    }
    iput(dev_i);                        //free inode of hd1 device file
    if (!(dir_i = namei(dir_name)))  //get inode of mnt directory file
        return -ENOENT;
    if (dir_i->i_count != 1 || dir_i->i_num == ROOT_INO) {
//only if inode of mnt is referred once and it is not root inode, it is available
        iput(dir_i);
        return -EBUSY;
    }
    if (!S_ISDIR(dir_i->i_mode)) {   //confirm that mnt is directory file
        iput(dir_i);
        return -EPERM;
    }
    if (!(sb=read_super(dev))) {     //get super block of device from device id
        iput(dir_i);
        return -EBUSY;
    }
    if (sb->s_imount) {
        iput(dir_i);
        return -EBUSY;
    }
    if (dir_i->i_mount) {
        iput(dir_i);
        return -EPERM;
    }
    sb->s_imount = dir_i;
    dir_i->i_mount = 1;
    dir_i->i_dirt = 1;                  /* NOTE! we don't iput(dir_i) */
    return 0;                           /* we do that in umount */
}
```

Here, mnt is available to mount the file system.

5.1.3 Mount the Super Block with the Root File System

Make sure that the mount point and the mounted point are clear before mounting; that is, the file system of the device hd1 is not installed and other file systems are not installed in the directory file mnt. After these, the system mounts them all. The code is as follows:

```
//code path:fs/super.c:

int sys_mount(char * dev_name, char * dir_name, int rw_flag)

{
    ......
    if (!(sb = read_super(dev))) {              //get super block of device from device id
        iput(dir_i);
        return -EBUSY;
    }
    if (sb->s_imount) {                         //determine the file system of hd1 is not
                                                //installed
        iput(dir_i);                                        //in other places
        return -EBUSY;
    }
```

```
        if (dir_i->i_mount) {               //determine the inode of mnt is not installed
            iput(dir_i);                     //with other file system
            return -EPERM;
        }
        sb->s_imount = dir_i;                //mount dir_i in root file system with
                                             //s_imount in super block
        dir_i->i_mount = 1;                  //mark dir_i indicate that inode has been
                                             //mounted with file system
        dir_i->i_dirt = 1;                   //mark dir_i indicate that the information
                                             //of inode has been modified
/* NOTE! we don't iput(dir_i) */
    return 0;                    /* we do that in umount */
}
```

We will explain how the file system works through three examples about file operation in Sections 5.2 and 5.8.

Example 1: the user process opens a file in the hard disk and reads out the content.

Example 2: the user process creates a new file in the hard disk and writes the content.

Example 3: the user process closes the file and deletes it.

Example 1: the user process opens a file that exists in the hard disk and reads out the content. This example is divided into two parts: open file and read file. The code is as follows:

```
void main()
{
//open file
char buffer[12000];
int fd = open("/mnt/user/user1/user2/hello.txt", O_RDWR,0644));
//read out file
int size = read(fd,buffer,sizeof(buffer));
return;
}
```

▪ 5.2 Opening a File

The first step to open a file is to find out which file is to be operated by the process. This process of finding is divided into two stages:

1. *Filp[20] in the user process task_struct is bind with the file_table[64] in the kernel.

2. I node corresponding to the file opened by the user process is registered in file_table[64].

The OS accesses a file according to the demand of user process. The kernel can control the process of opening a file many times or many files once through *filp[20]. Once a file (the same or a different one) is opened, an item in *filp[20] is occupied (e.g., if the file "hello.txt" is opened twice by the user process, two items in *filp[20] are occupied) to store the pointer. Hence, in one process, the total numbers of opening a file at the same time cannot be more than 20.

In the OS, file_table[20] is the data structure that manages all processes used to open a file. It records the following information: different processes open different files, different processes open the same file, and different files are opened many times by the same process. Similar to filp[20], once a file is opened, it is recorded in file_table[64].

The i node is the most important data structure that records file profile. In the OS, the i node corresponds to files one by one; hence, the i node uniquely identifies a file. The kernel keeps track of these file i nodes in use through inode_table[32], and each file i node in use is recorded. The nature of opening a file is to build up the relationship among filp[20], file_table[64], and inode_table[32], that is, to build up the relationship represented by the orange line in Figure 5.2.

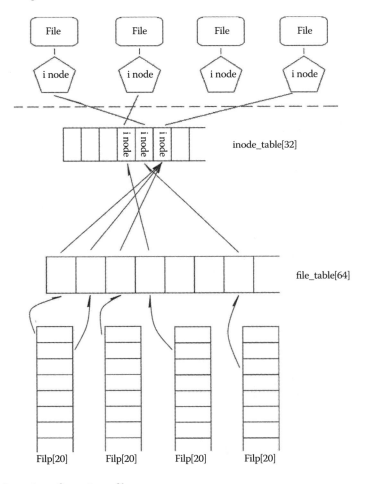

Figure 5.2 Overview of opening a file.

There are three steps in this process.

Step 1: bind *filp[20] in the user process task_struct with file_table[64] in the kernel.

Step 2: use the directory name "mnt/user/user1/user2/hello.txt" given by the user as a clue to locate the i node of the file "hello.txt."

Step 3: the i node corresponding to hello.txt is registered in file_table[64].

Call the function open() to complete the task of opening the file. This function is eventually mapped to sys_open(). The process of mapping and the basic implementation of the function sys_open() are introduced in Section 4.4.1. We will explain the implementation details of sys_open() and analyze its design.

5.2.1 Mount *Filp[20] in the User Process to File_table[64]

In sys_open, the code, which realize the bind *filp[20] with file_table[64], is as follows:

```
//code path:include/linux/fs.h:
#define NR_OPEN 20                      //max mount of files to be opened by process
#define NR_FILE 64                      //max mount of files to be opened by OS
……
struct file {
  unsigned short f_mode;                //mode of file operating
  unsigned short f_flags;               //lag for file open or control
  unsigned short f_count;               //number of file handles
  struct m_inode * f_inode;             //inode pointing to corresponding file
  off_t f_pos;                          //file position(read and write offset)
};


//code path:include/linux/sched.h:
struct file * filp[NR_OPEN];            //pointer array of manage process to use file


//code path:fs/file_table.c:
struct file file_table[NR_FILE];        //record controlling information that OS has open
                                        //files


//code path:fs/open.c:
int sys_open(const char * filename,int flag,int mode)
{
  struct m_inode * inode;
  struct file * f;
  int i,fd;


  mode & = 0777 & ~current->umask;      //set mode as available to user
  for(fd = 0 ; fd<NR_OPEN ; fd++)       //find free item in *filp[20] of current process
    if (!current->filp[fd])
        break;
  if (fd>=NR_OPEN)                       //check structure *filp[20] is beyond use limits or not
      return -EINVAL;
```

```
current->close_on_exec &= ~(1<<fd);   //set close-flag as 0 (will be explained in Chapter 6)
f = 0+file_table;
for (i=0 ; i<NR_FILE ; i++,f++)        //fine free item in file_table[64]
    if (!f->f_count) break;
if (i>=NR_FILE)                        //check file_table[64] is beyond limits or
                                       //not(Maximum is 64)

    return -EINVAL;
(current->filp[fd] = f)->f_count++;    //bind *filp[20] of current process with corresponding
                                       //item in file_table[64] and add up amount of file
......                                 //handle

}
```

To achieve the task, free items should be found in *filp[20] and file_table[64] independently. The system then binds *filp[20] in the current process with the corresponding item in file_table[64] and adds up the mount of the file handles of the corresponding item in file_table[64] (file handle will be explained in Chapter 7).

Note that it is so complex and unable to pre-estimate in situation of many processed using files. For example, the free items of *filp[20] and file_table[64] cannot always be found. That is to say, the error information will be given by the kernel when beyond the using limitation of the two data structure. So the designing that check firstly and use later is throughout.

5.2.2 Get the File's i node

This section analyzes the path name "/mnt/user/user1/user2/hello.txt" to find the i node of the hello.txt file.

The difference with the i_node finding method introduced in Section 4.1.1 is that the hello.txt file is stored in the hard disk and the search process will start from the root i node and find the file in the hard disk through the Ramdisk. The whole process is shown below.

As we can see from Figure 5.3, the parsing process has an obvious isomorphism and the process is as follows:

Look up the i node → Find the directory file through the i node →

Find the directory entry by directory file → Find the i node number of the directory file by directory entry →

Find the directory entry by directory file → Find the i node number of the directory file by directory entry →

......

Eventually, find the hello.txt file.

5.2.2.1 Get the i node of the Directory File

The process of program calling to get the i node is shown in Figure 5.4.

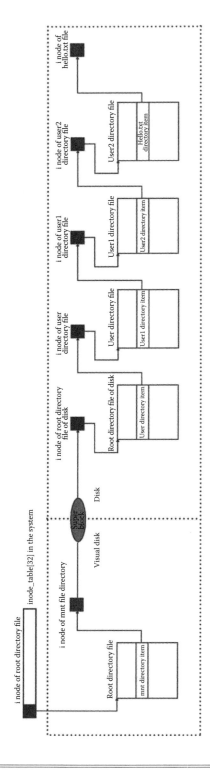

Figure 5.3 Process to parse the file path.

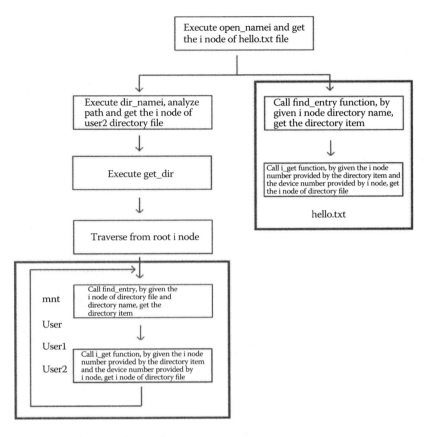

Figure 5.4 Process of getting the i node.

The goal of acquiring the i node of the directory file is achieved by calling open_ namei(). The code is as follows:

```
//path name:fs/open.c:
int sys_open(const char * filename,int flag,int mode)
{
.....
    if ((i = open_namei(filename,flag,mode,&inode))<0) {     //get inode of hello.txt file.
        current->filp[fd] = NULL;                             //*filp[20] are set Null if
                                                              //inode is not found
        f->f_count = 0;                                       //citation count in file_
                                                              //table[64] is set 0 if inode
                                                              //is not found.
        return i;
    }
.....
}
```

Open_namei() will first set the flag and mode of the opened file as per user's request. The code is as follows:

```
//path name:include/fcntl.h:              //octal form:
.....
#define O_ACCMODE         00003                              //file access mode mask
#define O_RDONLY          00                                 //read-only flag
#define O_WRONLY          01                                 //write-only flag
#define O_RDWR            02                                 //read-write flag
#define O_CREAT           00100     /* not fcntl */          //create new file flag
#define O_EXCL            00200     /* not fcntl */          //process exclusive flag
#define O_NOCTTY          00400     /* not fcntl */          //no control terminal flag
#define O_TRUNC           01000     /* not fcntl */          //truncate flag
#define O_APPEND          02000                              //append flag
#define O_NONBLOCK        04000     /* not fcntl */          //non-block flag
#define O_NDELAYO_NONBLOCK
.....


//path name:include/fcntl.h://binary form:(notice the rule in setting flag)
.....
#define O_ACCMODE         0000 0000 0000 0011
#define O_RDONLY          0000 0000 0000 0000
#define O_WRONLY          0000 0000 0000 0001
#define O_RDWR            0000 0000 0000 0010
#define O_CREAT           0000 0000 0100 0000/* not fcntl */
#define O_EXCL            0000 0000 1000 0000/* not fcntl */
#define O_NOCTTY          0000 0001 0000 0000 /* not fcntl */
#define O_TRUNC           0000 0010 0000 0000 /* not fcntl */
#define O_APPEND          0000 0100 0000 0000
#define O_NONBLOCK        0000 1000 0000 0000 /* not fcntl */
#define O_NDELAYO_NONBLOCK
.....


//path name:fs/namei.c:
int open_namei(const char * pathname, int flag, int mode,
    struct m_inode ** res_inode)          //pathname is/mnt/user/user1/user2/hello.txt
{
    const char * basename;        //basename records the address of'/'
    int inr,dev,namelen;
    struct m_inode * dir, *inode;
    struct buffer_head * bh;
    struct dir_entry * de;                  //de points to directory content

    if ((flag & O_TRUNC) && !(flag & O_ACCMODE))    //if file is read-only and length is 0
        flag | = O_WRONLY;                          //set the file to write-only
    mode & = 0777 & ~current->umask;
    mode | = I_REGULAR;                             //set the file to regular
    if (!(dir = dir_namei(pathname,&namelen,&basename)))    //parse path name and get topmost inode
        return -ENOENT;
    if (!namelen) {                 /* special case: '/usr/' etc */
        if (!(flag & (O_ACCMODE|O_CREAT|O_TRUNC))) {
            *res_inode = dir;
            return 0;
        }
        iput(dir);
        return -EISDIR;
    }
    bh = find_entry(&dir,basename,namelen,&de);       //find directory entry of target file
                                                      //through topmost inode
    .....
}
```

After setting, dir_namei() is called to analyze the file path and traverse the i nodes of all directory files to find the i node of the last directory file, namely, the topmost i node.

Dir_namei() will call get_dir() to get the i node. The code is as follows:

```
//path name:fs/namei.c:
static struct m_inode * dir_namei(const char * pathname,
    int * namelen, const char ** name)   //pathname points to/mnt/user/user1/user2/hello.txt
{
```

```
char c;
const char * basename;
struct m_inode * dir;

if (!(dir = get_dir(pathname)))              //call get_dir() to parse path name and get inode
    return NULL;
basename = pathname;
while (c=get_fs_byte(pathname++))            //after tranversing, pathname points to '/0' in string.
    //tranverse each string in "/mnt/user/user1/user2/hello.txt" and copy one character to c in
    //each cycle
    if (c=='/')
        basename = pathname;                //after tranversing string, basename points to the last '/'
*namelen = pathname-basename-1;             //compute the name length of "hello.txt"
*name = basename;                           //get the address of '/' before hello.txt
return dir;
}
```

Get_dir() will get the i node content. The process has been introduced preliminarily in Section 4.1.1: the work is complete through "find directory entry and get i node through directory entry" continuously.

The corresponding function in finding the directory entry is find_entry().

The corresponding function in getting the i node is iget().

These two functions are introduced in detail here. The code is as follows:

```
//pathname:fs/namei.c:
static struct m_inode * get_dir(const char * pathname)
{
    char c;
    const char * thisname;
    struct m_inode * inode;
    struct buffer_head * bh;
    int namelen,inr,idev;
    struct dir_entry * de;

    if (!current->root || !current->root->i_count)    //current root inode does not exist or
        panic("No root inode");                       //the citation count is 0
    if (!current->pwd || !current->pwd->i_count)      //current directory root inode does not exist or
        panic("No cwd inode");                        //the citation count is 0
    if ((c = get_fs_byte(pathname)) = ='/') {         //identify the first character of
        inode = current->root;                        //"/mnt/usr/usr1/usr2/hello.tet" is '/'
        pathname++;
    } else if (c)
        inode = current->pwd;
    else
        return NULL;   /* empty name is bad */
    inode->i_count++;                                 //citation count increases by 1


    while (1) {                                       //cycle the statements below until find topmost inode
        thisname = pathname;                          //thisnamepoints to 'm' first
        if (!S_ISDIR(inode->i_mode) || !permission(inode,MAY_EXEC)) {
            iput(inode);
            return NULL;
        }
        for(namelen = 0;(c = get_fs_byte(pathname++))&&(c! = '/');namelen++)
            //the loop breaks each time when finding '/' in string or c is '\0'
            /* nothing */;                            //notice this ';'
        if (!c)
            return inode;
```

```
    if (!(bh = find_entry(&inode,thisname,namelen,&de))) {//get directory entry through inode
        iput(inode);                          //release the inode if assigned directory entry is not found
        return NULL;                          //and return NULL
    }
    inr = de->inode;//get inode number from directory entry
    idev = inode->i_dev;//get device number from inode
    brelse(bh);
    iput(inode);                              //release all inodes of each directory file after used
                                              //to avoid wasting space in inode_table
    if (!(inode = iget(idev,inr)))            //get inode
        return NULL;
    }
}
```

The main task of find_entry() is as follows: First, the function determines the amount of directory entries in the directory file by the i node. Then, begins from the first logic block corresponding to the directory file, the logic blocks are continuously loaded into the buffer from the peripherals, and the function searches the specified directory entry until it is found.

The code is as follows:

```
//code path:include/linux/fs.h:
  #define BLOCK_SIZE 1024
//path name:fs/namei.c:
static struct buffer_head * find_entry(struct m_inode ** dir,
  const char * name, int namelen, struct dir_entry ** res_dir)
//get directory entry of mnt
{
   int entries;
   int block,i;
   struct buffer_head * bh;
   struct dir_entry * de;
   struct super_block * sb;


#ifdef NO_TRUNCATE
   if (namelen > NAME_LEN)//return "NULL" if the name length exceeds 14 under the premise of NO_TRUNCATE
        return NULL;
#else
   if (namelen > NAME_LEN)//or truncate the name length
        namelen = NAME_LEN;
#endif
   entries = (*dir)->i_size/(sizeof (struct dir_entry));
//calculate the amount of directory entries according to file length information namely i_size
*res_dir = NULL;
if (!namelen)//examine the file name length is 0 or not
        return NULL;
/* check for '..', as we might have to do some "magic" for it */
   if (namelen = =2 && get_fs_byte(name) = ='.' && get_fs_byte(name+1) = ='.') {
   ......//handle the case if directory entry is..
   }


   if (!(block = (*dir)->i_zone[0]))
//determine the first logic block number of directory file is not 0
        return NULL;
   if (!(bh = bread((*dir)->i_dev,block)))//read logic blocks into specified buffer
        return NULL;
   i = 0;
   de = (struct dir_entry *) bh->b_data;//de points to the head address of buffer
   while (i < entries) {//search for mnt in all directory entries
        if ((char *)de > = BLOCK_SIZE+bh->b_data) {
//if specified directory entry is not found in the logic block
        brelse(bh);
        bh = NULL;
```

```
//then continue to search for mnt directory file after reading the next logic block into buffer
        if (!(block = bmap(*dir,i/DIR_ENTRIES_PER_BLOCK)) ||
            !(bh = bread((*dir)->i_dev,block))) {
            i += DIR_ENTRIES_PER_BLOCK;
            continue;
        }
        de = (struct dir_entry *) bh->b_data;
    }
    if (match(namelen,name,de)) {//match the directory entry
        *res_dir = de;//if mnt is found, pass it to *res_dir
        return bh;
    }
    de++;
    i++;
}
brelse(bh);
return NULL;//return NULL if mnt is not found after all directory file are examined
}
```

The main task of iget() is to get the i node according to the i node id and the device id of the directory entry. The specific access is as follows: First, the function searches the i node in inode_table[32] and uses it if the specified i node already exists. Since each file has only one i node and the same file could be referred by multiple processes, if the specified i node is already loaded by other processes, then loading the i node repeatedly would not only cause confusion but also waste time.

Besides, if any i node is mounted with the file system, the root i node of the file system would be loaded and it becomes the starting point for searching files in another file system.

The i node of "mnt" is the first one to be obtained. According to Section 5.1, the file system is mounted with the i node of mnt; thus, the root i node of the file system need to be loaded in the i node table.

The code is as follows:

```
//code path:fs/namei.c:
struct m_inode * iget(int dev,int nr) //get inode of mnt, dev and nr specify device id
//and inode id
{
//struct m_inode * inode, * empty;

    if (!dev)//if device number is null
        panic("iget with dev = =0");
    empty = get_empty_inode();              //get an free inode item from inode_table[32]
    inode = inode_table;
    while (inode < NR_INODE+inode_table) {
//examine specified inode is loaded already or not, in this case the inode of mnt is loaded before
        if (inode->i_dev ! = dev || inode->i_num ! = nr) {
//compare device id and inode id to specified one
            inode++;
            continue;
        }
        wait_on_inode(inode);
//wait until the inode is unlocked
        if (inode->i_dev ! = dev || inode->i_num ! = nr) {//this inode may have been released
            inode = inode_table;           //thus traverse inode_table[32] and if not removed
            continue;                      //the inode could be used, the inode of mnt is not
                                           //removed in this case
        }
        inode->i_count++;
        if (inode->i_mount) {              //if the inode is mount with file system(in mnt case)
            int i;
```

```
        for (i = 0 ; i<NR_SUPER ; i++)        //search for peripheral of file system, namely the
                                              //super block of hd1
                if (super_block[i].s_imount==inode)
                break;
        if (i > = NR_SUPER) {                 //inode is not mount with file system
            printk("Mounted inode hasn't got sb\n");
            if (empty)
                iput(empty);
            return inode;
        }
        iput(inode);
        dev = super_block[i].s_dev;           //get device id by super block of hd1
        nr = ROOT_INO;                        //determine root inode of peripheral and ROOT_INO is1
        inode = inode_table;                  //traverse inode of peripheral(hard disk) again and
                                              //determine
                                              //it has been mount already

        continue;
        }
            if (empty)
                iput(empty);
            return inode;
        }
    if (!empty)          //there's no free item in inode_table[32]
            return (NULL);
//root inode of hd1 is not found so that it will be loaded
    inode = empty;
    inode->i_dev = dev;
    inode->i_num = nr;
    read_inode(inode);              //read inode;
    return inode;                   //because inode of mnt is mount with file system then root
                                    //inode of hd1 is returned

}
```

After preparation, read_inode() is called to read i nodes from peripherals (hard disk), and the i nodes are loaded into inode_table[32].

The code is as follows:

```
//code path:fs/inode.c:
static void read_inode(struct m_inode * inode)        //read inode
{
    struct super_block * sb;
    struct buffer_head * bh;
    int block;

    lock_inode(inode);                                //lock specified inode in inode_table[32]
    if (!(sb = get_super(inode->i_dev)))              //get super block of inode, which has been loaded
            panic("trying to read inode without dev");
    block = 2 + sb->s_imap_blocks + sb->s_zmap_blocks +
        (inode->i_num-1)/INODES_PER_BLOCK;            //determine the logic block which stores the
                                                      //specific inode
    if (!(bh = bread(inode->i_dev,block)))            //load the logic block into specified buffer
            panic("unable to read inode block");
    *(struct d_inode *)inode =                        //load inode into specified location in
                                                      //inode_table[32]

        ((struct d_inode *)bh->b_data)
            [(inode->i_num-1)%INODES_PER_BLOCK];
    brelse(bh);
    unlock_inode(inode);                              //unlock inode after table item operation
}
```

After acquiring the root i node of the file system in the hard disk, get_dir() will continuously call find_entry() and iget() to get the i node of user and user1, that is, the directory files, in order to get the i node of user2, namely, the topmost i node. The execution procedure is the same as finding the i node of mnt; the difference lies in the fact that the i nodes of these directory files are not mounting with the file system, and there is also disparity in the execution route.

The code is as follows:

```
//code path:fs/namei.c:
struct m_inode * iget(int dev,int nr)    //get inode of following directory files
{
  struct m_inode * inode, * empty;


  if (!dev)//if device id is 0, system crashes.
        panic("iget with dev = =0");
  empty = get_empty_inode();       //get an free item from inode_table[32]
inode = inode_table;
  while (inode < NR_INODE+inode_table) {
  //examine whether the inode has been load already, inodes of other directory files are
  //never loaded.
        if (inode->i_dev ! = dev || inode->i_num ! = nr) {
//the loop breaks after compare
        inode++;
        continue;
        }
        ....
  }
  if (!empty)
        return (NULL);
  //prepare to load the inode beacause it is not found in other directory files
  inode = empty;
  inode->i_dev = dev;
  inode->i_num = nr;
  read_inode(inode);    //read inode
  return inode;         //continue to search and return the inode of user, user1 and user2
                        //successively
}
```

The function returns the i node of user2 after execution and gets back to dir_namei(). The code is as follows:

```
//code path:fs/namei.c:
static struct m_inode * dir_namei(const char * pathname,
  int * namelen, const char ** name)    //pathname is the pointer to/mnt/user/user1/user2/
                                        //hello.txt
{
  char c;
  const char * basename;
  struct m_inode * dir;


  if (!(dir = get_dir(pathname)))       //the function to get inode
        return NULL;
  while (c = get_fs_byte(pathname++))   //after traverse, pathname points to '/0' at the end
//of string traverse each string in "/mnt/user/user1/user2/hello.txt" and copy one character
//to c in each loop
        if (c = ='/')
                basename = pathname;    //basename points to the last '/' after traverse
  *namelen = pathname-basename-1;       //calculate the name length of "hello.txt"
  *name = basename;                     //get the address of '/' before hello.txt


  return dir;
}
```

Finally, the function gets back to open_namei() and returns the i node of user2, that is, the topmost i node.

```
//code path:fs/namei.c:
int open_namei(const char * pathname, int flag, int mode,
  struct m_inode ** res_inode)
{
  ......
  if (!(dir = dir_namei(pathname,&namelen,&basename)))   //get topmost inode by analyzing pathname
      return -ENOENT;
  ......
}
```

After getting the topmost i node by analyzing the path name, the main task of open_namei() is completed. The next procedure is to identify the i node of hello.txt through the topmost i node.

5.2.2.2 Get the i node of the Target File

The procedure of getting the i node of hello.txt is basically the same as getting the topmost i node in Section 5.2.2.1, that is, getting the i node by calling find_entry() and iget().

The code is as follows:

```
//code path:fs/namei.c:
int open_namei(const char * pathname, int flag, int mode,
    struct m_inode ** res_inode)
{
  ......
  if (!(dir = dir_namei(pathname,&namelen,&basename)))    //get topmost inode by analyzing
                                                          //pathname
      return -ENOENT;
  if (!namelen) {                                          //if name length of target file
                                                          //is 0
      if (!(flag & (O_ACCMODE|O_CREAT|O_TRUNC))) {         //refer the flag to that in
                                                          //Section 5.2.2.1
          *res_inode = dir;
          return 0;
      }
      iput(dir);
      return -EISDIR;
  }


  bh = find_entry(&dir,basename,namelen,&de);
  //load hello.txt into buffer, de points to hello.txt
  if (!bh) {                      //after hello.txt is loaded the buffer block is not null
      ......
  }
  inr = de->inode;                //get inode number
  dev = dir->i_dev;               //get device number of hd1
  brelse(bh);
  iput(dir);                      //release the inode of user2
      if (flag & O_EXCL)          //refer the flag to that in Section 5.2.2.1
      return -EEXIST;
  if (!(inode = iget(dev,inr)))                            //get inode of hello.txt
  return -EACCES;
  if ((S_ISDIR(inode->i_mode) && (flag & O_ACCMODE)) ||    //refer the flag to that in
                                                          //Section 5.2.2.1
      !permission(inode,ACC_MODE(flag))) {                //examine the access permission
                                                          //of user
      iput(inode);
      return -EPERM;
  }
```

```
    inode->i_atime = CURRENT_TIME;
    if (flag & O_TRUNC)                          //refer the flag to that in Section 5.2.2.1
        truncate(inode);
    *res_inode = inode;                          //pass inode to sys_open
    return 0;
}
```

After getting the i node of hello.txt, the i node is mounted to file_table[64].

5.2.3 Bind File i node with File_table[64]

In Section 5.2.2.2, the i node of hello.txt has been loaded into inode_table[32]. The i node should be bind with file_table[64] now so that file_table[64] could find the i node through the pointer of the item in inode_table[32]. In addition, the OS will set the attributes, citation count, and read–write pointer offset of hello.txt.

The code is as follows:

```
//code path:fs/open.c:
int sys_open(const char * filename,int flag,int mode)
{
    .....
    if (S_ISCHR(inode->i_mode))                  //hello.txt is not character device file
        if (MAJOR(inode->i_zone[0]) = =4) {
            if (current->leader && current->tty<0) {
                current->tty = MINOR(inode->i_zone[0]);
                tty_table[current->tty].pgrp = current->pgrp;
            }
        } else if (MAJOR(inode->i_zone[0]) = =5)
            if (current->tty<0) {
                iput(inode);
                current->filp[fd] = NULL;
                f->f_count = 0;
                return -EPERM;
            }
/* Likewise with block-devices: check for floppy_change */
    if (S_ISBLK(inode->i_mode))                  //hello.txt is not block device file
        check_disk_change(inode->i_zone[0]);
    f->f_mode = inode->i_mode;                   //set file attribute by inode
    f->f_flags = flag;                           //set file operating mode by flag
    f->f_count = 1;                              //citation count increases by 1
    f->f_inode = inode;                          //build reference between file and inode
    f->f_pos = 0;                                //set read-write pointer to 0
    return (fd);                                 //return file handle to user space
}
```

Until now, file_table[64] is bound to the pointer of filp[20] of the current process on one hand and to the i node of hello.txt in inode_table[32] on the other hand. The OS retuns fd, which is the offset of the mount point in file_table[64], that is, file handle, to the user process. The system could determine which file is demanded by the process after that process transfers fd to the OS. Take the following case as an example:

```
int size = read(fd,buffer,sizeof(buffer));
```

This line is used to read hello.txt: the actual parameter fd is the tag of hello.txt. After this parameter is transferred to the kernel, the OS will find the mount point by fd and operate next.

Details on reading the file operation will be introduced in the next section.

∎ 5.3 Reading a File

Reading a file means reading data from the file opened by the user process. It is completed by the function read().

5.3.1 Locate the Position of the Data Block in the Peripherals

The function read() is eventually mapped to sys_read() to execute. Before executing the main content, the system will first check the feasibility of this operation, including whether the file handle passed by the user process and bytes of number read are in a reasonable range, whether the page where the user process data are is written into the data is not read-only, and so on. After these checks, begin to perform the main content, that is, call the function file_read() and read the file data specified by the process. The code is as follows:

```
//file path:fs/read_write.c:
int sys_read(unsigned int fd,char * buf,int count)       //read data from the file "hello.txt"
{    //fd is the file handle, buf is a user space pointer, and count is the number of bytes
    //to read
    struct file * file;
    struct m_inode * inode;

    if (fd> = NR_OPEN || count<0 || !(file = current->filp[fd]))//whether fd and count is
                                                        //within reasonable range,file
                                                        //is opened or not
        return -EINVAL;
    if (!count)                          //if number of bytes is 0, return
        return 0;
    verify_area(buf,count);              //verify the property of page where buf is. If it is
                                         //read-only, copy this page(refer to chapter 6)
    inode = file->f_inode;
    if (inode->i_pipe)
        return (file->f_mode&1)?read_pipe(inode,buf,count):-EIO;
    if (S_ISCHR(inode->i_mode))
        return rw_char(READ,inode->i_zone[0],buf,count,&file->f_pos);
    if (S_ISBLK(inode->i_mode))
        return block_read(inode->i_zone[0],&file->f_pos,buf,count);
    if (S_ISDIR(inode->i_mode) || S_ISREG(inode->i_mode)) {  //analyze node-i property of file
                                                     //"hello.txt" and it is common file
        if (count+file->f_pos > inode->i_size)
            count = inode->i_size - file->f_pos;
        if (count< = 0)
            return 0;
        return file_read(inode,file,buf,count);              //read data specified by process
    }
    printk("(Read)inode->i_mode =%06o\n\r",inode->i_mode);
    return -EINVAL;
}
```

In file_read(), the system locates the logic block number of the specified file data block in the peripheral by bmp(). The code is as follows:

```
//code path:include/linux/fs.h:
#define BLOCK_SIZE 1024
```

```
//code path:fs/file_dev.c:
int file_read(struct m_inode * inode, struct file * filp, char * buf, int count) {
    int left,chars,nr;
    struct buffer_head * bh;
```

```
      if ((left = count)< = 0)
      return 0;
      while (left) {               //not more than data about one buffer block(1KB) is copied into
                                   //buf memory in every loop
      if (nr = bmap(inode,(filp->f_pos)/BLOCK_SIZE)) {
          //file operation pointer offset divided by BLOCK_SIZE(1024) is where the data operated
          //locates
          //in this case, filp->f_pos is 0
//based on the data block number in file, find the logic block number in the peripheral
          if (!(bh = bread(inode->i_dev,nr)))      //read data from the peripheral
                  break;
      } else
          bh = NULL;
      ......
}
```

Note that when the function bmp() calls the function _bmp(), add another parameter. The code is as follows:

```
//code path:fs/inode.c:
int bmap(struct m_inode * inode,int block)
{
  return _bmap(inode,block,0);          //last parameter is creating flag. 0
                                        //means operating a existed block. 1
                                        //means creating a new block.

}
```

We will first introduce how the i node manages files.

The i node manages file data block through its structure i_zone. The diagram is shown in Figures 5.5 through 5.7.

I_zone[9] records the file data block context info. When the number of file data block is more than 9, Linux has to find another tactic: it continues to store the index value of the logic block in the data block of the data area to manage the data block hierarchically, in order to enlarge the number of data blocks for management.

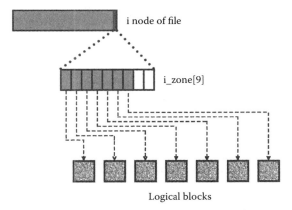

The total amount of file data block is less than or equal to 7 KB

Figure 5.5 Management schematic diagram of the i node when file data is less than 7 blocks.

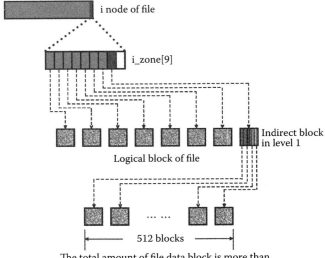

Figure 5.6 Management schematic diagram of the i node when file data is between 7 blocks and (7 + 512) blocks.

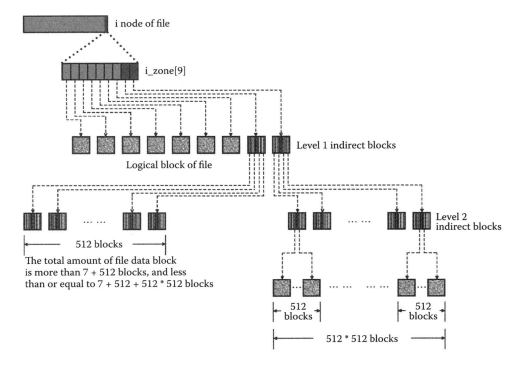

Figure 5.7 Management schematic diagram of the i node when file data is between (7 + 512) blocks and Minix.

When the total amount of data is not more than 7 KB, the first seven members of i_zone[9] are used, recording the block number of these seven data blocks in the data area.

When the total amount of data is more than 7 KB, one should start a one-level indirect management program. The eighth member of i_zone[9] records the block number of a data block; however, it stores the logic block number of the next 512 data blocks in the peripherals, not the file data context. On the basis of these block numbers, find the corresponding data block. Because the amount of data block is 1024 bytes and each block number occupies 2 bytes, a data block can store a block number of 512. In this way, the management limit is 7 + 512 data blocks, that is, (7 + 512) KB.

When the total amount of data is more than (7 + 512) KB, we use two-level indirect management instead. The ninth member of i_zone[9] records the block number of a data block; however, it stores the logic block number of the next 512 data blocks in the peripherals, not the file data context. These 512 data blocks store another 512 data blocks. In this way, the maximum blocks of management is 7 + 512 + 512 * 512 data blocks, that is, (7 + 512 + 512 * 512) KB.

In case 1, it is in the process of reading the first data block in the file "hello.txt." It is in the situation of having less than seven logic blocks. The code is as follows:

```
//code path:fs/inode.c:
static int _bmap(struct m_inode * inode,int block,int create)
{
    struct buffer_head * bh;
    int i;

    if (block<0)                        //if operating file data block number is less than 0
        panic("_bmap: block<0");
    if (block > = 7+512+512*512)        //if operating file data block number is greater than
                                        //allowable maximum
        panic("_bmap: block>big");

//= = = = = = = = = = = = = = =not more than 7 logic blocks = = = = = = = = = = = = = = = =

    if (block<7) {                      //operating file data block number is less than 7
        if (create && !inode->i_zone[block])       //create a new data block
            if (inode->i_zone[block] = new_block(inode->i_dev)) {
                inode->i_ctime = CURRENT_TIME;
            inode->i_dirt = 1;
            }
        return inode->i_zone[block];    //return value of logic block number recorded in
                                        //block item of i_zone
    }

// = = = = = = = = = = = = between 7 and (7+512) logic blocks = = = = = = = = = = = = = = = =

    block - = 7;
    if (block<512) {
        if (create && !inode->i_zone[7])           //creat a new data block
            if (inode->i_zone[7] = new_block(inode->i_dev)) {
                inode->i_dirt = 1;
                inode->i_ctime = CURRENT_TIME;
            }
        if (!inode->i_zone[7])          //one-level indirect block has no index number, stop
                                        //finding, return 0
            return 0;
        if (!(bh = bread(inode->i_dev,inode->i_zone[7])))  //get one-level indirect block
            return 0;
        i = ((unsigned short *) (bh->b_data))[block];  //get logic block number of item
                                        //block in indirect block
        if (create && !i)               //whether create a new data block
                                        //or not
```

```
                    if (i = new_block(inode->i_dev)) {
                            ((unsigned short *) (bh->b_data))[block] = i;
                            bh->b_dirt = 1;
                    }
            brelse(bh);
            return i;
    }

//= = = = = = = = = = = between (7+512) and (7+512+512*512)logic blocks = = = = = = = = = = =

    block - = 512;
    if (create && !inode->i_zone[8])                    //whether create a new data block
        if (inode->i_zone[8] = new_block(inode->i_dev)) {
                inode->i_dirt = 1;
                inode->i_ctime = CURRENT_TIME;
        }
    if (!inode->i_zone[8])                              //one-level indirect block has no index
                                                        //number, stop finding, return 0
        return 0;
    if (!(bh = bread(inode->i_dev,inode->i_zone[8])))     //get one-level indirect block
        return 0;
    i = ((unsigned short *)bh->b_data)[block>>9]; //get logic block number of item block/512
                                                  //in indirect block
    if (create && !i)
if (i = new_block(inode->i_dev)) {
                    ((unsigned short *) (bh->b_data))[block>>9] = i;
                    bh->b_dirt = 1;
        }
    brelse(bh);
    if (!i)
        return 0;
    if (!(bh = bread(inode->i_dev,i)))                  //get two-level indirect block
            return 0;
    i = ((unsigned short *)bh->b_data)[block&511];//get logic block number of item block&512
                                                  //in second level of indirect block
    if (create && !i)
        if (i = new_block(inode->i_dev)) {
                    ((unsigned short *) (bh->b_data))[block&511] = i;
                    bh->b_dirt = 1;
        }
    brelse(bh);
    return i;
}
```

5.3.2 Data Block Is Read into the Buffer Block

By calling read(), the first data block of the file "hello.txt" is read into the specified buffer from the hard disk. The scenario is shown in Figure 5.8.

The code is as follows:

```
//code path:fs/file_dev.c:
int file_read(struct m_inode * inode, struct file * filp, char * buf, int count)
{
    ......
while (left) {                      //not more than data about one buffer block(1KB) is copied into
//buf memory in every loop
        if (nr = bmap(inode,(filp->f_pos)/BLOCK_SIZE)) {  //find logic block number in
//device based on data block number in file
                if (!(bh = bread(inode->i_dev,nr)))        //read data from peripherals
                        break;
        } else
                bh = NULL;
    ......
}
```

For more about bread(), refer to Section 3.3.1.

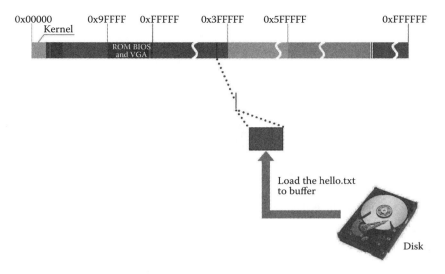

Figure 5.8 Read data from the file into the buffer.

5.3.3 Copy Data from the Buffer into the Process Memory

After loading the data block to the buffer, the system will copy it into a specified user process data memory (*buf) from the buffer. The code is as follows:

```
//code path:fs/file_dev.c:
int file_read(struct m_inode * inode, struct file * filp, char * buf, int count)
{
  ......
  while (left) {
    ......
    } else
        bh = NULL;
    nr = filp->f_pos% BLOCK_SIZE;                //calculate amount of data needing to be
                                                 //copied in next 4 lines

    chars = MIN(BLOCK_SIZE-nr, left);
    filp->f_pos + = chars;
    left - = chars;
    if (bh) {                                    //get data from peripheral successfully
        char * p = nr + bh->b_data;
        while (chars—  >0)                       //copy data of chats bytes into specified
                                                 //memory
        put_fs_byte(*(p++),buf++);
        brelse(bh);
    } else {                                     //otherwise copy 0 with amount of chars
        while (chars—  >0)
        put_fs_byte(0,buf++);
    }
  }
  inode->i_atime = CURRENT_TIME;
  return (count-left)?(count-left):-ERROR;
}
```

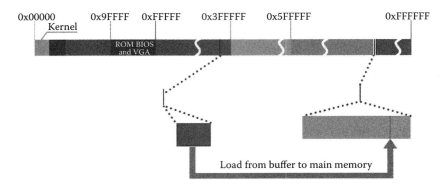

Figure 5.9 Read data from the buffer into the main memory.

The process of copying data stored in the buffer to a specified memory is shown in Figure 5.9.

Here, the system only reads data of a data block (1 KB) from the beginning of the file "hello.txt." The "while" loop will complete the process that loads data of a specified amount into area *buf.

The process of reading a file is completed, and we then explain the operation of creating a new file and writing the file based on example 2.

Example 2: the user process creates a new file in the hard disk and writes the content into this file. The example is divided into two parts: creating a new file and writing. The code is as follows:

```
void main()
{
    char str1[] = "Hello, world";
    //create new file
    int fd = creat("/mnt/user/user1/user2/hello.txt",0644));
    //write
    int size = write(fd,str1,strlen(str1));
}
```

5.4 Creating a New File

Creating a new file is the process of creating a file that does not exist in the file system based on user process requirements. It is performed by the function creat().

5.4.1 Searching a File

The function creat() is mapped to sys_creat() eventually. The code for creating a new file is similar with that for opening a file; hence, the system will directly call the function sys_open() to create a new file after entering the function sys_creat().

The code is as follows:

```
//code path:fs/file_dev.c:
int sys_creat(const char * pathname, int mode)          //create a new file
{
    return sys_open(pathname, O_CREAT | O_TRUNC, mode);
//notice: both creating flag O_CREAT and exclusive flag O_TRUNG is set, parameter
//flag is different from that in 5.2.2
}
```

The system acquires the i node of the file "hello.txt" by calling the function open_namei().

The code is as follows:

```
//code path:fs/open.c:
int sys_open(const char * filename,int flag,int mode)
{
    ......
        mode &= 0777 & ~current->umask;   //set mode of file as user-available state
    for(fd=0 ; fd<NR_OPEN ; fd++)
        if (!current->filp[fd])
    ......
        return -EINVAL;
    (current->filp[fd]=f)->f_count++;
    if ((i=open_namei(filename,flag,mode,&inode))<0) {      //get i-node of file
                                                            //"hello.txt"
        current->filp[fd]=NULL;
    ......
}
```

In this example, because the file does not exist, the execution of open_namei() differs from that in Section 5.2.2. If the "hello.txt" directory item cannot be searched after getting the i node by calling dir_namei() to analyze the directory name, the value of bh is set as NULL.

The code is as follows:

```
//code path:fs/namei.c:
int open_namei(const char * pathname, int flag, int mode,
    struct m_inode ** res_inode)
{
    ......
    mode &= 0777 & ~current->umask;
    mode |= I_REGULAR;                              //set this file as regular file

    if (!(dir = dir_namei(pathname,&namelen,&basename)))     //analyze path,get i-node
            return -ENOENT;
    if (!namelen) {                      /* special case: '/usr/' etc */
        if (!(flag & (O_ACCMODE|O_CREAT|O_TRUNC))) {
                *res_inode=dir;
                return 0;
        }
        iput(dir);
        return -EISDIR;
```

```
        }
        bh = find_entry(&dir,basename,namelen,&de);      //search content item of file "hello.txt"
    through topmost i-node
    ......
    }


//code path:fs/namei.c:
static struct buffer_head * find_entry(struct m_inode ** dir,
    const char * name, int namelen, struct dir_entry ** res_dir)
{
    ......
    i = 0;
    de = (struct dir_entry *) bh->b_data;                //de points to the first address of buffer
        while (i < entries) {                            //search "hello.txt" from all directory items
                                                         //of buffer block
            if ((char *)de >= BLOCK_SIZE+bh->b_data) {        //if directory item can't be found
                brelse(bh);
                bh = NULL;
                if (!(block = bmap(*dir,i/DIR_ENTRIES_PER_BLOCK)) ||
                        !(bh = bread((*dir)->i_dev,block))) {   //continue to search
                                                               //while loading directory
                                                               //item

                    i += DIR_ENTRIES_PER_BLOCK;
                    continue;
                }
                de = (struct dir_entry *) bh->b_data;
            }
            if (match(namelen,name,de)) {        //confirm the match of directory item
*res_dir = de;                                   //if "hello.txt" is found, it is passed to pointer
                *res_dir
                return bh;
            }
            de++;
            i++;
        }
    brelse(bh);
    return NULL;                                 //"hello.txt" directory item can't be found eventually
}
```

Note that in Section 5.2.1, the mode parameter has not been used when a file is open. However, this time, it is used to set the property of the i node.

5.4.2 Create a New i node for a File

Not finding the directory item of the file "hello.txt" does not mean that the user process aims at creating a new file (maybe the path is wrong). Before creating a new i node, the system needs to check whether the flag O_CREAT is set or not. If it is set, the user process actually aims at creating a new file (the set process is introduced in Section 5.4.1). Otherwise, create a new i node for the file "hello.txt" and write new directory item information corresponding to the file "hello.txt" into the directory file named user2. Check whether this process has write permission. Then, call the function new_inode() to create a new i node and set the information such as the property of the i node.

The code is as follows:

```
//code path:fs/namei.c:
int open_namei(const char * pathname, int flag, int mode,
    struct m_inode ** res_inode)
{
    ......
    if (!(dir = dir_namei(pathname,&namelen,&basename)))   //analyze path and get i-node
        return -ENOENT;
```

```
        if (!namelen) {                         /* special case: '/usr/' etc */
                if (!(flag & (O_ACCMODE|O_CREAT|O_TRUNC))) {
                        *res_inode = dir;
                        return 0;
                }
                iput(dir);
                return -EISDIR;
        }
        bh = find_entry(&dir,basename,namelen,&de);    //find directory item of aimed file through
                                                        //topmost i-node

if (!bh) {                                       //buffer block is empty when no item is get
        if (!(flag & O_CREAT)) {                 //confirm that user actually aims at
                                                 //creating a new file
                iput(dir);
                return -ENOENT;
        }
        if (!permission(dir,MAY_WRITE)) {        //confirm that user has write permission to
                                                 //directory file "user2"
                iput(dir);
                return -EACCES;
        }
        inode = new_inode(dir->i_dev);           //create new i-node
        if (!inode) {
                iput(dir);
                return -ENOSPC;
        }
        inode->i_uid = current->euid;            //set id of i-node user
        inode->i_mode = mode;                    //set i-node as access mode
        inode->i_dirt = 1;                       //set revised flag of i-node as 1
        bh = add_entry(dir,basename,namelen,&de); //create new directory item
        if (!bh) {
                inode->i_nlinks-- ;
                iput(inode);
                iput(dir);
                return -ENOSPC;
        }
        de->inode = inode->i_num;
        bh->b_dirt = 1;
        brelse(bh);
        iput(dir);
        *res_inode = inode;
        return 0;
    }
.....
}
```

The task that the function new_inode() performs to create a new i node is divided into two steps:

1. In the i node bitmap, the bit corresponding to the new i node is identified.

2. Load part of the property information of the i node into a specified table item of inode_table[32].

The code is as follows:

```
//code path:fs/bitmap.c:
struct m_inode * new_inode(int dev)
{
    struct m_inode * inode;
    struct super_block * sb;
    struct buffer_head * bh;
    int i,j;
```

```
        if (!(inode = get_empty_inode()))  //get free i-node item in inode_table[32]
            return NULL;
        if (!(sb = get_super(dev)))             //get device super block(loaded when installing file system)
            panic("new_inode with unknown device");
//below set i-node bitmap based on information about i-node bitmap from super block
        j = 8192;
        for (i = 0 ; i<8 ; i++)
            if (bh = sb->s_imap[i])
                    if ((j = find_first_zero(bh->b_data))<8192)
                        break;
        if (!bh || j > = 8192 || j+i*8192 > sb->s_ninodes) {
            iput(inode);
            return NULL;
        }
        if (set_bit(j,bh->b_data))
            panic("new_inode: bit already set");
        //above set i-node bitmap based on information about i-node bitmap from super block
        bh->b_dirt = 1;                         //1set revised flag of buffer block where i-node bitmap is as 1
        //below set property of i-node
        inode->i_count = 1;
        inode->i_nlinks = 1;
        inode->i_dev = dev;
        inode->i_uid = current->euid;
        inode->i_gid = current->egid;
        inode->i_dirt = 1;
        inode->i_num = j + i*8192;
        inode->i_mtime = inode->i_atime = inode->i_ctime = CURRENT_TIME;
        return inode;
}
```

5.4.3 Create a New Content Item

The directory item of the file "hello.txt" is loaded into directory file user2. We first introduce the schematic diagram of the directory file (Figure 5.10).

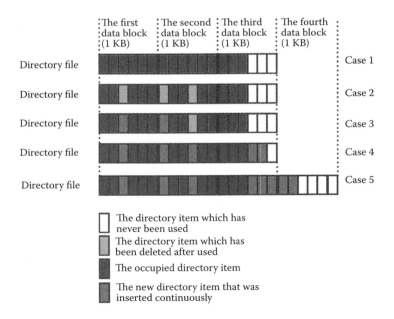

Figure 5.10 Schematic diagram of the directory file.

Situation 1 is the initial state of a content file. Situation 2 concerns deleting one of the directory items (i.e., clear the i node number of directory items as 0). Situations 3, 4, and 5 involve loading directory items continuously.

The system calls the function add_entry() to create a new directory item.

The code is as follows:

```
//code path:fs/namei.c:
int open_namei(const char * pathname, int flag, int mode,   struct m_inode **
res_inode)
{
    ......
        inode = new_inode(dir->i_dev);               //create new i-node
        if (!inode) {
                iput(dir);
                return -ENOSPC;
        }
        inode->i_uid = current->euid;               //set id of i-node user
        inode->i_mode = mode;                       //set i-node as access mode
        inode->i_dirt = 1;                          //set use-flag of i-node as 1
        bh = add_entry(dir,basename,namelen,&de);   //add directory item
        if (!bh) {
                inode->i_nlinks-  ;
                iput(inode);
                iput(dir);
                return -ENOSPC;
        }
        de->inode = inode->i_num;            //add i-node number in directory item
        bh->b_dirt = 1;
        brelse(bh);
        iput(dir);
        *res_inode = inode;
        return 0;
    }
    ......
}
```

The task of the function add_entry() is to load a new directory item if an free item can be found in the directory file. If not, the system will create a new data block in the peripherals to load. The scenario of loading is shown previously.

The code is as follows:

```
//code path:fs/namei.c:
static struct buffer_head * add_entry(struct m_inode * dir,
    const char * name, int namelen, struct dir_entry ** res_dir)    //add directory item in
                                                                    //directory file user2
{
    int block,i;
    struct buffer_head * bh;
    struct dir_entry * de;


    *res_dir = NULL;
#ifdef NO_TRUNCATE
    if (namelen > NAME_LEN)
            return NULL;
#else
    if (namelen > NAME_LEN)
            namelen = NAME_LEN;
```

```
#endif
    if (!namelen)
        return NULL;
    if (!(block = dir->i_zone[0]))                      //confirm logic block number on
//device of the first file block in directory file user2(not 0)
            return NULL;
    if (!(bh = bread(dir->i_dev,block)))        //load content of directory file into a
                                                //data block
        return NULL;
    i = 0;
    de = (struct dir_entry *) bh->b_data;
    while (1) {                                 //search idle directory item in directory file
// = = = =load next data block to continue searching when whole data block has no free item
//create new data block on device to load new content item when all have no free item = = = = = =
        if ((char *)de >= BLOCK_SIZE+bh->b_data) {
                brelse(bh);
                bh = NULL;
                block = create_block(dir,i/DIR_ENTRIES_PER_BLOCK);
                if (!block)
                        return NULL;
                if (!(bh = bread(dir->i_dev,block))) {
                        i += DIR_ENTRIES_PER_BLOCK;
                        continue;
                }
                de = (struct dir_entry *) bh->b_data;
        }
//= = = = = = = = = = = = = = = =find free item at end of data block, and load
//directory item where it is idle = = = = = = = = = = = = = = = = = = = =
        if (i*sizeof(struct dir_entry) >= dir->i_size) {
                de->inode=0;
                dir->i_size = (i+1)*sizeof(struct dir_entry);
                dir->i_dirt = 1;
                dir->i_ctime = CURRENT_TIME;
        }
//= = = = = = = = = = = = = = = = = = =find free item in middle of data block, and load
//directory item there = = = = = = = = = = = = = = = = = = = =
        if (!de->inode) {
                dir->i_mtime = CURRENT_TIME;
                for (i=0; i < NAME_LEN ; i++)
                        de->name[i]=(i<namelen)?get_fs_byte(name+i):0;
                bh->b_dirt = 1;
                *res_dir = de;
                return bh;
        }
        de++;
        i++;
    }
    brelse(bh);
    return NULL;
}
```

The code of the function create_block() is as follows:

```
//code path:fs/inode.c:
int create_block(struct m_inode * inode, int block)
{
    return _bmap(inode,block,1);
        //last parameter is creating flag,here it is set as 1,meaning
//creating new data block probably, which is different in chapter 5.3.1
}
```

After entering the function _bmp(), the code below is very important:

```
//code path:fs/inode.c:
static int _bmap(struct m_inode * inode,int block,int create)
{
    struct buffer_head * bh;
    int i;


    if (block<0)                            //if data block number of file to be operated is less
                                            //than 0
        panic("_bmap: block<0");
    if (block > = 7+512+512*512)            //if data block number of file to be operated is less
                                            //than allowable limits
        panic("_bmap: block>big");
//= = = = = = = = = = = = =not more than 7 logic blocks = = = = = = = = = = = = = = = = = = = =
    if (block<7) {                          //file block number of data block to be operated is
                                            //less than 7
        if (create && !inode->i_zone[block])    //if it is to create a new data block,
                                                //execute below code
            if (inode->i_zone[block] = new_block(inode->i_dev)) {
                inode->i_ctime = CURRENT_TIME;
                inode->i_dirt = 1;
            }
        return inode->i_zone[block];            //return value of logic block number
                                                //recorded in block item of i_zone
    }
//= = = = = = = = = = = = between 7 and (7+512) logic blocks = = = = = = = = = = = = = = = = = =
    block - = 7;
    if (block<512) {                            //if file block number of data block to be
//operated is less than 512, block number of one-level indirect search file is needed
        if (create && !inode->i_zone[7])                    //if it is to create a
//new data block, execute below code
            if (inode->i_zone[7] = new_block(inode->i_dev)) {
                inode->i_dirt = 1;
                inode->i_ctime = CURRENT_TIME;
            }
        if (!inode->i_zone[7])                  //return 0 directly if one-level block has
                                                //no index number
            return 0;
        if (!(bh = bread(inode->i_dev,inode->i_zone[7])))   //get one-level indirect block
            return 0;
        i = ((unsigned short *) (bh->b_data))[block];   //get logic block number of block
                                                        //item in direct block
        if (create && !i)                       //execute below code if it is to
                                                //create a new data block
            if (i = new_block(inode->i_dev)) {
                ((unsigned short *) (bh->b_data))[block] = i;
                bh->b_dirt = 1;
            }
        brelse(bh);
        return i;
    }
//= = = = = = = = = = between 7+512 and 7+512+512*512 logic blocks = = = = = = = = = = = = = =
    block - = 512;
    if (create && !inode->i_zone[8])            //execute below code if it is to create a
                                                //new data block
        if (inode->i_zone[8] = new_block(inode->i_dev)) {
            inode->i_dirt = 1;
            inode->i_ctime = CURRENT_TIME;
        }
    if (!inode->i_zone[8])      //return 0 if one-level indirect block has no index
        return 0;
    if (!(bh = bread(inode->i_dev,inode->i_zone[8])))       //get one-level indirect block
        return 0;
    i = ((unsigned short *)bh->b_data)[block>>9];           //get logic block number of
                                                            //block/512 item in indirect block
```

```
        if (create && !i)                                  //if it is to create a new data
                                                           //block, execute below code
            if (i = new_block(inode->i_dev)) {
                    ((unsigned short *) (bh->b_data))[block>>9] = i;
                    bh->b_dirt = 1;
            }
        brelse(bh);
        if (!i)
                return 0;
        if (!(bh = bread(inode->i_dev,i)))                 //get two-level indirect block
                return 0;
        i = ((unsigned short *)bh->b_data)[block&511];//get logic block number of block&512 item
in indirect block


        if (create && !i)                  //if it is to create a new data block, execute below code
            if (i = new_block(inode->i_dev)) {
                    ((unsigned short *) (bh->b_data))[block&511] = i;
                    bh->b_dirt = 1;
            }
        brelse(bh);
        return i;
}
```

When the create flag is set, it's not means creating a new data block without any condition. Furthermore, we should ensure that the next file block does not exist, that is, !inode->izone[......] or !i is true; thus, apply a new data block. Similar to this example, when loading the content of a directory item with no idle item found in a data block, the next data block might have one idle item. If the data block is forced to be allocated, the existing block will be overwritten, leading to directory file management confusion.

The task of creating a new data block is finished in the function new_block(). We will introduce it in detail in Section 5.5.

The scenario of creating a new directory item is shown in Figure 5.11.

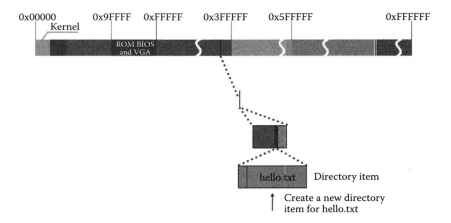

Figure 5.11 Find idle directory item and add directory data.

5.5 Writing a File

The process of writing a file by the OS is as follows: First, write data into the buffer from the process memory; then, synchronize data from the buffer to the peripherals under the appropriate conditions. Meanwhile, the OS synchronizes data in units of data block (1 KB) from the buffer (1 KB) to the peripherals. This requires the buffer and logic block need to be written in the peripherals should bind together before synchronizing. Make sure that data to be written in the buffer block of the user memory can be exactly synchronized to the specified logic block.

We first introduce how to determine the binding relationship.

5.5.1 Locate the Position of the File to Be Written In

The function write() is eventually mapped to sys_write(). This function checks the parameters. Then, call the function file_write() to write the file.

The code is as follows:

```
//code path:fs/read_write.c:
int sys_write(unsigned int fd,char * buf,int count)//write file
{


    struct file * file;
    struct m_inode * inode;


    if (fd> = NR_OPEN || count <0 || !(file = current->filp[fd]))   //whether fd, count is within
                                                                     //reasonable range and file
                                                                     //is open
        return -EINVAL;
    if (!count)                                              //f amount of bytes written
                                                            //in is 0, return directly
        return 0;
    inode = file->f_inode;
    if (inode->i_pipe)
        return (file->f_mode&2)?write_pipe(inode,buf,count):-EIO;
    if (S_ISCHR(inode->i_mode))
        return rw_char(WRITE,inode->i_zone[0],buf,count,&file->f_pos);
    if (S_ISBLK(inode->i_mode))
        return block_write(inode->i_zone[0],&file->f_pos,buf,count);
    if (S_ISREG(inode->i_mode))                             //make sure that file
                                                            //to be written is regular file
        return file_write(inode,file,buf,count);           //write file
    printk("(Write)inode->i_mode =%06o\n\r",inode->i_mode);
        return -EINVAL;
}
```

The parameter flags passed by the user process to determine the position of the data to be written. Within the function file_write(), the system checks flag f_flags to determine the position where data are written at first and then calls create_block() function, which creates a peripheral logic block corresponding to the position of this file and returns the logic block number.

The code is as follows:

```
//code path:fs/file_dev.c:
int file_write(struct m_inode * inode, struct file * filp, char * buf, int count)
{
    off_t pos;
    int block,c;
    struct buffer_head * bh;
    char * p;
    int i = 0;


/*
* ok, append may not work when many processes are writing at the same time
* but so what. That way leads to madness anyway.
*/
    if (filp->f_flags & O_APPEND)        //if you set add-write flag of the end of file
        pos = inode->i_size;             //pos is moved to the end of file
    else
        pos = filp->f_pos;               //begin to write in data directly at the position that
                                         //file pointer f_pos points to(in this example, f_pos is 0)
    while (i<count) {
        if (!(block = create_block(inode,pos/BLOCK_SIZE)))      //create logic block and
                                                                //return the number
            break;
        if (!(bh = bread(inode->i_dev,block)))           //apply for buffer block
                                                         //(no need for reading)
            break;
    ……
}
```

The code for creating a new data block corresponding to the specified i_zone[9] in the i node is as follows:

```
//code path:fs/inode.c:
int create_block(struct m_inode * inode, int block)
{
    return _bmap(inode,block,1);         //last parameter is to create flag. When it is set as
                                         //1, new block is created
}


//code path:fs/inode.c:
static int _bmap(struct m_inode * inode,int block,int create)
{
    struct buffer_head * bh;
    int i;

    if (block<0)                                    //if data block number of file to be
                                                    //operated is less than 0
        panic("_bmap: block<0");
    if (block > = 7+512+512*512)                    //if data block number of file to be
                                                    //operated is more than available maxim
        panic("_bmap: block>big");
    if (block<7) {                      //block为0if data block number "block"of data block
//file to be operated is less than 0. In this example, it is 0
        if (create && !inode->i_zone[block])                //create a new data block
                if (inode->i_zone[block] = new_block(inode->i_dev)) {//data block created
newly is corresponded to specified i_zone[9] in i-node.
                inode->i_ctime = CURRENT_TIME;
                inode->i_dirt = 1;
        }
        return inode->i_zone[block];            //return value of logic block number
                                               //recorded in item block in i_zone[9]
    }
    ……
}
```

The creation of the new block is executed in the function new_block(). The content is divided into two parts:

1. Set the bit in logic block bitmap corresponding to new created data block as 1.

2. Apply for buffer block for new created data block in buffer area, used to load contents written in.

The code is as follows:

```
//code path:fs/bitmap.c:
int new_block(int dev)//create a new data block
{
    struct buffer_head * bh;
    struct super_block * sb;
    int i,j;


    if (!(sb = get_super(dev)))              //get super block of device
        panic("trying to get new block from nonexistant device");
    j = 8192;
//= = = = = below is to set logic block bitmap of new data block based on information about
//logic block bitmap in super block
    for (i = 0 ; i<8 ; i++)
        if (bh = sb->s_zmap[i])
            if ((j = find_first_zero(bh->b_data))<8192)
                break;
    if (i> = 8 || !bh || j> = 8192)
        return 0;
    if (set_bit(j,bh->b_data))
        panic("new_block: bit already set");
//= = =above is to set logic block bitmap of new data block based on information about
//logic block bitmap in super block


    bh->b_dirt = 1;                          //set use-flag of buffer block where logic
                                             //block bitmap is as 1
    j + = i*8192 + sb->s_firstdatazone-1;    //find logic block number of data block
    if (j > = sb->s_nzones)
        return 0;
    if (!(bh = getblk(dev,j)))               //apply for new idle buffer block for new
                                             //data block in buffer area
        panic("new_block: cannot get block");
    if (bh->b_count ! = 1)
        panic("new_block: count is ! = 1");
    clear_block(bh->b_data);                 //clear data in this logic block
    bh->b_uptodate = 1;                      //set update-flag as 1
    bh->b_dirt = 1;                          //set rewrite-flag as 1
    brelse(bh);
    return j;
}
```

5.5.2 Apply for a Buffer Block

The system calls bread(). Because a new buffer block is created by the function new_block(), it is unnecessary to load the logic block from the peripherals. The code is as follows:

```
//code path:fs/file_dev.c:
int file_write(struct m_inode * inode, struct file * filp, char * buf, int count)
{
    ......
    while (i<count) {
        if (!(block = create_block(inode,pos/BLOCK_SIZE)))          //create new data block
            break;
        if (!(bh = bread(inode->i_dev,block)))                      //load buffer block
            break;
        c = pos% BLOCK_SIZE;
    ......
}


//code path:fs/buffer.c:
struct buffer_head * bread(int dev,int block)
{
    struct buffer_head * bh;
    if (!(bh = getblk(dev,block)))                  //data block is hooked to hash
                                                    //table and no need to read from peripherals
            panic("bread: getblk returned NULL\n");
    if (bh->b_uptodate)                             //set b_uptodate as 1 in
                                                    //new_block(),and return directly
            return bh;
    ll_rw_block(READ,bh);
    wait_on_buffer(bh);
    if (bh->b_uptodate)
            return bh;
    brelse(bh);
    return NULL;
}
```

5.5.3 Copy Specified Data from the Process Memory to the Buffer Block

Figure 5.12 shows an instance of copying specified data from the process memory to the buffer block.

The characters "Hello, world" is about to be written and one buffer block is enough to load it. So the while loop once runs one round.

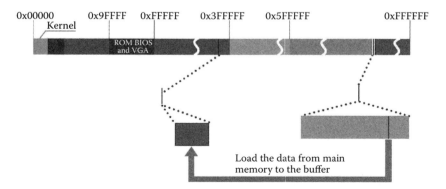

Figure 5.12 Copy data from the memory to the buffer.

The code is as follows:

```
//code path:fs/file_dev.c:
int file_write(struct m_inode * inode, struct file * filp, char * buf, int count)
{
    ......
        if (!(bh = bread(inode->i_dev,block)))          //apply for buffer block
                break;
        c = pos% BLOCK_SIZE;                            //calculate the number of bytes
                                                        //to be written into buffer block

        p = c + bh->b_data;
        bh->b_dirt = 1;
        c = BLOCK_SIZE-c;
        if (c > count-i) c = count-i;
        pos + = c;
        if (pos > inode->i_size) {
                inode->i_size = pos;
                inode->i_dirt = 1;
        }
        i + = c;
        while (c-- >0)
                *(p++) = get_fs_byte(buf++);            //write data into specified
                                                        //buffer block

        brelse(bh);
    }
    inode->i_mtime = CURRENT_TIME;
    if (!(filp->f_flags & O_APPEND)) {
        filp->f_pos = pos;
        inode->i_ctime = CURRENT_TIME;
    }
    return (i?i:-1);
}
```

At this point, data specified by the user process is not written into the hard disk, only at the buffer. Next, we talk about how to synchronize data from the buffer to the hard disk.

5.5.4 Two Ways to Synchronize Data from the Buffer to the Hard Disk

Here are two ways to synchronize data from the buffer area to the hard disk. One is regular synchronization "updata" and the other is that the OS forces synchronization because the buffer area is limited.

The first way is as follows:

It is designed such that when the shell process runs for the first time, the update process is started. This process will reside in the memory. Its function is to synchronize data from the buffer area to the peripherals.

This process will call pause(), which is eventually mapped to the function sys_pause(), resulting in the process being in an interruptible wait state. The OS will wake the updata process intervally. When it runs, call the function sync() and synchronize data from the buffer area to the peripherals.

The function sync() is eventually mapped to the system calling the function sys_sync() to run. In order to guarantee the integrity of the file synchronization contents, it needs to synchronize the file i node bitmap, the file i node, the file data block, and the logic block bitmap corresponding to data block. Sys_sync() writes the modified file i node into the buffer area (others are already in the buffer area) and then traverses the entire buffer. As soon as the content of the buffer block is modified (b_dirt is set as 1), all are synchronized to the peripherals.

The code is as follows:

```
//code path:fs/buffer.c:
int sys_sync(void)
{
    int i;
    struct buffer_head * bh;


    sync_inodes();                            //write i-node into buffer area
    bh = start_buffer;
    for (i=0 ; i<NR_BUFFERS ; i++,bh++) {     //traverse the entire buffer area
        wait_on_buffer(bh);                   //\if buffer block is in-use, wait for
                                              //unlocking this buffer block
        if (bh->b_dirt)                       //as soon as content of this buffer block
                                              //is modified
            ll_rw_block(WRITE,bh);            //synchronize content of buffer block to
                                              //peripherals
    }
    return 0;
}
```

The task that synchronizes the i node is completed by the function sync_inode().
The code is as follows:

```
//code path:fs/inode.c:
void sync_inodes(void)
{
    int i;
    struct m_inode * inode;


    inode = 0+inode_table;
    for(i=0 ; i<NR_INODE ; i++,inode++) {     //traverse all i-node
        wait_on_inode(inode);                 //if i-node traversed is in use,
                                              //wait for this i-node to be unlocked
        if (inode->i_dirt && !inode->i_pipe)  //if content of i-node has been
                                              //modified and it is not i-node of pipe file
            write_inode(inode);               //synchronize i-node to buffer area
    }
}


//code path:fs/inode.c:
static void write_inode(struct m_inode * inode)
{
    struct super_block * sb;
    struct buffer_head * bh;
    int block;


    lock_inode(inode);                        //lock up i-node to avoid
                                              //interruption
    if (!inode->i_dirt || !inode->i_dev) {
        unlock_inode(inode);
        return;
    }
    if (!(sb = get_super(inode->i_dev)))      //get super block of peripherals
        panic("trying to write inode without device");
    block = 2 + sb->s_imap_blocks + sb->s_zmap_blocks +
        (inode->i_num-1)/INODES_PER_BLOCK;    //logic block number of i-node bitmap in
                                              //peripherals
    if (!(bh = bread(inode->i_dev,block)))    //load logic block where i-node is into
                                              //buffer area
        panic("unable to read i-node block");
```

```
    ((struct d_inode *)bh->b_data)                       //synchronize i-node to buffer area
        [(inode->i_num-1)%INODES_PER_BLOCK] =
                  *(struct d_inode *)inode;
    bh->b_dirt = 1;                                       //set b_dirt of buffer block as 1
    inode->i_dirt = 0;                                    //set i_dirt of i-node as 0
    brelse(bh);
    unlock_inode(inode);                                  //unlock i-node
}
```

After synchronization is completed, the update process will be suspended, and continues to synchronize the buffer block after the next waking up.

The second way is as follows:

Example 2 is simple because data written in the buffer area is less. We may alter it slightly. The code is as follows:

```
void main()
{
    char str1[] = "Hello, world";
    int i;
    //create new file
    int fd = creat("/mnt/user/user1/user2/hello.txt",0644));
    //write in file
  for(i = 0;i<1000000;i++)
{
    int size = write(fd,str1,strlen(str1));
  }
}
```

Consider the following scenario: the data to be written is more than 10 MB, but the buffer area is certainly not more than 10 MB. How can data be written then if the buffer area is full before process update is woken up? For data to continue to be written, data in the buffer area must be forced to synchronize with the hard disk, in order to leave enough space to write on.

This task is completed by the function getblk(), introduced in Section 3.3.1.2. When all free blocks in the buffer area are unable to be written in data(b_dirt is 1), it means it needs more space.

The code is as follows:

```
//code path:fs/buffer.c:
struct buffer_head * getblk(int dev,int block)
{
    struct buffer_head * tmp, * bh;

repeat:
    if (bh = get_hash_table(dev,block))
        return bh;
    tmp = free_list;
    do {
```

```
                if (tmp->b_count)
                        continue;
                if (!bh || BADNESS(tmp)<BADNESS(bh)) {
                        bh = tmp;
                        if (!BADNESS(tmp))
                                break;
                }
/* and repeat until we find something good */
        } while ((tmp = tmp->b_next_free) != free_list);        //find free buffer block(not
                                                                //equal to b_dirt is 0)
        if (!bh) {
                sleep_on(&buffer_wait);
                goto repeat;
        }
        wait_on_buffer(bh);
        if (bh->b_count)
                goto repeat;
        while (bh->b_dirt) {                    //though there is free buffer block, buffer area has
//no usable buffer block because b_dirt is 1, and it needs to synchronically in order to more space
                sync_dev(bh->b_dev);            //synchronize data
                wait_on_buffer(bh);
                if (bh->b_count)
                        goto repeat;
        }
/* NOTE!! While we slept waiting for this block, somebody else might */
/* already have added "this" block to the cache. check it */
        if (find_buffer(dev,block))
                goto repeat;
/* OK, FINALLY we know that this buffer is the only one of it's kind, */
/* and that it's unused (b_count = 0), unlocked (b_lock = 0), and clean */
        bh->b_count=1;
        bh->b_dirt=0;
        bh->b_uptodate=0;
        remove_from_queues(bh);
        bh->b_dev=dev;
        bh->b_blocknr=block;
        insert_into_queues(bh);
        return bh;
}
```

Those are two ways to synchronize data.

They are worth discussing below.

In Section 5.5.3, the data block that p points to is newly applied so that writing data from the beginning of a specified data block does not affect existing data. However, if the file "hello.txt" is not a newly created file but an existing file, writing data in any data block that p points to will overwrite the existing data beyond the writing point in this data block (unless p points to end).

It means that the user can only add in data at the end of the file. If data is modified in the middle of the file, relying solely on the function sys_write() is not enough. Thus, how does OS handle more complex situations of modifying data? It is explained in detail below.

■ 5.6 Modifying a File

The nature of modifying files is to insert and delete data anywhere without affecting the existing data in the file. The solution to this problem is to call the functions sys_read(), sys_write(), and sys_lseek(). The functions sys_read() and sys_write() have been described in Sections 5.3 and 5.5. Now, we will first introduce the function sys_lseek() and then describe how to use it in combination with the other functions.

5.6.1 Reposition the Current Operation Pointer of the File

The user processes call the function lseek() to reposition the current operation f_pos; it is eventually mapped to the function sys_lseek() to execute.

The code is as follows:

```
//the code path:include/Unistd.h:
#define SEEK_SET    0 //indicate that shift from the start of the file
#define SEEK_CUR    1 //indicate that shift from the current place
#define SEEK_END    2 //indicate that shift from the end of the file


//the code path:fs/read_write.c:
int sys_lseek(unsigned int fd,off_t offset, int origin)
//adjust the file operation pointe, offset is the bytes shifted from f_pos to the end of the
//file
{
    struct file * file;
    int tmp;


    if (fd >= NR_OPEN || !(file=current->filp[fd]) || !(file->f_inode)
    || !IS_SEEKABLE(MAJOR(file->f_inode->i_dev)))
        return -EBADF;
    if (file->f_inode->i_pipe)
        return -ESPIPE;
    switch (origin) {
        case 0:             //set the file starting place as the starting point, set
                            //file->f_pos
                    if (offset<0) return -EINVAL;
                    file->f_pos=offset;
                    break;
        case 1:             //set file->f_pos as the current file operation place
                    if (file->f_pos+offset<0) return -EINVAL;
                    file->f_pos += offset;
                    break;
        case 2:             //set the file ending place as the starting point,set
                            //file->f_pos
                    if ((tmp = file->f_inode->i_size+offset) < 0)
                            return -EINVAL;
                    file->f_pos = tmp;
                    break;
        default:
                    return -EINVAL;
    }
    return file->f_pos;
}
```

5.6.2 Modifying Files

Now, let us assume that hello.txt is an existing file in your hard disk, and its content is "Hello,world." Here, using sys_read(), sys_write(), and sys_lseek() in combination, we insert the data to the file hello.txt.

The code is as follows:

```
#include <fcntl.h>
#include <stdio.h>
#include <string.h>
```

```
#define LOCATION 6

int main(char argc, char **argv)
{
    char str1[] = "Linux";
    char str2[1024];
    int fd, size;

    memset(str2, 0, sizeof(str2));
    fd = open("hello.txt", O_RDWR, 0644);
    lseek(fd, LOCATION, SEEK_SET);
    strcpy(str2, str1);
    size = read(fd, str2+5, 6);


    lseek(fd, LOCATION, SEEK_SET);
    size = write(fd, str2, strlen(str2));


close(fd);
return 0;
}
```

This program is to insert the string "Linux" into the hello.txt file; eventually, the hello. txt file should be "Hello, Linuxworld."

```
fd = open("hello.txt", O_RDWR, 0644);
```

The function open() maps to the function sys_open() and opens the file you will operate.

```
lseek(fd, LOCATION, SEEK_SET);
```

The function lseek() maps to the function sys_lseek(); the third parameter is SEEK_SET, which indicates that the current operation pointer is 6 bytes from the beginning of the file.

```
strcpy(str2, str1);
```

This line means copy string "Linux" to the beginning of the array str2[1024].

```
size = read(fd, str2+5, 6);
```

The function read() maps to the function sys_read(); it reads the content of the file hello.txt. The parameter "str2+5" means to copy the content of the file hello.txt to the sixth element of the array str2. The parameter "6" indicates that it will read out the file's six characters. The function lseek(FD, LOCATION, SEEK_SET) has shifted the current operation pointer to 6 bytes from the beginning of the file; hence, the content to be read out is the string "world." Finally, the result is "Linuxworld."

```
lseek(fd, LOCATION, SEEK_SET);
```

This line is the same as the earlier one. They changed the current operation pointer to determine where to write the files.

```
size = write(fd, str2, strlen(str2));
```

The function write() maps to the function sys_write(). It writes the string "Linuxworld" to the file hello.txt, and the final result is "Hello, Linuxworld."

Example 3: close the file and then remove it from the file system. We may rewrite the code in Section 5.6. The new code is as follows:

```
#include <fcntl.h>
#include <stdio.h>
#include <string.h>

#define LOCATION 6

int main(char argc, char **argv)
{
    char str1[] = "Linux";
    char str2[1024];
    int fd, size;

    memset(str2, 0, sizeof(str2));
    fd = open("/mnt/user/user1/user2/hello.txt", O_RDWR, 0644);
    lseek(fd, LOCATION, SEEK_SET);
    strcpy(str2, str1);
    size = read(fd, str2+5, 6);

    lseek(fd, LOCATION, SEEK_SET);
    size = write(fd, str2, strlen(str2));

    //close the file
    close(fd);
    //delete the file
    unlink("/mnt/user/user1/user2/hello.txt");
    return 0;
}
```

▮ 5.7 Closing a File

Closing a file is completed by close().

5.7.1 Disconnecting Filp and File_table[64] in the Current Process

The function close() maps to the function sys_close(), and it disconnects the current processes' file_table[64] and *filp[20] in the task_struct, as shown in Figure 5.13.

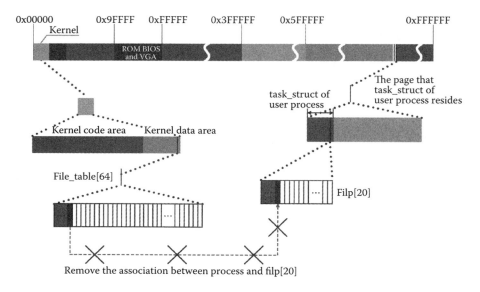

Figure 5.13 Overview of closing a file.

The code is as follows:

```
//the code path:fs/open.c:
int sys_close(unsigned int fd)
{
    struct file * filp;

    if (fd > = NR_OPEN)
        return -EINVAL;
    current->close_on_exec & = ~(1<<fd);
    if (!(filp = current->filp[fd]))
        return -EINVAL;
    current->filp[fd] = NULL;        //set fd in filp[20] to NULL
    if (filp->f_count = = 0)
        panic("Close: file count is 0");
    if (- filp->f_count)  //decline the file handle reference counting in
                          //file_table[64]
return (0);
    iput(filp->f_inode);  //disconnecting the node i with file_table[64]
    return (0);
}
```

Note:

The structure file_table[64] manages all file operations. Other processes may be in operation on the file hello.txt at this time and use the same structure (which we have introduced in Section 5.2.1). Filp->f_count reduces the reference count, instead of being simply emptied. Of course, in example 3, if there is no process operating on the file, filp->f_count will decrease to 0 and the list item in file_table[64] becomes free.

5.7.2 Releasing the Files' i node

The releasing procedure is as follows: First, by checking the various properties of the i node, in example 3, one can determine whether the contents of the i node have been changed. Therefore, the i node should be synced to the specified buffer block at first. Then, by decreasing i_count to 0, the i node in inode_table[32] becomes available.

The code is as follows:

```
//the code path:fs/open.c:
void iput(struct m_inode * inode)        //releasing the i-node of files
{
    if (!inode)
        return;
    wait_on_inode(inode);                //the i-node is probably being used, so waiting
if (!inode->i_count)                     //if the releasing i-node's reference count is 0
        panic("iput: trying to free free inode");
    if (inode->i_pipe) {                 //if the i-node is a pipe file's i-node
wake_up(&inode->i_wait);
        if (-- inode->i_count)
            return;
        free_page(inode->i_size);
        inode->i_count = 0;
        inode->i_dirt = 0;
        inode->i_pipe = 0;
        return;
    }
    if (!inode->i_dev) {                 //if the device number is 0
        inode->i_count-- ;               //decline the count
        return;
    }
    if (S_ISBLK(inode->i_mode)) {        //if the i-node is a block device file's i-node
        sync_dev(inode->i_zone[0]);      //sync it to the peripheral
        wait_on_inode(inode);
    }
repeat:
    if (inode->i_count>1) {              //the reference count of i-node is bigger then 1
        inode->i_count-- ;               //decline the count


        return;
    }
    if (!inode->i_nlinks) {              //if the i-node's link count is 0
        truncate(inode);                 //release all the logical block of the i-node
        free_inode(inode);               //release this i-node
        return;
    }
    if (inode->i_dirt) {
//for this case,the content of the i-node is changed, sync it to the peripheral
write_inode(inode); /* we can sleep - so do again */
        wait_on_inode(inode);
        goto repeat;
    }
    inode->i_count-- ;                   //decline the i-node's reference count
    return;
}
```

■ 5.8 Deleting a File

Deleting files is different from closing files. Closing files only disconnects the binding point in file_table[64] of current process with the file hello.txt, but deleting a file means all the processes in the computer would have no access to the file.

Tip:

In Linux 0.11, using the system call sys_link to set the path "/mnt/user/Zhang/chengxu.c" pointing to the path "/mnt/user/hello.txt" file is permitted, and it is similar to the shortcuts under Windows. It allows different users to build their own familiar path name and file name to access the files they want, rather than having to remember the original path name. In the i node, use the i_nlinks to identify how many path names (directory) link to a file. When establishing such a link, i_nlinks increases by 1.

5.8.1 Checking the Deleting Conditions of Files

In example 3, the function unlink() eventually maps to the sys_unlink() system call. Getting the i node of the file hello.txt and then checking the information of the file's property and permissions will determine whether the file can be deleted.

The code is as follows:

```
//the code path:fs/namei.c:
int sys_unlink(const char * name)
{
    const char * basename;
    int namelen;
    struct m_inode * dir, * inode;
    struct buffer_head * bh;
    struct dir_entry * de;

    if (!(dir = dir_namei(name,&namelen,&basename)))
//analysing the path name, finding the topmost i-node of the deleting files
        return -ENOENT;
    if (!namelen) {                              //if namelen is 0
        iput(dir);                               //release the topmost i-node
        return -ENOENT;
    }
    if (!permission(dir,MAY_WRITE)) {
//if the user process has no writing authority to the file
        iput(dir);                               //release the topmost i-node
        return -EPERM;
    }
    bh = find_entry(&dir,basename,namelen,&de);  //get the file's directory entry
    if (!bh) {
        iput(dir);
        return -ENOENT;
    }
    if (!(inode = iget(dir->i_dev, de->inode))) {
//get the i-node of the deleting file
        iput(dir);
        brelse(bh);
        return -ENOENT;
    }
    if ((dir->i_mode & S_ISVTX) && !suser() &&
        current->euid != inode->i_uid &&
        current->euid != dir->i_uid) {
//if the user process has no writing authority to the file
        iput(dir);   //release the topmost i-node
        iput(inode); //release the i-node of the target file
        brelse(bh);
        return -EPERM;
    }
    if (S_ISDIR(inode->i_mode)) {                //if the target file is a directory file
        iput(inode);                             //release the i-node of the target file
        iput(dir);                               //release the topmost i-node
        brelse(bh);
        return -EPERM;
    }
    if (!inode->i_nlinks) {
```

```
//if this i-node's link is 0, then set it to 1
        printk("Deleting nonexistent file (%04x:%d),%d\n",
               inode->i_dev,inode->i_num,inode->i_nlinks);
        inode->i_nlinks=1;
    }
//the following delete the files
    de->inode = 0;
    bh->b_dirt = 1;
    brelse(bh);
    inode->i_nlinks-  ;
    inode->i_dirt = 1;
    inode->i_ctime = CURRENT_TIME;
    iput(inode);
    iput(dir);
    return 0;
}
```

5.8.2 Specific Deleting Work

The process of deleting the hello.txt file is shown in Figure 5.14.

The code is as follows:

```
//the code path:fs/namei.c:
int sys_unlink(const char * name)
{
    const char * basename;
    int namelen;
    struct m_inode * dir, * inode;
    struct buffer_head * bh;
    struct dir_entry * de;

    ......
    //the following delete the files
    de->inode = 0;                         //clear the directory item of hello.txt in user2
    bh->b_dirt = 1;                        //set the buffer block b_dirt to 1
    brelse(bh);
    inode->i_nlinks-  ;                    //decline the links of the target file
    inode->i_dirt = 1;                     //set the target file's i-node to 1
    inode->i_ctime = CURRENT_TIME;
    iput(inode);                           //release the i-node of file hello.txt
    iput(dir);                             //release the i-node of user2 directory file
    return 0;
}
```

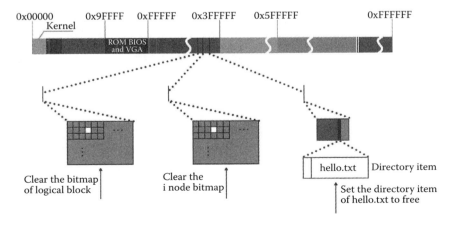

Figure 5.14 Delete the file hello.txt.

Note that the execution of the function iput() is different from that in Section 5.7.2.
The code is as follows:

```
//the code path:fs/open.c:
void iput(struct m_inode * inode)          //release the target file's i-node
{
    ......
repeat:
    if (inode->i_count>1) {                //the reference count of i-node is bigger than 1
        inode->i_count- ;                  //decline the reference count


        return;
    }
    if (!inode->i_nlinks) {
//now, the link number is 0, it means there is no process connecting to the i-node
        truncate(inode);
//according to i-node's i_zone[9], release the logical block of the file
        free_inode(inode);
//clear the bit in the i-node's bitmap, and clear the inode_table[32]
        return;
    }
    if (inode->i_dirt) {
//for this example, the content of i-node has changed, sync it to peripheral
        write_inode(inode); /* we can sleep - so do again */
        wait_on_inode(inode);
        goto repeat;
    }
    inode->i_count- ;                      //decline the i-node's referenc
    return;
}
```

The system calls the function truncate(), according to the i node's i_zone[9], and releases all logic blocks of the file on the peripherals.
The code is as follows:

```
//the code path:fs/open.c:
void truncate(struct m_inode * inode)
{
    int i;

    if (!(S_ISREG(inode->i_mode) || S_ISDIR(inode->i_mode)))
//if the file hello.txt is not a normal or directory file
        return;                //return directly
    for (i=0;i<7;i++)
        if (inode->i_zone[i]) {
                free_block(inode->i_dev,inode->i_zone[i]);
//set the former 7 bit of i_zone to 0
                inode->i_zone[i]=0;
        }
    free_ind(inode->i_dev,inode->i_zone[7]);
//set the logical blocks of level 1 indirect block and the manager
//logical block to 0
    free_dind(inode->i_dev,inode->i_zone[8]);
//set the logical blocks of level 2 indirect block and the manager
//logical block to 0

    inode->i_zone[7] = inode->i_zone[8] = 0;
    inode->i_size = 0;
    inode->i_dirt = 1;
    inode->i_mtime = inode->i_ctime = CURRENT_TIME;
}
```

The system calls the function free_inode() to clear the i node bitmap and table item. The code is as follows:

```
//the code path:fs/bitmap.c:
void free_inode(struct m_inode * inode)
{
        struct super_block * sb;
        struct buffer_head * bh;


        if (!inode)                 //if the i-node is NULL
                return;
        if (!inode->i_dev) {        //if the device number is 0
                memset(inode,0,sizeof(*inode));
                return;
        }
        if (inode->i_count>1) {     //if the i-node is multiple referenced
                printk("trying to free inode with count =%d\n",inode->i_count);
                panic("free_inode");
        }
        if (inode->i_nlinks)        //if the i-node is connected to the process
                panic("trying to free inode with links");
        if (!(sb = get_super(inode->i_dev)))
//if the i-node's file system has no superblock
                panic("trying to free inode on nonexistent device");
        if (inode->i_num < 1 || inode->i_num > sb->s_ninodes) //check i-node number
                panic("trying to free inode 0 or nonexistant inode");
        if (!(bh = sb->s_imap[inode->i_num>>13]))
//if the i-node's has no bitmap
                panic("nonexistent imap in superblock");
        if (clear_bit(inode->i_num&8191,bh->b_data))
//clear the bit corresponding to hello.txt in the i-node's bitmap
                printk("free_inode: bit already cleared.\n\r");
        bh->b_dirt = 1;
//set the buffer block b_dirt to 1
        memset(inode,0,sizeof(*inode));
//clear the file hello.txt's i-node to 0 in the i-node table
}
```

The OS syncs the emptied i node bitmap, logical block bitmap, and i node table information to your hard disk (but does not clear its content in the logical block). These are management information from the file hello.txt. This information are no longer exists, and even if the logical block contents of file were stored in the hard disk, you would no longer have access to them.

6 The User Process and Memory Management

The important feature of modern operating systems is that they support real-time multitasking, that is, running multiple programs simultaneously. The running programs are called processes. In the viewpoint of the designers of the UNIX system, the core of the operating system is the process, the so-called OS is actually a number of running processes. According to this principle, the creation of process can only be borne by process, that is, the parent-child process creation mechanism. In any case, there is at least one process in the OS, that is, process 0. Also, a special process is responsible for users interacting with the computer, that is, the shell process. In short, everything is the process.

When one computer has only one with only one core, the essence of multiple processes running simultaneously is time shared running by turn. To ensure multiple processes running at the same time in a correct way, you must solve two key issues: one is how to prevent one process's code and data from interacting with another; the other is how to make it possible for the multiple process to run in an orderly way.

The first problem involves the protection of the process, and the second problem is for scheduling of the process.

In Intel IA-32 architecture, process protection embodies the protection of the memory space, and protection of process memory space is achieved by linear address protection and physical address protection.

■ 6.1 Linear Address Protection

Now, computers basically follow the Von Neumann system. In the system, instruction and data are stored in the same memory. Memory designed as random-access memory (RAM) can read and write data or instructions arbitrarily. When there is no protected mode, different user program codes and data have no physical difference; they are formed by a series of 0s and 1s. There is no mechanism to stop mutual interference between different user programs.

When supporting real-time multitasking, the first problem is how to ensure that every process has no interference with other processes, that is, ensure one process has no access to the other process's codes and data.

6.1.1 Patterns of the Process Linear Address Space

In the intel IA-32 CPU architecture, as long as it opens PE and PG, all programs that are running on your computer use only the linear address and turn it into a physical address; the conversion is done by the hardware automatically.

The linear address is the address that the CPU can address. Under the IA-32 architecture, the linear address space ranges from 0 to 4 GB when the address bus is 32-bit. In order to separate the address memory space, Linux 0.11 separates the 4 GB linear address space into 64 portions; every portion is 64 MB, and every process owns one portion, up to open 64 processes. It requires that the process cannot cross the starting point and the ending point. In this way, the linear address space of the processes are not overlapping each other, achieving the protection of process memory space. This is the core design of OS Linux 0.11; any other designs should be subordinated to this pattern.

Task[64] is the basic point of this pattern; the registration and cancellation of all processes are centrally managed by it; only positioned in task[64], a process can be arranged in linear address space. According to nr in task[64], the OS can find corresponding LDT in the GDT. Task[64] has a key role to control the total processes and connect the process with LDT and TSS in the GDT.

Although planning out the 64 divided 4 GB equally in the linear address space's structure, can it effectively stop the visit of access across a 64 MB linear address space? In other words, can it ensure that the linear address spaces of the process do not overlap each other?

While operating system kernels make out a structure about the linear address space of process, it cannot only rely on algorithms and controlling logic to block cross-boundary processes. The reason is that CPU can perform only one instruction at a time, furthermore, it cannot execute kernel instruction when it is implementing the instruction of process. So, no matter how beautiful the algorithm to control cross-boundary processes, it isn't executing, and it can't control cross-boundary processes when the process implement visits a cross-boundary process.

The software does not work; it can only rely on the hardware.

Intel IA-32 architecture designed a method that was based on the hardware of the CPU process control method of access across borders.

6.1.2 Segment Base Addresses, Segment Limit, GDT, LDT, and Privilege Level

The protection of Intel IA-32 to the linear address space is based on the segment.

Historically, as the function (subroutine) link needed, the divide segment method in memory was invented. All designs are based on segments. Linear address space is one-dimensional, so we only need to look at both ends of a linear address space, making the procedure work in segment space without overstepping the boundary; it won't interfere with other segments.

Early Intel CPUs, in order to reduce costs, were only designed with the starting position of head register without an ending register. In order to compatible with early CPUs, Intel IA-32 (head) structure designed a segment limit in head register. One register acts as two registers.

With the help of Intel IA-32 CPU architecture providing a segment base and limit, the Linux 0.11 operating system stops the crossing of the border behavior in the segments. For example, JMP x, if x is large and exceeds a limit, hardware will block this act and report a general protection (GP) fault immediately.

To the ljmp code across segment boundaries in the process, the base address and segment limit cannot prevent the 1jmp crossing boundary process code. What method does the Linux 0.11 operating system use to block illegal access across a process?

There are two ways of illegally crossing the border. One is one process crosses to another process illegally; the other is a process crosses into the kernel.

One process crossing to another process illegally. From a IA-32 perspective, 1jmp instructions illegally cross one process to another, the code segments of two processes are all 3 privilege level, and all the processes of Linux 0.11 are arranged in a linear address space of 4 GB. So, this 1jmp instruction is permitted to execute. Segment base addresses and limits can't prevent illegal trans-border effects. Linux 0.11 stopped illegal ljmp instruction execution, which was supported by LDT.

In Chapter 2, we explained GDT, LDT's design of the Linux 0.11 operating system. There are 64 processes, and each process consumes two GDT items: one TSS; another is LDT. All processes of LDT are designed the same. Each LDT has three items; the first item is empty, the second is the process of the code segment, and the third is the process data segment. If there is an illegal cross-process jump instruction in the process code, for example, when the ljmp instruction executes, the following instruction operation is "offset within segment selectors." Segment selectors of the code segments are inside the CS. Look carefully; it can be seen that the content of all processes CS are same in Linux 0.11 operating system; in the binary expressed form it is: 0000000000001111. CPU hardware is unable to identify CS belongs to any process, so it isn't able to select the specific segment descriptor, and only can use the current LDT as default segment descriptors. As the ljmp instructions, which can jmp between segments, no matter how the operands are written, it is unable to cross the current process code, and it also will not be able to jump between segments; it is only the implementation of this segment. This shows that Linux 0.11 designs what appears to be duplicate of LDT, but genius.

Imagine if Linux 0.11 is not designed as this, but write all the code segment descriptors of process directly into the GDT. To the Linux 0.11, all processes share a 4 GB linear address space; the illegal jump instruction across processes can be performed unimpeded.

According to this thinking, you can see that Linux 0.11 is not very good in preventing illegal long jumps between processes. We have introduced TSS and LDT in the Chapter 2 that the limits of them are the same, 104 B; the limit for TSS is appropriate but too long for LDT; LDT has only three entries; each entry is 8 bytes; the total is only 24 B. We can see from the INIT_TASK of process 0 that the LDT is immediately followed by TSS, and this data structure would be given to the child process when it is created, so all process's LDT and TSS in the task_struct are the same. If the process code is like this:

Ljmp offsets, CS (CS is 0000000000111111, namely: privilege level in the 3, LDT table of the 8th).

This instruction will still be performed within a segment, and the content of LDT base with offset 8 is unpredictable; occurring errors are unpredictable. No matter what the errors, they are unable to cross process boundaries nor to change the LDT.

Looking at this issue in turn, even if an illegal long jump instruction across the process can be executed, just the code jump, data, and stack segments do not transform. Code executes in one process, and data and stack execute in another process under these conditions, and the code will generally perform dead. From the reverse angle, we can gain a deeper understanding of why the normal process of switching is using TSS to transform all code, data, and stack. To make a correct process switch, you must save the execution state of the process and switch to another process fully and completely.

The above explanation describes how to use ljmp illegal crossing from one process to another process, and a procedure is discussed below about ljmp crossing into the kernel illegally.

Crossing into the kernel from an illegal process. The user process privilege level is 3, and the kernel privilege level is 0. Intel IA-32 forbids the program to jump across the privileged level, and privilege level 3 jumps to privilege level 0 are forbidden. Also, privilege level 0 jumps to privilege level 3 are forbidden. So it is clear that the CPU would prevent the long jump effectively, and the border of the processes and kernel has an effective protection. The code of privilege level 0 has access to the data of privilege level 3; however, the code of privilege level 3 has no access to the data of privilege level 0. These prohibitions are very rigid by hardware.

As is seen from the explanation above, the settings of GDT and LDT could prevent the illegal visiting of one process to another. Could a user process modify the GDT and LDT? The answer is no. Because Linux 0.11 put the GDT and LDT structures into the kernel data area, they are at the privilege level 0, and only privilege level 0 code can modify them.

However, could a user process create the GDT and LDT in their own data segment based on their willingness? If they only form a set of data structures like GDT and LDT, it's, of course, OK, but they can't play the real role of GDT and LDT. The real GDT and LDT must be recognized by the CPU, both their first addresses should be hooked on the CPU's GDTR, LDTR, in the running time, and the CPU only recognizes the data structures that the GDTR and LDTR point to, even if there are other data structures called GDT and LDT that the CPU cannot recognize. The Linux 0.11 kernel attached GDT, LDT to GDTR, LDTR at the initialization phase of the process.

Can user processes attach their own GDT, LDT to GDTR, LDTR? The answer is no. Because the set instructions of LGDT and LLDT, which load GDTR and LDTR respectively, they could only run in the privilege level 0.

Now, we can see clearly that the Linux operating system designs a set of hardware protection mechanisms based on the Intel IA-32 architecture, including the segment base address, segment limit, GDT, LDT and privilege. It creates a solid boundary between process and process and process and kernel in the linear address and prevents the illegal visit from being effective.

Then, how to solve the reasonable data communication across the border between processes? How to operate it when switching between processes or when the process needs the reasonable support of the operating system kernel?

The first question, we will introduce in Chapter 8 on communication between processes. The second question relates to a TSS and CPU hardware interrupt.

The process switching of Linux 0.11 is completed by schedule()?, and its technology route likes the task gate (but not the task gate). It is in the privilege level 0, using instruction ljmp jump directly to the TSS of switching process (it seems strange to jump from instruction to data, but actually, the CPU does a lot of the work, eventually jumping to the target process's code segment) to achieve process switching.

When the processes want to be supported by the kernel (such as read), it can use the interrupt technique that the Intel IA-32 architecture provides, which could support the jump from privilege level 3 to privilege level 0. Note that the jump is not an ordinary jump; it requires the CPU's interrupt mechanism, unlike the flat, normal jump in memory address. Once you have been supported by the kernel, use the iret instruction to jump from privilege level 0 to privilege level 3 to continue your own process.

▇ 6.2 Paging

6.2.1 Linear Address to Physical Address

Previously, we introduced linear address, and the linear address has to convert to a physical address eventually. Linux 0.11 open PG before idling, the linear address mapped to the physical address through the three mapping modes of page directory table - page table - page. Code is shown below:

```
//Code path:boot/head.s:
......
        xorl %eax,%eax     /* pg_dir is at 0x0000 */
        movl %eax,%cr3     /* cr3 - page directory start */
        movl %cr0,%eax
        orl $0x80000000,%eax
        movl %eax,%cr0     /* set paging (PG) bit */     //set CR0, open PG
        ret                /* this also flushes prefetch-queue */
......
```

Through the introduction in the first chapter, we learned that PE has already opened before opening the PG and switched to protected mode. The CPU hardware default, in protected mode, the linear address equally maps to the physical address. If you open the PG, the linear address needs to be resolved through the MMU and mapped to the physical address through the three mapping modes of page directory table - page table - page.

In protected mode, whether opened PG, the influence of the linear address map to the physical address is shown in Figure 6.1.

Why does Linux 0.11 open PG? We have introduced that in the IA-32 system the linear address space ranges from 0 to 4 GB and has been divided equally by 64 processes; each has 64 MB, and if the PG is not open, the linear address can only map to the physical address on the basis of the CPU default rules, and Linux 0.11 only supports 16 MB physical

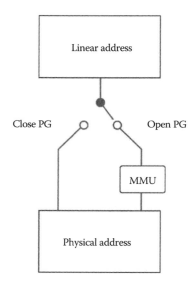

Figure 6.1 Influence of PG on linear address mapping.

memory, so apparently most of the linear address space are wasted and cannot support multiple processes executed simultaneously, so the open PG, according to the actual carrying capacity of the physical memory, maps the linear address of the process to the physical address, in order to support multiple process execution.

The progress of linear address mapping to the physical address is like this: The value of each linear address is 32, and the MMU identifies a linear address value according to the 10-10-12 length and analyzes it to the page directory item number, page table item number, the page offset, and finally maps to the physical address. The progress is shown in Figure 6.2.

Linux 0.11 only has a page directory table; the CR3 stores the base address of the page directory table. The MMU should find out the information in CR3 when analyzing the linear address; then it can find the page directory table and have the following resolution, so the most important thing is to make the page directory table base address load to the CR3 before opening the PG.

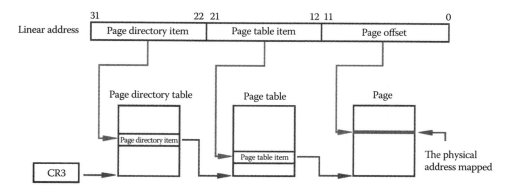

Figure 6.2 Linear address mapping to a physical page based on page directory, page table.

Code is shown in below:

```
//Code path:boot/head.s:
......
        stosl           /* fill pages backwards - more efficient :-) */
        subl $0x1000,%eax
        jge 1b
        xorl%eax,%eax   /* pg_dir is at 0x0000 */
        movl%eax,%cr3   /* cr3 - page directory start */ //load the base
//address 0 of page directory table to CR3
        movl%cr0,%eax
        orl $0x80000000,%eax
        movl%eax,%cr0   /* set paging (PG) bit */      //set CR0, open PG
        ret             /* this also flushes prefetch-queue */
    ......
```

We can find the page directory item in the page directory table through parsing the page directory item's 10 bits of data of the linear address value. The page directory item records the physical address of the page table, and we can find the location of the page table accordingly. Then we can find the page table item through parsing the 10 bits of data of the linear address value which represents the page table item. Similarly, the page table item records the physical address value of the page, and we can find the location of the page; then we can eventually find the physical address after analyzing the 12 bit in the linear address value which represents the value of page offset.

The page directory table, page tables, and the page's three mapping relationships are established by the kernel, and the kernel establishes the mapping relationship that allows a different linear address to map to a different physical address and can also map to the same physical address. Next we take the execution of the process and paging, for example, to describe the different linear address mapping to the different physical address.

6.2.2 Process Execution Paging

The kernel needs to be enough to do the following when paging and mapping to the physical page.

1. It can only allocate a new page from the free page and cannot be assigned the page that is being used by other processes and interfere with the execution of other processes. The page of the kernel area cannot be diverted for other purposes.

We learned from the introduction of the second chapter, the kernel manages to page more than 1 MB memory space through a mem_map structure before idling, and the reference count of each page in the main memory is initialized to 0, which defaults to the free pages.

The code is shown below:

```
//Code path:mm/memory.c:
......
#define LOW_MEM 0x100000                              //1MB
#define PAGING_MEMORY (15*1024*1024)
```

```
#define PAGING_PAGES (PAGING_MEMORY>>12)                  //the total
                                                          //number of page
#define MAP_NR(addr) (((addr)-LOW_MEM)>>12)
#define USED 100
......
void mem_init(long start_mem, long end_mem)
{
        int i;

        HIGH_MEMORY = end_mem;
        for (i=0 ; i<PAGING_PAGES ; i++)
                mem_map[i] = USED;
        i = MAP_NR(start_mem);
        end_mem -= start_mem;
        end_mem >>= 12;
        while (end_mem-- >0)                    //Set reference count to 0
                mem_map[i++]=0;
}
```

It only operates in the control range of mem_map when allocating a page for process and only selects the page with reference count 0. If applied successfully, it will set the reference count to 1 to prevent diverting for other purposes and causing confusion.

The code is shown below:

```
//Code path:mm/memory.c:
......
#define PAGING_MEMORY (15*1024*1024)    //don't proceed page management below 1MB
......
#define MAP_NR(addr) (((addr)-LOW_MEM)>>12)
......
unsigned long get_free_page(void)
{
register unsigned long __res asm("ax");


__asm__("std ; repne ; scasb\n\t"    //only choose the page with reference count 0
        "jne 1f\n\t"
        "movb $1,1(%%edi)\n\t"       //set reference count to 1 after apply
        "sall $12,%%ecx\n\t"
        "addl %2,%%ecx\n\t"
        ......
        "1:"
        :"=a" (__res)
        :"0" (0),"i" (LOW_MEM),"c" (PAGING_PAGES),
        "D" (mem_map+PAGING_PAGES-1)          //find the empty page in the limits
                                              //of mem_map managed
        :"di","cx","dx");
return __res;
}
```

If it is not assigned a page, it will intervene forcibly to terminate the execution.

```
//Code path:kernel/fork.c:
int copy_process(int nr,long ebp,long edi,long esi,long gs,long none,
                 long ebx,long ecx,long edx,
                 long fs,long es,long ds,
                 long eip,long cs,long eflags,long esp,long ss)
{
        ......
        struct task_struct *p;
        int i;
        struct file *f;
        p = (struct task_struct *) get_free_page(); //assign free page for
//task_struct process and kernel stack
        if (!p)              //if not assgin page, return error, stop execution
                return -EAGAIN;
        task[nr] = p;
        *p = *current;       /* NOTE! this doesn't copy the supervisor stack */
        ......
}


int copy_page_tables(unsigned long from,unsigned long to,long size)
{
        unsigned long * from_page_table;
        unsigned long * to_page_table;
        unsigned long this_page;
        unsigned long * from_dir, * to_dir;
        unsigned long nr;
{
......
        if (!(1 & *from_dir))
                continue;
        from_page_table = (unsigned long *) (0xfffff000 & *from_dir);
        if (!(to_page_table = (unsigned long *) get_free_page())) //apply free
//page for the copying page table
                return -1;          /* Out of memory, see freeing */  //if not apply,
//return -1,stop execution
        *to_dir = ((unsigned long) to_page_table) | 7;
        nr = (from==0)?0xA0:1024;
        ......
}


void do_no_page(unsigned long error_code,unsigned long address)
{
        ......
        if (share_page(tmp))
                return;
        if (!(page = get_free_page()))     //apply free page for the process
                                           //loading program
                oom();                     //if not apply, exit the process
/* remember that 1 block is used for header */
        block = 1 + tmp/BLOCK_SIZE;
        for (i=0 ; i<4 ; block++,i++)
                nr[i] = bmap(current->executable,block);
        ......
}
```

```
static inline volatile void oom(void)
{
        printk("out of memory\n\r");
        do_exit(SIGSEGV);                              //exit the process
}


#define PAGING_MEMORY (15*1024*1024)    //don't proceed page management below
                                        //1MB
......
#define MAP_NR(addr) (((addr)-LOW_MEM)>>12)
......
unsigned long get_free_page(void)
{
register unsigned long __res asm("ax");
__asm__("std ; repne ; scasb\n\t"
    "jne 1f\n\t"
    ......
    "1:"
    :"=a" (__res)
    :"0" (0),"i" (LOW_MEM),"c" (PAGING_PAGES),
    "D" (mem_map+PAGING_PAGES-1) //find the empty page in the limit of mem_map
    :"di","cx","dx");
return __res;
}
```

2. When to apply a new page to the process and when you should not.

From the introduction to the first chapter, we learn that the last three bits of each page directory entry and page table entry mark the properties of the page (a page table itself also takes a page) that it manages. They are U/S, R/W, and P. Determining whether to apply a page is determined when parsing the linear address, and the key depends on P flag.

A page directory entry or page table entry, if it relates to a page, the P flag will be set to 1. If not create a mapping relationship, the flag is 0. The linear address value will be parsed by the MMU when executing a process. If you parse out a table P bit to 0, it indicates that the item doesn't have a corresponding page and will generate a page fault. The page fault which we introduced earlier generated. If the P bit is 1, it indicates the entry corresponding to the specific page. It can find the specific page according to the address value recorded in the item. So this bit is very important. The designer must ensure that this bit of information is clear when designing the kernel and definitely not a garbage value because the garbage value is equal to the error.

It sets a page directory table and four page tables to 0, and sets P-bit to 1 when paging for kernel.

```
//Code path:boot/head.s:
......
setup_paging:                       //clear 0
    movl $1024*5,%ecx               /* 5 pages - pg_dir+4 page tables */
    xorl %eax,%eax
    xorl %edi,%edi                  /* pg_dir is at 0x000 */
    cld;rep;stosl
    movl $pg0+7,_pg_dir             /* set present bit/user r/w */
```

```
        movl $pg1+7,_pg_dir+4          /*- - - - - " "- - - - - */
        movl $pg2+7,_pg_dir+8          /*- - - - - " "- - - - - */
        movl $pg3+7,_pg_dir+12         /*- - - - - " "- - - - - */
        movl $pg3+4092,%edi
        movl $0xfff007,%eax            /* 16Mb - 4096 + 7 (r/w user,p) */
        std
    1:  stosl                         /* fill pages backwards - more efficient :-) */
        subl $0x1000,%eax
        jge 1b
    ......
```

The binary of 7 is 111, and the P-bit is setted to 1.

When it creates a process, it will apply for paging. As long as calling the get_free_page() function, it will set the memory to 0 because we cannot predict the usage of this page memory. If it is used as a page table, unclear 0 will have garbage value, and it is a hidden danger.

The code is shown below:

```
//Code path:mm/memory.c:
unsigned long get_free_page(void)
{
......
    "leal 4092(%%edx),%%edi\n\t"
    "rep ; stosl\n\t"                 //clear page to 0
......
}
```

You have to establish the mapping relationship when copying a page table. After creating the mapping, set the P-bit to 1.

```
//Code path:mm/memory.c:
int copy_page_tables(unsigned long from,unsigned long to,long size)
{
    ......
    from_page_table = (unsigned long *) (0xfffff000 & *from_dir);
    if (!(to_page_table = (unsigned long *) get_free_page()))
    return -1;/* Out of memory, see freeing */
    *to_dir = ((unsigned long) to_page_table) | 7; //Set the P-bit of page
                                                   //directory table item to 1
    nr = (from==0)?0xA0:1024;
    for (; nr-- > 0 ; from_page_table++,to_page_table++) {
    this_page = *from_page_table;
    if (!(1 & this_page))
            continue;
        this_page &= ~2; //Set the bit of page table item to 1,the binary of
                         //~2 is 101
    *to_page_table = this_page;
        if (this_page > LOW_MEM) {
        *from_page_table = this_page;
        ......
}
```

The page table item will clear 0 after relieving the relationship of the page table and page, and after relieving the relationship of the page directory item and page table, the page directory item is also clear 0, so it is equal to clear P_0.

```
//Code path:mm/memory.c:
int free_page_tables(unsigned long from,unsigned long size)
{
    ......
        if (1 & *pg_table)
            free_page(0xfffff000 & *pg_table);
        *pg_table = 0; //clear page table item to 0
        pg_table++;
    }
    free_page(0xfffff000 & *dir);
    *dir = 0;              //clear page directory table item to 0
    ......
}}
```

In the program loading stage in the process, it first calls the free_page_tables () function to clear the P-bit of the corresponding page table entry or page directory entry to 0, and it indicates that the corresponding page of the linear address does not exist and generates a page fault when the process executes the program.

It builds a mapping relationship with the new page after loading the program in the process, and the P-bit is set to 1. The code is shown below:

```
//Code path:mm/memory.c:
unsigned long put_page(unsigned long page,unsigned long address)
{
    ......
    if ((*page_table)&1)
        page_table = (unsigned long *) (0xfffff000 & *page_table);
    else {
        if (!(tmp=get_free_page()))
            return 0;
        *page_table = tmp|7;      //Set the P-bit of page directory
                                  //entry to 1
        page_table = (unsigned long *) tmp;
    }
    page_table[(address>>12) & 0x3ff] = page | 7; //Set the bit of page
                                                  //table entry to 1
    ......
}
```

3. Map the new application page to the linear address in the process.

Linux 0.11 creates the paging foundation on the basis of the segmentation foundation. If each linear address space of the process is limited without interfering with each other, then the page shouldn't be chaos. We have introduced a process linear address space overall pattern, and in the IA-32 system, it divides a 4 GB linear address space into 64 portions, and each processes one portion without interfering with one another, and the page directory entry's design fully complies with this pattern. The Linux 0.11 page directory table only has one, and a page directory table can control 1024 page tables, and a page table controls 1024 pages. A page has 4 KB, and such a page directory table can control 1024 * 1024 * 4 KB size = 4 GB memory space. Divide a page directory table into 64 portions, and each process can take a 16-page directory items, control a 16-page tables, namely an occupied 64 MB physical page. This makes for each process page to be mapped to a different page table entry, and the page table is also mapped to a different page directory entry, so when the MMU analyzes the linear address of any process, finally, it can be mapped to a different physical address. Of course, for sharing page needs, a different linear address is allowed to mapping to the same page, but that is just the practical application demand, a kind of strategy. A page directory table, page table, page, and this mapping mode are enough to support the only page mapping to the linear address space of the process.

To the sharing page problem, we will introduce you below.

6.2.3 Process Sharing the Page

Each process page will map to its own linear address space when process paging, and process execution will not interfere with each other. But, in some cases, a process needs to share the page, such as the father and child process needs to share the page. The most obvious example is that the process 1 creates process 2, and before the process 2 load shell, they share code. It is shown below:

```
//Code path:init/main.c:
void init(void)
{
        ......
        if (!(pid=fork())) {
            close(0);            //These codes share with the process
            if (open("/etc/rc",O_RDONLY,0))
                _exit(1);
            execve("/bin/sh",argv_rc,envp_rc);
                _exit(2);
        }
        if (pid>0)
            while (pid != wait(&i))
        ......

}
```

The best choice is when the child processes have been created, it uses the parent process code at first, and the child process shares the pages that belongs to the father. Then, the child process remaps when loading its program. This raises a question: Multiple processes operate on the same page and have read and written, and this is equivalent to break a hole the process-enclosed environment. Therefore, we need to do something to make the hole blocked.

Linux 0.11 uses two bits of a page table to make the hole blocked.

First, introduce the U/S bit, and if the U/S bit is set to 0, it indicates a program of the privilege level of 3 cannot access this page while another privilege level can. If set to 1, it indicates all programs of the privilege level of 3 can access this page. Its function is watching the user processes, preventing the page, which only accessed by kernel, from using by a user process. Of course, the protection of Linux 0.11 is more stress to the use of "segment."

U/S bit is set to 1 when the kernel pages before idling; the code is as follows:

```
//Code path:boot/head.s:
......
setup_paging:
    movl $1024*5,%ecx              /* 5 pages - pg_dir+4 page tables */
    xorl %eax,%eax
    xorl %edi,%edi                 /* pg_dir is at 0x000 */
    cld;rep;stosl
    movl $pg0+7,_pg_dir            /* set present bit/user r/w */
    movl $pg1+7,_pg_dir+4          /*- - - - - " "- - - - - */
    movl $pg2+7,_pg_dir+8          /*- - - - - " "- - - - - */
    movl $pg3+7,_pg_dir+12         /*- - - - - " "- - - - - */
    movl $pg3+4092,%edi
    movl $0xfff007,%eax            /* 16Mb - 4096 + 7 (r/w user,p) */
    std
1:  stosl                /* fill pages backwards - more efficient :-) */
    subl $0x1000,%eax
    jge 1b
......
```

The binary of 7 is 111 in the code; it indicates that the U/S-bit is set to 1.

The U/S-bit of the child processes page directory entry and page table is set to 1 when creating the process; the code is shown below:

```
//Code path:mm/memory.c:
int copy_page_tables(unsigned long from,unsigned long to,long size)
{
    ......
    from_page_table = (unsigned long *) (0xfffff000 & *from_dir);
    if (!(to_page_table = (unsigned long *) get_free_page()))
        return -1;          /* Out of memory, see freeing */
    *to_dir = ((unsigned long) to_page_table) | 7; //Set the U/S-bit of page
                                                   //directory table entry to 1
    nr = (from==0)?0xA0:1024;
    for (; nr-- > 0 ; from_page_table++,to_page_table++) {
        this_page = *from_page_table;
        if (!(1 & this_page))
```

```
            continue;
        this_page &= ~2;              //Set the U/S-bit of page table entry to 1, the
                                      //binary of ~2 is 101
    *to_page_table = this_page;
        if (this_page > LOW_MEM) {
            *from_page_table = this_page;
        ......
}
```

The new application page of the process maps to the linear address space of the process will set the U/S-bit of the corresponding page table entry to 1. If it is a new page table, it will also set the U/S-bit of the corresponding page directory entry to 1.

```
//Code path:mm/memory.c:
unsigned long put_page(unsigned long page,unsigned long address)
{
  ......
  if ((*page_table)&1)
      page_table = (unsigned long *) (0xfffff000 & *page_table);
  else {
        if (!(tmp = get_free_page()))
              return 0;
        *page_table = tmp|7;         //Set the U/S-bit of page directory
                                     //entry to 1
        page_table = (unsigned long *) tmp;
  }
  page_table[(address>>12) & 0x3ff] = page | 7;    //Set the U/S-bit of page
                                                   //table entry to 1
  ......
}
```

Next, we introduce the R/W. If it is set to 0, it indicates the page can only read and can't write. If it is set to 1, it indicates that it can read and write.

The process can share the page that will bring you a question, if multiple processes write the data to one page, this page will appear chaotic, so it needs protection. The R/W bit provides this kind of protection.

The father and child process share pages when create the child process, and the shared page cannot be written into the data; the R/W bit is set to 0. The code is shown below:

```
//Code path:mm/memory.c:
int copy_page_tables(unsigned long from,unsigned long to,long size)
{
  ......
  this_page = *from_page_table;
  if (!(1 & this_page))
      continue;
  this_page &= ~2; //Set the R/W-bit of page table item to 1,the
                   //binary of ~2 is 101
  *to_page_table = this_page;
  if (this_page > LOW_MEM) {
      *from_page_table = this_page;
      ......
}
```

Furthermore, the processes without father and child relationship can also share the page and do not need load again. At this time, it will set the R/W to 0 and prohibit writing data.

```c
//Code path:mm/memory.c:
void do_no_page(unsigned long error_code,unsigned long address)
{
    ......
    if (!current->executable || tmp >= current->end_data) {
        get_empty_page(address);
        return;
    }
    if (share_page(tmp))
        return;
    if (!(page = get_free_page()))
        oom();
    ......
}


static int share_page(unsigned long address) //ready to share page
{
    ......
    if ((*p)->executable ! = current->executable)
        continue;
    if (try_to_share(address,*p))
        return 1;
    }
    return 0;
}
static int try_to_share(unsigned long address, struct task_struct * p)
//detect whether can share page
{
    ......
    to &= 0xfffff000;
    to_page = to + ((address>>10) & 0xffc);
    if (1 & *(unsigned long *) to_page)
        panic("try_to_share: to_page already exists");
/* share them: write-protect */
    *(unsigned long *) from_page &= ~2;          //Set the R/W-bit of page
                                                  //table item to 1,the
                                                  //binary of ~2 is 101
    *(unsigned long *) to_page = *(unsigned long *) from_page;
    invalidate();
    ......
}
```

Through the above introduction, it is not difficult to locate a process sharing page, and there are only two possible operations, either read or write. Although read will not cause data chaos, it will result in literally reading. If it is written, it is possible to cause chaos, and it needs to be banned. To the writing requirements, Linux 0.11 takes the write-on-copy strategy to solve, namely to copy the written data page to process, and the two processes each have one, and each writes each page, so it won't result in chaos. We will use an operating example to explain the write-on-copy mechanism at the end of this chapter section.

Linux 0.11 does have such demand like pipeline, and two processes in the same page can read and write. We will introduce how to ensure that process operating does not produce data of chaos in Chapter 8.

6.2.4 Kernel Paging

For the kernel, it pages itself at first after entering protection mode. Paging is built on the basis of linear address space. In the front section, we introduced that the kernel's segment base is 0, and the segment limit of the code segment and data segment are 16 MB. Each page size is 4 KB, each page table can manage 1024 pages, and each page directory can manage 1024 page tables. Because the segment limit is 16 MB; thus it needs the four-page table below the 4-page directory entries to manage the 16 MB memory. The code is as follows:

```
//Code path:boot/head.s:
......
setup_paging:
    movl $1024*5,%ecx          /* 5 pages - pg_dir+4 page tables */
    xorl%eax,%eax
    xorl%edi,%edi              /* pg_dir is at 0x000 */
    cld;rep;stosl
    movl $pg0+7,_pg_dir        /* set present bit/user r/w */
    movl $pg1+7,_pg_dir+4      /*- - - - - " "- - - - - */
    movl $pg2+7,_pg_dir+8      /*- - - - - " "- - - - - */
    movl $pg3+7,_pg_dir+12     /*- - - - - " "- - - - - */
    movl $pg3+4092,%edi
    movl $0xfff007,%eax        /* 16Mb - 4096 + 7 (r/w user,p) */
    std
1:stosl                   /* fill pages backwards - more efficient :-) */
    subl $0x1000,%eax
    jge 1b
......
```

From Figure 6.3, we can see that the linear address of the kernel is equal to the physical address. The objective is that the kernel can visit the memory area of all the processes.

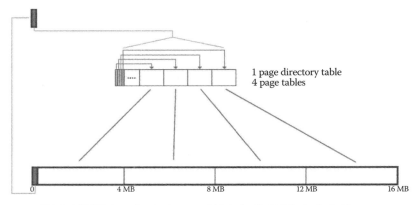

1 page directory table
4 page tables

The 0—16 MB is kernel control space, which is also 0—16 MB physical address

Figure 6.3 Kernel paging.

Identity mapping mode is not the only mode; the kernel chose linear addresses to physical addresses of identity mapping because it's the most convenient to kernel. For example, when the kernel applies a page for the process; the page always need to map to a page table entry, and this needs to write the physical address to the page table entry. If it's identity mapping mode, it obtains a linear address value, which directly can use as physical addresses after calling get_free_page() function, so it is more convenient.

The kernel not only controls all the memory page access rights, but also has the ability to set each page's reading and writing attributes and to record the information on the entries in page directory table and page table. The code is shown below:

```
//Code path:boot/head.s:
......
setup_paging:
    movl $1024*5,%ecx           /* 5 pages - pg_dir+4 page tables */
    xorl%eax,%eax
    xorl%edi,%edi               /* pg_dir is at 0x000 */
    cld;rep;stosl
    movl $pg0+7,_pg_dir         /* set present bit/user r/w */
    movl $pg1+7,_pg_dir+4       /*-  - - - -  - " "- - - -  - */
    movl $pg2+7,_pg_dir+8       /*-  - - - -  - " "- - - -  - */
    movl $pg3+7,_pg_dir+12      /*-  - - - -  - " "- - - -  - */
    movl $pg3+4092,%edi
    movl $0xfff007,%eax         /* 16Mb - 4096 + 7 (r/w user,p) */
    std
1:stosl                        /* fill pages backwards - more efficient :-) */
    subl $0x1000,%eax
    jge 1b
......
```

The meanings of "7" have introduced in the first chapter.

Note: It should find the page directory table firstly when the CPU hardware analyzes the linear address value, and if it can't find it, a follow-up about the page table and page analysis is unable to be done. This base address of page directory default stores in CR3 by hardware; as long as it's analyzing the linear address, go to CR3 to find the base address, so the kernel loads the base address into CR3.

```
//Code path:boot/head.s:
......
xorl %eax,%eax                 /* pg_dir is at 0x0000 */
movl %eax,%cr3                 /* cr3 - page directory start */
......
```

In this line of CR3 operation instruction, only 0 privilege level code can execute, which means that, in the future process started, even if it imitates the kernel to make a page directory data structure, in the result of the 3 privilege level, it can't put this structure articulate to CR3 and can't find the page that is used by other processes. This will protect the other processes.

Note: Although the kernel linear address space is not similar to the user process, the kernel cannot directly access the process across linear address space. But it occupies all the pages, and the privilege level is 0, so the kernel in enforcement can change all the contents of a page and equals the operation of the page of all processes. But this is different from the kernel directly visiting the process through the linear address segment. A typical example, if the process reads the disk, it always writes the data in the buffer into user space, and this matter is completed by the kernel.

```
//Code path:mm/memory.c:
int file_read(struct m_inode * inode, struct file * filp, char * buf, int count)
{
......
    chars = MIN(BLOCK_SIZE-nr, left);
    filp->f_pos += chars;
    left -= chars;
    if (bh) {
        char * p = nr + bh->b_data;
        while (chars-- >0)
            put_fs_byte(*(p++),buf++);//copy data
        brelse(bh);
    } else {
        while (chars-- >0)
            put_fs_byte(0,buf++);
    }
}
......
}


//Code path:include/asm/Segment.h:
extern inline void put_fs_byte(char val,char *addr){
__ asm__ ("movb%0,%%fs:%1"::"r" (val),"m" (*addr));//store a byte in the memory
//address of segment which is recorded in fs register
}


//Code path:kernel/system_call.s
......
_system_call:
    ......
    movl $0x10,%edx              # set up ds,es to kernel space
    mov%dx,%ds
    mov%dx,%es
    movl $0x17,%edx              # fs points to local data space
    mov%dx,%fs //kernel use fs register to store the data segment descriptor of
              //user process LDT
    call _sys_call_table(,%eax,4)
......
```

From the code, we can see the kernel can directly access the process LDT, which corresponds to the page of the memory address, but it does not mean that the kernel can cross segment of the linear address, and access to the linear address space of the process. The base protection of the segment, is not broken because of paging.

▮ 6.3 Complete Process of User Process from Creation to Exit

Based on the principle explained before, we take an example, practicing with theory, to explain the complete process of the user process from creation to exit in detail.

6.3.1 Create Process str1

Prepare conditions for the creation of process str1.

First, let's introduce the source code of process str1:

```
#include <stdio.h>
int foo(int n)
{
    char text[2048];
    if (n = =0)
        return 0;
    else{
        int i = 0;
        for (i; i<2048; i++)
        text[i] = '\0';
        printf("text_%d = 0x%x, Pid =%d\n", n, text, getpid());
        sleep(5);
        foo(n-1);
    }
}
int main(int argc, char **argv)
{
    foo(6);
    return 0;
}
```

There is an executable file called str1 on the disk. Users input a command in the interface of shell.

```
./str1, shell
```

The program will respond and analyze this command and create a user process starting from this.

By analyzing, we need to perform program str1 now, and then shell calls the function fork to start creating the process to produce a soft interrupt of int 0x80, eventually mapped to the function of sys_fork. The function find_empty_process() is called for process str1 to apply for an available process ID and a free position in task[64] in the process. We here assume that process str1 is the first applied user process after the operating system has been idling. According to previous chapter introduced, the applied process ID is 5, and the idle position found in the task[64] is 5.

Take access to the process ID and idle situation of task[64] as well as the position occupied by process str1 in task[64] (Figure 6.4).

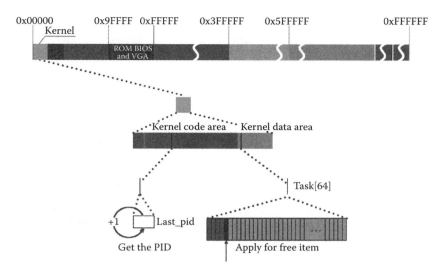

Figure 6.4 Take access to the process ID and idle situation of task[64].

Later, according to the item number in task[64], determine process str1 is in which 64 MB linear address space, and its LDT and TSS is bind with which two GDT. Let's look at the following implementation.

Find storage space for the management structure of process str1. Function copy_process() first needs to apply a page for process str1, and this page will be used to store task_struct and kernel stack of the process. We learn from the former introduction that in order to achieve the protection of the process the system designs a special structure for the management of each process, and this is task_struct. Each process has an account in order to ensure noninterfering. After the process turns into the kernel, the code of implementation is the kernel code, but the execution path is not necessarily the same. This will result in a different order and content of data pushed in the stack. These stacks cannot be stored in the user space of each process, so it is easy to be overwritten or altered, which requires a specially prepared set of kernel stack for each process.

Through the earlier explanation of the kernel paging strategy, all the pages have mapped to the 16M linear address space of the kernel when entering the protected mode. Now, it calls get_free_page() function, which executes in the kernel and gets the task_struct and kernel stack page, which can only be in the kernel linear address space. From the operating system's subsequent program, we cannot find codes that map the page to another process linear address space. Although this page is distributed for managing the str1 process, this page does not map to the linear address space of the str1 process, and the str1 process can't visit this page because the page is always grasped in the hand of the kernel.

From the strategy of applying the page by the get_free_page() function, we can see the operating system make the page-intensive accumulation to the high address so as to improve efficiency in the use of memory. When the process executes, and especially multiple processes execute, the release of the page is random, which often causes the memory to spread the release of the free page, and the get_free_page() function always traverses all pages from the high address to a lower address as long as it finds a free page to apply until there is no free page position. This will ensure that all application pages in memory are closely arranged and make a 4 GB linear address space dispersion in the process memory, intensive to limited physical memory to execute.

Of course, if it does not apply to a free page, it indicates the memory has no page for process use, so it directly returns an error message, and the process's creation ends. The system has a large number of free pages in the memory after idling, and the str1 process is just created after idling, so it can apply for a free page. According to the item number of task[64], it mounts the process task_struct to task[64], and the item of task[64] conforms to 64 equal portions of layout of linear address space. Each creates a process and loads the address pointer of task_struct into task[64], and if the system searches the process, just find the task[64]; then it can find the task_struct with no chaos.

The code is shown as follows:

```
//Code path:kernel/fork.c:
int copy_process(int nr,long ebp,long edi, //The nr is the item number of task[64]
        long esi,long gs,long none,
        long ebx,long ecx,long edx,
        long fs,long es,long ds,
        long eip,long cs,long eflags,long esp,long ss)
{
    struct task_struct *p;
    int i;
    struct file *f;
    p = (struct task_struct *) get_free_page(); //apply free page for str1 process
    if (!p)              //if not apply, return error
        return -EAGAIN;
    task[nr] = p; //mount the task_struct of str1 process to task[64]
    *p = *current;         /* NOTE! this doesn't copy the supervisor stack */
    p->state = TASK_UNINTERRUPTIBLE;
    p->pid = last_pid;
    ......
}
```

The free pages applied in the main memory shown in Figure 6.5 mark in the mem_ map of the kernel data area. The articulated situation of task[64] and the free page of use as the str1 process task_struct is shown in Figure 6.5.

Process str1 copy task_struct from the shell. In Linux 0.11, at any time, there should be a process at work; hence, the *current* pointer is pointed to the current process. When a process is going to be forked, the task is finished by a process; furthermore, it is finished by the current process. The shell copies the *task_struct* of itself to process *str1*, and this is also the extension of the designing philosophy.

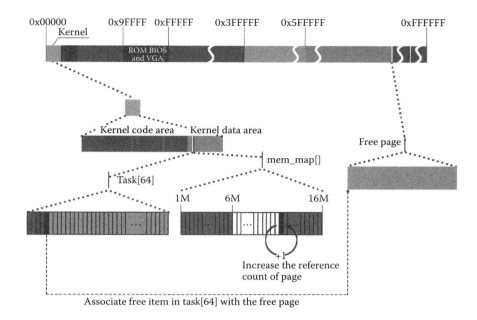

Figure 6.5 Apply the page for task_struct of str1.

The code is as follows:

```
//code path: kernel/fork.c:
int copy_process(int nr,long ebp,      //nr corresponds to id of task[64]
     long edi,long esi,long gs,long none,
     long ebx,long ecx,long edx,
     long fs,long es,long ds,
     long eip,long cs,long eflags,long esp,long ss)
{
     ......
     if (!p)
          return -EAGAIN;
     task[nr] = p;
     *p = *current;      /* NOTE! this doesn't copy the supervisor stack */
//copy task_struct to process str1
     p->state = TASK_UNINTERRUPTIBLE;
     p->pid = last_pid;
     ......
}
```

Figure 6.6 illustrates the copy procedure.

When *task_struct* is copied to *str1*, the process *str1* inherits all the management information from the shell. However, because the structure information of each process is different, it is necessary to personalize the structure information. First, set the status of the process to be uninterruptible. When the kernel is processing, Linux 0.11 disallows process interchange, so the setting of status is not a must. In the situation in which process schedule is allowed when the kernel is at work, the status must be set uninterruptible. That's

---

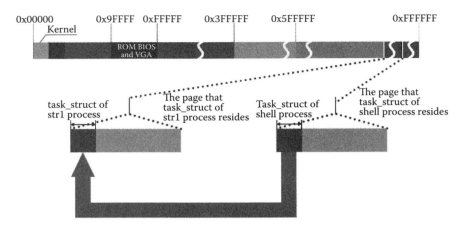

Figure 6.6 Copy the task_struct.

because the task_struct structure is already mounted in the task[64] structure, and when interruption occurred in the procedure of the structure personalization, this process will be put into run although its personalization is unfinished. When this process is put into run, processes will be in disorder.

The code is as follows:

```
//code path: kernel/fork.c:
int copy_process(int nr,long ebp,long edi,long esi,long gs,long none,
                 long ebx,long ecx,long edx,
                 long fs,long es,long ds,
                 long eip,long cs,long eflags,long esp,long ss)
{
    ......
    task[nr] = p;
    *p = *current;   /* NOTE! this doesn't copy the supervisor stack */
    p->state = TASK_UNINTERRUPTIBLE;   //process str1 is set to be uninterruptible state
    p->pid = last_pid;
    p->father = current->pid;
    ......
}
```

The procedure is illustrated in Figure 6.7.

Copy the process page table of str1 and set its page directory entry. Task_struct also contains other fields that need to be personalized. Process str1 has different pids compared with the shell process, furthermore, pid of shell is also different from it's parent. All this information needs personalization. The code is as follows:

```
//code path: kernel/fork.c:
int copy_process(int nr,long ebp,long edi,long esi,long gs,long none,
                 long ebx,long ecx,long edx,
                 long fs,long es,long ds,
                 long eip,long cs,long eflags,long esp,long ss)
{
        ......
        *p = *current;       /* NOTE! this doesn't copy the supervisor stack */
```

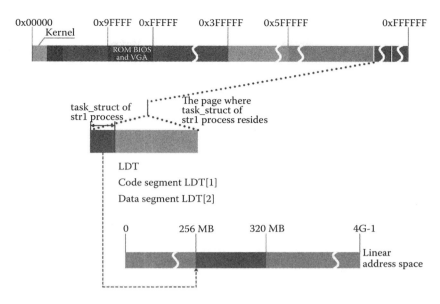

Figure 6.7 Determine the location of process in linear space.

```
        p->state = TASK_UNINTERRUPTIBLE;
        p->pid = last_pid;                    //set the pid of process str1
        p->father = current->pid;             //set shell to be the parent process of str1
        p->counter = p->priority;
        p->signal = 0;
        ......
}
```

Process str1 inherits its time slice value from the shell process, when the shell has been processing for a while; thus, the time slice of str1, which inherits from shell has been reduced. However, we shall not make this happen, so str1 shall define its time slice value due to the priority of the shell rather than inheriting the time slice value from the shell directly. If the priority of the shell is not set by the user, its time slice value will be 15 by default.

The code is shown as follows:

```
//code path: kernel/fork.c:
int copy_process(int nr,long ebp,long edi,long esi,long gs,long none,
                 long ebx,long ecx,long edx,
                 long fs,long es,long ds,
                 long eip,long cs,long eflags,long esp,long ss)
{
        ......
        *p = *current;       /* NOTE! this doesn't copy the supervisor stack */
        p->state = TASK_UNINTERRUPTIBLE;
        p->pid = last_pid;
        p->father = current->pid;
        p->counter = p->priority;       //time slice value of str1 is set due to the priority
                                        //of current process
        p->signal = 0;
        p->alarm = 0;
        ......
}
```

The next section follows the personalization of the signal. In the task_struct structure, there are three fields related to the signal: signal, sigaction[32], and blocked, which respectively correspond to the signal bitmap, the mount point of the signal handler function, and the signal blocking code. When the process str1 is forked, only the signal is reset, and other information is not set. This is because if the signal of str1 is not set to 0, it will inherit its signal information from the parent process. When str1 is processing, if the kernel is turned into running before return, the signal will be checked. Process str1 should not have received a signal, but because of the misuse of the signal information, an unnecessary signal process will occur. In order to process signal, there will need to modify the information of user stack and to bind the signal process handler of a specific process, while process str1 has no preparation for these action. When the process turned from the kernel to the current process with these uncertainties, the process will come into disorder.

Now that no signal is received, we do not care about the mount point of the signal handler function and blocking code, so they are not personalized. The specified code is as follows:

```
//code path: kernel/fork.c:
int copy_process(int nr,long ebp,long edi,long esi,long gs,long none,
            long ebx,long ecx,long edx,
            long fs,long es,long ds,
            long eip,long cs,long eflags,long esp,long ss)
{
    ......
    p->father = current->pid;
    p->counter = p->priority;
    p->signal = 0;                              //reset signal bitmap
    p->alarm = 0;
    p->leader = 0;              /* process leadership doesn't inherit */
    ......
}
```

A detailed signal process procedure will be introduced in Chapter 8.

Then, we will introduce the personalization of other fields. Similarly, reset and inherit by default actions also apply to the time setting and session organization of str1.

The specified code is as follows:

```
//code path: kernel/fork.c:
int copy_process(int nr,long ebp,long edi,long esi,long gs,long none,
        long ebx,long ecx,long edx,
        long fs,long es,long ds,
        long eip,long cs,long eflags,long esp,long ss)
{
    ......
    p->counter = p->priority;
    p->signal = 0;
    p->alarm = 0;   //reset alarm time
    p->leader = 0; /* process leadership doesn't inherit */ //reset the session leader field
    p->utime = p->stime = 0;
    p->cutime = p->cstime = 0;
    p->start_time = jiffies;
    p->tss.back_link = 0;
    p->tss.esp0 = PAGE_SIZE + (long) p;
    ......
}
```

Other fields related to time settings and session organizations are all inherited. The fields above are set for kernel management.

The next section comes with an introduction to the TSS field, which is designed for process switch. Process switch is guaranteed by process protection. Different process protection designs correspond to different process switch modes. When the process is running, various registers are used. As a consequence, process switch is a switch of a series of register values rather than a simple jump. To guarantee the order of the process, the status before and after process switch shall be consistent. Thereby, Linux 0.11 records all registers in the task_struct, which is TSS. Process switch shall be consistent with the mechanism: Before process switch, TSS saves the current key state (i.e., the current status of each registers), and after switching back, restore register value from TSS.

The code is as follows:

```
//code path: kernel/fork.c:
int copy_process(int nr,long ebp,long edi,long esi,long gs,long none,
                 long ebx,long ecx,long edx,
                 long fs,long es,long ds,
                 long eip,long cs,long eflags,long esp,long ss)
{
        ......
        p->cutime = p->cstime = 0;
        p->start_time = jiffies;
        p->tss.back_link = 0;                       //code follows set TSS fields
        p->tss.esp0 = PAGE_SIZE + (long) p;
        p->tss.ss0 = 0x10;
        p->tss.eip = eip;
        p->tss.eflags = eflags;
        p->tss.eax = 0;
        p->tss.ecx = ecx;
        p->tss.edx = edx;
        p->tss.ebx = ebx;
        p->tss.esp = esp;
        p->tss.ebp = ebp;
        p->tss.esi = esi;
        p->tss.edi = edi;
        p->tss.es = es & 0xffff;
        p->tss.cs = cs & 0xffff;
        p->tss.ss = ss & 0xffff;
        p->tss.ds = ds & 0xffff;
        p->tss.fs = fs & 0xffff;
        p->tss.gs = gs & 0xffff;
        p->tss.ldt = _LDT(nr);                      //codes above set TSS fields
        p->tss.trace_bitmap = 0x80000000;
        if (last_task_used_math = = current)
               __asm__ ("clts ; fnsave%0"::"m" (p->tss.i387));
        ......
}
```

As we can see from the code, most parameters of the copy_process function is used to set register status. When str1 begins to run, it must be caused by a process switch. Once a process switch happens, all values stored in TSS will be restored to initialize the value of CPU registers and determine the start status of process str1.

It is worth noticing that these register values are automatically set by the CPU, so we can't find any code corresponding to register assignment. Then how does the CPU know the right value set to each register? The only possibility is that CPU circuits have a default order for register assignment, that is, the order listed in the above code if the order is different from the default order, the process will run into disorder.

Process protection is not only within the kernel's management to process and process switch; when the process is running, measures shall be taken to guard the boundary of the process at any time. In details, pagination and segmentation are introduced, which will be explained in the following sections.

Copy str1's page table and set the corresponding page directory entry. Now the copy_mem() function is called to segment for the process, which will define its linear address space.

Through the knowledge we learned before, the key to defining a linear address space is to define the segment base address and segment limit.

The code is as follows:

```
//code path: kernel/fork.c:
int copy_mem(int nr,struct task_struct * p)
{
    unsigned long old_data_base,new_data_base,data_limit;
    unsigned long old_code_base,new_code_base,code_limit;

    code_limit=get_limit(0x0f);              //length of code segment of current process(shell)
    data_limit=get_limit(0x17);              //length of data segment of current process(shell)
    old_code_base = get_base(current->ldt[1]);
    old_data_base = get_base(current->ldt[2]);
    if (old_data_base !=old_code_base)
            panic("We don't support separate I&D");
    if (data_limit < code_limit)
            panic("Bad data_limit");
    new_data_base = new_code_base = nr * 0x4000000; //define new segment base according to nr
                                          //in task[64]
    p->start_code = new_code_base;
    set_base(p->ldt[1],new_code_base);       //define its LDT refer to str1's code segment base
    set_base(p->ldt[2],new_data_base);       //define its LDT refer to str1's data segment base
    if (copy_page_tables(old_data_base,new_data_base,data_limit)){
            free_page_tables(new_data_base,data_limit);
            return -ENOMEM;
    }
    return 0;
}
```

It is worth noticing, as we can infer from the code, str1's segment base is set according to item number nr in task[64], and str1's LDT is set according to its segment base address while we didn't see the setting of segment limit. To our knowledge, the segment limit of a process stores in LDT, and when task_struct is copied, LDT is also copied without any modification, that is to say, str1 inherits its parent process, shell's LDT. The reason we do this is when str1 begins to run, its code will be executed sooner or later, but its own program is not loaded yet (perhaps this might not happen ever). Thus str1 can only share the code with its parent process, and by inheriting the segment limit of parent process, str1 can share all code and data with its parent process.

After segmentation, we begin to consider paging. Paging is based on segmentation, and this is because the segment base address and segment limit have defined copy from where, copy to where, and the number of entries needs to copy from the page table entry information. The specified code is as follows:

```
//code path: kernel/fork.c:
int copy_mem(int nr,struct task_struct * p)
{
    ......
    new_data_base = new_code_base = nr * 0x4000000;
    p->start_code = new_code_base;
    set_base(p->ldt[1],new_code_base);
    set_base(p->ldt[2],new_data_base);
    if (copy_page_tables(old_data_base,new_data_base,data_limit)){ //call this function
                                                                   //to page for str1
            free_page_tables(new_data_base,data_limit);
            return -ENOMEM;
    }
    return 0;
}
```

As we mentioned in our introduction to segmentation, after str1 is forked, it doesn't own its code yet and shares code with its parent process shell. Correspondently, str1 shares its page with the shell; in other words, we shall create a set of new page directory entries and page table entries for str1 so that it points to the same page with shell. The code is as follows:

```
//code path: mm/memory.c:
int copy_page_tables(unsigned long from,unsigned long to,long size)
{
    ......
    for(; size-  >0 ; from_dir++,to_dir++) {          //pagination is based on segmentation
        if (1 & *to_dir)
            panic("copy_page_tables: already exist");
        if (!(1 & *from_dir))
            continue;
        from_page_table = (unsigned long *) (0xfffff000 & *from_dir);
        if (!(to_page_table = (unsigned long *) get_free_page()))//allocate a new page for
                                                                 //created page
            return -1;/* Out of memory, see freeing */
        *to_dir = ((unsigned long) to_page_table) | 7;       //set the page directory entry
        nr = (from = =0)?0xA0:1024;
        for (; nr-  > 0 ; from_page_table++,to_page_table++) { //copy page table
            this_page = *from_page_table;
            if (!(1 & this_page))
                continue;
            this_page & = -2;                        //make the share to be read-only for shell
            *to_page_table = this_page;              //make the share to be read-only for str1
            if (this_page > LOW_MEM) {
                *from_page_table = this_page;
                this_page - = LOW_MEM;
                this_page >> = 12;
                mem_map[this_page]++;
            }
        }
    }
    invalidate();
    return 0;
}
```

Figure 6.8 illustrates the procedure of copying page table and settings of page directory entry.

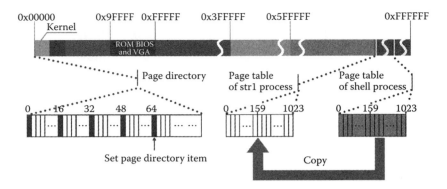

Figure 6.8 Copying page table and setting the page directory for str1.

It is worth noticing that, when a page table is created for a new process, the function get_free_page() should be called to allocate free pages.

The pages we allocated here, from the perspective of need, will be used to load the page table entries of the new process. These page table entries are used to manage the page possessed by str1 rather than being used by the process directly. So we only allocated the page and didn't map it to the linear space address of process str1. Similar to allocating pages for the task_struct or kernel stack of process, the program is executed in kernel when allocating pages, running within the linear address space of kernel. At this time, the allocated pages have already mapped to the kernel's linear address space, and the kernel is capable of accessing these pages. Similarly, pages allocated when preparing for loading a page table are all used for kernel management, and they can only be accessed by the kernel but are not accessible for the process. The fundamental reason of such accessibility is that the kernel didn't map these pages to the linear address space.

After segmentation and paging, we shall handle the issue of file inheritance. Files opened by shell shall be inherited by its child process. Specifically, we accumulate the counter of file reference and counter of the i node reference counter. When the child process needs to use these files, they can be processed without a reopen. For example, if file tty is opened and the handler is copied by shell, then its child process can use tty directly, and there's no need to reload the file. The code for aggregating reference counter is as follows:

```
//code path: kernel/fork.c:
int copy_process(int nr,long ebp,long edi,long esi,long gs,long none,
        long ebx,long ecx,long edx,
        long fs,long es,long ds,
        long eip,long cs,long eflags,long esp,long ss)
{
    ......
    if (copy_mem(nr,p)) {
        task[nr] = NULL;
        free_page((long) p);
        return -EAGAIN;
    }
    for (i = 0; i<NR_OPEN;i++)
        if (f = p->filp[i])
            f->f_count++;                 //accumulate the file reference counter
    if (current->pwd)
        current->pwd->i_count++;          //accumulate the reference of current working
                                          //directory i-node
```

6. The User Process and Memory Management

```
    if (current->root)
        current->root->i_count++;        //accumulate the reference of root directory i-node
    if (current->executable)
        current->executable->i_count++; //accumulate the reference of executable file i-node
    set_tss_desc(gdt+(nr<<1)+FIRST_TSS_ENTRY,&(p->tss));
    set_ldt_desc(gdt+(nr<<1)+FIRST_LDT_ENTRY,&(p->ldt));
    ......
}
```

Create the relationship between str1 and GDT (global description table). Now that we have resolved the file inheritance issue, then we shall mount the TSS and LDT of process str1 to the specified position of GDT. The specified code is as follows:

```
//code path: kernel/fork.c:
int copy_process(int nr,long ebp,long edi,long esi,long gs,long none,
        long ebx,long ecx,long edx,
        long fs,long es,long ds,
        long eip,long cs,long eflags,long esp,long ss)
{
    ......
    if (current->pwd)
        current->pwd->i_count++;
    if (current->root)
        current->root->i_count++;
    if (current->executable)
        current->executable->i_count++;
    set_tss_desc(gdt+(nr<<1)+FIRST_TSS_ENTRY,&(p->tss));  //mount TSS of str1 to GDT and
                                                          //set segment information
    set_ldt_desc(gdt+(nr<<1)+FIRST_LDT_ENTRY,&(p->ldt));  //mount LDT of str1 to GDT and
                                                          //set segment information
    p->state = TASK_RUNNING;  /* do this last, just in case */
    return last_pid;
}
```

The setting is illustrated in Figure 6.9.

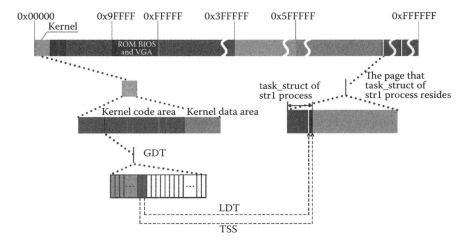

Figure 6.9 Mount the TSS and LDT of process str1 to GDT.

TSS and LDT are critical to process protection. The essence of protection is to prevent the process from interfering with other process when it is running. In the term of segment, there are two ways to jump to another process:

The first, as we mentioned before, is carrying out a jump instruction within a segment while the jump value exceeds the segment length limit. The hardware is always guarding it, and LDT keeps a record of the process's segment base address and segment limit. Each instruction, when executed, will be checked by the hardware to determine whether it exceeds the specified length limit. If so, it will be reported to GP and come to interception.

The second is when an inter-segment jump instruction is executed to implement an inter-segment jump when the process is running. In Linux 0.11, each process keeps its own LDT, in which situation the process is executed in privilege level 3, and the LDT provides a segment descriptor. Hence, when an inter-segment jump is conducted, the current LDT shall be replaced by the LDT of another segment, in order to modify the segment descriptor. This must be caused by the instruction "LLDT" in which the base address of LDTR and LDT are needed. However, the instruction LLDT can only be executed under privilege level 0. So LDT cannot be modified at this time. Furthermore, there is no way that can a current process jump to another segment; in other words, the process cannot jump to other processes.

Assuming Linux 0.11 takes any other different process protection pattern, in which all processes record their segment descriptor by using GDT rather than LDT, then modify GDT by LGDT instruction is not the only way to realize inter-segment jump. Thereby, an inter-segment jump will be possible, which will disrupt the process protection. As we can see, the segment level protection is well designed by the designer of Linux.

Both protections have been guaranteed, and the segment level protection is finished completely. On the basis of segment level protection, we will implement the page level protection.

As we can infer from two invocations of function get_free_page(), the whole pagination procedure is finished by kernel, and if the pages are not mapped to the processes' linear address space, they will be not accessible for the processes. When considering mapping, the page directory table and page table must be specified. And the page directory entry in the directory table page is determined by the linear address space of the process. So as long as the linear address spaces are not overlapped, the processes memory disorder will not happen.

Set the status of str1 to ready. So far, the procedure to create the process str1 is finished. We will now set its status to be "ready," which means that process str1 is ready for the schedule.

The code is as follows:

```
//code path: kernel/fork.c:
int copy_process(int nr,long ebp,long edi,long esi,long gs,long none,
        long ebx,long ecx,long edx,
        long fs,long es,long ds,
        long eip,long cs,long eflags,long esp,long ss)
{
    ......
    set_tss_desc(gdt+(nr<<1)+FIRST_TSS_ENTRY,&(p->tss));
    set_ldt_desc(gdt+(nr<<1)+FIRST_LDT_ENTRY,&(p->ldt));
    p->state = TASK_RUNNING;  /* do this last, just in case */ //set the status to be ready
    return last_pid;
}
```

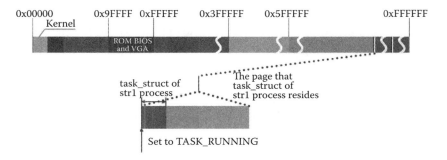

Figure 6.10 Set the status of str1 to be ready.

The procedure is illustrated in Figure 6.10, in which the state is set to be TASK_ RUNNING.

6.3.2 Preparation to Load str1

Preparations for loading user process str1. Preparations for loading user process str1 and loading shell are similar, including the following steps: detection of external environments, such as parameters and environmental variables; detection of the executable code of str1; specified adjustment to the task_struct of process str1; and at last, settings of EIP and ESP.

After entering the do_execve function, external preparations shall be made. First, setting up the pages for parameters and environmental variables of process str1. Second, read the i node of str1 file, which stores the code of str1, and check whether the file has problems by detecting the i node's information. Through the i node, find the file and check the record of the length of the code segment and data segment to determine whether the code and data can be contained within a linear address space of 64 MB.

The code is as follows:

```
//code path: fs/exec.c:
int do_execve(unsigned long * eip,long tmp,char * filename,
   char ** argv, char ** envp)
{
    ......
    if (N_MAGIC(ex) ! = ZMAGIC || ex.a_trsize || ex.a_drsize ||
        ex.a_text+ex.a_data+ex.a_bss>0x3000000 ||    //length of code, data and heap shall be
                                                      //less than 48MB
        inode->i_size < ex.a_text+ex.a_data+ex.a_syms+N_TXTOFF(ex)) {
        retval = -ENOEXEC;
        goto exec_error2;                            //if the length exceeds 48M, go to error
    }
    ......
}
```

Passing all these checks means that the code of str1 meets the executable file regulation and can be contained in a linear address space of 64 MB. Only when such criteria are met, the following adjustments make sense.

As we already know, when creating process str1, some opened files and signal fields are inherited from the shell process. Now it's time to load str1's own program, so some relationships shall be released, and some shall be reset.

The specified code is as follows:

```
//code path: fs/exec.c:
int do_execve(unsigned long * eip,long tmp,char * filename,
        char ** argv, char ** envp)
{
    ......
    if (!sh_bang) {
        p = copy_strings(envc,envp,page,p,0);
        p = copy_strings(argc,argv,page,p,0);
        if (!p) {
            retval = -ENOMEM;
            goto exec_error2;
        }
    }
/* OK, This is the point of no return */
    if (current->executable)                    //we are loading program from str1's
                                                //executable file, no longer need to
                                                //sharing shell's i-node
            iput(current->executable);          //release the relationship with shell's
                                                //executable file
    current->executable = inode;                //replace with the executable file's i-node
    for (i = 0 ; i<32 ; i++)
            current->sigaction[i].sa_handler = NULL;    //clear signal handler
                                                        //loading the user defined signal
                                                        //processing program

    for (i = 0 ; i<NR_OPEN ; i++)
            if ((current->close_on_exec>>i)&1)
                    sys_close(i);
    current->close_on_exec = 0;                         //reset the blocking code of the opened file
    free_page_tables(get_base(current->ldt[1]),get_limit(0x0f));
    free_page_tables(get_base(current->ldt[2]),get_limit(0x17));......
}
```

Release the page table of str1. As introduced before, the process str1 is now sharing the same pages with shell. Now str1 is loading its own program, so the sharing relationship shall be cancelled. This is finished by calling the free_page_tables() function.

The code is as follows:

```
//code path: fs/exec.c:
int do_execve(unsigned long * eip,long tmp,char * filename,
        char ** argv, char ** envp)
{
    ......
    for (i = 0 ; i<NR_OPEN ; i++)
        if ((current->close_on_exec>>i)&1)
            sys_close(i);
    current->close_on_exec = 0;
    free_page_tables(get_base(current->ldt[1]),get_limit(0x0f));    //release sharing pages
                                                                    //of code segment
    free_page_tables(get_base(current->ldt[2]),get_limit(0x17));    //release sharing pages
                                                                    //of data segment

    if (last_task_used_math == current)
            last_task_used_math = NULL;
    current->used_math = 0;
    ......
}
```

```
//code path: mm/memory.c:
int free_page_tables(unsigned long from,unsigned long size)
{
    ......
        if (1 & *pg_table)
            free_page(0xfffff000 & *pg_table);     //release sharing pages
        *pg_table = 0;                             //reset page table
        pg_table++;
    }
    free_page(0xfffff000 & *dir);                  //release page taken by page
                                                   //table itself
    *dir = 0;                                      //reset page table index
    ......
}
```

The procedure of releasing the page table is shown in Figure 6.11; please notice the change of page directory entry.

It is worth noticing that, as we mentioned, str1 and shell share their pages; thus, these pages are all read-only to them. Now that the sharing relationship of str1 has been cancelled, the pages are still read-only to shell. Will this influence the processing of shell? This will be explained in the following sections related to the procedure of write-on-copy.

Resetting the code segment and data segment of str1. Process str1 is now loading its own program, and LDT shall be reset according to the length of the program. The specified code is as follows:

```
//code path: fs/exec.c:
int do_execve(unsigned long * eip,long tmp,char * filename,
  char ** argv, char ** envp)
{
    ......
    p += change_ldt(ex.a_text,page)-MAX_ARG_PAGES*PAGE_SIZE; //re-set the segment limit
    ......
}


static unsigned long change_ldt(unsigned long text_size,unsigned long * page)
{
    ......
    code_limit = text_size+PAGE_SIZE -1;
    code_limit &= 0xFFFFF000;              //re-set the code segment limit according
                                           //to the code length
    data_limit = 0x4000000;                //set the length of data segment to be 64MB
    code_base = get_base(current->ldt[1]);
    data_base = code_base;                 //segment base address keeps unchanged
    set_base(current->ldt[1],code_base);
    set_limit(current->ldt[1],code_limit);
    set_base(current->ldt[2],data_base);
    set_limit(current->ldt[2],data_limit);
    ......
}
```

This is the last setting for str1's segment limit, which is always less than 64 MB. If a new process is forked from str1, according to the process copying mechanism, the segment length limit of str1's child processes will be less than 64 MB. Hence, each process created by the system will be limited within its own 64 MB memory space.

The procedure is shown in Figure 6.12.

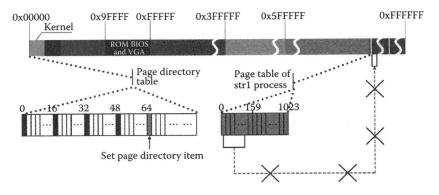

Figure 6.11 Release the pages of process str1.

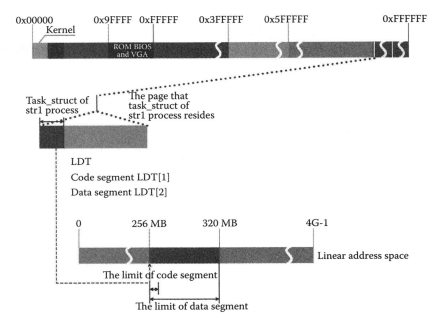

Figure 6.12 Re-set str1's code segment and data segment.

Adjust task_struct of process str1. The intention of setting fields, such as brk, start_stack in task_struct of str1, is to avoid mistakes during the procedure of process. The essence of such setting is management but not protection.

The code is as follows:

```
//code path: fs/exec.c:
int do_execve(unsigned long * eip,long tmp,char * filename,
    char ** argv, char ** envp)
{
    ......
    current->used_math = 0;
    p += change_ldt(ex.a_text,page)-MAX_ARG_PAGES*PAGE_SIZE;
    p = (unsigned long) create_tables((char *)p,argc,envc);
    current->brk = ex.a_bss +        //set up control fields of the process
            (current->end_data = ex.a_data + //according to the ex information in the file
            (current->end_code = ex.a_text));
    current->start_stack = p & 0xfffff000;
    current->euid = e_uid;
    current->egid = e_gid;
    i = ex.a_text+ex.a_data;
    while (i&0xfff)
            put_fs_byte(0,(char *) (i++));
    eip[0] = ex.a_entry;                /* eip, magic happens :-) */
    eip[3] = p;
    ......
}
```

The procedure of these adjustment in task_struct of str1 is shown in Figure 6.13.

As last mentioned, we shall adjust EIP and ESP to make the soft interrupt return and put the first instruction of str1's code into run. Because str1 and shell had released the page-sharing relationship, and the page table has been released, which means its mapping relationship with str1 has been cut off. It means that the content of the page directory entry is 0, including the P-bit. Once str1 execute, MMU will find the correspondent page directory entry's P-bit is 0 by mapping the linear address. Hence, page fault is invoked.

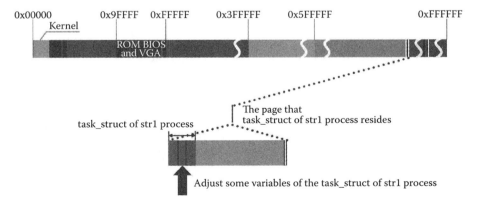

Figure 6.13 Adjust the task_struct of process str1.

6.3.3 Running and Loading of Process str1

Generation of interrupt and OSs responding. After the generation of page fault interruption, the response will be by the page_fault service. Eventually, the interruption will be processed by page fault handler _do_no_page by calling _do_no_page in _page_fault.

The code is as follows:

```
//code path: mm/page.s:
 _page_fault:
        ...
        testl $1,%eax
        jne 1f
 1:    call _do_no_page
 ......
```

After entering the do_no_page() function, before loading str1, two detections shall be made. First is whether str1 has loaded its code and whether the linear address value caused page fault is out of the end of the code. Obviously, neither condition is true, so the code of str1 will be loaded from the hard disk.

The code is as follows:

```
//code path: mm/memory.c:
void do_no_page(unsigned long error_code,unsigned long address)
{
     ......
     address &= 0xfffff000;
     tmp = address - current->start_code;
     if (!current->executable || tmp>= current->end_data){   //executable is the i node of
                                                              //str1's code file
                                                              //end_data is the end of code
          get_empty_page(address);
                      return;
     }
     if (share_page(tmp))
          return;
     ......
}
```

Second, str1 possibly shares code with a current process, for example, has any other process already loaded str1? This is also obviously impossible in this case.

The code is as follows:

```
//code path: mm/memory.c:
void do_no_page(unsigned long error_code,unsigned long address)
{
     ......
     if (!current->executable || tmp > = current->end_data) {
          get_empty_page(address);
          return;
     }
     if (share_page(tmp))           //detect whether it is sharing pages with other process
          return;
     if (!(page = get_free_page()))
          oom();
     ......
}
```

The current situation is the same with the situation when we load shell, and the process needed to be loaded from the hard disk. The following comes allocating free pages in memory and load str1.

Allocate a memory page for str1. Allocate a free page in main memory, and load the first part of str1 to the allocated page. The code is as follows:

```
//code path: mm/memory.c:
void do_no_page(unsigned long error_code,unsigned long address)
{
    ......
    if (share_page(tmp))
        return;
    if (!(page = get_free_page()))  //allocate page for str1
        oom();                       //if the allocation fails, let str1 exit
/* remember that 1 block is used for header */
    block = 1 + tmp/BLOCK_SIZE;
    ......
}
```

The procedure of allocating a free page and the registration of management structure mem_map is shown in Figure 6.14.

As we can infer from the former introduction, all pages allocated to the process have two mapping relationships, one is mapped to the kernel's linear address space, and another is mapped to the process' linear address space. The mapping relationship

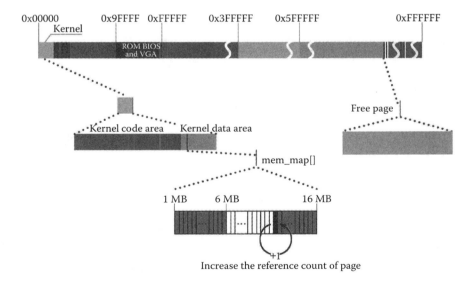

Figure 6.14 Allocate a memory page for str1.

between the kernel and the pages always exists. Consider the pages' mapping to kernel is cut off after the pages are mapped to process, it means that the kernel will not be able to access these pages.

Loading the program of str1 to newly allocated pages. Now the program is loaded into the newly allocated pages from the hard disk, 4 KB content per loop.

The code is as follows:

```
//code path: mm/memory.c:
void do_no_page(unsigned long error_code,unsigned long address)
{
    ......
    if (!(page = get_free_page()))
        oom();
    /* remember that 1 block is used for header */
    block = 1 + tmp/BLOCK_SIZE;
    for (i = 0 ; i<4 ; block++,i++)
        nr[i] = bmap(current->executable,block);
    bread_page(page,current->executable->i_dev,nr);  //read str1's information
                                                      //from hard disk
    i = tmp + 4096 - current->end_data;
    tmp = page + 4096;
    ......
}
```

In the above code, the function bmap() has been introduced in Chapter 5, Section 5.5. The procedure of function bread_page() is same with bread() in essence.

The procedure is shown in Figure 6.15.

Because the page has already mapped to the kernel's linear address space, when data are loaded in, they can be modified by the kernel at any time needed. This also suitable for the data loaded in the future.

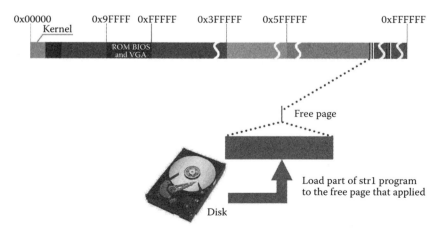

Figure 6.15 Loading the initial part for process str1 to newly allocated page.

Mapping the physical memory address process of str1 to its linear address space.
After str1 is loaded, we shall map it to str1's linear address space.

The specified code is as follows:

```
//code path: mm/memory.c:
void do_no_page(unsigned long error_code,unsigned long address)
{
    ......
    while (i-- > 0) {
        tmp--;
        *(char *)tmp = 0;
    }
    if (put_page(page,address))        //mapping to str1's linear address space
        return;
    free_page(page);
    oom();
}
```

The mapping procedure is illustrated in Figure 6.16; please notice that the correspondent page directory entry is set up in this procedure.

Only after the mapping, process will be able to execute the loaded code.

Loading complete content of str1 by repeating page fault. Given that the program is larger than the size of a page, when other parts of the program are needed during execution, page fault will be invoked again and again in order to load the required program.

Until now, the loading process of str1 has been completed. Next, we are going to introduce the situation after str1 is executing.

The program str1 begins to push stack. Once the program begins to execute, pushing stack actions begin.

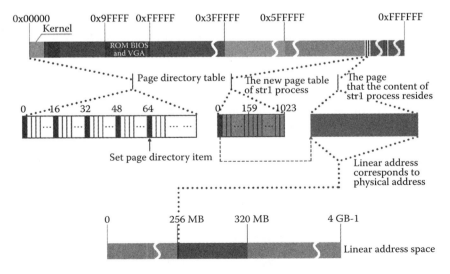

Figure 6.16 Mapping str1's physical address to its linear address.

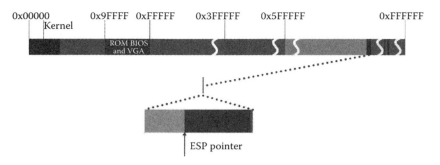

0x00000   0x9FFFF 0xFFFFF   0x3FFFFF   0x5FFFFF   0xFFFFFF

Kernel

ROM BIOS
and VGA

ESP pointer

Figure 6.17 The first time str1 pushing stack.

The foo function in the str1 program is called recursive. In this case, we set up a char array, namely "text," with the length of 2048 bytes to accelerate the increasing speed of str1's stack space. Therefore, page fault will be invoked more quickly (after only two stack pushing, a page fault will be invoked). Each time the foo function is called, the stack of str1 (ESP) increases by 2048 bytes.

Stack pushing when process str1 calls foo for the first time. The first time foo function is called, ESP increases by 2048 bytes. Before increasing, the stack ESP pointed to has taken up some place in the page to store the process's parameters and environment variables. So after expanding 2048 bytes, adding to the space already in use, the ESP is still within 4 KB—the size of a page. In other words, the program is still within the capacity of one physical page. As illustrated in Figure 6.17, the more black part in the lower right corner stands for parameters and environmental variables already in the page, and we can see that they are contained in the same page with part of the stack data.

Page fault invoked when str1 pushing stack for the second time. The second time that function foo is called, it will be a different case. Add with the data already in the physical page, another 2048 bytes will exceed the capacity of the page. When MMU is mapping the linear address value, the P-bit of a new page table entry is 0, and page fault is invoked again, making preparations for allocating a new page.

Handling the page fault invoked in the second stack pushing. A new physical page will be mapped to str1's linear address space eventually in order to support addressing. The function do_no_page is again called when handling the page fault this time, but the code to execute will be different, and the following code will be executed:

```
//code path: mm/memory.c:
void do_no_page(unsigned long error_code,unsigned long address)
{
    ……
    address &= 0xfffff000;
    tmp = address - current->start_code;
    if (!current->executable || tmp > = current->end_data)  {//this conditions is true
        get_empty_page(address);            //allocate free space when pushing stack
        return;
    }
    ……
}
```

This is because the condition tmp > = current->end_data becomes true this time. The program is executing to a linear address that exceeds the end_data of the process. Therefore, call function get_empty_page(), and no extra data are loaded into the page this time. Pushing stack also invokes page fault, having nothing with peripheral.

After entering get_empty_page(), the required page will be allocated and mapped to the linear address space of process str1.

The code is as follows:

```
//code path: mm/memory.c:
void get_empty_page(unsigned long address)
{
    unsigned long tmp;


    if (!(tmp=get_free_page()) || !put_page(tmp,address)) {    //allocating page and
                                                               //mapping to str1's linear
                                                               //address space

        free_page(tmp);         /* 0 is ok - ignored */
        oom();
    }
}
```

Process str1 continues to process, repeating pushing stack, and invoking page fault. The process continues to run, and such procedure is repeated: "pushing stack → if the P-bit of the page table entry is 0 → invoke page fault → allocating physical memory → pushing stack·····". When the function foo is called for the nth time, the mapping relationship between the user process stack and physical memory is shown in Figure 6.18. Please notice the memory page change of stack data.

Clear the stack after str1 is finished. After the program is finished, the recursion of function foo comes to an end (if (n = =0) return 0). At this time, the function return will lead to the clearing of the process stack. ESP shrinks up to the higher address direction, and the space for the user process to use is actually reduced. Thus, the former physical page mapped to linear space in the stack should be freed. Nevertheless, in our analysis and test to the Linux 0.11 source code, such procedure is not actually conducted. The reason is as follows: When the process is working, the kernel is not at work, and the pages discarded by the process during its processing can't be detected by the kernel in time. Besides, no circuit in the CPU is designed for such staff; there is no mechanism for discarded page detection. Even if the function is implemented by the kernel, there is no chance to carry out such a function. Thereby, pages are not freed after clearing the stack.

The result is shown in Figure 6.19.

6.3.4 Exiting of Process str1

Here, we introduce the exiting of process str1, including how to release the operation process of the occupied memory space, how to deal with the occupied space of its task_struct, and so on. In fact, the exiting of the str1 and shell process is generally identical, all through

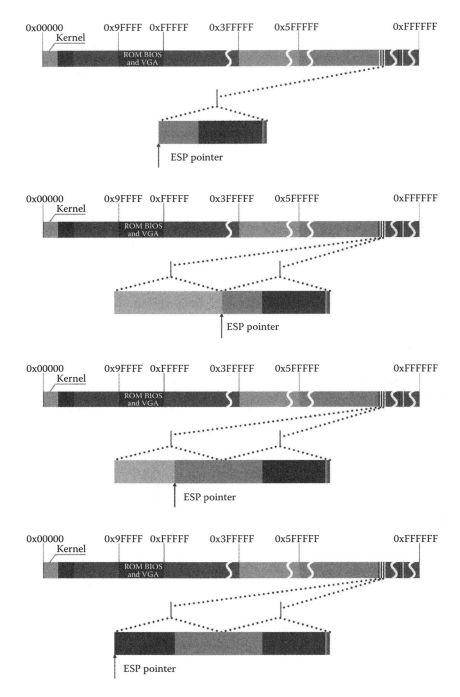

Figure 6.18 Reparation of str1's pushing stack.

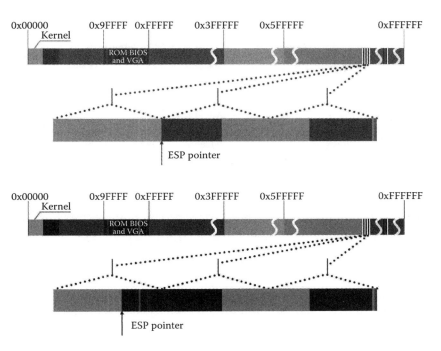

Figure 6.18 (Continued) Reparation of str1's pushing stack.

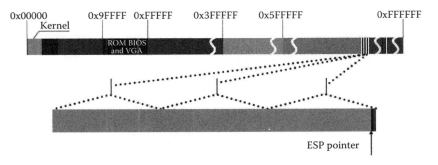

Figure 6.19 Clearing the stack after process str1 is finished.

calling exit() function to realize. The parent is responsible to release the page where the task_struct is located. Now we come to the concrete process.

The str1 process is ready to exit. The str1 process calls exit() function to exit, eventually mapping to the sys_exit() function to carry out, and calling the do_exit() function to deal with the related affairs of str1 process exit.

The specific code is as follows:

```
//code path:include/unistd.h:
volatile void exit(int status);


//code path:kernel/exit.c:
int sys_exit(int error_code)
{
    return do_exit((error_code&0xff)<<8);
}
```

There are two aspects of the content related to process exits, which include, first, releasing the physical memory that the code and data of str1 process occupied and removing the relationship with str1. By this, the str1 process is self-responsible. Second, release the physical memory, which is occupied by the str1 process's management structure task_struct and withdraw its relationship with task[64]. This is done by the parent process shell.

Release the page occupied by str1 process. While executing the do_exit() function, the system uses the free_page_tables() function to release the page that the str1 program takes, which includes the pages that have been clear stack but not been released, and release the page table and the page directory that manages these pages. These pages are still kept in the garbage data of the str1 process but the mapping relationship has been released. Process str1 will not be able to find these pages.

The code is as follows:

```
//code path:kernel/exit.c:
int do_exit(long code)
{
    int i;
    free_page_tables(get_base(current->ldt[1]),get_limit(0x0f));    //release the page of
                                                                     //str1 code segment
                                                                     //occupied
    free_page_tables(get_base(current->ldt[2]),get_limit(0x17));    //release the page of
                                                                     //str1 data segment
                                                                     //occupied

    for (i=0 ; i<NR_TASKS ; i++)
        if (task[i] && task[i]->father = = current->pid) {
            task[i]->father = 1;
            if (task[i]->state = = TASK_ZOMBIE)
                /* assumption task[1] is always init */
                (void) send_sig(SIGCHLD, task[1], 1);
        }
    ……
}
```

The procedure is shown in Figure 6.20.

Remove file-related contents of str1 and send a signal to the parent process. The specific performance of how to remove the relationship between this process and the str1 program's executable file is that the file shared with the parent process is released first, and then the kernel sets the str1 process to zombie state and sends a signal to the parent

Release page and page table

Figure 6.20 Release the page of str1 program takes.

process shell that the child process has exited. The problem of signal processing will be introduced in the Chapter 8 in detail.

The code is as follows:

```
//code path:kernel/exit.c:
int do_exit(long code)
{
    ......
    for (i=0 ; i<NR_OPEN ; i++)            //following release the file shared with
                                            //the parent process
        if (current->filp[i])
                sys_close(i);
    iput(current->pwd);
    current->pwd=NULL;
    iput(current->root);
    current->root=NULL;
    iput(current->executable);
    current->executable=NULL;              //above release the file shared with the
                                            //parent process
    ......
    current->state = TASK_ZOMBIE;          //set str1 to zombie states
    current->exit_code = code;
    tell_father(current->father);          //send a signal to the parent process shell
    ......
}
```

The process of removing a relationship and sending a signal to the parent process is shown in Figure 6.21.

Implement the process scheduling after the exiting of str1 program. So far, the rehabilitation work of the str1 process for the exiting has been finished. The str1 process will switch to other processes to execute. Because only one user process is created, now in the system there are process 0, process 1, updata process, shell process, and the str1 user process.

The code is as follows:

```
//code path:kernel/exit.c:
   int do_exit(long code)
   {
       ......
       current->state = TASK_ZOMBIE;
       current->exit_code = code;
       tell_father(current->father);
       schedule();                          //ready to switch to the shell execution
       return (-1);          /* just to suppress warnings */
   }
```

The process of the switching effect is shown in Figure 6.22.

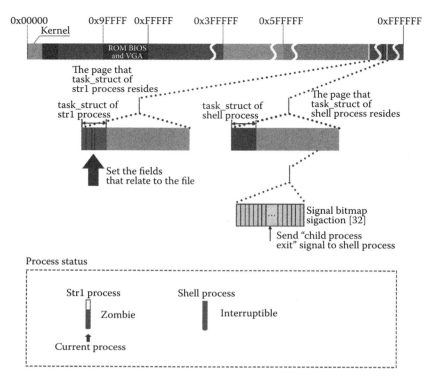

Figure 6.21 Remove the str1 procedure's content, which is related to the document.

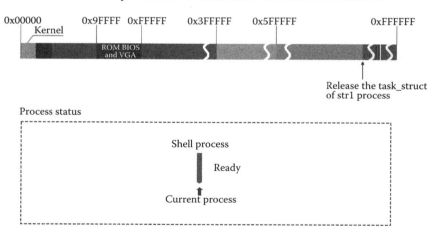

Figure 6.22 Str1 process exit, switch to shell process.

The shell process receives the signal transmitted by the str1 and waked up, which means set to the ready state, then switching to the shell process to execute. After the shell process executing into the kernel, the kernel will release the page, which is occupied by the str1 process task_struct, and remove the relationship between task[64] and the str1 process. So str1 is completely withdrawn from the system. The empty task[64] position can be used by another process, and the process, which takes up this position, will have the same linear address space and a page directory entry with str1.

6.4 Multiple User Processes Run Concurrently

In this section, we will have a look at how to execute and switch among multiple processes with three user processes str1, str2, and str3 as examples.

6.4.1 Process Scheduling

Create str1, str2, and str3 processes in order. We assume that there is no user process running in the system. There are three executable files, str1, str2, and str3, in the peripheral, and the program in the file is the same as the str1 process code, which was introduced before. Under this premise, we create three user processes: str1, str2, and str3 in order.

Now, last_pid has accumulated to 4, so the pid of the three processes should be: 5, 6, and 7 in order. Now, the first four has been occupied in the task[64], and the number in task[64] is 4, 5, and 6 in order. From this, we can further conclude that their position in the linear address space should be: 4*64 MB to 5*64 MB, 5*64 MB to 6*64 MB, and 6*64 MB to 7*64 MB, respectively.

The distribution of these three processes in a linear space is shown in Figure 6.23.

Figure 6.24 shows the distribution of task_struct of the three processes and the data pushed into the stack in the physical memory.

The implementation effect of the str1 process pushing into the stack. Suppose that it is the str1 process's turn to execute at this time. Str1 starts to call foo function, and then a page-fault exception is produced. During the page-fault handling, kernel applies a free physical page for str1 process, and it was mapped into the linear address space of the

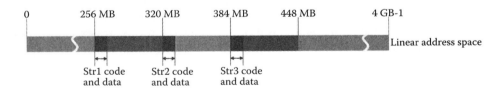

Figure 6.23 Distribution of str1, str2, and str3 processes in a linear space.

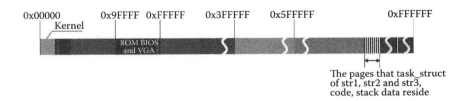

Figure 6.24 Distribution of task_struct of the three processes and the data information to be pressed into the stack in the main memory area.

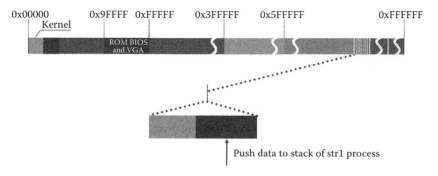

0x00000   0x9FFFF 0xFFFFF   0x3FFFFF   0x5FFFFF   0xFFFFFF

Kernel

ROM BIOS
and VGA

Push data to stack of str1 process

Figure 6.25 Effect of str1 process push stack.

str1 process. After that, process settings for text array, contents are written in the newly allocated physical pages.

The result is shown in Figure 6.25.

During srt1 running, timer interrupt generated and switches to str2. In Linux 0.11, there are two cases leading to process switch. One is the timer interrupt, which has no relationship with the running process at all. No matter which process is running, on privilege level 0 or privilege level 3, a timer interrupt will be generated. If switch requirements, switches with no doubt, it switches. Another is invoked by the process running. When the process runs in the kernel, if the process run programs need to read data in hard disk, the process cannot continue to execute before data reads, and it suspend the current process and switches to other processes. But in both cases, the full set of information in TSS and LDT follows the process. Let's first look at the switching caused by timer interrupt.

While str1 is running, timer interrupt will generate every 10 ms, which will reduce its time slice. Therefore, we call the sleep() function in a program in order to have an effect of time delay. When the time slice of the current process is cut into 0, the program is not finished, and the privilege level is 0 or 3. If the str1 process was executing user programs, and the privilege level is 3, then it will call the schedule function to prepare for process switching.

The code is as follows:

```
//code path:kernel/sched.c:
void do_timer(long cpl)
{
    ......
    if ((-- current->counter)>0) return;       //judge whether time slice is cut into 0
        current->counter=0;
    if (!cpl) return;                          //only in the 3 privilege level can be
                                               //switched, 0 privilege levels cannot
    schedule();
}
```

When switching to run str2 process, it also performed the same logic program. Notably, when setting the text array, the logical address of the print screen and the str1 program is the same. But their linear addresses are different, and the process of str2 did not overlap str1 in physical memory.

The effect of str2 pushing into the stack is shown in Figure 6.26.

During the running of str2, it will switch to str3 when encountering a timer interrupt.

When str2 runs after a period of time, the time slice cuts into 0 and then switches to the str3, and it will also push into the stack, and str3 starts running. The code of implementation is the same as the str2 process. It is also pushed into the stack and sets up text.

The effect of str3 pushing into the stack is shown in Figure 6.27.

We may change the code of str3 a little and call the open(), read(), and close() functions to read a file from the hard disk, which then maps to sys_read() function. After reading the instruction in the disk, the data does not immediately enter the buffer zone. str3 cannot continue without data. At this time it will suspend itself and then switch to other processes to execute.

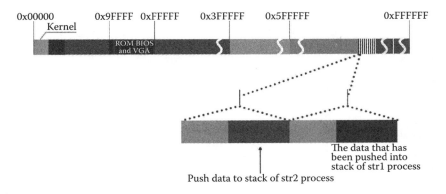

Figure 6.26 Effect of str2 pushing into the stack.

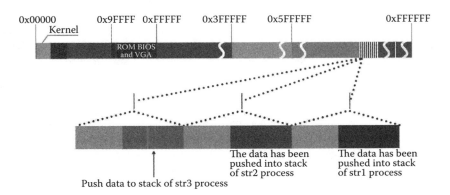

Figure 6.27 Effect of str3 pushing into the stack.

The code is as follows:

```
//code path:fs/buffer.c:
struct buffer_head * bread(int dev,int block)
{
    struct buffer_head * bh;


    if (!(bh=getblk(dev,block)))
            panic("bread: getblk returned NULL\n");
    if (bh->b_uptodate)
            return bh;
    ll_rw_block(READ,bh);
    wait_on_buffer(bh);                         //check whether need to wait for the buffer
                                                //block unlock and therefore suspend the
                                                //process

    if (bh->b_uptodate)
            return bh;
    brelse(bh);
    return NULL;
}



    static inline void wait_on_buffer(struct buffer_head * bh)
{
    cli();
    while (bh->b_lock)
            sleep_on(&bh->b_wait);              //the buffer block is still locking, so it
                                                //is necessary to suspend the process

    sti();
}


    void sleep_on(struct task_struct **p)
{
    .....
    tmp = *p;
    *p = current;
    current->state = TASK_UNINTERRUPTIBLE;      //suspend the current process, it is str3
    schedule();                                 //switch to other processes in this case
    if (tmp)
            tmp->state=0;
}
```

When the three procedures run over a period of time, what is the distribution pattern in main memory? When str3 executes after a period of time, the time slice also used up. Although these three user processes still need to continue to run, the time slice has used up. If a timer interrupt happens again, do_timer will call a schedule() function to switch the process once again, and the system will re-allocate a time slice for them.

From the end of the task[], the kernel makes a redistribution of a time slice to all processes (including the sleep process but except the process 0) in the current system. The size of the time slice is counter/2 + priority. Priority is the priority of the process, so if the process has a higher priority level, the value of priority is larger and it will gain more time slice and then reselect the process to run according to the time slice and such repeated.

The code is as follows:

```
//code path:kernel/sched.c:
void schedule(void)
{
    ......
        for(p = &LAST_TASK ; p > &FIRST_TASK ; --p)
            if (*p)
                (*p)->counter = ((*p)->counter >> 1) +
                    (*p)->priority;
    ......
}
```

It is worth mentioning that, when redistributing the time slices, there is no need to distribute for process 0. The reason is that as long as all processes in the system currently do not have condition to execute, the system will automatically switch to process 0. Process 0 will run even if its time slice is cut into 0. Because if there is no other process running, the system relies on process 0 to continue. Thus, the time slice has no meaning for process 0. Therefore, process 0 is a special one, its execution is decided by the current demand of the system, and the mechanism of the time slice rotation does not apply to it. They will continue to constantly push stack as shown in Figure 6.35. The data pushed into their respective stack. In the linear address space, the data in the stack is continuous respectively, but in the physical space, the data is completely "staggered" allocated.

When these three procedures run over a period of time, the distribution in the main memory area of the data, which is pressed into their respective stack by themselves is shown in Figure 6.28.

It is not difficult to find that, at any time, only one process is running. There is no multiple processes executing at the same time. The simultaneous running of multiple processes is only the subjective feeling of people. The data does not cover each other, and no matter what kind of situation produces process switch, it is all switched by calling the schedule() function. When this function is doing process switch, it will use the full set of data of TSS and LDT to follow the process in order to protect the process.

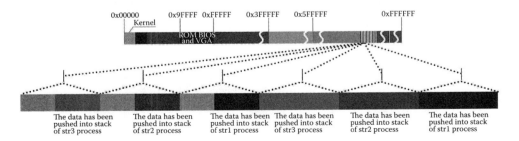

Figure 6.28 Distribution in the main memory area of the data that are pressed into stack during a period of time when these three procedures run.

6.4.2 Page Protection

Process A and B share page. Suppose now the system has one user process (process A), and the corresponding program code of it has been loaded into memory. The number of the page reference that is occupied in the memory of this process is "1," and then it begins execution, creating a new process (process B) by calling the fork() function. While creating a process, the system copies all page table entries of process A to process B and sets the page directory entry (PDE) of process B. At this time, the two processes share the page, citing the shared page accumulated to 2, and the shared page is all set to "read only" attribute, which means that either process A or B can only run the read operation for these shared pages, rather than write operation.

The code is as follows:

```
//code path:mm/memory.c:
int copy_page_tables(unsigned long from,unsigned long to,long size)
{
    ......
    for (; nr— > 0 ; from_page_table++,to_page_table++) {
        this_page = *from_page_table;
        if (!(1 & this_page))
            continue;
        this_page &= ~2;                    //the page's operation attribute of Process A
                                            //is set to read-only
        *to_page_table = this_page;         //the page's operation attribute of Process B
                                            //is set to read-only
        if (this_page > LOW_MEM) {
            *from_page_table = this_page;
            this_page -= LOW_MEM;
            this_page >>= 12;
            mem_map[this_page]++;           //reference counting record in the mem_map,
                                            //and accumulate to 2
        }
    }
    ......
}
```

The page sharing situation is shown in Figure 6.29.

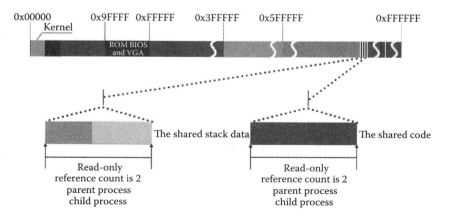

Figure 6.29 Page sharing situation of process A and B.

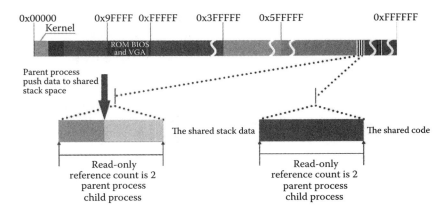

Figure 6.30 Process A ready for pushing.

Process A prepare for pushing operation. We assume that process A executes next, and it is a push action. Let us see what will happen.

Now all the pages of the program of process A are read only. It means that whether the page occupied by the code or the corresponding page of the original push data can only do the read operation rather than write operation. However, the push action is a write operation. After parsing the corresponding linear address value during push, it must be mapped to a read-only page and will produce a "page write protect" interrupt. It is shown in Figure 6.30.

The push action of process A triggers page write protection. The corresponding function of page fault interrupt when it happens page write protection is un_wp_page() function. It performs as follows. The first step is to apply for a free page in the main memory (in the following, we call it the new page) to make a backup for all the data of the page (in the following, we call it the original page) in the location of push stack. Then we subtract 1 from the citing count of the original page. This is because the data in the original page will be backed up to a new page, and the process A will go to a new page to operate data, and no longer need to maintain relations with the original page, so the citing count of the original page subtracts 1.

The code is as follows:

```
//code path:mm/memory.c:
void un_wp_page(unsigned long * table_entry)
{
    ......
    if (!(new_page = get_free_page()))      //get a new page
        oom();
    if (old_page >= LOW_MEM)
        mem_map[MAP_NR(old_page)]--;         //citing count of page is
                                             //decremented for 1
    ......
}
```

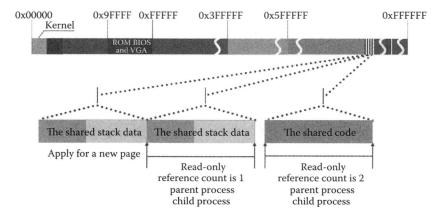

Figure 6.31 Apply for a new page for the process A to store the push data.

The main distribution of memory after performing page write protection for process A to apply for a new page is shown in Figure 6.31.

What is notable is that we just make the citing count of original page subtract 1 but do not completely release it. This is because, in the operating system, all resources may be shared by multiple processes, for example, the file i node, file management, memory page table, and so on, need to represent the state through the citing count. When a process terminates a relationship with them, other processes are not doing the same things; then simple "release" is not appropriate.

Putting the page table of process A points to the new application pages. Although has been applied for the new page, the page table entry in the page table of process A, which corresponds to the original page, still points to the original page. Because there is no page table entry corresponding to the new page, then it is unable finally to find the physical address. So it also lets the page table entry, which points to the original page in the page of process A, point to a new page. And changes the attribute from the "read-only" to "read/write," so the process A has an ability to process the data in the new page.

The code is as follows:

```
//code path:mm/memory.c:
void un_wp_page(unsigned long * table_entry)
{
    ......
    if (old_page >= LOW_MEM)
        mem_map[MAP_NR(old_page)]--;
    *table_entry = new_page | 7;              //the binary form of 7 is
                                              //111, it means a new
                                              //page can read and write.

    invalidate();
    copy_page(old_page,new_page);
}
```

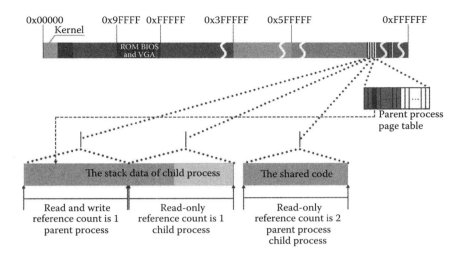

Figure 6.32 Page table of process A corresponds to the new application page.

When this operation is done, the state of the new page that is allocated to process A is shown in Figure 6.32.

Copy the contents of the original page to the new application page of process A. When everything is ready, you can copy the contents of the original page to the new page. After this action, process A will complete the push action in the new page.

The code is as follows:

```
//code path:mm/memory.c:
void un_wp_page(unsigned long * table_entry)
{
    ......
    if (old_page >= LOW_MEM)
            mem_map[MAP_NR(old_page)]—;
    *table_entry = new_page | 7;
    invalidate();
    copy_page(old_page,new_page);        //here we copy the data
                                         //of original page to the
                                         //new page, let process A
                                         //using

}
```

After the copy operation, the storage case in the new memory page, the process A application is shown in Figure 6.33.

Process B is preparing for operation of the shared page. After process A has been running for a period of time, it should turn to its child process, process B. Process B still uses the original page, assuming that it will do a write operation in the original page, but now the original page attribute is still "read only." This is arranged when process A creates process B and has never changed. So in this case, it needs page-write protection again, and it is still mapped to the un_wp_page() function. Because the citing count of the original

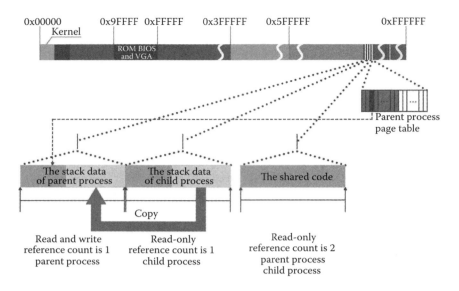

0x00000 0x9FFFF 0xFFFFF 0x3FFFFF 0x5FFFFF 0xFFFFFF

Kernel

ROM BIOS
and VGA

Parent process
page table

The stack data
of parent process

The stack data
of child process

The shared code

Copy

Read and write
reference count is 1
parent process

Read-only
reference count is 1
child process

Read-only
reference count is 2
parent process
child process

Figure 6.33 Copy the content of the original page to a new page process A application.

page has been reduced to 1, now set the original page attribute to "read/write." The code
is as follows:

```
//code path:mm/memory.c:
void un_wp_page(unsigned long * table_entry)
{
    ......
    old_page = 0xfffff000 & *table_entry;
    if (old_page >= LOW_MEM && mem_map[MAP_NR(old_page)]==1){   //found that the citing
                                                                //count of original
                                                                //page is 1, do not share
        *table_entry |= 2;                                      //the binary form of 2
                                                                //is 010, the R/W bit is
                                                                //set to 1, read/write
        invalidate();
        return;
    }
    ......
}
```

The process A and B can operate different pages for each other in stack data processing, and these pages are all read/write, and the citing count is 1; they will not interfere with
each other later (Figure 6.34).

Now the process B does not have its own procedures, and if it has in the future, it will
relieve the relationship with the original page. The citing count of the original page will
continue to subtract 1, so it becomes 0, and then the system will recognize it as the "free
page."

Assuming that the processes B execute the push operation first. We now again
assume that it is not the parent process (process A) to implement first but the child process
(process B); then what would happen?

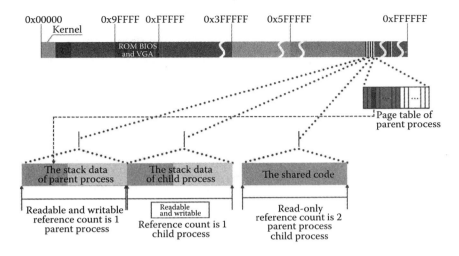

Figure 6.34 Process B changes the character of the original shared page.

This case is symmetrical with the front, and the system applies for a page for the process B; then let the page table entry, which is corresponding to the original page in the page table of process B, point to the new page. Finally, it copies the content of the original page to a new page for process B to operate. When turning to process A to implement, the original page that is set to "read/write" the process A still uses the original page to execute data operation.

The memory allocation of process B implementing the push operation first is shown in Figure 6.35.

What is also worth noting is that page-write protection is an action performed by the kernel. While the whole action occurs, the user process remains normal execute. It does not know it is duplicated in memory or which page to be copied either.

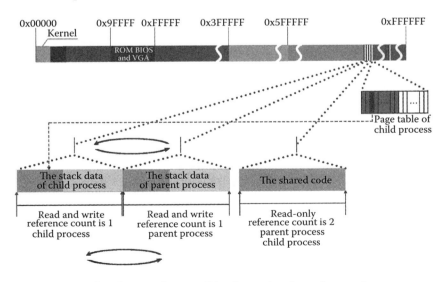

Figure 6.35 Memory distribution of process B implementing the push operation.

7 Buffer and Multiprocess File

The preceding chapters have explained the process, file, and memory management. Based on these explanations, the readers can understand the operating system, the complex relationship among process, the file system, and the buffer which is across the above three parts. If we to understand the complex relationship among OS, process, file system and memory management deeply, we must make clear what the function of the buffer is.

7.1 Function of Buffer

In order to make clear what the function of the buffer is, we want to ask: Is it alright without a buffer, and what problems will come out without it?

From the physical aspect of the computer, the buffer is a space that is opened in the physical memory. There is no essential difference in the physical property between this memory space and the memory space that is occupied by a process. Exchanging data between the block device (for convenience, this chapter discusses the hard disk only) and the buffer is the same as the process between the hard disk and memory space of process in the physical aspect. It does not affect the correctness of data interaction or the transmission speed. In this view, even without the buffer, it can also complete the data interface between process and hard disk.

Therefore, the buffer is not necessary. Designing a buffer is sure to make the operating system run better, thus adding a beautiful thing to a contrasting beautiful thing.

What benefits can be brought to the operation of an operating system by designing a buffer?

We think that it is mainly reflected in two aspects:

1. It forms a uniform distribution of all block devices and makes the designing of the operating system more convenient and flexible.

2. It makes the file operations of the block device run more efficiently.

The first aspect is relatively easy to understand, and the second is one of the difficult problems to understand the operating system, so in this chapter, we will explain the design in detail about the buffer in improving the running efficiency of operation files of the block device through two examples of files operated by multiprocess.

In Figure 7.1, we can find that there seems to be a problem in which the process memory space and the buffer memory space are the same. When exchanging the data between the process memory space and the hard disk, a buffer is added, and it only adds to the time of the data changing hands in memory once, but this data changing hands is without any data processing. It is just simply changing hands and should only increase CPU resource consumption. But why is it faster than the process of directly exchanging data from the hard disk?

The reason is buffer sharing. In the computer, the speed of data interaction between memory and memory is faster 2 levels than that between the memory and the hard disk. If the process A has read the data from the hard disk to the buffer, and process B also needs to read this data, then it does not need to read it from the hard disk, and it can be directly read from the buffer. Then the time process B takes is only about one percent of the process A time for reading this data, so efficiency is increased by two level of magnitude. If there are processes C, D, and E, etc. that all need to read this data, the whole efficiency of the computer will be greatly improved. This is a model of buffer sharing; it means that different processes share the same data in the buffer. If the process A reads the data, uses this data, and reads the data again after a period of time, and it is still in

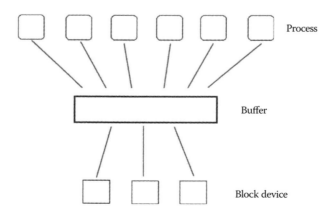

Figure 7.1 Pattern picture of process, buffer, and block device.

the buffer, process A can directly read it from the buffer, and it doesn't spend the time from the hard disk. It is another mode of sharing, and that is the same process multiple shares the same data in the buffer at different times. Another is the combination of these two patterns. What we analyze above is the sharing of a read operation that is the same as a write operation.

From the above analysis, we can find that if we want to improve the overall efficiency of file read-and-write, we should share the data in the buffer as much as possible. If we want to do this, **the most effective and direct way is to let the data of the buffer stay in it as long as possible!**

We can say that the kernel design of the codes, which manage the buffer, is how to ensure the correctness of the interactive data and how to make the data in the buffer stay as long as possible. In this chapter, we'll explain how the operating system code achieves this goal of making the data stay in the buffer as long as possible through two examples.

■ 7.2 Structure of Buffer

The buffer relates to process, memory, and file. It has a lot of content and complex codes, and it is not easy to understand. It is one of the difficult problems to understand in the operating system. In order to learn and master buffer design better, first, let's look at the buffer structure (Figure 7.2).

In Linux, to support buffer, we design two pieces of important management information: buffer_head and request. Buffer_head is mainly responsible for the data interaction of the buffer block between the process and the buffer. Under the condition of making sure data interaction correct, let the data in the buffer stay as long as possible. Request is mainly responsible for the interaction between the data in the buffer and the block device. Under the circumstances of the correctness of data interaction, let the data that is modified by the process in the buffer block be synchronized into the block devices as soon as possible.

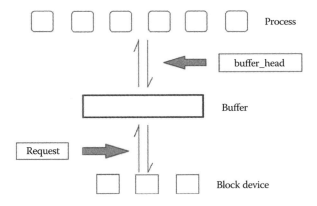

Figure 7.2 Pattern chart of buffer, buffer_head, and request.

The code of the data structure of the two management information is as follows:

```
//code path:include/linux/fs.h:
struct buffer_head {
        char * b_data;                    /* pointer to data block (1024 bytes) */
        unsigned long b_blocknr;          /* block number */
        unsigned short b_dev;             /* device (0 = free) */
        unsigned char b_uptodate;
        unsigned char b_dirt;             /* 0-clean,1-dirty */
        unsigned char b_count;            /* users using this block */
        unsigned char b_lock;             /* 0 - ok, 1 -locked */
        struct task_struct * b_wait;
        struct buffer_head * b_prev;
        struct buffer_head * b_next;
        struct buffer_head * b_prev_free;
        struct buffer_head * b_next_free;
};


//code path:kernel/blk_drv/blk.h:
struct request {
        int dev;           /* -1 if no request */
        int cmd;           /* READ or WRITE */
        int errors;
        unsigned long sector;
        unsigned long nr_sectors;
        char * buffer;
        struct task_struct * waiting;
        struct buffer_head * bh;
        struct request * next;
};
```

We will explain in detail why this data structure is designed and how this data structure achieves this goal of letting the data stay in the buffer as long as possible next.

7.3   The Function of b_dev, b_blocknr, and Request

b_dev and b_blocknr are very important members in buffer_head structure and are the foundation of supporting of the multiple process sharing file. They are both the foundation of correctness, and also the foundation that the data stay in the buffer as long as possible. We first introduce how these two members ensure the correctness.

7.3.1   Ensure the Correctness of the Data Interaction between Processes and Buffer Block

Process and buffer make the interactive data not in units of files but in a buffer block. Several blocks interact at one time, and the data that is less than the size of one block still occupies one buffer block. Interaction between buffer and disk is still in a block, and a buffer block has the same size as a hard block. When a process operates files, the request of document operation, which is proposed by the process, is implemented by the operating system to interact with a specific data block in the hard disk. Because there is a buffer, the data block in the process and hard disk is not in interaction directly but through a buffer.

If we want to ensure the correctness of data interaction, first we have to ensure that the data block of the hard disk must strictly correspond with the buffer block.

Because the hard disk device number and block number can only identify a specific hard block, and from the second chapter, we know that each block has only one buffer_head to manage, the strategy of the operating system is as follows: The kernel binds the relationship between the buffer block and the hard disk through b_dev and b_blocknr in the buffer_head structure, and this will ensure the uniqueness of the relationship between the disk block and the buffer block, furthermore, it is equivalent in data interaction between the buffer block and the hard disk and the interaction between process and buffer, so as to ensure data interaction without confusion. The code is as follows:

```
//code path:fs/buffer.c:
struct buffer_head * getblk(int dev,int block)        //apply for buffer block
{
repeat:
        if (bh = get_hash_table(dev,block))           //if it is found that buffer
                                                      //block has been bound with
                                                      //the specified device (DEV)
                                                      //and the data block (block)
        return bh;           //return, use it directly
        tmp = free_list;                              //if bound buffer block
                                                      //which is in standard is
                                                      //not found, apply for a new
                                                      //buffer block
        do {
            if (tmp->b_count)
        continue;
            if (!bh || BADNESS(tmp)<BADNESS(bh)) {
                bh = tmp;
                if (!BADNESS(tmp))
        break;
/* and repeat until we find something good */
        } while ((tmp = tmp->b_next_free) != free_list);
        ......
/* OK, FINALLY we know that this buffer is the only one of it's kind, */
/* and that it's unused (b_count = 0), unlocked (b_lock = 0), and clean */
        bh->b_count = 1;
        bh->b_dirt = 0;
        bh->b_uptodate = 0;
        remove_from_queues(bh);
        bh->b_dev = dev;                              //set up device number of
                                                      //new buffer block
        bh->b_blocknr = block;                        //set up block number of new
                                                      //buffer block
        insert_into_queues(bh);
        return bh;
}
```

From the code, we can see that when applying for a new one, it will lock in the relationship between the buffer block and the data block. This makes the kernel in the process direction and determines the location of the file and switches it to b_dev and b_blocknr. Do not consider the relationship between the hard disk data block and the buffer block because the interaction with the hard disk is definitely right finally.

When reading the file, the kernel calculates b_dev and b_blocknr where the file data content is through a file pointer. In the process, it goes to the buffer block. After implementing the bread() function, it should no longer deal with the data block of the hard disk directly. The code is as follows:

```
//code path:fs/file_dev.c:
int file_read(struct m_inode * inode, struct file * filp, char * buf, int count)      //read file
{
......
if ((left = count)< = 0)
          return 0;
          while (left) {
          if (nr = bmap(inode,(filp->f_pos)/BLOCK_SIZE) {   //through the file offset
                                                            //pointer, calculate the
                                                            //block number
               if (!(bh = bread(inode->i_dev,nr)))          //in the actual parameters inode->i_dev is
                                                            //device number, nr is block number
          break;
          } else
          bh = NULL;
          nr = filp->f_pos% BLOCK_SIZE;
          chars = MIN(BLOCK_SIZE-nr, left);
......
}
......
}


//code path:fs/buffer.c:
struct buffer_head * bread(int dev,int block)      //read the equipment data of bottom block
{
          struct buffer_head * bh;
          if (!(bh = getblk(dev,block)))            //when apply for buffer block, the number
                                                    //device of equipment and block we will use
          panic(«bread: getblk returned NULL\n»);
          if (bh->b_uptodate)
          return bh;
          ......
}
```

It is the same as reading a file. When writing a file, the kernel calculates b_dev and b_blocknr where the file data content is through a file pointer. In the process, it goes to the buffer block. The code is as follows:

```
//code path:fs/file_dev.c:
int file_write(struct m_inode * inode, struct file * filp, char * buf, int count)
//write file
{
......
if (filp->f_flags & O_APPEND)
          pos = inode->i_size;
          else
          pos = filp->f_pos;
          while (i<count) {
          if (!(block = create_block(inode,pos/BLOCK_SIZE)))  //through the file offset
                                                              //pointer, calculate the
                                                              //block number
          break;
          if (!(bh = bread(inode->i_dev,block)))  //in the actual parameters inode->i_dev is
                                                  //device number, nr is block number
          break;
          c = pos% BLOCK_SIZE;
          p = c + bh->b_data;
          bh->b_dirt = 1;
```

```
       ......
       }
......
}

//code path:fs/buffer.c:
struct buffer_head * bread(int dev,int block)    //read the equipment data of bottom block
                                                 //device
{
       struct buffer_head * bh;
       if (!(bh = getblk(dev,block)))            //when apply for buffer block, the number
                                                 //of equipment and block we will use
       panic("bread: getblk returned NULL\n");
       if (bh->b_uptodate)
       return bh;
       ......
}
```

The direction of extending interchange file is the same as the content and management.

When the kernel reads the i node, it calculates the b_dev of the i node and the b_blocknr through the number of the i node and the information in the super block without operating the hard disk data blocks across the buffer directly. The code is as follows:

```
//code path:fs/inode.c:
static void read_inode(struct m_inode * inode)    //read the i node
{
       ......
lock_inode(inode);
if (!(sb = get_super(inode->i_dev)))
       panic("trying to read inode without dev");
       block = 2 + sb->s_imap_blocks + sb->s_zmap_blocks +   //determine the block (number)
                                                             //through the number of the
                                                             //i node and the information of
                                                             //the super block
       (inode->i_num-1)/INODES_PER_BLOCK;
       if (!(bh = bread(inode->i_dev,block)))                //the inode->i_dev in the actual parameter is
                                                             //the device number, nr is the block number
       panic("unable to read i-node block");
       *(struct d_inode *)inode =
       ((struct d_inode *)bh->b_data)
       [(inode->i_num-1)%INODES_PER_BLOCK];                  //extract the i node from the buffer
                                                             //and load it into the inode_table[32]
       brelse(bh);
       unlock_inode(inode);
}


//code path:fs/buffer.c:
struct buffer_head * bread(int dev,int block)    //read the underlying block device data
{
       struct buffer_head * bh;
       if (!(bh = getblk(dev,block)))            //the device number and the block number
                                                 //needed when allocate the buffer
       panic(«bread: getblk returned NULL\n»);
       if (bh->b_uptodate)
       return bh;
       ......
}
```

Similarly to the kernel reading the i node, it calculates the b_dev of the i node and the b_blocknr through the number of the i node and the information in the super block when writing into the i node. The action stops here. The code is as follows:

```
//code path:fs/inode.c:
static void write_inode(struct m_inode * inode)    //write the i node
{
        ......
if (!(sb = get_super(inode->i_dev)))
        panic("trying to write inode without device");
        block = 2 + sb->s_imap_blocks + sb->s_zmap_blocks + //determine the block (number)
                                                  //through the i node
                                                  //number and the information
                                                  //of the super block
        (inode->i_num-1)/INODES_PER_BLOCK;
        if (!(bh = bread(inode->i_dev,block)))   //the inode->i_dev in the actual parameter
                                                  //is the device number, and nr is the
                                                  //block number
        panic("unable to read i-node block");
        ((struct d_inode *)bh->b_data)
        [(inode->i_num-1)%INODES_PER_BLOCK] =
        *(struct d_inode *)inode;                 //extract the i node from the inode_table[32]
                                                  //and load it into the buffer
bh->b_dirt = 1;
        inode->i_dirt = 0;
        ......
}


//code path:fs/buffer.c:
struct buffer_head * bread(int dev,int block)     //read the underlying block device data
{
        struct buffer_head * bh;
        if (!(bh = getblk(dev,block)))            //the device number and the block
                                                  //number needed when allocate the buffer
        panic("bread: getblk returned NULL\n");
        if (bh->b_uptodate)
        return bh;
        ......
}
```

Similarly, when the kernel loads the super block, it calculates the b_dev and b_blocknr of the super block, the i node bitmap, and the logical block bitmap through the device number and the block number specified; the action continues here. The code is as follows:

```
//code path:fs/super.c:
static struct super_block * read_super(int dev)   //read the super block
{
        ......
s->s_time = 0;
        s->s_rd_only = 0;
        s->s_dirt = 0;
        lock_super(s);
        if (!(bh = bread(dev,1))) {               //1 is the block number, super block
                                                  //is the first data block of the
                                                  //device
        s->s_dev = 0;
        free_super(s);
        return NULL;
        }
```

```
                *((struct d_super_block *) s) =
                *((struct d_super_block *) bh->b_data);
brelse(bh);
                if (s->s_magic != SUPER_MAGIC) {
                s->s_dev = 0;
                free_super(s);
                return NULL;
                }
                ......
                block = 2;              //2 is the block number of the first i node bitmap
                for (i = 0 ; i < s->s_imap_blocks ; i++)
                if (s->s_imap[i] = bread(dev,block))
                block++;
                else
                break;
                for (i = 0 ; i < s->s_zmap_blocks ; i++)   //block continue to
                                                           //accumulate, load the super
                                                           //block bitmap according to
                                                           //this
                if (s->s_zmap[i] = bread(dev,block))
                block++;
                else
                break;
if (block != 2+s->s_imap_blocks+s->s_zmap_blocks) {
                for(i = 0;i<I_MAP_SLOTS;i++)
                brelse(s->s_imap[i]);
                ......
}


//code path:fs/buffer.c:
struct buffer_head * bread(int dev,int block)          //read the underlying block
                                                       //device data
{
        struct buffer_head * bh;
        if (!(bh = getblk(dev,block)))         //the device number and the block
                                               //number needed when allocate the
                                               //buffer
        panic(«bread: getblk returned NULL\n»);
        if (bh->b_uptodate)
        return bh;
        ......
}
```

The code above shows that, in the direction of the process, the accuracy is assured by making sure the device number and the block number correspond to the buffer. And the getblk() function achieves the binding function.

From the hard disk direction, the kernel supports the interaction between the buffer and the hard disk through another request data structure, the device number dev and the first sector number of the block (the block is the operating system concept, and the hard drive only has the concept of a sector) in the request to determine the position of the data interaction, and the value of these two fields is also set by the values of b_dev and b_blocknr in the buffer_head. This shows that, as long as the device number and the block number of the buffer are determined, it is enough to consider the buffer when the kernel interacts with the hard disk through the request. There is no need to extend to the process of considering the file operations.

The code is as follows:

```
//code path:kernel/blk_drv/ll_rw_blk.c:
void ll_rw_block(int rw, struct buffer_head * bh) //operate the underlying block device
{
        unsigned int major;
        if ((major = MAJOR(bh->b_dev)) > = NR_BLK_DEV ||
        !(blk_dev[major].request_fn)) {
        printk("Trying to read nonexistent block-device\n\r");
        return;
        }
        make_request(major,rw,bh);      //set the request item
}
static void make_request(int major,int rw, struct buffer_head * bh)
{
        ......
if (req < request) {
        if (rw_ahead) {
        unlock_buffer(bh);
        return;
        }
        sleep_on(&wait_for_request);
        goto repeat;
        }
        req->dev = bh->b_dev;            //use the b_dev in the Buffer block to set the
                                         //request item
        req->cmd = rw;
        req->errors = 0;
        req->sector = bh->b_blocknr<<1;            //use the b_blocknr in the Buffer block to
                                                   //set the request item
        req->nr_sectors = 2;
        req->buffer = bh->b_data;
        req->waiting = NULL;
        req->bh = bh;
        req->next = NULL;
        add_request(major+blk_dev,req);        //load the request item
}
static void add_request(struct blk_dev_struct * dev, struct request * req)
{
        ......
if (!(tmp = dev->current_request)) {
        dev->current_request = req;
        sti();
        (dev->request_fn)();               //make hard disk operation command
        return;
        }
......
}


//code path:kernel/blk_drv/hd.c:
void do_hd_request(void)
{
        ......
INIT_REQUEST;
        dev = MINOR(CURRENT->dev);     //get the device number from the request
block = CURRENT->sector;               //get the block number from the request
if (dev > = 5*NR_HD || block+2 > hd[dev].nr_sects) {
        end_request(0);
        goto repeat;
        }
......
__asm__("divl%4":" = a" (block)," = d" (sec):"0" (block),"1" (0), //calculate the heads,
                                                                  //sectors and the cylinders
                                                                  //by the block number
        "r" (hd_info[dev].sect));
__asm__("divl%4":" = a" (cyl)," = d" (head):"0" (block),"1" (0),
        "r" (hd_info[dev].head));
sec++;
nsect = CURRENT->nr_sectors;
......
}
```

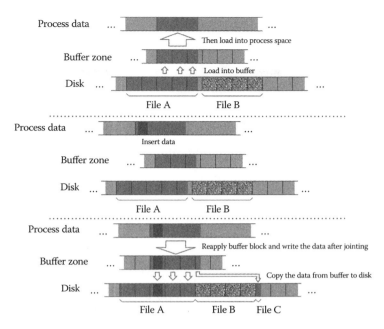

Figure 7.3 Add data within the block.

In summary, in the direction of the process, any complex file operation, such as modifying, inserting, and deleting data in any part of the file, could ensure the accuracy as long as these two fields (b_dev and b_blocknr) and data block are locked. From the direction of the process, the interaction with the buffer is equivalent to the interaction with the data block in the hard disk.

The situation that additional data is just within a block is shown in Figure 7.3. The additional data between blocks is shown in Figure 7.4.

7.3.2 Let the Data Stay in the Buffer as Long as Possible

The b_dev and b_blocknr not only ensure accuracy, but also lay the foundation for letting the data stay longer in the buffer.

Whether the data stays in the buffer depends on whether there is a binding relationship between the buffer and the data block of the hard disk. The code is as follows:

```
//code path:fs/buffer.c:
struct buffer_head * getblk(int dev,int block)      //allocate the buffer
{
    struct buffer_head * tmp, * bh;

repeat:
if (bh = get_hash_table(dev,block))                 //try to continue to use from the existing
                                                    //binding relationship of the the buffer
        return bh;
    tmp = free_list;
    ......
}

struct buffer_head * get_hash_table(int dev, int block)
```

```
{
    ......
    for (;;) {
            if (!(bh = find_buffer(dev,block)))     //find the buffer whose device number and
                                                    //the block number meets the request
                return NULL;
            bh->b_count++;
        wait_on_buffer(bh);
        ......
    }
}

static struct buffer_head * find_buffer(int dev, int block)
{
    struct buffer_head * tmp;
    for (tmp = hash(dev,block) ; tmp ! = NULL ; tmp = tmp->b_next) //go through the hash
                                                                   //table to make comparison
        if (tmp->b_dev = =dev && tmp->b_blocknr = =block)
                return tmp;                          //if find a existing one, return tmp
        return NULL;                                 //return NULL if not find a existing one
}
```

We can see from the code above that the kernel only uses the device number and the block number when searching the existing buffer from the hash table. The kernel maintains that the data in the data block still stays in the buffer and can be used directly without reading from the hard disk as long as the binding relationship between the buffer and the hard disk data still exists. It saves 100 times the time reading from the hard disk.

After going through the buffer, all the buffers have a binding relationship with the data in the disk, but b_dev and b_blocknr of blocks in the buffer are not needed by the process. If we still cannot find the proper one, then the kernel uses a free buffer not being

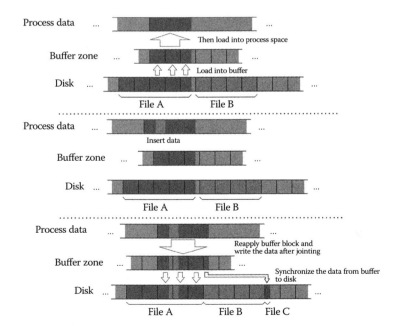

Figure 7.4 Add data between two different blocks.

used by the process temporarily (b_count is 0), abolishes the existing binding relationship, and replaces it with a new binding relationship, that is, a new-built buffer block. Until now, the data in the disk data block does not stay in the buffer. The code is as follows:

```
//code path:fs/buffer.c:
struct buffer_head * getblk(int dev,int block)        //allocate the buffer
{
    ......
    if (find_buffer(dev,block))
        goto repeat;
    bh->b_count = 1;
    bh->b_dirt = 0;
    bh->b_uptodate = 0;
    remove_from_queues(bh);
    bh->b_dev = dev;
    bh->b_blocknr = block;
    insert_into_queues(bh);
    return bh;
}
```

The meaning of these two lines of code is to build the binding relationship of the buffer just allocated and the data block. There will be two cases when allocating a new buffer. There will be two cases; in the first case, when the system just boots, the buffer does not build any binding relationship with a data block. In the other case, the operating system has been running for some time and has done enough file to read and write operations, so all the buffers have established a binding relationship with the hard disk data block and all the buffers cannot be shared because they do not assort with the b_dev and b_blocknr of the new buffer. So we could only occupy a buffer forcefully from the buffers not used (b_count is 0) by the process. In this situation, these two lines of code have two meanings:

1. To build a new binding relationship between the buffer and the hard disk data block.

2. At the same time, to abolish the existing binding relationship between the buffer and the data block of the hard disk.

It is worth noting that there is not any mechanism or code in the kernel that could release the binding relationship established between the buffer and the hard disk data block deliberately and proactively. Only in compelling circumstances is it replaced by the newly established binding relationship forcefully. The purpose of all these is only to let the data stay in the buffer as long as possible. Now we can see that b_dev and b_blocknr are very important management information of the hard disk data block to stay in the buffer longer.

The design idea of the request is just opposite to the buffer. Its purpose is to let the buffer interact data with the hard disk as soon as possible. As we introduced earlier, there are fields similar to the b_dev and b_blocknr in the request, which are the device number "dev" and the first sector number "sector", and they can not only ensure the accuracy of the interaction between the buffer and the hard disk data block, but can let the buffer and the data block interact as soon as possible. Let's look at the following code:

```
//code path:kernel/blk_drv/ll_rw_blk.c:
void ll_rw_block(int rw, struct buffer_head * bh) //the underlying block device operation
{
    unsigned int major;

    if ((major = MAJOR(bh->b_dev)) > = NR_BLK_DEV ||
    !(blk_dev[major].request_fn)) {
        printk("Trying to read nonexistent block-device\n\r");
        return;
    }
    make_request(major,rw,bh);                      //set the request
}


static void make_request(int major,int rw, struct buffer_head * bh)
{
    .....
        if (req < request) {
            if (rw_ahead) {
                unlock_buffer(bh);
                return;
            }
            sleep_on(&wait_for_request);
            goto repeat;
        }
    req->dev = bh->b_dev;                    //use the b_dev in the buffer to set the request
    req->cmd = rw;
    req->errors = 0;
    req->sector = bh->b_blocknr<<1;          //use the b_blocknr set in the buffer to set the request
    req->nr_sectors = 2;
    req->buffer = bh->b_data;
    req->waiting = NULL;
    req->bh = bh;
    req->next = NULL;
    add_request(major+blk_dev,req);          //load the request item
}

static void add_request(struct blk_dev_struct * dev, struct request * req)
{
    struct request * tmp;
    req->next = NULL;
    cli();
    if (req->bh)
        req->bh->b_dirt = 0;
    if (!(tmp = dev->current_request)) {//let the current buffer corresponding to the request
                                        //interact with the hard disk immediately as long as
                                        //the hard disk is free
        dev->current_request = req;
        sti();
        (dev->request_fn)();
        return;
    }
    for (; tmp->next ; tmp = tmp->next) //load the request into the request queue if the hard
                                        //disk is busy
        if ((IN_ORDER(tmp,req) ||
        !IN_ORDER(tmp,tmp->next)) &&
        IN_ORDER(req,tmp->next))
        break;
    req->next = tmp->next;                   //next pointer is used to set up the queue
    tmp->next = req;
    sti();
}
```

Two scenarios could emerge when performing the add_request function: If the hard disk is free, then use it to process the current request. If the hard disk is busy processing a request at the moment, here comes a new request and it is inserted into the request queue. The "next" pointer in the request structure is used to build the request, as Figure 7.5 shows.

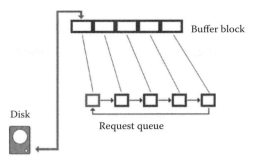

Buffer block

Disk

Request queue

Figure 7.5 Build the request queue.

Now, have a look at the code processing the request in the queue:

```
//code path:kernel/blk_drv/hd.c:
static void read_intr(void)
{
    if (win_result()) {
        bad_rw_intr();
        do_hd_request();
        return;
        }
    port_read(HD_DATA,CURRENT->buffer,256);
    CURRENT->errors = 0;
    CURRENT->buffer + = 512;
    CURRENT->sector++;
    if (-- CURRENT->nr_sectors) {
        do_hd = &read_intr;
        return;
    }
    end_request(1);            //cope with the aftermath after processing a request
    do_hd_request();           //keep giving interaction command if there remain
                               //many requests; else, return
}


static void write_intr(void)
{
    if (win_result()) {
        bad_rw_intr();
        do_hd_request();
        return;
    }
    if (-- CURRENT->nr_sectors) {
        CURRENT->sector++;
        CURRENT->buffer + = 512;
        do_hd = &write_intr;
        port_write(HD_DATA,CURRENT->buffer,256);
        return;
    }
    end_request(1);            //cope with the aftermath after processing a request
    do_hd_request();           //keep giving interaction command if there remain
                               //many requests; else, return
}


void do_hd_request(void)
{
    int i,r;
    unsigned int block,dev;
    unsigned int sec,head,cyl;
    unsigned int nsect;
```

```
INIT_REQUEST;                               //determine whether there remaining requests right here
    dev = MINOR(CURRENT->dev);
    block = CURRENT->sector;
    if (dev > = 5*NR_HD || block+2 > hd[dev].nr_sects) {
        end_request(0);
        goto repeat;
    ......
}


//code path:kernel/blk_drv/hd.c:

extern inline void end_request(int uptodate)
{
    ......
        wake_up(&CURRENT->waiting);
        wake_up(&wait_for_request);
    CURRENT->dev = -1;
    CURRENT = CURRENT->next;                //set the current request be the next, make
                                            //preparations for processing the left requests
}

#define INIT_REQUEST \
repeat: \
    if (!CURRENT) \                         //CURRENT is empty meaning there is no request left
        return; \
    if (MAJOR(CURRENT->dev) ! = MAJOR_NR) \
        panic(DEVICE_NAME ": request list destroyed"); \
    if (CURRENT->bh) {\
        if (!CURRENT->bh->b_lock) \
            panic(DEVICE_NAME ": block not locked"); \
    }
```

We can see from the code that, no matter the read interrupt service routine or the write interrupt service routine, they will all call the end_request() function and the do_hd_request() function after processing the interaction of a buffer and the data block. This produces the loop operation processing the requests in the queue. The macro INIT_REQUEST in the do_hd_request() function is used to determine whether the loop is completed. If the request is not empty currently, which means there remains buffer space corresponding to the requested need to interact, keep giving the interaction command until all the tasks in the request are processed, and the CURRENT is empty, then return. This loop performs as shown in Figure 7.6.

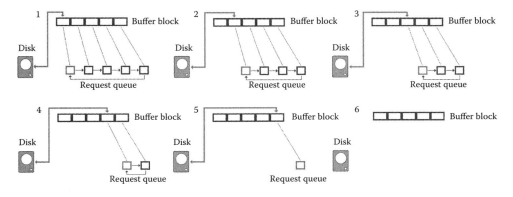

Figure 7.6 OS process the request queue.

The only purpose of the request design is to let the buffer and the hard disk data block interact with each other as soon as possible.

It is noteworthy that the size of the request is 32 as request[32], so why is it 32 and not 16 or 64?

This is because the data interaction in the host computer has a speed 100 times quicker than in the hard disk, which means that, on average, 100 pieces of buffer data interact with the process while only 1 piece of buffer data interacts with the hard disk. The maximum number of the buffer blocks in the host computer is 3000. The ratio of the buffer to the request is exactly 100, which matches the ratio of their interaction speed. If the request is too great for the hard disk to handle, the request will be idle and waste the memory. If the number of the requests is too small, there is not enough request, leading to the new command cannot be given, and the hard disk is free while the process has no proper buffer to use and suspend frequently; this will reduce the operating efficiency of the entire system. And 32 is just the right size.

▌■ 7.4 Function of Uptodate and Dirt

As was introduced in the previous section, the b_dev and the b_blocknr are the basis of the process of sharing the buffer, and they are the signs of whether data in the buffer still stays. If it stays, then it will be shared, and the use will be extended to two directions: One is the process direction, which can be shared and which can be not shared by the process; another is the hard disk direction, which needs to be synchronized to the hard disk and which needn't. And the core task of these two use directions is to ensure the accuracy of the data in the buffer and the data block.

The two fields b_uptodate and b_dirt in buffer_head are all used to ensure the accuracy of the data in the buffer and the data block.

b_uptodate aims at the process direction; it tells the kernel that it could support the data shared by the process safely as long as the b_uptodate of the buffer is assigned 1 and the data in the buffer is the latest of the data block. Otherwise, the b_uptodate is 0, which warns the kernel that the buffer is not updated by the binding data of the data block and should not support the process to share the buffer.

b_dirt aims at the hard disk direction; when the b_dirt of the buffer is assigned 1, it tells the kernel that the buffer has been rewritten by the data of the process direction and needs to be synchronized to the hard disk or else it is 0, and it needn't be synchronized.

7.4.1 Function of b_uptodate

First, we have a look at the process direction and what happens without the control of the b_uptodate.

Without the control of the b_uptodate, the buffer binds with the hard disk block, and an error may occur when the process operates the data in the buffer directly to read the file, for example, as Figure 7.7 shows.

From the diagram, it is not difficult to find that the data in the buffer is not updated due to the data of the data block. b_uptodate is 0, and the data in the buffer is garbage data, so the data read by the process is also garbage data, and the data in the hard disk is not read at all. This is not the original intention that the process read the hard disk data, and the data is wrong.

To write the file, an example is shown in Figure 7.8.

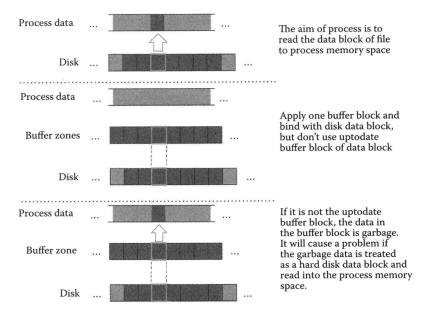

Figure 7.7 Read file if OS do not use b_uptodate to control file operation.

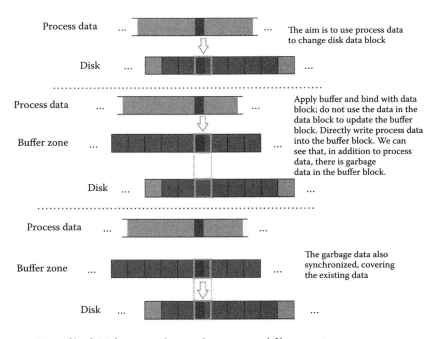

Figure 7.8 Write file if OS do not use b_uptodate to control file operation.

From the diagram, it is not difficult to find that the size of the data that the process wants to write to the file is smaller than a block. Without updating the buffer by the data in the data block, b_uptodate is 0, and the garbage data of the buffer is not only written into the data block when synchronizing the data, but it also overwrites the original data, leading to an error. And it is not the real intention of the process.

It is thus clear that if we don't update the data in the buffer by the data in the hard disk data block, the subsequent read file and write file to the buffer are not built on the basis of data in the hard disk data block, and it may lead to the data error. Setting b_uptodate to be 1, means that the data in the buffer is based on the hard disk data block, and the kernel could support data interaction of the process and the buffer safely.

Therefore, when we execute an interrupt service routine in the hard disk, read the data from the hard disk to the buffer, or synchronize from the buffer to the hard disk, set the b_uptodate to be 1. The code is as follows:

```
//code path:kernrl/blk_drv/hd.c:
static void read_intr(void)          //read interrupt service routine
{
    ......
        CURRENT->buffer + = 512;
    CURRENT->sector++;
    if (- CURRENT->nr_sectors) {
        do_hd = &read_intr;
        return;
    }
    end_request(1);                  //cope with the aftermath after
                                     //processing a request
    do_hd_request();
}


//code path:kernrl/blk_drv/hd.c:
static void write_intr(void)         //write interrupt service routine
{
    ......
        if (- CURRENT->nr_sectors) {
        CURRENT->sector++;
        CURRENT->buffer + = 512;
        do_hd = &write_intr;
        port_write(HD_DATA,CURRENT->buffer,256);
        return;
        }
        end_request(1);              //cope with the aftermath after
                                     //processing a request
        do_hd_request();
}


//code path:kernrl/blk_drv/blk.h:
extern inline void end_request(int uptodate)
{
        DEVICE_OFF(CURRENT->dev);
        if (CURRENT->bh) {
        CURRENT->bh->b_uptodate = uptodate;//set b_uptodate to be 1, data is
                                        //updated and synchronized
        unlock_buffer(CURRENT->bh);
    }
    ......
}
```

It is worth noting that the b_uptodate assigned 1 tells the kernel the data in the buffer has been updated by the data in the data block, but it does not mean the two should be absolutely identical. For example, building a new data block for the file needs to build a new buffer and build the binding relationship with the data block just built. Building the binding relationship clears the buffer; then set the b_uptodate of the buffer to be 1. Of course, now the data is not virtually synchronized, and the data of the buffer and hard disk block is inconsistent, but this does not affect the synchronization of the data correctly.

We learned from Chapter 5 that the new built data block only has two uses: to store the contents of the files or to store the indirect block management information of the i_zone of the file. If it is used to store the contents of the files, the new built data block and the new built hard disk data block are all the garbage data, and they are not the process needed; no matter whether the data is updated, the consequence is "equivalent" to solving the problem. So set the b_uptodate of the buffer to be 1. (Just think about it; it does not matter if the buffer is empty or not).

If it is the indirect block management information, it must be clear 0, meaning it does not index the indirect data block; otherwise, the garbage data will lead to the index error and damage the accuracy of the file operations. Although the data of the buffer and the hard disk data block is different by now, according to the same reason, the b_uptodate could be assigned 1.

The designer gives an overall consideration and takes this strategy: as long as we allocate the buffer for the new data block, no matter what the buffer is used for in the future, the process does not need the data in it now, so just clear up 0 altogether. Thus, it does not matter what information the data block bounded stores, set the b_uptodate of the buffer to be 1, and the update problem "is equivalent" to be solved.

The code is as follows:

```
//code path:fs/inode.c:
int create_block(struct m_inode * inode, int block) //create a new
                                                     //data block
{
    return _bmap(inode,block,1);
}

static int _bmap(struct m_inode * inode,int block,int create)
{
    ......
    if (block<7) {
        if (create && !inode->i_zone[block])
            if (inode->i_zone[block] = new_block(inode->i_dev)) {
                inode->i_ctime = CURRENT_TIME;
                inode->i_dirt = 1;
            }
        return inode->i_zone[block];
    }
    ......
}

//code path:fs/Bitmap.c:
int new_block(int dev)           //allocate a data block in the device dev
```

```
{
    ......
    if (bh->b_count ! = 1)
        panic("new block: count is ! = 1");
clear_block(bh->b_data);
bh->b_uptodate = 1;                        //set the buffer to be updated
bh->b_dirt = 1;
brelse(bh);
return j;
}
```

After b_uptodate is assigned 1, there could be only two conditions to the buffer. Let's see what happens.

For reading, the buffer is newly built although it has garbage data inside. In view of its being the newly built file, there is no logic requirement of reading the empty file data block, and the kernel won't do such a stupid action.

In the write circumstances, because the newly built buffer is cleared, and the hard disk data block is garbage data, the data of the buffer and the data block are all not what the process needs, and it does not matter if they are updated or overwritten. It can be seen as updated already equivalently. So executing the write operations is not against the process's purpose.

Let's look at the diagram given in Figure 7.9.

Above is the scenario that the b_uptodate of the kernel is assigned 1. The figure shows that the hard disk data block is used to store the file content. The white parts mean clearing 0, and it does not matter if it stores the file data block or the information of the indirect block.

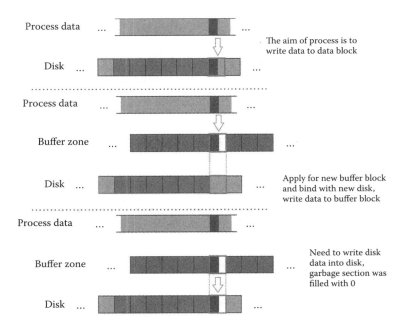

Figure 7.9 Read file if the OS uses b_uptodate to control file operation.

7.4 Function of Uptodate and Dirt

On the contrary, if the data in the buffer is not updated, and the b_uptodate is 0, the kernel will prevent the process from sharing the data in the buffer no matter whether it is read or write with the purpose of preventing the data corruption caused by no-update as we discussed above. For example, it judges for two times when reading the block device data, and the code is as follows:

```
//code path:fs/Buffer.c:
struct buffer_head * bread(int dev,int block)
{
        struct buffer_head * bh;
        if (!(bh = getblk(dev,block)))
            panic(«bread: getblk returned NULL\n»);
        if (bh->b_uptodate)     //see if it is updated when allocating
                                //the buffer to determine whether return
                                //to use the buffer
        return bh;
        ll_rw_block(READ,bh);
        wait_on_buffer(bh);
        if (bh->b_uptodate)     //check if it is updated again after
                                //reading from the hard disk to determine
                                //whether return to use the buffer
            return bh;
        brelse(bh);
        return NULL;
}
```

In this code, the getblk() function is very likely to have found a buffer block from the buffer, which already built the binding relationship—both b_dev and b_blocknr match—and just enough to be used by the current process; however, this buffer cannot be used and is only to be released because the b_uptodate is 0.

In another example, allocating a new buffer block is to interact with the data block that exists in the file. Set the b_uptodate to be 0, meaning this buffer data has not been updated and cannot be shared by the process. The code is as follows:

```
//code path:fs/Buffer.c:
struct buffer_head * getblk(int dev,int block)
{
......
if (find_buffer(dev,block))
        goto repeat;
        bh->b_count = 1;
        bh->b_dirt = 0;
        bh->b_uptodate = 0;     //data is not updated yet and can not be
                                //shared by the process
        remove_from_queues(bh);
        bh->b_dev = dev;
        bh->b_blocknr = block;
        insert_into_queues(bh);
        return bh;
}
```

The code has been introduced in Section 7.1, and a new buffer comes up right here the first time it comes into being, the data of it and the hard disk data block are different, so set the b_uptodate to be 0 to avoid the process misusing it.

7.4.2 Function of the b_dirt

After setting b_uptodate to be 1, the kernel could support the process to share the data of the buffer block, read and write. The read operation won't change the data in the buffer, but the write operation changes the buffer data, so set the b_dirt to be 1, such as write data into the block device file, write into the common file, etc. The specific code is as follows:

```
//code path:fs/blk_dev.c:
int block_write(int dev, long * pos, char * buf, int count)//write
                             //block device file content into the buffer
{
    ......
    offset = 0;
    *pos + = chars;
    written + = chars;
    count - = chars;
    while (chars- >0)
            *(p++) = get_fs_byte(buf++);
    bh->b_dirt = 1;
            brelse(bh);
    ......
}

//code path:fs/file_dev.c:
int file_write(struct m_inode * inode, struct file * filp, char * buf,
int count)              //write common file content into the buffer
{
    ......
    c = pos% BLOCK_SIZE;
    p = c + bh->b_data;
    bh->b_dirt = 1;
    c = BLOCK_SIZE-c;
    if (c > count-i) c = count-i;
    pos + = c;
    if (pos > inode->i_size) {
            inode->i_size = pos;
            inode->i_dirt = 1;
    }
    i + = c;
    while (c- >0)
            *(p++) = get_fs_byte(buf++);
    ......
}

//code path:fs/file_dev.c:
static struct buffer_head * add_entry(struct m_inode * dir,
const char * name, int namelen, struct dir_entry ** res_dir)
//directory file use write buffer block when loading the directory entry
{
```

```
        if (i*sizeof(struct dir_entry) > = dir->i_size) {
        de->inode = 0;
        dir->i_size = (i+1)*sizeof(struct dir_entry);
        dir->i_dirt = 1;
        dir->i_ctime = CURRENT_TIME;
    }
    if (!de->inode) {
        dir->i_mtime = CURRENT_TIME;
        for (i = 0; i < NAME_LEN ; i++)
        de->name[i] = (i<namelen)?get_fs_byte(name+i):0;
        bh->b_dirt = 1;
        *res_dir = de;
        return bh;
    }
}
```

Should the b_uptodate be assigned 0 again and forbid the kernel supporting the process to share the buffer after changing the buffer data? Let's look at Figure 7.10.

From the diagram, it is not difficult to find that the data of this buffer has been updated by the data of the hard disk data block, so after writing the new data into the buffer, the part not written into it is still the same as the corresponding part of the hard disk data block. When synchronizing to the data block in the future, all the data in the process hopes to synchronize to the hard disk data block, and it won't synchronize the garbage data to the data block. So the b_uptodate still is 1, and there is no need to change it, and the data of this buffer block could still be shared by the process, no matter whether it is read or write. Let's look at the sketches to continue writing data (Figure 7.11).

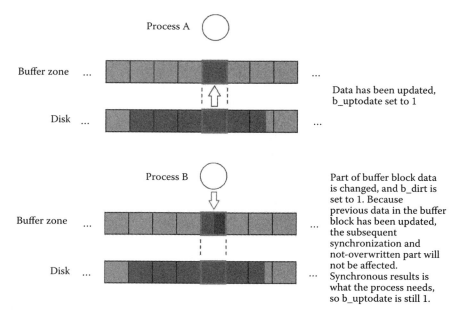

Figure 7.10 Write data into buffer.

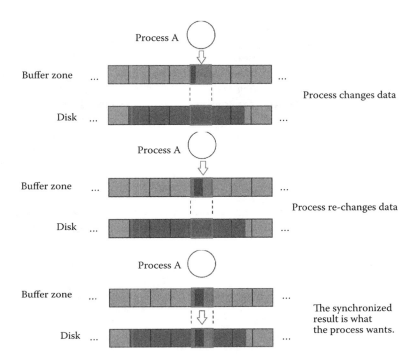

Figure 7.11 Continue to write data into buffer.

By that analogy, the data in the buffer is changing naturally when writing data into the buffer constantly, and in the future, these new data will be naturally synchronized to the hard disk data block as the process hopes.

Buffer_head set the two fields b_uptodate and b_dirt on the process direction and the hard disk direction respectively, and the structure of the request also takes the two directions into account. Compared with the write operation, the read operations are more urgent to the users, so the request sets different sizes for the two operations, and the code is as follows:

```
//code path:kernel/blk_drv/ll_rw_blk.c:
static void make_request(int major,int rw, struct buffer_head * bh)
{
    ……
    lock_buffer(bh);
    if ((rw = = WRITE && !bh->b_dirt) || (rw = = READ && bh->b_uptodate)) {
        unlock_buffer(bh);
        return;
    }
repeat:
    if (rw = = READ)
        req = request+NR_REQUEST;
    else
        req = request+((NR_REQUEST*2)/3);
    while (- req > = request)
        if (req->dev<0)
            break;
    ……
}
```

It is not difficult to find, from the code above, that there is only two thirds the space the request[32] could be used to write, and all that is left could be used to read. In the same condition, executing the read operation has a better chance.

In addition, through carefully evaluating b_uptodate and b_dirt, we could find that the process can share the data inside as long as the b_uptodate is assigned 1. If there is no buffer block that can be shared by the process in the buffer, and it can be used for other purposes as long as the b_count is 0. Bind the buffer with the other data block for another use and not the data error. But if the b_dirt is assigned 1, things will be different, and the data of this buffer is already different from that of the data block and needs to be synchronized. Although there is no need to synchronize it right away, but it cannot be misdirected before synchronizing. Otherwise these data will be overwritten, and data in the hard disk data block does not reflect the rewrite of the process, leading to data corruption. If the buffer is not enough to be used by the process, then the process has to wait until the synchronization finishes. The kernel will set the b_dirt to be 0 immediately when the synchronization has been finished, making more buffer for the process. The code is as follows:

```
//code path:kernel/blk_drv/ll_rw_blk.c:
static void add_request(struct blk_dev_struct * dev, struct request *
req)
{
        struct request * tmp;

        req->next = NULL;
        cli();
        if (req->bh)
            req->bh->b_dirt = 0;
        if (!(tmp = dev->current_request)) {
            dev->current_request = req;
            sti();
            (dev->request_fn)();
            return;
        }
    ......
}
```

7.4.3 Function of the i_update, i_dirt, and s_dirt

Controlling the accuracy of the file content is described above, and the content ensures the accuracy of the buffer data and hard disk data block data by b_uptodate and b_dirt. The file management information has similar fields, such as the i node stored in the inode_table[32]. When different processes are operating the same file, they share the information of the i node file. So its data structure has two fields, i_update (actually not used in the Linux 0.11) and i_dirt. The code is as follows:

```
//code path:include/linux/fs.h:
struct m_inode {
        unsigned short i_mode;
        unsigned short i_uid;
        unsigned long i_size;
```

```
        unsigned long i_mtime;
        unsigned char i_gid;
        unsigned char i_nlinks;
        unsigned short i_zone[9];
/* these are in memory also */
        struct task_struct * i_wait;
        unsigned long i_atime;
        unsigned long i_ctime;
        unsigned short i_dev;
        unsigned short i_num;
        unsigned short i_count;
        unsigned char i_lock;
        unsigned char i_dirt;
        unsigned char i_pipe;
        unsigned char i_mount;
        unsigned char i_seek;
        unsigned char i_update;
};
```

It is not hard to understand designing the i_dirt, such as changing the file size, so the file i node should change the size record. Then the i node in the inode_table[32] is different from that of the hard disk, and it needs to be synchronized. The i_update in the i node is not used in the system, and this is because the file management information in the hard disk is stored in the shape of the data block and loaded into the buffer in the shape of a block. It is the same as the hard disk data block after loading it into the buffer, which is equivalent to being updated. It could be shared directly without setting the i_update in the management structure.

There are also sharing problems of the super block in the super_block[8]. The super block stores the management information of the entire file system, and it will be used when multiprocessing the file. Its data structure has a s_dirt, and the code is as follows:

```
//code path:include/linux/fs.h:
struct super_block {
        unsigned short s_ninodes;
        unsigned short s_nzones;
        unsigned short s_imap_blocks;
        unsigned short s_zmap_blocks;
        unsigned short s_firstdatazone;
        unsigned short s_log_zone_size;
        unsigned long s_max_size;
        unsigned short s_magic;
/* These are only in memory */
        struct buffer_head * s_imap[8];
        struct buffer_head * s_zmap[8];
        unsigned short s_dev;
        struct m_inode * s_isup;
        struct m_inode * s_imount;
        unsigned long s_time;
        struct task_struct * s_wait;
        unsigned char s_lock;
        unsigned char s_rd_only;
        unsigned char s_dirt;
};
```

The reason why there are no fields similar to the uptodate is the same as that the i_update is not be used in the i node. They are also loaded into the buffer in the shape of a block. There is no need to use the uptodate in the management structure because after loading it into the buffer it is equivalent to being updated. The s_dirt fields have not been used only when reading the super block and are set to be 0. There is no s_dirt in the Linux 0.11 because the process reads from super_block[8] to share the super block information without writing it into the table entry.

■ 7.5 Function of the Count, Lock, Wait, Request

After staying in the buffer, the problem of the data used in the process direction goes on. This section will introduce the b_count, b_lock, and *b_wait.

7.5.1 Function of b_count

When the process applies to the kernel, it could only make the choice from the following two conditions: 1) Let the process share the same buffer with the other processes, using all the value of the control fields or 2) apply a buffer not to be used by any other process for this process and reset all the control fields.

The process needs to know which buffer has been occupied and which is not in order to make the choice. Some buffers might be shared by more than one process, and then a field should be set in the buffer to let the kernel know at any time "how many processes of each buffer are shared," and b_count is the field.

There is no process using the buffer block during the initialization of the buffer, so the b_count of each buffer is assigned 0.

The code is as follows:

```
//code path:fs/buffer.c:
void buffer_init(long buffer_end)
{
        ......
        h->b_dev = 0;
        h->b_dirt = 0;
        h->b_count = 0;          //there is no process using the buffer
                                 //block, set b_count = 0

        h->b_lock = 0;
        h->b_uptodate = 0;
        h->b_wait = NULL;
        h->b_next = NULL;
        h->b_prev = NULL;
        h->b_data = (char *) b;
        h->b_prev_free = h-1;
        h->b_next_free = h+1;

        ......
}
```

The buffer block should not be used by any other process when allocating a new buffer block. Set b_count 0, and the buffer is shared by the first process and b_count is assigned 1 after that. The code is as follows:

```
//code path:fs/buffer.c:
struct buffer_head * getblk(int dev,int block)
{
      ......
      tmp = free_list;
   do {
      if (tmp->b_count)                          //Reference technology must
                                                 //be zero
            continue;
      if (!bh || BADNESS(tmp)<BADNESS(bh)) {     //take into account the
                                                 //application again
            bh = tmp;
      if (!BADNESS(tmp))
            break;
   }
/* and repeat until we find something good */
   } while ((tmp = tmp->b_next_free) ! = free_list);
      ......
   bh->b_count = 1;        //the new buffer, meaning only the current process is
                          //using it, so b_count is forcefully assigned 1
      bh->b_dirt = 0;
      bh->b_uptodate = 0;
      remove_from_queues(bh);
      bh->b_dev = dev;
      bh->b_blocknr = block;
      insert_into_queues(bh);
      return bh;
   }
```

The buffer is shared by the process one after another. The value of the b_count is gradually accumulated on the basis of the original data. The code is as follows:

```
//code path:fs/buffer.c:
struct buffer_head * getblk(int dev,int block)
{
      struct buffer_head * tmp, * bh;
repeat:
      if (bh = get_hash_table(dev,block))        //go through the hash table
                                                 //to see if the buffer could
                                                 //share with other process
      return bh;
......
}

struct buffer_head * get_hash_table(int dev, int block)
{
      struct buffer_head * bh;

      for (;;) {
      if (!(bh = find_buffer(dev,block)))
      return NULL;
      bh->b_count++;                             //if the buffer can be shared then one
                                                 //more process use it, b_count increase
      wait_on_buffer(bh);
      if (bh->b_dev = = dev && bh->b_blocknr = = block)
      return bh;
      bh->b_count- ;
      }
}
```

After one process reads the file, there is no need to share the buffer, and the kernel will release the relationship of the process and the buffer, b_count minus one. If all the relationships of the process and the buffer are released, the b_count decreases to 0, and then the buffer can be allocated as a new one. The code is as follows:

```
//code path:fs/file_dev.c:
int file_read(struct m_inode * inode, struct file * filp, char * buf, int count) //readfile
{
    ......
    while (chars-->0)
        put_fs_byte(*(p++),buf++);
        brelse(bh);              //the reference count decrease
    } else {
        while (chars-->0)
            put_fs_byte(0,buf++);
    ......
}


int file_write(struct m_inode * inode, struct file * filp, char * buf, int count) //writefile
{
    ......
    while (c-->0)
        *(p++) = get_fs_byte(buf++);
        brelse(bh);              //the reference count decrease
    }
    inode->i_mtime = CURRENT_TIME;
    if (!(filp->f_flags & O_APPEND)) {
    filp->f_pos = pos;
    inode->i_ctime = CURRENT_TIME;
    }
    ......
}


//code path:fs/buffer.c:
void brelse(struct buffer_head * buf)
{
    if (!buf)
        return;
    wait_on_buffer(buf);
        if (!(buf->b_count-- ))
    panic("Trying to free free buffer");
        wake_up(&buffer_wait);
}
```

It is worthy to note that when all processes sharing the buffer are released from the share relationship, although the b_count is absolutely 0, it does not mean the binding relationship of the buffer and the data block is released. If a process operates this buffer again in the future, there is no need to read from the hard disk again, and the process could continue to use the buffer as long as the b_dev and b_blocknr of the buffer are not changed.

7.5.2 Function of i_count

It is the content data of the file that is shared between the process and the buffer block. Not only the b_count field is needed to administer the content data of the file, some similar fields are also needed to refer to all the conditions that data structures like "search for a free entry" and "be repurposed after the research" are needed in the file management information, for example, inode_table[32]. The specific code is as follows:

```
//code path:include/linux/fs.h:
struct m_inode {
        unsigned short i_mode;
        unsigned short i_uid;
        unsigned long i_size;
        unsigned long i_mtime;
        unsigned char i_gid;
        unsigned char i_nlinks;
        unsigned short i_zone[9];
/* these are in memory also */
        struct task_struct * i_wait;
        unsigned long i_atime;
        unsigned long i_ctime;
        unsigned short i_dev;
        unsigned short i_num;
        unsigned short i_count;
        unsigned char i_lock;
        unsigned char i_dirt;
        unsigned char i_pipe;
        unsigned char i_mount;
        unsigned char i_seek;
        unsigned char i_update;
};
```

Inode_table[32] is file management information. The process references the file data block corresponding to the buffer block. So the process inevitably references the i node entry in inode_table[32]. And both are synchronized. So inode_table[32] also needs the field i_count to identify how many processes are sharing the i node entry. If it is not shared, then i_count turns out to be 0, and it can be regarded as a free entry. For example, when a process wants to open a file that had never been opened, but the i node entry cannot be shared with other processes at the same time, this free i node entry can be used to load the i node.

However super_block[8] is quiet different from this. A device only owns a super block, and the entire system can be installed in only eight super blocks, which is fixed. From loading the file system to uninstalling it, the superblock represents only one device. So there is no need to consider whether it is free or use it for any other intentions. More than one process can load the same file system, and operation on the same superblock is required, but a field like count is not needed to record the number of the super_block cited. The specific code is as follows:

```
//code path:include/linux/fs.h:
struct super_block {
        unsigned short s_ninodes;
        unsigned short s_nzones;
        unsigned short s_imap_blocks;
        unsigned short s_zmap_blocks;
        unsigned short s_firstdatazone;
        unsigned short s_log_zone_size;
        unsigned long s_max_size;
        unsigned short s_magic;
/* These are only in memory */
        struct buffer_head * s_imap[8];
        struct buffer_head * s_zmap[8];
        unsigned short s_dev;
        struct m_inode * s_isup;
        struct m_inode * s_imount;
        unsigned long s_time;
        struct task_struct * s_wait;
        unsigned char s_lock;
        unsigned char s_rd_only;
        unsigned char s_dirt;
};
```

As we can see from the code, no field like count exists.

It is worth noting that except for i node and super blocks, file management information also includes i node bitmap and logical block bitmap. These two types of file management information do not have a dedicated data structure. But they also need to support share. They are stored in the buffer block, you might say, permanently. These buffer blocks are used only by the i node's bitmap and the logical block bitmap.

```
//code path:fs/super.c:
static struct super_block * read_super(int dev)
{
    ......
    for (i = 0 ; i < s->s_imap_blocks ; i++)              //load I-node bitmap into the buffer block
        if (s->s_imap[i] = bread(dev,block))
            block++;
        else
            break;
    for (i = 0 ; i < s->s_zmap_blocks ; i++)              //load logical block bitmap into buffer block
        if (s->s_zmap[i] = bread(dev,block))
            block++;
        else
            break;
            if (block ! = 2+s->s_imap_blocks+s->s_zmap_blocks) {//release if Abnormal
situations appear
            for(i = 0;i<I_MAP_SLOTS;i++)
                brelse(s->s_imap[i]);
            for(i = 0;i<Z_MAP_SLOTS;i++)
                brelse(s->s_zmap[i]);
            s->s_dev = 0;
            free_super(s);
            return NULL;
    }
    s->s_imap[0]->b_data[0] | = 1;
    s->s_zmap[0]->b_data[0] | = 1;
    free_super(s);
    return s;
}


//code path:fs/buffer.c:
struct buffer_head * bread(int dev,int block)          //Read the underlying block device data
{
    struct buffer_head * bh;
    if (!(bh = getblk(dev,block))) //Device number and a block number is needed when applying
buffer block
            panic("bread: getblk returned NULL\n");
    if (bh->b_uptodate)
            return bh;
    ......
}

struct buffer_head * getblk(int dev,int block)
{
    ......
    if (find_buffer(dev,block))
        goto repeat;
        bh->b_count = 1;           //Reference count is 1
    bh->b_dirt = 0;
    bh->b_uptodate = 0;
    ......
}
```

As can be seen from the code, after the i node's bitmap and the logical block bitmap are loaded into the buffer blocks, the b_count in these buffer blocks is set to 1, never to be released later. So the count of the buffer block cannot be reduced to 0, as a result of which these buffer blocks are not available when any process wants to apply for a new buffer block. So these buffer blocks become dedicated.

7.5.3 Function of b_lock and *b_wait

The kernel applies a buffer block for the process, especially when the b_count in the buffer block turns out to be 0, and considering the synchronization, there is great possibility that this buffer block is transacting data with the hard disk. So the b_lock field is set in this buffer_head structure. If this field is set to be 1, it means this buffer block is interacting data with the hard disk. The kernel will stop the process from conducting operations to the buffer block until the end of the interaction with the hard disk. The interception will be relieved when the field is set to 0.

If the b_lock field in the buffer block, which is applied by the process, is set to 1, the process also needs to be suspended even though the process has already got the buffer block. The buffer block can only be accessed until it is unlocked. When the buffer block is locked, no matter how many processes had applied the buffer block, they cannot immediately operate the buffer block. All these processes should be suspended and switch to other processes to execute. We need to record which processes are suspended while waiting for this buffer block. Due to the use of a waiting queue of the process, a field can solve this record. The field is *b_wait.

These two fields are often used in combination. The specific code is as follows:

b_lock is set to 0, and *b_wait is set to null when we initialize the buffer block.

```
//code path:fs/buffer.c:
void buffer_init(long buffer_end)
{
        ......
        h->b_dev = 0;
    h->b_dirt = 0;
    h->b_count = 0;
    h->b_lock = 0;
    h->b_uptodate = 0;
    h->b_wait = NULL;
    h->b_next = NULL;
    h->b_prev = NULL;
    h->b_data = (char *) b;
    h->b_prev_free = h-1;
    h->b_next_free = h+1;
    ......
}
```

After the buffer block is applied, this block should be locked before the operation on the bottom layer, which means b_lock should be set to 1. The specific code is as follows:

```
//code path:kernel/blk_drv/ll_rw_block.c:
static void make_request(int major,int rw, struct buffer_head * bh)
{
    ......
    if (rw! = READ && rw! = WRITE)
        panic("Bad block dev command, must be R/W/RA/WA");
        lock_buffer(bh);                        //lock the buffer block
    if ((rw = = WRITE && !bh->b_dirt) || (rw = = READ && bh->b_
uptodate)) {
```

```
        unlock_buffer(bh);
        return;
    }
    ......
}

static inline void lock_buffer(struct buffer_head * bh)
{
        cli();
        while (bh->b_lock)      //if the buffer block is already locked
            sleep_on(&bh->b_wait);      //suspend the process directly
        bh->b_lock = 1;                 //lock the buffer block
        sti();
}
```

Before the hard disk data blocks start transacting data with the buffer blocks, the function lock_buffer() will judge whether the buffer block is locked. If it is locked, it is possible that this buffer block is already applied by other processes, and it is transacting data with the hard disk. So we could call function sleep_on() to suspend the process and switch to the other processes to execute. Lock the buffer block again to prevent it from being misused by other process when we switch back to the current process later. B_lock and *b_wait's combination is not only reflected here, but also all the conditions when the buffer block's state should be determined. The specific code is as follows:

```
//code path:fs/buffer.c:
struct buffer_head * bread(int dev,int block)
{
        struct buffer_head * bh;

        if (!(bh = getblk(dev,block)))
            panic("bread: getblk returned NULL\n");
        if (bh->b_uptodate)
            return bh;
        ll_rw_block(READ,bh);
        wait_on_buffer(bh);     //Detect whether process need to
                                //wait for the buffer block to be
                                //unlock or not
if (bh->b_uptodate)
            return bh;
        brelse(bh);
        return NULL;
}

static inline void lock_buffer(struct buffer_head * bh)
{
        cli();
        while (bh->b_lock)      //if the buffer block is already locked
            sleep_on(&bh->b_wait);   //suspend the process
        bh->b_lock = 1;                 //lock the buffer block
        sti();
}
```

They should be used in combination when we lock the buffer and suspend the process. And they are also used in combination when we unlock the buffer block and wake the process. The specific code is as follows:

```
//code path:kernel/blk_drv/ll_rw_block.c:
static void make_request(int major,int rw, struct buffer_head * bh)
{
    ......
        lock_buffer(bh);
        if ((rw = = WRITE && !bh->b_dirt) || (rw = = READ && bh->b_uptodate)) {
            unlock_buffer(bh);              //unlock the buffer block and wake up the process
            return;
        }
        if (rw = = READ)
        req = request+NR_REQUEST;
    ......
}


static inline void unlock_buffer(struct buffer_head * bh)    //unlock the buffer block and
                                                             //wake up the process
{
    if (!bh->b_lock)
        printk("ll_rw_block.c: buffer not locked\n\r");
    bh->b_lock = 0;
    wake_up(&bh->b_wait);
}
```

After transacting the data, an interrupt service routine will run. And this will unlock the buffer block. The processes waiting for this buffer block will be awakened later. The specific code is as follows:

```
//code path:kernel/blk_drv/blk.h:
extern inline void end_request(int uptodate)    //Process the rehabilitation work after the
                                                //completion of the request operation
    DEVICE_OFF(CURRENT->dev);
    if (CURRENT->bh) {
        CURRENT->bh->b_uptodate = uptodate;
        unlock_buffer(CURRENT->bh);             //unlock the buffer block and wake up the
                                                //process
    }
if (!uptodate) {
        printk(DEVICE_NAME " I/O error\n\r");
        printk("dev%04x, block%d\n\r",CURRENT->dev,
            CURRENT->bh->b_blocknr);
    }
    ......
}


static inline void unlock_buffer(struct buffer_head * bh)    //unlock the buffer block and
                                                             //wake up the process
{
    if (!bh->b_lock)
        printk(DEVICE_NAME ": free buffer being unlocked\n");
    bh->b_lock = 0;                  //release the lock of buffer block
    wake_up(&bh->b_wait);           //wake up the process waiting for the buffer block
}
```

7.5.4 Function of i_lock, i_wait, s_lock, and *s_wait

When we share the contents of the file, the b_lock and *b_wait fields are stored in the buffer block. Sharing the management information of the file and sharing the contents of the file are corresponding. So there are similar fields in the data structure of the file management information, for example, inode_table[32] and super_block[8]. The specific code is as follows:

```
//code path:include/linux/fs.h:
struct m_inode {
        unsigned short i_mode;
        unsigned short i_uid;
        unsigned long i_size;
        unsigned long i_mtime;
        unsigned char i_gid;
        unsigned char i_nlinks;
        unsigned short i_zone[9];
/* these are in memory also */
        struct task_struct * i_wait;
        unsigned long i_atime;
        unsigned long i_ctime;
        unsigned short i_dev;
        unsigned short i_num;
        unsigned short i_count;
        unsigned char i_lock;
        unsigned char i_dirt;
        unsigned char i_pipe;
        unsigned char i_mount;
        unsigned char i_seek;
        unsigned char i_update;
};

struct super_block {
        unsigned short s_ninodes;
        unsigned short s_nzones;
        unsigned short s_imap_blocks;
        unsigned short s_zmap_blocks;
        unsigned short s_firstdatazone;
        unsigned short s_log_zone_size;
        unsigned long s_max_size;
        unsigned short s_magic;
/* These are only in memory */
        struct buffer_head * s_imap[8];
        struct buffer_head * s_zmap[8];
        unsigned short s_dev;
        struct m_inode * s_isup;
        struct m_inode * s_imount;
        unsigned long s_time;
        struct task_struct * s_wait;
        unsigned char s_lock;
        unsigned char s_rd_only;
        unsigned char s_dirt;
};
```

Fields like lock and wait both exist in the file management information, and they are used in combination because they should serve the sharing service. Situations in which i_lock and i_wait are used in combination in inode_table[32] are as follows. The specific code is as follows:

```
//code path:fs/inode.c:
static void read_inode(struct m_inode * inode)//read the i-node
{
        ......
        lock_inode(inode);              //lock the i-node
        if (!(sb = get_super(inode->i_dev)))
                panic("trying to read inode without dev");

        ......
        *(struct d_inode *)inode =
                ((struct d_inode *)bh->b_data)
                        [(inode->i_num-1)%INODES_PER_BLOCK];
        brelse(bh);
        unlock_inode(inode);            //unlock the i-node
}

static void write_inode(struct m_inode * inode)//write the i-node
{
        ......
        lock_inode(inode);              //lock the i-node
        if (!inode->i_dirt || !inode->i_dev) {
                unlock_inode(inode);
        return;
        }
        ......
        bh->b_dirt = 1;
        inode->i_dirt = 0;
        brelse(bh);
        unlock_inode(inode);            //unlock the i-node
}


static inline void lock_inode(struct m_inode * inode)
{
        cli();
        while (inode->i_lock)           //if i-node is locked
        sleep_on(&inode->i_wait);       //suspend the process
        inode->i_lock = 1;              //lock the i-node
        sti();
}
static inline void unlock_inode(struct m_inode * inode)
{
        inode->i_lock = 0;              //unlock the i-node
        wake_up(&inode->i_wait);        //wake up the processes waiting
for i-node to be unlocked
}
```

Situations in which s_lock and *s_wait are used in combination in super_block[8] are as follows. The code is as follows:

```
//code path:fs/inode.c:
static struct super_block * read_super(int dev)//read the super block
{
    ......
    s->s_time = 0;
    s->s_rd_only = 0;
    s->s_dirt = 0;
    lock_super(s); //lock the super block
    if (!(bh = bread(dev,1))) {
    s->s_dev = 0;
    free_super(s);
    return NULL;
    }
    ......
    s->s_imap[0]->b_data[0] | = 1;
    s->s_zmap[0]->b_data[0] | = 1;
    free_super(s); //unlock the super block
return s;
}

void put_super(int dev)//release the super block
{
    ......
    if (sb->s_imount) {
    printk("Mounted disk changed - tssk, tssk\n\r");
    return;
    }
    lock_super(s); //lock the super block
    sb->s_dev = 0;
    for(i = 0;i<I_MAP_SLOTS;i++)
    brelse(sb->s_imap[i]);
    for(i = 0;i<Z_MAP_SLOTS;i++)
    brelse(sb->s_zmap[i]);
    free_super(sb);
    free_super(s); //lock the super block
......
}

static void lock_super(struct super_block * sb)
{
    cli();
    while (sb->s_lock)          //if the super block locked
    sleep_on(&(sb->s_wait));    //suspend the process
    sb->s_lock = 1;             //lock the super block
    sti();
}

static void free_super(struct super_block * sb)
{
    cli();
    sb->s_lock = 0;             //unlock the super block
    wake_up(&(sb->s_wait));     //wake up the process waiting
for the unlocked super block
    sti();
}
```

7.5.5 Function of Request

Fields in the buffer block, i nodes, and super block establish a foundation of sharing the buffer block for the process. And they solved the problem about whether the buffer block could be shared or not. Here is how to share the buffer block more efficiently.

We have presented problems about using the buffer blocks concerning the process above. Then we will present the problems about using the buffer blocks concerning the hard disk. Let's look at the data structure of request. Codes are as follows:

```
//code path:kernel/blk_drv/Blk.h:
struct request {
        int dev;                /* -1 if no request */
        int cmd;                /* READ or WRITE */
        int errors;
        unsigned long sector;
        unsigned long nr_sectors;
        char * buffer;
        struct task_struct * waiting;
        struct buffer_head * bh;
struct request * next;
}
```

Request needs to interact with the hard disk. So the cmd field is designed to determine whether it needs to write or read. Besides we need to be clear about which buffer block needs to interact. For example the *bh and *buffer fields are designed for this. We also need to consider the mapping rules of the data blocks and sectors, for example, the sector and nr_sectors fields are designed for this. We also need to consider what to do if the interaction is wrong. We use errors to record the times that problems emerge. All these fields are designed for interaction with the hard disk.

The transaction is totally about one buffer block and one data block. So we don't need to consider the sharing problems. As a result, there is no field like b_count in the request. There are only two states in the record about the interaction condition, busy and free. So the dev field is not only used to present the device number, but it is also used to judge whether the request is being occupied. Codes are as follows:

```
//code path:kernel/blk_drv/ll_rw_block.c:
void blk_dev_init(void)
{
    int i;
    for (i = 0 ; i<NR_REQUEST ; i++) {
        request[i].dev = -1;            //The device number is set to -1, which means the
                                        //request entry is free
request[i].next = NULL;
    }
}

static void make_request(int major,int rw, struct buffer_head * bh)
{
    .....
    /* find an empty request */
    while (- req > = request)           //find a free request
        if (req->dev<0)                 //That must be -1, if it is less than 0, which means
                                        //it is free
```

```
            break;
            ......
            req->dev = bh->b_dev;                    //set dev using equipment number, It can't be -1, not
                                                     //-1 this value device number
req->cmd = rw;
            req->errors = 0;
            req->sector = bh->b_blocknr<<1;
            req->nr_sectors = 2;
            req->buffer = bh->b_data;
            req->waiting = NULL;
            req->bh = bh;
            req->next = NULL;
            add_request(major+blk_dev,req);
}

//code source:kernel/blk_drv/Blk.h:
extern inline void end_request(int uptodate)
{
......
wake_up(&CURRENT->waiting);
wake_up(&wait_for_request);
CURRENT->dev = -1;                   //set the request to free once it completed its mission
CURRENT = CURRENT->next;
}
```

Besides it is worth noting that request is set to achieve the balance of data interaction between the host and hard disk as far as possible. But this balance is not absolute. For example, if the writing operation is too frequent or the hard disk itself incurred an error as a result of which data transacting failed, and there is great possibility that data may be backlogged in request. This may eventually lead to lack of request. Even if the kernel has obtained the buffer blocks for the process, the process can only be suspended due to the absence of request. A field is also needed to record which process is suspended. *waiting is the field used to record which process is suspended. The specific code is as follows:

```
//code path:kernel/blk_drv/ll_rw_block.c:
static void make_request(int major,int rw, struct buffer_head * bh)
{
    ......
        if (req < request) {          //can't find a free request
            if (rw_ahead) {
                unlock_buffer(bh);
                return;
            }
            sleep_on(&wait_for_request);  //process is suspended
            goto repeat;
        }
}
```

When free request is available, the process will then be woken up. The specific code is as follows:

```
//code source:kernel/blk_drv/blk.h:
extern inline void end_request(int uptodate)
{
    ......
        wake_up(&CURRENT->waiting);
    wake_up(&wait_for_request);          //process waiting for request is woken up
    CURRENT->dev = -1;
    CURRENT = CURRENT->next;
}
```

Similarly, more than one process may be suspended due to waiting for some one request. Only *waiting one field is not capable of recording this. So we need process waiting queue to solve this problem. It is also mentioned earlier that it is used to record processes waiting for the buffer block. Process waiting queue techniques are needed to complete the recording of more than one waiting process.

■ 7.6 Example 1: Process Waiting Queue of Buffer Block

Below we present a case in which more than one process operates the same file at the same time. We use this to embody the problem of the sharing problem and explain clearly the principle of the process waiting queue.

Suppose there is a file named hello.txt on your hard disk. The file's size is 700 B (which is smaller than the size of a data block). A buffer block can carry the entire contents of this file when it is loaded in. Once three processes start operating, this file is equivalent to that they are operating the same buffer block relying on the system. This will produce the process waiting queue. This section will detail the process of generating the queue and waking up the processes in the queue.

Here we introduce the scene of example 1. The three processes are as follows:

Process A is about reading the disk. The purpose is to read 100 bytes in the hello.txt file into the buffer[100]. The specific code is as follows:

```
void FunA();
void main()
{
    ......
    FunA();
    ......
}
void FunA()
{
        char buffer[100];
        int i,j;
        //open the file
        int fd = open("/mnt/user/user1/user2/hello.txt", O_RDWR,0644));
        //read the file
        read(fd,buffer,sizeof(buffer));
        //close the file
        close(fd);
        for(i=0;i<1000000;i++)//Time-consuming piece
        {
            for(j=0;j<1000000;j++)
            {
                ;
            }
        }
    return;
}
```

Process B is about reading the disk too. The purpose is to read 200 bytes in the hello. txt file into the buffer[200]. The specific code is as follows:

```
void FunB();
void main()
{
        ......
        FunB();
        ......
}


void FunB()
{
        char buffer[200];
        int i,j;
        //open file
        int fd = open("/mnt/user/user1/user2/hello.txt",O_RDWR,0644));
        //read the file
        read(fd,buffer,sizeof(buffer));
        //close the file
        close(fd);
        for(i=0;i<1000000;i++)//Time-consuming piece
        {
                for(j=0;j<1000000;j++)
                {
                        ;
                }
        }
        return;
}
```

Process C is about writing the disk. The purpose is to write characters "ABCDE" in str1[] to the hello.txt file. The specific code is as follows:

```
void FunC();
void main()
{
        ......
        FunC();
        ......
}


void FunC()
{
        char str1[]="ABCDE";
        int i,j;
        //open file
        int fd = open("/mnt/user/user1/user2/hello.txt", O_RDWR,0644));
        //write file
        write(fd,str1,strlen(str1));
        //close file
        close(fd);
        for(i=0;i<1000000;i++)//Time-consuming piece
        {
                for(j=0;j<1000000;j++)
                {
                        ;
                }
        }
        return;
}
```

The execution order of these three processes is process A first, process B second, and process C the last. These three processes have no parent-child relationship.

Let's look at the specific implementation process.

Process A is suspended after reading the file. After it is started, process A executes the sentence "int fd = open ("/mnt/user/user1/user2/hello.txt", O_RDWR,0644))". Function open() will eventually be mapped to sys_open() function to execute. Function sys_open()'s implementation is introduced in Chapter 5. The specific code is as follows:

```
//code source:      fs/open.c:
int sys_open(const char * filename,int flag,int mode)
{
   ......
   (current->filp[fd] = f)->f_count++;          //bind *filp[20] in process A with items
                                                //corresponding to file_table[64],and add
                                                //file handle count

   ......
   if ((i = open_namei(filename,flag,mode,&inode))<0) {   //To obtain the I node in
                                                          //hello.txt file
   ......
      f->f_mode = inode->i_mode;                //set file attributes using i-node
                                                //attributes,
      f->f_flags = flag;                        //set file operations with the flag
                                                //parameter
      f->f_count = 1;                           //File reference count plus 1
      f->f_inode = inode;                       //build relationships between the i-node
                                                //and the file.
      f->f_pos = 0;                             //File read and write pointer is set to 0
      return (fd);                              //return the file handle to the user space
}
```

Implementation is shown in Figure 7.12.

Then the sentence "read(fd, buffer, sizeof (buffer))" is executed. The function read() will eventually be mapped to function sys_read() to execute. The function sys_read() will call function file_read() to read the contents of the file. Function file_read() calls function bread() to read data from the hard disk. The specific code is as follows:

```
//code source:      fs/read_write.c:
int sys_read(unsigned int fd,char * buf,int count)          //Reading data from hello.txt file
                                      //fd is the file handle, buf is a user-space pointer,
                                      //and count is the number of bytes to read
      if (S_ISDIR(inode->i_mode) || S_ISREG(inode->i_mode)) {
         if (count+file->f_pos > inode->i_size)
               count = inode->i_size - file->f_pos;
         if (count< = 0)
               return 0;
         return file_read(inode,file,buf,count);          //Read specified data of process
      }
      printk("(Read)inode->i_mode =%06o\n\r",inode->i_mode);
      return -EINVAL;
}

//code source:fs/file_dev.c:
int file_read(struct m_inode * inode, struct file * filp, char * buf, int count)
{
      ......
      if (nr = bmap(inode,(filp->f_pos)/BLOCK_SIZE)) {
         if (!(bh = bread(inode->i_dev,nr)))          //read data from the hard disk
         break;
      } else
         bh = NULL;
      ......
}
```

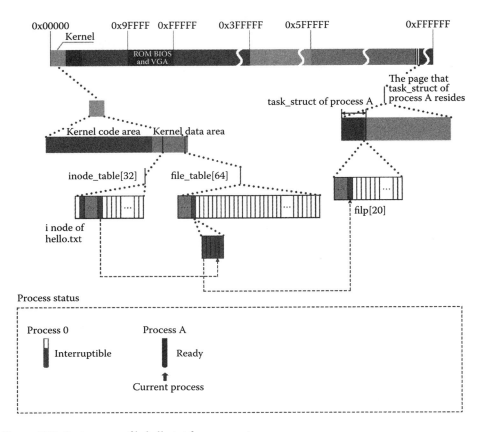

Figure 7.12 System open file hello.txt for process A.

The implementation process after entering function bread() has been described in detail in Section 3.3.1. The code is as follows:

```
//code source:fs/buffer.c:
struct buffer_head * bread(int dev,int block)      //read data from the hard disk
{
        .....
        if (!(bh = getblk(dev,block)))//Apply for a free buffer block
        ll_rw_block(READ,bh);              //The buffer block is locked and is bound with
                                          //request item, sending disc reading instruction
        wait_on_buffer(bh);                //suspend the process waiting for unlocked
                                          //buffer block,
        if (bh->b_uptodate)
                return bh;
        .....
}
```

Process A is suspended in function wait_on_buffer(). The code is as follows:

```
//code source:fs/buffer.c:
static inline void wait_on_buffer(struct buffer_head * bh)//suspend
the process waiting for unlocked buffer block,
{
        cli();//Interrupt off
        while (bh->b_lock)      //Detect whether the buffer block is locked
            sleep_on(&bh->b_wait);      //suspend the buffer block process
                                        //(A process), and switch to
                                        //other process
        sti();//Open interrupt
}
```

The buffer block has been locked when ll_rw_block() function is being executed (as is described in Section 3.3.1.3). If the result of (bh->b_lock) is true, function sleep_on() is called. Arguments that is transported is &bh->b_wait and bh->b_wait, which represents a pointer of the process that is waiting for the unlocking of the buffer block. All the b_wait in all the buffer blocks are set to NULL (as mentioned in Section 2.10) when the system is initialized. And this buffer block is a new application, which has never been used by other processes. So the value of bh->b_wait is NULL at this time. Next, the process enters the following function sleep_on(). The code is as follows:

```
//code source:kernel/sched.c:
void sleep_on(struct task_struct **p)
{
    struct task_struct *tmp;
    if (!p)
        return;
    if (current = = &(init_task.task))
        panic("task[0] trying to sleep");
    tmp = *p;                                //at this time tmp stores
                                             //NULL
    *p = current;                            //*p stores pointer of
                                             //process A
    current->state = TASK_UNINTERRUPTIBLE;   //set process A to
                                             //uninterruptible state
    schedule();                              //switch process
    if (tmp)
        tmp->state = 0;
}
```

From the introduction of arguments in sleep_on() function we learned that *p points to bh->b_wait. *p stores the pointer of process A, which means that process A is waiting for buffer block bh to be unlocked.

Calling function schedule() and switching to execute process B after the process A is suspended. At the same time, the hard disk is also transporting data to the data register port. This situation is shown below:

The progress bar representing process A in Figure 7.13 is turned into gray, which means process A is suspended.

It is worth noting that tmp in the code is stored in the kernel stack of the process A as NULL. Bh->b_wait stores the pointer of process A (Figure 7.14).

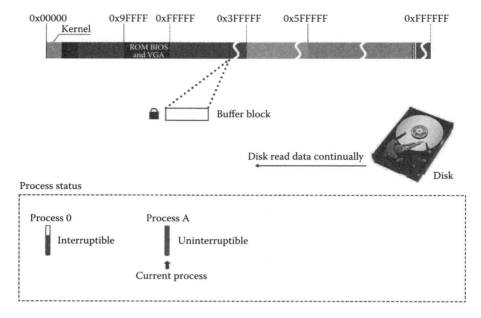

Figure 7.13 System reads data in hello.txt and suspends process A.

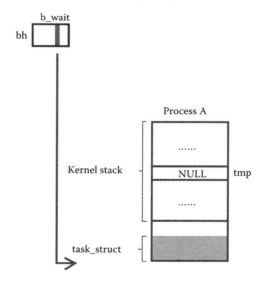

Figure 7.14 Set process A into wait queue.

Process B was suspended after reading the file. Process B first executes the sentence int fd = open ("/mnt/user/user1/user2/hello.txt", O_RDWR,0644)). Function open() will eventually be mapped to function sys_open() to execute. Function sys_open() will apply for a free new entries in the file management table file_table[64] to mount[20] file_table[64] empty entries mount and the *filp in task_struct in process B. Although the process B and process A are opening the same file, these two processes' operation of the file are not related to each other. As a result, two sets of books are needed. The specific code is as follows:

```
//code source:fs/open.c:
int sys_open(const char * filename,int flag,int mode)
{
    ......
    for(fd = 0 ; fd<NR_OPEN ; fd++)
        if (!current->filp[fd])
            break;
    ......
    for (i = 0 ; i<NR_FILE ; i++,f++)
        if (!f->f_count) break;
    ......
        (current->filp[fd] = f)->f_count++;        //bind *filp[20] in process B and items
                                                   //corresponding to file_table[64],and add file handle count
        if ((i = open_namei(filename,flag,mode,&inode))<0) {        //To obtain the I-node in
                                                                    //hello.txt file
    ......
        f->f_mode = inode->i_mode;        //set file attributes using i-node attributes
        f->f_flags = flag;                //set file operations with the flag parameter
        f->f_count = 1;                   //File reference count plus 1
        f->f_inode = inode;               //build relationships between the i-node and the file.
        f->f_pos = 0;                     //File read and write pointer is set to 0
        return (fd);                      //return the file handle to the user space
}
```

The scenario of binding is shown below:

The hard disk is constantly reading data, which means the request of reading the disk from process A is not yet completed (Figure 7.15).

The process calls function open_namei() and gets i node in hello.txt file and finally mounts the i node and file_table[64]. The specific code is as follows:

```
//code source:fs/open.c:
int sys_open(const char * filename,int flag,int mode)
{
    ......
        if ((i = open_namei(filename,flag,mode,&inode))<0) {//To obtain the I node in hello.txt file
    ......
        f->f_mode = inode->i_mode;        //set file attributes using i-node attributes
        f->f_flags = flag;                //set file operations with the flag parameter
        f->f_count = 1;                   //File reference count plus 1
        f->f_inode = inode;               //build relationships between the i-node and the file.
        f->f_pos = 0;                     //File read and write pointer is set to 0
        return (fd);                      //return the file handle to the user space
}
```

It is worth noting that the way to get the i node from the hello.txt file is different from the way process A gets i node. The specific code is as follows:

```
//code source:fs/namei.c:
int open_namei(const char * pathname, int flag, int mode,
    struct m_inode ** res_inode)
{
    ......
        if (flag & O_EXCL)
            return -EEXIST;
    if (!(inode = iget(dev,inr)))         //To obtain the I node
            return -EACCES;
    ......
}
```

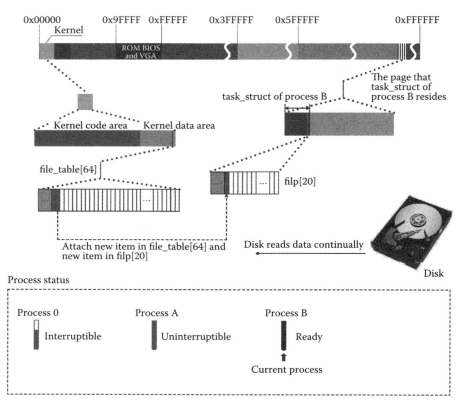

Figure 7.15 System build relationships between process B and the kernel file management table.

```
//code source:fs/namei.c:
struct m_inode * iget(int dev,int nr)
{
    ......
empty = get_empty_inode();    //apply for free entry in inode_table[32]
    ......
while (inode < NR_INODE+inode_table) {//Traversethe entire inode_table[32]
        if (inode->i_dev ! = dev || inode->i_num ! = nr) {//If can not find a ready-made
list, then keep looking
                continue;
        }
        wait_on_inode(inode);
        if (inode->i_dev ! = dev || inode->i_num ! = nr) {
            ......
            continue;
        }
        inode->i_count++;            //if ready-made i-node in hello.txt file can be find,
                                     //reference count increases
        ......
        if (empty)        //free entry found in inode_table[32] is useless, release it
                iput(empty);
        return inode;                //return i-node in hello.txt
}
    ......
}
```

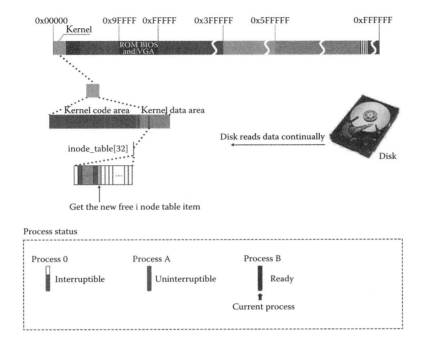

Figure 7.16 System creates the conditions for loading the i node in.

The application of a free i-node scenario is shown in Figure 7.16.

One file is only corresponding to one i node. Two sets of accounts are needed to record the operation to the file by process A and B. But there is only one i node that operates in hello.txt. Process A has loaded i node into inode_table[32]. Process B needs to continue to use the i node then.

The i node operation scenario of the above code is shown in Figure 7.17.

After opening the file, process B runs the sentence read(fd,buffer,sizeof(buffer)); and reads the content in the file hello.txt. Function read() will eventually be mapped to function sys_read() to execute. Then function sys_read() calls function file_read() to read the contents of the file. Function file_read() calls function bread() to read data from the hard disk. The specific code is as follows:

```
//code source:fs/read_write.c:
int sys_read(unsigned int fd,char * buf,int count)          //Reading data from hello.txt file
{                                                //fd is the file handle, buf is a user-
                                                 //space pointer, and count is the number of
                                                 //bytes to read
    if (S_ISDIR(inode->i_mode) || S_ISREG(inode->i_mode)) {
        if (count+file->f_pos > inode->i_size)
            count = inode->i_size - file->f_pos;
        if (count< = 0)
            return 0;
        return file_read(inode,file,buf,count);          //read specific data of process
    }
    printk("(Read)inode->i_mode =%06o\n\r",inode->i_mode);
    return -EINVAL;
}
```

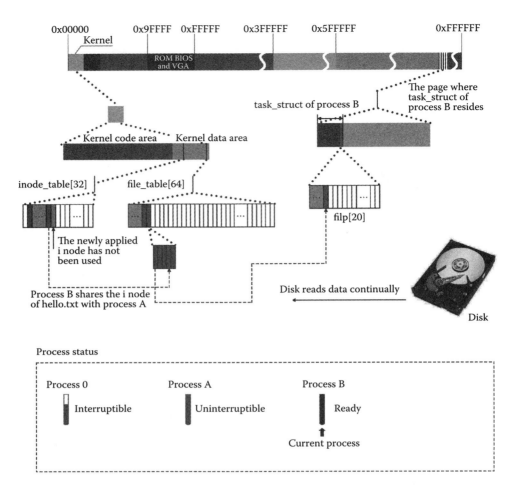

Figure 7.17 System finds the i node already loaded into file hello.txt for process B.

```
//code source:fs/file_dev.c:
int file_read(struct m_inode * inode, struct file * filp, char * buf, int count)
{
    ......
    if (nr = bmap(inode,(filp->f_pos)/BLOCK_SIZE)) {
        if (!(bh = bread(inode->i_dev,nr)))        //read data from the hard disk
break;
    } else
            bh = NULL;
    ......
}
```

The implementation process after entering the bread() function has been described in detail in Section 3.3.1. The specific code is as follows:

```
//code source:fs/buffer.c:
struct buffer_head * bread(int dev,int block)//read data from the hard disk
{
    ......
    if (!(bh = getblk(dev,block))) //Apply for a free buffer block
    ......
    ll_rw_block(READ,bh);           //The buffer block is locked and is bound
                                    //with request item, sending disc reading
                                    //instruction
    wait_on_buffer(bh);             //suspend the process waiting for unlocked
                                    //buffer block
    if (bh->b_uptodate)
        return bh;
    ......
}
```

The execution scenario of function getblk() and function ll_rw_block() is different. It returns immediately after entering function getblk() because the data block corresponding to the file hello.txt has been loaded into the buffer block. The specific code is as follows:

```
//code source:fs/buffer.c:
struct buffer_head * getblk(int dev,int block)        //apply for a buffer block
{
    ......
    if (bh = get_hash_table(dev,block))               //At this point the
                                                      //specified buffer block can
                                                      //be found in the hash table
    return bh;                          //return to the bh pointer directly
    ......
}
```

Then execute function ll_rw_block(). As the buffer block has been locked, process B will be suspended by the system due to waiting for the buffer block to be unlocked. The specific code is as follows:

```
//code source:kernel/blk_drv/ll_rw_block.c:
void ll_rw_block(int rw, struct buffer_head * bh)
{
    unsigned int major;

    if ((major = MAJOR(bh->b_dev)) > = NR_BLK_DEV ||
    !(blk_dev[major].request_fn)) {
        printk("Trying to read nonexistent block-device\n\r");
        return;
    }
    make_request(major,rw,bh);//set the request
}


static void make_request(int major,int rw, struct buffer_head * bh)
{
    ......
```

```
    lock_buffer(bh);//lock the buffer block the bh pointing to
    if ((rw == WRITE && !bh->b_dirt) || (rw == READ && bh->b_uptodate)) {
        unlock_buffer(bh);
        return;
    }
    ......
}


static inline void lock_buffer(struct buffer_head * bh)//lock the buffer block
{
    cli();
    while (bh->b_lock)              //if the buffer block is already locked
        sleep_on(&bh->b_wait);     //suspend the process waiting for the
                                   //buffer block
    bh->b_lock = 1;                //If program executed to here, it means the
                                   //buffer block is not locked. Then lock it
    sti();
}
```

Then the kernel executes function sleep_on(). It is the same file that is operated by processes A and B in Example 1. And it is corresponding to the same buffer block bh. The value of b_wait in the buffer block is set to the task_struct pointer of process A. So the scene of executing the function sleep_on() is completely different from the implementation of the previous process A. The specific code is as follows:

```
//code source:kernel/sched.c:
void sleep_on(struct task_struct **p)
{
    struct task_struct *tmp;

    if (!p)
        return;
    if (current == &(init_task.task))
        panic("task[0] trying to sleep");
    tmp = *p;                                //at this time tmp stores task_struct
                                             //pointer of process A
    *p = current;                            //*p stores pointer of process B
    current->state = TASK_UNINTERRUPTIBLE;   //set process B to uninterruptible
                                             //waiting state
    schedule();                              //switch process
    if (tmp)
        tmp->state = 0;
}
```

The kernel calls the function schedule() after process A is suspended and switches to process C to execute.

At the same time, the hard disk is transacting data to the data register port. This scenario is shown in Figure 7.18.

It is worth noting that tmp in the code is stored in the kernel stack of the process B and is stored as task_struct pointer of process A. At this time, bh-> b_wait stored the pointer of the process B as shown in Figure 7.19.

Process C is suspended after writing files. Process C is excuted, and in the same operation hello.txt file, the data is written to the file. The data is written to the hello.txt file after the process C starts to execute. The technical route of executing process C is

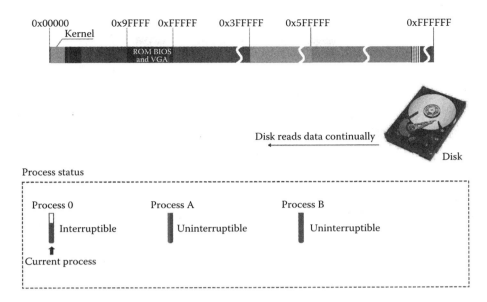

Figure 7.18 Process B was set to TASK_UNINTERRUPTIBLE.

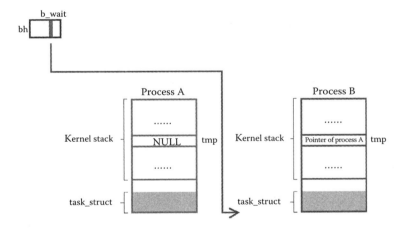

Figure 7.19 Process B was set to TASK_UNINTERRUPTIBLE and added to the process wait queue.

broadly consistent with the process B. Execute the sentence int fd = open("/mnt/user/user1/user2/hello.txt", O_RDWR,0644)) first. Function open() will eventually be mapped to function sys_open() to execute. The final results of the implementation of function sys_open() is that a free entry is reapplied in the file_table[64] and *filp[20] in task_struct of process C binds with file_table[64] in the free entry.

Then function sys_open() calls function open_namei(). The i node of this file will also be found in the i node table inode_table[32]. The number of references of the i node adds 1 again. The specific code is as follows:

```
//code source:fs/open.c:
int sys_open(const char * filename,int flag,int mode)
{
    ......
    (current->filp[fd] = f)->f_count++;            //mount *filp[20] in process c and items
                                                   //corresponding to file_table[64],and add
                                                   //file handle count
    ......
    if ((i = open_namei(filename,flag,mode,&inode))<0) {   //To obtain the I node in
                                                           //hello.txt file
    ......
     f->f_mode = inode->i_mode;          //set file attributes using i-node attributes
     f->f_flags = flag;                  //set file operations with the flag parameter
     f->f_count = 1;                     //File reference count plus 1
     f->f_inode = inode;                 //build relationships between the i-node and the file.
     f->f_pos = 0;                       //File read and write pointer is set to 0
     return (fd);                        //return the file handle to the user space
}
```

Process B continues to execute this sentence write (fd, str1, strlen (str1)) and writes data into file hello.txt (Figure 7.20).

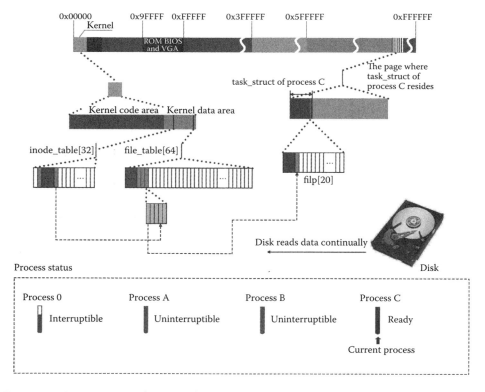

Figure 7.20 Process C is ready to read file hello.txt.

Function write() will eventually be mapped to function sys_write() to execute. The function sys_ write() calls function file_read() to read the contents of the file. Function file_read() calls function bread() to read data from the hard disk. The specific code is as follows:

```
//code source:fs/read_write.c:
int sys_write (unsigned int fd,char * buf,int count)          //write data into hello.txt file
{          //fd is the file handle, buf is a user-space pointer, and count is the number of
           //bytes to read
    ......
    if (S_ISBLK(inode->i_mode))
        return block_write(inode->i_zone[0],&file->f_pos,buf,count);
    if (S_ISREG(inode->i_mode))
        return file_write(inode,file,buf,count);              //write specified data in process
    printk("(Write)inode->i_mode =%06o\n\r",inode->i_mode);
    return -EINVAL;
}


//code source:fs/file_dev.c:
int file_write (struct m_inode * inode, struct file * filp, char * buf, int count)
{
    ......
    if (!(block = create_block(inode,pos/BLOCK_SIZE)))
        break;
    if (!(bh = bread(inode->i_dev,nr)))                       //write data into hard disk
        c = pos% BLOCK_SIZE;
    p = c + bh->b_data;
    bh->b_dirt = 1;
    ......
}
```

The implementation process after entering the function bread() is consistent with the process B. The code is as follows:

```
//code source:fs/buffer.c:
struct buffer_head * bread(int dev,int block)//read data from the hard disk
{
    ......
    if (!(bh = getblk(dev,block)))//Apply for a free buffer block
    ll_rw_block(READ,bh);                    //The buffer block is locked and is bound
                                             //with request item, sending disc reading
                                             //instruction
    wait_on_buffer(bh);                      //suspend the process waiting for unlocked
                                             //buffer block,
    if (bh->b_uptodate)
        return bh;
    ......
}
```

After entering function getblk(), it returns immediately because the data block corresponding to the file hello.txt is loaded into the buffer block.

```
//code source:fs/buffer.c:
struct buffer_head * getblk(int dev,int block)//apply for a buffer block
{
    struct buffer_head * tmp, * bh;
    repeat:
    if (bh = get_hash_table(dev,block))         //At this point the specified buffer block
                                                //can be found in the hash table
        return bh;                              //return to the bh pointer directly
    tmp = free_list;
    ......
}
```

Then execute function ll_rw_block(). As the buffer block is locked, process C will be suspended by the system due to waiting for the buffer block to be unlocked. The specific code is as follows:

```
//code source:kernel/blk_drv/ll_rw_block.c:
void ll_rw_block(int rw, struct buffer_head * bh)
{
    unsigned int major;

    if ((major = MAJOR(bh->b_dev)) > = NR_BLK_DEV ||
        !(blk_dev[major].request_fn)) {
            printk("Trying to read nonexistent block-device\n\r");
            return;
    }
    make_request(major,rw,bh);//set the request
}


static void make_request(int major,int rw, struct buffer_head * bh)
{
    ......
    lock_buffer(bh);//lock the buffer block the bh pointing to
    if ((rw = = WRITE && !bh->b_dirt) || (rw = = READ && bh->b_uptodate)) {
        unlock_buffer(bh);
        return;
    }
    ......
}


static inline void lock_buffer(struct buffer_head * bh)//lock the buffer block
{
    cli();
    while (bh->b_lock)                          //if the buffer block is already locked
        sleep_on(&bh->b_wait);                  //suspend the process waiting for the buffer block
    bh->b_lock = 1;                             //If program executed to here, it means the buffer
                                                //block is not locked. Then lock it
    sti();
}
```

Then execute function sleep_on(). It is the same file that is operated by processes A, B, and C in example 1. And it is corresponding to the same buffer block bh. The value of b_wait in the buffer block is set to the task_struct pointer of process B. So the scene of executing the function sleep_on() is completely different from the implementation of the previous process B. The code is as follows:

```
//code source:kernel/sched.c:
void sleep_on(struct task_struct **p)
{
    struct task_struct *tmp;

    if (!p)
        return;
    if (current == &(init_task.task))
        panic("task[0] trying to sleep");
    tmp = *p;                               //at this time tmp stores task_struct
                                            //pointer of process B
    *p = current;                           //*p stores pointer of process C
    current->state = TASK_UNINTERRUPTIBLE;  //set process c to uninterruptible state
    schedule();                             //switch process
    if (tmp)
        tmp->state = 0;
}
```

The schedule() function is called after process C is suspended. And the system has no ready process. So the kernel switches to process 0 to execute.

At the same time, the hard disk is transacting data to a data register port. This scenario is shown in Figure 7.21.

It is worth noting that the code tmp is stored in the kernel stack of the process C, and the storage is the task_struct pointer of the process B; the process C pointer is stored in the bh->b_wait at this time, for instance (Figure 7.22).

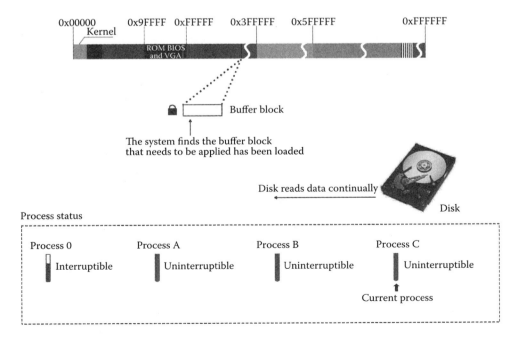

Figure 7.21 Process C was set to TASK_UNINTERRUPTIBLE.

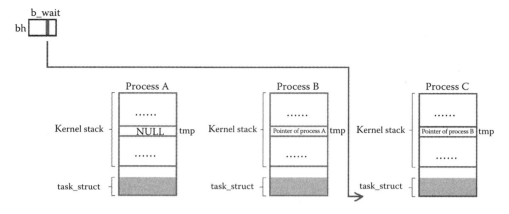

Figure 7.22 Process C was set to TASK_UNINTERRUPTIBLE and added to the process wait queue.

Now the situation is that three processes are suspended by the system due to waiting for the buffer block bh to unlock. Then it forms a waiting queue, before it is suspended, the task_struct pointer of the previous suspended process is stored in the kernel stack of each process, and the Picture performance is the waiting queue. The role of this queue is that until the buffer block unlocks, the operating system can wake up the suspended process before this process suspends according to the record in the kernel stack of each awakened process, in this way, all the processes waiting for the buffer block releases will be awakened in turn, and the specific process will be described in detail below.

The three processes are awakened in the reverse order. Now the process A, process B, and process C have been suspended, and all the processes in the system are not in ready state. Now it has switched to execute the process 0 by default until the data read is completed, and then the hard disk generates an interrupt as shown in Figure 7.23.

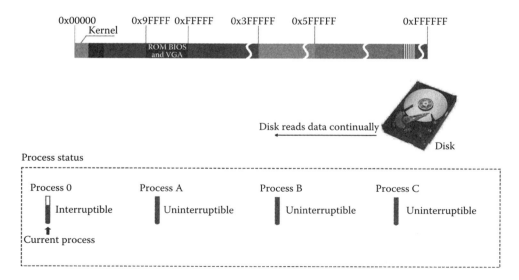

Figure 7.23 Switch again to execute process 0.

The interrupt service routine will start to work after a hard disk interrupt has generated. At this time, the hard disk has loaded all the data specified into the buffer block. After the interrupt service routine has started to work, the bh buffer block will unlock, and call function wake_up() to wake up the wait field in bh corresponding process (process C), and the code is as follows:

```
//code path:kernel/blk_drv/Blk.h:
extern inline void end_request(int uptodate)
{
    DEVICE_OFF(CURRENT->dev);
    if (CURRENT->bh) {
        CURRENT->bh->b_uptodate = uptodate;
        unlock_buffer(CURRENT->bh);          //unlock the buffer block
    }
    ......
}


extern inline void unlock_buffer(struct buffer_head * bh)

{

    if (!bh->b_lock)
        printk(DEVICE_NAME ": free buffer being unlocked\n");
    bh->b_lock = 0;               //unlock the buffer block
    wake_up(&bh->b_wait);         //wake up process waiting for buffer block unlock
}
```

When function wake_up() is called, the passed parameter is & bh-> b_wait, and from the process waiting queue graph, it is not difficult to find that the bh->b_wait direct to task_struct pointer of the process C, so process C is awakened.

The code of function wake_up() is as follows:

```
//code path:kernel/sched.c:
void wake_up(struct task_struct **p)
{
    if (p && *p) {
        (**p).state = 0;//process C is set to ready state
        *p = NULL;
    }
}
```

This setting scene is shown in Figure 7.24.

After the interrupt service routine, it will return to the process 0 once again and switch to the ready process C. Process C is in function sleep_on() and calls function schedule() to

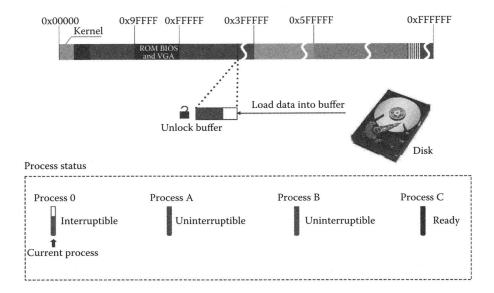

Figure 7.24 Process C is awakened.

switch the process; therefore, process C will eventually enter function sleep_on(), and the first code to be executed is as follows:

```
//code path:kernel/sched.c:
void sleep_on(struct task_struct **p)
{
    ......
    schedule();
    if (tmp)
        tmp->state = 0;//process that is related to tmp is set to ready state
}
```

We look at the diagram shown in Figure 7.25.

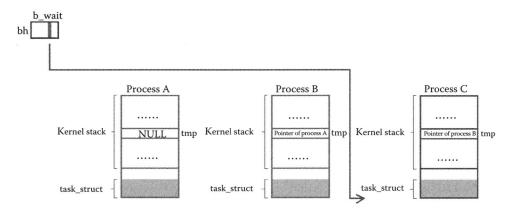

Figure 7.25 Process C was woken up and exited from the process wait queue.

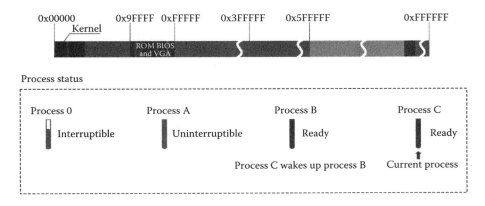

Figure 7.26 Process B is woken up.

Now the kernel program is in execution, using the kernel stack of the process C, so tmp corresponds to the task_struct pointer of the process B, and at this point, process B is set to a ready state.

Set the scene as shown in Figure 7.26.

Kernel continues to execute, and the data from character array str1 that the process C source program has specified will be written to the buffer block that is related to the file hello.txt, and the code is as follows:

```
//code path:fs/file_dev.c:
int file_write(struct m_inode * inode, struct file * filp, char * buf, int count)
{
......
if (pos > inode->i_size) {
        inode->i_size = pos;
        inode->i_dirt = 1;
    }
i + = c;
        while (c-->0)
        *(p++) = get_fs_byte(buf++);//write string to the buffer block
        brelse(bh);
        ......
}
```

The written scenario is shown in Figure 7.27.

Then return to the user program of process C. The code is as follows:

```
for(i = 0;i<1000000;i++)//time-consuming slice
{
        for(j = 0;j<1000000;j++)
{
        ;
}
}
```

In the implementation process, the timer interrupt continues to generate, and the time slice of process C is cut continuously as shown in Figure 7.28.

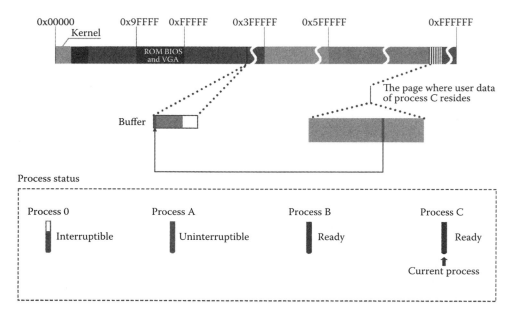

Figure 7.27 The system will write data to the specified buffer block for process C.

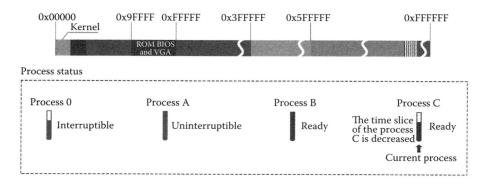

Figure 7.28 In the implementation process of process C, the time slice is cut continuously.

Pay attention to the picture; the progress bar of each process is in the execution state, the time slice of the process C is cut continuously (Figure 7.29).

The time slice of the process C has been reduced to zero and then switches the process. It has been introduced before, after process C is awoken, and the first thing that the system will do is setting process B to the ready state. At this time, both process B and process C in the system are in a ready state, and the time slice of the process C has been used up; then it will switch to the process B to perform as is shown in Figure 7.30.

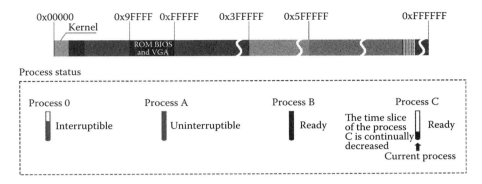

Figure 7.29 Time slice of the process C is reduced to zero.

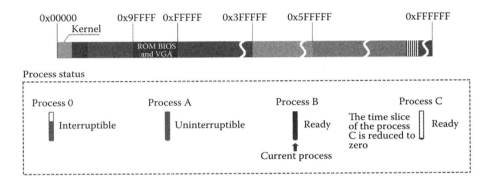

Figure 7.30 Switch to process B to perform.

Process B is also in the function sleep_on(), calling function schedule() to switch the process; therefore, the process B will eventually be in function sleep_on(), and the first code to be executed is as follows:

```
//code path:kernel/sched.c:
void sleep_on(struct task_struct **p)
{
    ......
    schedule();
    if (tmp)
        tmp->state = 0;//process that is related to tmp is set to ready state
}
```

We look at the diagram shown in Figure 7.31.

The kernel program is in the implementation, using the kernel stack of the process B, so tmp corresponds to the task_struct pointer of process A at this time, and process A is set to a ready state.

The scene of waking up process A is shown in Figure 7.32.

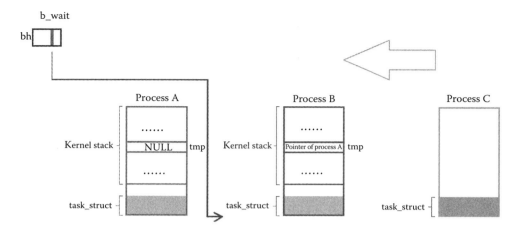

Figure 7.31 Process B was woken up and exited from the process wait queue.

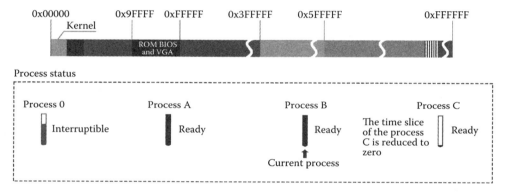

Figure 7.32 Wake up process A.

The current process is process B, and it will read data from the specified buffer block. The executable code is as follows:

```
//code path:fs/file_dev.c:
int file_read (struct m_inode * inode, struct file * filp, char * buf, int count)
{
......
if (bh) {
        char * p = nr + bh->b_data;
        while (chars- >0)
          put_fs_byte(*(p++),buf++); //data is read into user space of process B
        brelse(bh);
     } else {
        while (chars-->0)
          put_fs_byte(0,buf++);
     }
     ......
}
```

Then return to the program of process B; executable code is as follows:

```
for(i = 0;i<1000000;i++)//consuming time slice
{
for(j = 0;j<1000000;j++)
{
;
}
}
```

As the timer interrupt generates continuously, after the time slice of the process B is cut to 0 because only process A in the system is in a ready state, its time slice has not been cut to 0, so it will switch to process A to perform as shown in Figure 7.33.

Process A is also in the function sleep_on(), calling function schedule() to switch the process; therefore, the process A will eventually be in function sleep_on(), and the first code to be executed is as follows:

```
//code path:kernel/sched.c:
void sleep_on(struct task_struct **p)
{
    .....
    schedule();
    if (tmp)                 //tmp is NULL at this time
        tmp->state = 0;      //here the code isn't executed and do not wake up the process
}
```

The scene of the execution is not the same; we look at the diagram shown in Figure 7.34.

The kernel program is in the execution, using the kernel stack of the Process A, thus NULL, that is related to tmp will not wake up the process.

These are the processes that the process is awakened in the process waiting queue. The three processes are suspended in the order of process A, process B, and process C, and it has been introduced in Section 7.1.4 that the wake-up order is process C, process B, and process A, and it is just the opposite order of the suspended.

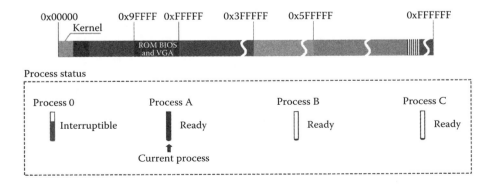

Figure 7.33 Switch to process A.

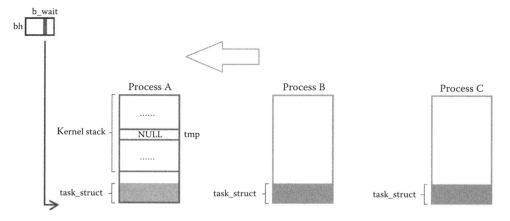

Figure 7.34 Process A was woken up and exited from the process wait queue.

▌ 7.7 Overall Look at the Buffer Block and the Request Item

The b_dev and b_blocknr are flags of data that stays in the buffer block in the practical application of the buffer block; the kernel did not remove these two fields intentionally. This means that, if it applies for the buffer block continuously, then all buffer blocks would be bound to the data block soon. At this time, if it continues to apply for the buffer block, it can only replace the old binding relationship with the new binding relationship, and the data in this buffer block has become invalid. **This reflects a strategy that lets the buffer data stay in the buffer as long as possible**.

In order to make the data stay for a long time, the kernel does as much as possible not to apply for the new buffer block, and it had better use the binding relationship that has been established, and if there is no other way to go, then apply for a new one. This approach is embodied in the code as follows:

```
//code path:fs/buffer.c:
struct buffer_head * getblk(int dev,int block)    //apply for the buffer block
{
repeat:
    if (bh = get_hash_table(dev,block))           //if it is found that a buffer block has
                                                  //already bound
                                                  //with the specify data block (block) of
                                                  //the specified
                                                  //device (dev)
            return bh;                            //use the off-the-shell directly
    tmp = free_list;                              //if the binding buffer block according
                                                  //with the specified standard
                                                  //can't be found, then apply for a
                                                  //new buffer block

    do {
        ......
/* and repeat until we find something good */
    } while ((tmp = tmp->b_next_free) ! = free_list);
    ......
}
```

From the code, it is not difficult to find that the kernel searches the hash table first, then compares b_dev and b_blocknr to analyze whether it can still be used. If not, then it executes the loop do... While and applies for a new buffer block.

Here we look at the scene of applying for a new buffer block.

The code is shown as below:

```
//code path:fs/buffer.c:
#define BADNESS(bh) (((bh)->b_dirt<<1)+(bh)->b_lock)
struct buffer_head * getblk(int dev,int block)       //apply for the buffer block
{
    ......
tmp = free_list;
do {
        if (tmp->b_count)                            //if the buffer block is occupied, then
                                                     //skip the cycle
            continue;
        if (!bh || BADNESS(tmp)<BADNESS(bh)) {       //weigh BADNESS and select the buffer block
            bh = tmp;
            if (!BADNESS(tmp))
                break;
        }
/* and repeat until we find something good */
    } while ((tmp = tmp->b_next_free) ! = free_list);
    ......
}
```

The present situation is that the hash table has been traversed, and all the buffer blocks in the buffer can't be used by the process, so the kernel must apply for a new buffer block. When the kernel apples for the new buffer block, it should start the search from the header of free_list without destroying the buffer block that has bound with the data block as much as possible. Let them remain in the buffer for a while. If there is really no other way (such as all buffer blocks in the buffer have bound with data blocks), it has to replace the old relationship the new relationship.

The implementation in the circulation starts under this premise.

It does not analyze the b_uptodate field in the circulation because the searching hash table in front has confirmed that no suitable buffer block can still be used. This means one thing for the current process that all the buffer blocks in the buffer are not available. It does not matter whether they are updated or not as long as b_uptodate is 1 or 0. So, at this time, there is no need to analyze values of b_uptodate.

It judges whether the b_count is 0 or not first in the loop. If not, it shows that the buffer block is shared by other processes. The current process can't abolish the buffer block that is being shared by another process, and this buffer block cannot be used, so the kernel should apply for a new buffer block for it. If the b_count 0 buffer block cannot be found in the buffer, this process can only be suspended.

The code is as shown below:

```
//code path:fs/buffer.c:
#define BADNESS(bh) (((bh)->b_dirt<<1)+(bh)->b_lock)
struct buffer_head * getblk(int dev,int block)               //apply for the buffer block
{
    ......
    tmp = free_list;
    do {
            if (tmp->b_count)                                //if the buffer block is
                                                             //occupied, skip the loop
```

```
continue;
    if (!bh || BADNESS(tmp)<BADNESS(bh)) {
        bh = tmp;
        if (!BADNESS(tmp))
            break;
    }
/* and repeat until we find something good */
    } while ((tmp = tmp->b_next_free) != free_list);
if (!bh) {                              //b_count 0 buffer block can't be found finally
        sleep_on(&buffer_wait);         //the current process has to be suspended
        goto repeat;
    }
    ......
}
```

If a buffer block with b_count as 0 has been found, there are about two fields that will be further chosen. The one is b_dirt, and the other is b_lock. If these two fields are 0, the buffer block is appropriate, and it can be used directly. If b_lock is 1 or b_dirt is 1, then which is more appropriate? Comparing the two choices, b_lock at 1 is the favorable one. The reason is that if there is a 1 in these two fields, the current process cannot be used certainly, and it has to wait. In contrast, the less time the better. B_lock is 1, indicating that the buffer block is interacting data with the hard disk. When it has finished, it will be used by the current process finally. However, when b_dirt is 1 it indicates that before creating a new binding relationship, it needs to synchronize data to the hard disk definitely. When it synchronizes the data, it should be locked definitely, and b_lock is set to 1. Therefore, the choice that b_lock is 1 to b_dirt is 1 is less waiting time than the choice that b_dirt is 1 to b_lock is 1. This can also be seen in the code.

The code is as follows:

```
//code path:fs/buffer.c:
#define BADNESS(bh) (((bh)->b_dirt<<1)+(bh)->b_lock)
struct buffer_head * getblk(int dev,int block)              //apply for the buffer block
{
    ......
tmp = free_list;
do {
        if (tmp->b_count)        //if the buffer block is occupied,skip the loop
            continue;
        if (!bh || BADNESS(tmp)<BADNESS(bh)) {
            bh = tmp;
            if (!BADNESS(tmp))
                break;
        }
/* and repeat until we find something good */
    } while ((tmp = tmp->b_next_free) != free_list);
if (!bh) {                              //b_count 0 buffer block can't be found finally
        sleep_on(&buffer_wait);         //the current process has to be suspended
        goto repeat;
    }
    ......
while (bh->b_dirt) {                     //if b_dirt 1 buffer block has been applied,
                                        //write directly to the disk.
                                        //If write outside, then use the current process
        sync_dev(bh->b_dev);
            wait_on_buffer(bh);
        if (bh->b_count)
            goto repeat;
    }
    ......
}
```

Visibly, not applying for the b_dirt 1 buffer block first will allow the process to implement as soon as possible, and it is more beneficial. So in #define BADNESS(bh) ((((bh)->b_dirt<<1)+(bh)->b_lock), we should move b_dirt one bit to the left in order to make it gain a higher weight. BADNESS(tmp)<BADNESS(bh), in this line of logic, make b_dirt be applied as late as possible when b_dev, b_blocknr, and b_count are under the same conditions.

∎ 7.8 Example 2: Comprehensive Examples of Multiprocess Operating File

Let's introduce the problems of the buffer block selection and the use of request through a set of cases of multiprocess operating files. The situations of the three processes are as follows. Process A is a write process in order to write characters "ABCDE" in str1[] to the file hello1.txt. The code is as follows:

```
void FunA();
void main()
{
    ......
    FunA();
    ......
}


void FunA()
{
    char str1[] = "ABCDE";
    int i;
    //open the file
    int fd = open("/mnt/user/user1/user2/hello1.txt", O_RDWR,0644));
    for(i=0;i<1000000;i++)
    {
        //write the file
        write(fd,str1,strlen(str1));
    }
    //close the file
    close(fd);
    return;
}
```

Process B is a write process in order to write characters "ABCDE" in str1[] to the file hello2.txt. The code is as follows:

```
void FunB();
void main()
{
    ......
    FunB();
    ......
}
```

```
void FunB()
{
    char str1[]="ABCDE";
    int i;
    //open the file
    int fd=open("/mnt/user/user1/user2/hello2.txt", O_RDWR,0644));
    for(i=0;i<1000000;i++)
    {
        //write the file
        write(fd,str1,strlen(str1));
    }
    //close the file
    close(fd);
    return;
}
```

Process C is a read process, and the purpose is read 20,000 bytes to the buffer from hello3. txt. The code is as follows:

```
void FunC();
void main()
{
    ......
    FunC();
    ......
}


void FunC()
{
    char buffer[20000];
    int i, j;
    //open the file
    int fd = open("/mnt/user/user1/user2/hello3.txt", O_RDWR,0644));
    //read the file
    read(fd,buffer,sizeof(buffer));
    //close the file
    close(fd);
    return;
}
```

The executive order of three processes are as follows:

At first, process A is executed; then process B is executed; process C is in the end. The three processes do not have a parent-child relationship.

The system will write data to the buffer continuously for process A. First, process A starts with performing the function write, assuming that there is nothing in file hello1.txt. Process A only needs to apply for a buffer block in the buffer and writes the specified data to the buffer block. The premise of applying the new buffer block is that the buffer block is free and not dirty. We assume that the system has all the buffer blocks free and not dirty and filled with data. Figure 7.35 shows the state of a system that is all free and not dirty as

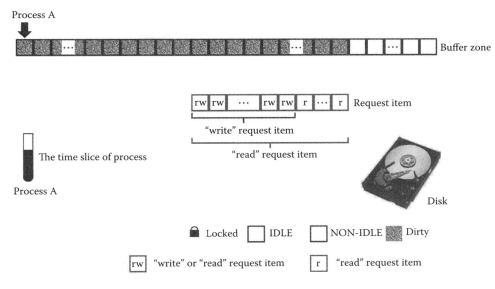

Figure 7.35 System continues to write data to process A.

a buffer block filled with data. Next, we will look at what circumstances applying for the new buffer block and writing operations will cause when the buffer is in the state Figure 7.35 shows.

Continuous performance will lead data of the buffer block to be synchronized. The current process is still process A, and the system is far from completing its request. It should continue to write data to the buffer. This requires the function getblk to find a free buffer block in the buffer, that is the buffer block with b_count as 0.

The executable code is as follows:

```
//code path:fs/buffer.c:
struct buffer_head * getblk(int dev,int block)
{
    ......
    tmp = free_list;
    do {
        if (tmp->b_count)              //find the free buffer block
            continue;
        if (!bh || BADNESS(tmp)<BADNESS(bh))  {//on the basis of the idle,
                                              //weigh BADNESS
            bh = tmp;
            if (!BADNESS(tmp))
                break;
        }
/* and repeat until we find something good */
    } while ((tmp = tmp->b_next_free) ! = free_list);
    ......
}
```

But now the situation is that the buffer has no free and not dirty buffer blocks but only a free but dirty buffer block. This means that the next step is to synchronize data from the buffer to the hard disk by force in order to hollow out more space in the buffer and provide support for a subsequent write disk. The executable code is as follows:

```
//code path:fs/buffer.c:
struct buffer_head * getblk(int dev,int block)
{
    ......
    if (bh->b_count)
      goto repeat;
    while (bh->b_dirt) {             //if all the free buffer blocks are dirty,
                                     //it indicates there is too much data needed
                                     //to be synchronized to the hard disk
      sync_dev(bh->b_dev);          //synchronize immediately
      wait_on_buffer(bh);
      if (bh->b_count)
        goto repeat;
    }
    ......
}
```

Synchronize the data from the buffer to the hard disk. At this time, the function sync_dev() is used to synchronize data from the buffer to the hard disk. After entering sync_dev function, the executable code is as follows:

```
//code path:fs/buffer.c:
int sync_dev(int dev)
{
    ......
    bh = start_buffer;
    for (i=0 ; i<NR_BUFFERS ; i++,bh++) {     //all have to be traversed
        if (bh->b_dev != dev)
          continue;
        wait_on_buffer(bh);
        if (bh->b_dev == dev && bh->b_dirt)   //as long as the device number matches and
                                              //it is dirty, then
                                              //synchronization
          ll_rw_block(WRITE,bh);
    }
    ......
}
```

The function sync_dev will traverse the entire buffer, and all the "dirty" blocks in the buffer block will be synchronized to the hard disk. The synchronous step of each "dirty" buffer block is like this:

First, the buffer block will be bound with free request items that have been applied, and the records in the claims will be used as the unique basis for data synchronization.

Second, if there is no hard disk working at this time, then the command of the writing disk will be issued, and the data will be synchronized. If the hard disk is working, then the request will be inserted in the request queue. When the hard disk has finished the data synchronization and triggered an interrupt, the interrupt service routine will send command to the hard disk continuously in order to make the data correspond to each item in the request queue synchronized to the hard disk one after another.

Function Sync_dev will keep on executing the above work until it can't apply for a free request.

The synchronization process of each buffer block is completed in function ll_rw_block. In this process, the buffer block will be locked. The lock can only prevent the data interaction between the process and the buffer block and prevent data interaction between the system itself and the buffer block, but it doesn't stop the data interaction between the buffer block and the hard disk. Before sending sync command, the dirty flag b_dirt of the buffer block that needs to be synchronized will be set to 0, indicating that it is no longer a "dirty" buffer block.

The specific route of the implementation: After entering function ll_rw_block, it will call function make_request to bind the buffer block with the request. First the buffer block will be locked in function make_request and load request through function add_request. After the completion of the loading request, the system will send write disk command to the hard disk through calling function do_hd_request. Function do_hd_request is an interactive underlying function between the system and the hard disk, and according to the data in the request, it will write the data of the specified buffer block to the specified hard disk block ultimately. The executable code is as follows:

```
//code path:kernel/blk drv/ll rw blk.c:
static void make_request(int major,int rw, struct buffer_head * bh)
{
    ......
    if (rw! = READ && rw! = WRITE)
        panic("Bad block dev command, must be R/W/RA/WA");
    lock_buffer(bh);                                        //lock the buffer block
    if ((rw = = WRITE && !bh->b_dirt) || (rw = = READ && bh->b_uptodate)) {
        unlock_buffer(bh);
        return;
    }
    ......
    req->buffer = bh->b_data;
    req->waiting = NULL;
    req->bh = bh;
    req->next = NULL;
    add_request(major+blk_dev,req);                         //load claims
}
static void add_request(struct blk_dev_struct * dev, struct request * req)
{
    ......
    if (req->bh)
    req->bh->b_dirt = 0;           //the buffer block is synchronized and it will not be dirty
    ......
    (dev->request_fn)();           //this line of code corresponds to the function do_hd_request
    ......
}
```

The performance of synchronizing a buffer block is as shown in Figure 7.36, and this buffer block is locked in make_request, but the dirty flag of the buffer block has been set to 0 in the function add_request. At this time, the buffer block has become a buffer block which is free but not dirty. In contrast with Figure 7.35, pay attention to the state change of the buffer block.

The final result of function sync_dev continuously synchronizes the buffer block as is shown in Figure 7.37. Note that all the request items which have been left to the write operation have been occupied, and at the same time, the status of the buffer block corresponds to the write request item, has also been set to the free and not the dirty state. The hard disk is constantly processing the claims.

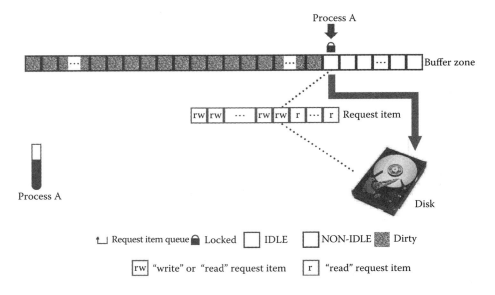

Figure 7.36 Writing request is inserted into the requesting queue.

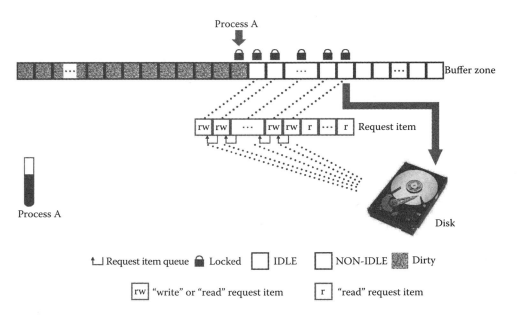

Figure 7.37 Space in the structure of the claims for the write request has run out.

The code for this process is as follows:

```
//code path:fs/buffer.c:
int sync_dev(int dev)
{
        int i;
        struct buffer_head * bh;
        bh = start_buffer;
        for (i=0 ; i<NR_BUFFERS ; i++,bh++) {  //traverse all buffer
                                                //blocks
        if (bh->b_dev ! = dev)
              continue;
        wait_on_buffer(bh);
        if (bh->b_dev = = dev && bh->b_dirt)
              ll_rw_block(WRITE,bh);
        }
        ......
}


//code path:kernel/blk_drv/ll_rw_blk.c:
void ll_rw_block(int rw, struct buffer_head * bh)
{
        unsigned int major;
        if ((major = MAJOR(bh->b_dev)) > = NR_BLK_DEV ||
        !(blk_dev[major].request_fn)) {
              printk("Trying to read nonexistent block-device\n\r");
              return;
        }
        make_request(major,rw,bh);
}

static void make_request(int major,int rw, struct buffer_head * bh)
{
        ......
        if (rw! = READ && rw! = WRITE)
        panic("Bad block dev command, must be R/W/RA/WA");
        lock_buffer(bh);        //it is locked here
        ......
        add_request(major+blk_dev,req);
}

static void add_request(struct blk_dev_struct * dev, struct request *
req)
{
        ......
req->next = NULL;
cli();
if (req->bh)
        req->bh->b_dirt = 0;   //here the dirty flag is set to 0
        ......
}
```

Although there are free request items in the structure of the request, the request items that left to the "write" operation only account for two thirds of the total number of request items. The corresponding code is as follows:

```
//code path:kernel/blk_drv/ll_rw_blk.c:
static void make_request(int major,int rw, struct buffer_head * bh)
{
  ......
  if (rw = = READ)
    req = request+NR_REQUEST;          //all request items can be used
                                       //for read operations
  else
    req = request+((NR_REQUEST*2)/3);  //only 2/3 of the claims can be
                                       //used for write operations
  ......
}
```

Because two thirds of the request items have all been occupied, now no free request item can serve the "sync." The write request is as shown in Figure 7.37.

Process A is suspended by the system because of waiting for free request. There is no free request item for write, but function sync_dev() will still continue to be called. After re-entering the function make_request(), it will execute the following code:

```
//code path:kernel/blk_drv/ll_rw_blk.c:
static void make_request(int major,int rw, struct buffer_head * bh)
{
      ......
      while (-- req >= request)
      ......
      if (req < request) {   //indicate that there is no free request
                             //item here
      ......
      sleep_on(&wait_for_request);
      }
      ......
}
```

The function of these codes is when suitable free claim can't be found in the end, the current process will be suspended. After calling the function sleep_on(), process A has become the process of waiting for free request, and it will be suspended. This process is shown in Figure 7.38. The hard disk is still processing the request constantly while process A has been in the suspended state despite its time slice.

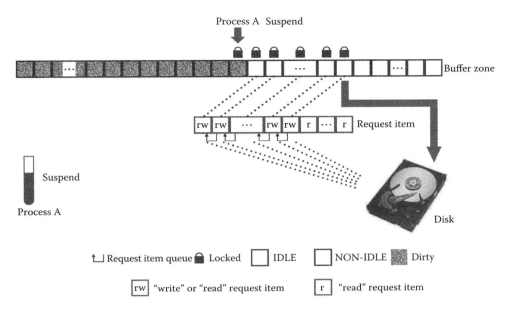

Figure 7.38 Process A is suspended.

Start to execute Process B. Process B starts to be executed, which is also a write disk process. The system should also apply for the buffer block for process B so that it can write data. The executable code is as follows:

```
//code path:fs/buffer.c:
struct buffer_head * getblk(int dev,int block)
{
......
        tmp = free_list;
do {
        if (tmp->b_count)
                continue;
        if (!bh || BADNESS(tmp)<BADNESS(bh)) {
                bh = tmp;
                if (!BADNESS(tmp))
                        break;
        }
/* and repeat until we find something good */
        } while ((tmp = tmp->b_next_free) != free_list);
        ......
}
```

As can be seen in Figure 7.38, the state of each free buffer block in the buffer is different at this time. The system will comprehensively analyze the state of all the free buffer blocks in the current case in order to determine which buffer block will be applied for

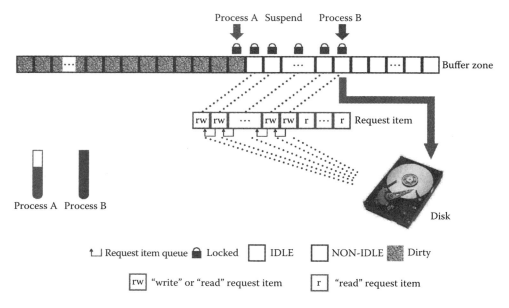

Figure 7.39 System has applied for a buffer block for process B.

process B. The system uses the BADNESS (tmp) to carry on a comprehensive analysis. BADNESS (tmp) is defined as follows:

```
#define BADNESS(bh) (((bh)->b_dirt<<1)+(bh)->b_lock).
```

Through the above analysis. we know that its role is to divide the buffer block in the buffer into four levels according to the principle more favorable for process executing. From favorable to unfavorable in order are

Level 1: There is a not "dirty" and not "locked" free buffer block, and the value of BADNESS in such a buffer block is 0.

Level 2: There is a not "dirty" but "locked" free buffer block, and the value of BADNESS in such a buffer block is 1.

Level 3: There is a "dirty" but not "locked" free buffer block, and the value of BADNESS in such a buffer block is 2.

Level 4: There is a "dirty" and "locked" free buffer block, and the value of BADNESS in such a buffer block is 3.

The smaller the value of BADNESS is, the more convenient the buffer block is to use. Otherwise, it is inconvenient.

The system has locked some buffer blocks, and their "dirty" flags are set to 0. Thus, it makes their BADNESS values become 1. In the present circumstance, this is the most convenient buffer block to use. Therefore, the system applies for a buffer block whose BADNESS value is 1 for process B. This buffer block is locked, which means that the buffer block cannot be operated immediately. But it's better than applying for a dirty buffer block. Figure 7.39 shows the buffer block that the system has applied for process B.

Process B is also suspended. The buffer block the system has applied is a "locked" buffer block, and it leads to the process or system not being able to exchange data with the buffer block immediately. Thus, the system will directly call function wait_on_buffer() and process B will also be suspended as is shown in Figure 7.40. Note that the system and the hard disk continue to process the request.

The code is as follows:

```
//code path:fs/buffer.c:
struct buffer_head * getblk(int dev,int block)
{
......
        if (!bh) {
        sleep_on(&buffer_wait);
        goto repeat;
}
        wait_on_buffer(bh);     //process B is suspended here
        if (bh->b_count)
        goto repeat;
        ......
}
```

The process C starts to execute and then subsequently is suspended. Process C starts to execute, which is a read disk process, and the system should also apply a buffer block for it. Based on the condition of buffer, the system applies for the same buffer block for process C and process B. From the introduction of Section 7.2.6, we learned that this buffer block

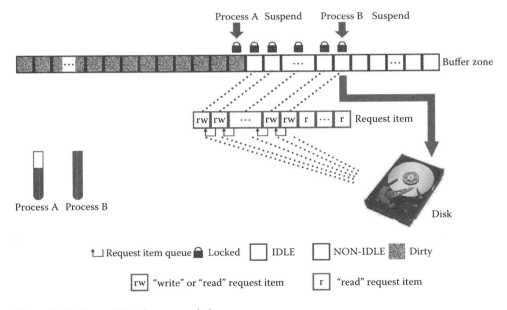

Figure 7.40 Process B is also suspended.

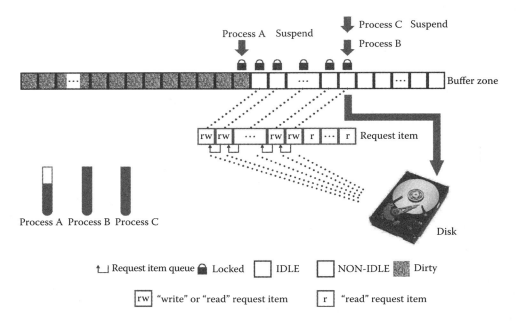

Figure 7.41 Waiting queue in which the processes A, B, and C are and their running state.

is locked, and the buffer block cannot be operated, but it can be applied. So the process C will also be suspended.

Process C and process B are now suspended because of waiting for the same buffer block to unlock. These two processes form a process waiting queue.

Until now, three user processes are suspended in example 2, so it switches to process 0 to execute by default. The situation that they are suspended in is shown in Figure 7.41. Process A is in the waiting queue of waiting for free request, but process B and process C are in the queue waiting for the same buffer block to unlock.

Process A and process C are awakened. Here we will introduce the process of the three user processes that are waken up. After they have been waken up, the system will continue to determine what user process will execute according to the various aspects of the situation of the buffer block and request items.

After a while, the hard disk has completed the synchronization task delivered by the request, and will produce a hard disk interrupt. The interrupt service routine begins to execute. The code is as follows:

```
//code path:kernel/blk_dev/blk.h:
extern inline void end_request(int uptodate)
{
        ......
        unlock_buffer(CURRENT->bh);
        ......
        wake_up(&wait_for_request);
        ......
```

```
}
extern inline void unlock_buffer(struct buffer_head * bh)
{
......
        bh->b_lock = 0;
wake_up(&bh->b_wait);
}
```

Process A is suspended for waiting for free request item. Then wake_up (&wait_for_request), and this line of code will wake up process A as shown in the process A in the left bottom of Figure 7.42.

Process B and process C form a process waiting queue. Process C is waken up first because it is suspended later than process B as shown in the process C in the left bottom of Figure 7.42.

In addition, the operation of the data in the specified buffer block has already been completed, so the interrupt service routine will unlock the buffer block. The interrupt service routine will continue to call function do_hd_request after the above work has been done. If there are request items to deal with, it will send a write disk command to the hard disk again. Obviously, the hard disk continues to the subsequent synchronization. As can be seen from the right part of Figure 7.42, the hard disk is processing the next request item. And, at the moment, there is an available free "write" request item.

We can see in Figure 7.42 that the time slice of process C is more than that of process A. Therefore, the system switches the current process from process 0 to process C.

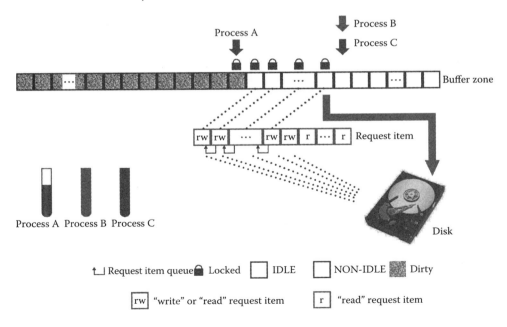

Figure 7.42 State of each process after the synchronization of data in the buffer block has completed.

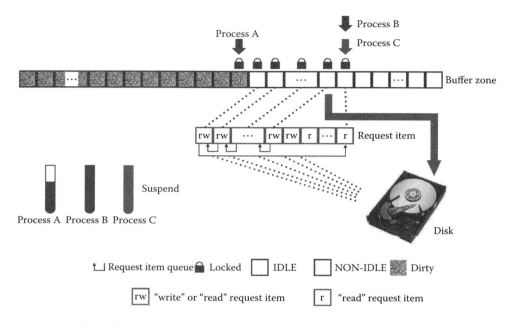

Figure 7.43 State of each process after the read request has been inserted into a queue request by process C.

The first thing is to wake up the process B as shown in the left bottom of Figure 7.43. The code is as follows:

```
//code path:fs/buffer.c:
struct buffer_head * getblk(int dev,int block)
{
......
        if (!bh) {
        sleep_on(&buffer_wait);
        goto repeat;
}

        wait_on_buffer(bh); //after waking up the process C, it
                            //continues to execute and wake up the
                            //process B firstly.
        if (bh->b_count)
                goto repeat;
        ......
}
static inline void wait_on_buffer(struct buffer_head * bh)
{
        cli();
        while (bh->b_lock)
                sleep_on(&bh->b_wait);
        sti();
}
```

The buffer block that the system has applied for process C is unlocked now, and it can be used. First, the system will set the buffer block, including set its reference number to 1. The code is shown below:

```
//code path:fs/buffer.c:
struct buffer_head * getblk(int dev,int block)
{
......
        if (!bh) {
        sleep_on(&buffer_wait);
        goto repeat;
}
        wait_on_buffer(bh);      //after waking up process B, process C
                                 //continues to execute from here
        if (bh->b_count)
                goto repeat;
        ......
        bh->b_count = 1;         //reference count is set to 1
        bh->b_dirt = 0;
        bh->b_uptodate = 0;
        ......
}
```

So the buffer block is no longer a free buffer block. And then apply for a free request item in the request [32], which is bound with the buffer block, and the buffer block is locked again. But it does not mean that the request item can be handle immediately, even if it has been set completely. The hard disk is busy processing other request items synchronously, and now the read disk request item can only be inserted into the request queue. The code is as shown below:

```
//code path:kernel/blk_dev/ll_rw_blk.c:
static void add_request(struct blk_dev_struct * dev, struct request *
req)
{
        ......
        for (; tmp->next ; tmp = tmp->next)  //device is busy and the
                        //request item will be inserted into the queue
                if ((IN_ORDER(tmp,req) ||
                    !IN_ORDER(tmp,tmp->next)) &&
                    IN_ORDER(req,tmp->next))
                        break;
        req->next = tmp->next; //next is used to form the request queue
        tmp->next = req;
        sti();
}
```

Process C will be suspended by the system.

Now the process status in the system is as shown in Figure 7.43, and the read request is the last item in the request queue, and the first item pointer in the request item arrays points to it.

The process B switches to the process A to execute. After process C is suspended, the time slice of process B is clearly more than that of process A, so switch to the process B. The system has already applied for the buffer block for process B. At that time, the buffer block is locked, so process B has to be suspended. Now the buffer block is still locked, so process B will be suspended again, and the system switches to process A as is shown in Figure 7.44.

Now the current process is A, which is suspended because of lacking free request items when it synchronizes the buffer block. So after it is waken up, the system will continue to synchronize buffer block. As can be seen in Figure 7.44, now the system has free claims for writing disk. So this request item is bound with the block buffer that will be synchronized soon, and it is inserted into the request queue. Then there is no free request item, so process A will be suspended again as is shown in Figure 7.45.

Next, the above steps will be repeated. On the one hand, as long as the hard disk has completed a synchronous operation, it will release a request item, and the corresponding buffer block will be unlocked. The process waiting for idle request or for the buffer block to unlock is waken up, caused by these. On the other hand, these awakened processes cause data interaction between the buffer and the hard disk constantly so that these processes are suspended constantly as is shown in Figure 7.46.

Until the last three processes have completed each read disk and write disk tasks as is shown in Figure 7.47.

The depth understanding of the buffer is the key to the understanding of multiprocess operating files. Now, as can be seen more clearly, that buffer design guideline is to **make the data in the buffer stay in the buffer as long as possible.** The interaction between the process and the hard disk had better be in the buffer, and it is better when there is less read and write hard disk data. Starting from the design guideline, carefully examine the source

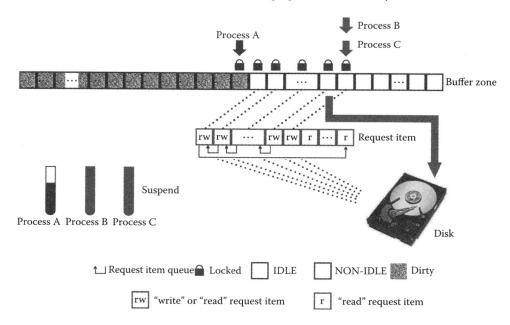

Figure 7.44 Process B is suspended, and the system switches to the process A to execute.

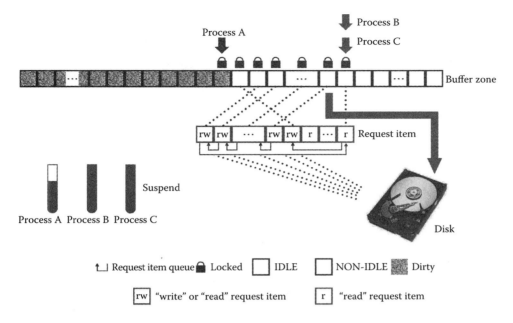

Figure 7.45 Process A is suspended again.

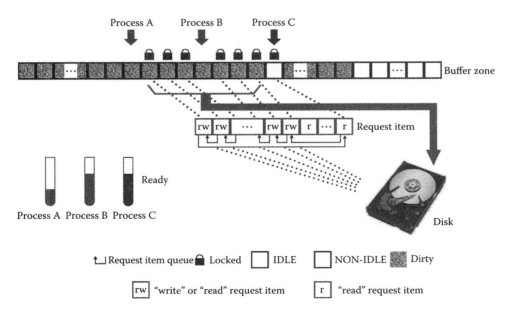

Figure 7.46 Wake up the process B when the synchronization of the buffer block has completed again.

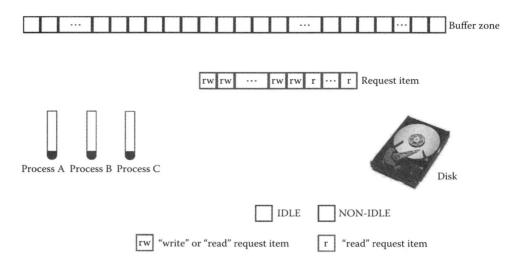

Figure 7.47 All the requests of processes have been processed.

code of Linux. As can be seen, the design of synchronization code has some deviation from this design guiding ideology.

```
//code path:fs/buffer.c:
int sys_sync(void)
{
        int i;
        struct buffer_head * bh;
        sync_inodes(); /* write out inodes into buffers */
        bh = start_buffer;
        for (i=0 ; i<NR_BUFFERS ; i++,bh++) { //traverse the entire
                                //buffer and do not miss a buffer block
                wait_on_buffer(bh);
                if (bh->b_dirt)
                        ll_rw_block(WRITE,bh);
        }
        return 0;
}


int sync_dev(int dev)
{
        int i;
        struct buffer_head * bh;
        bh = start_buffer;
        for (i=0 ; i<NR_BUFFERS ; i++,bh++) { //traverse the entire
                                //buffer and do not miss a buffer block
        if (bh->b_dev != dev)
                continue;
        wait_on_buffer(bh);
        if (bh->b_dev == dev && bh->b_dirt)
                ll_rw_block(WRITE,bh);
        }
```

```
        sync_inodes();
        bh = start_buffer;
        for (i=0 ; i<NR_BUFFERS ; i++,bh++) { //traverse the entire
                            //buffer and do not miss a buffer block
            if (bh->b_dev != dev)
            continue;
    wait_on_buffer(bh);
    if (bh->b_dev == dev && bh->b_dirt)
            ll_rw_block(WRITE,bh);
    }
    return 0;
}
```

B_count is not in the code. No matter whether it is 0 or not, the buffer block should be synchronized as long as b_dirt is 1. It is not very consistent with the design guideline of shared buffers as many as possible and read and write hard disks as little as possible.

8 Inter-Process Communication

The previous chapters explain that the processes are not allowed to cross the border to access other process's codes and data in Linux 0.11, which is the core content of the protected-mode of the operating system.

From the practical point of view, the processes often need to work cooperatively and share mutual information, which seems to be contrary to the process protection. The problem is how to achieve the reasonable requirements of interprocess communication without destroying the process protection? The Linux 0.11 operating system designs two sets of mechanism to provide services to the requirements. One is the "pipe mechanism," and another is the "signal mechanism." In this chapter, we will give a detailed introduction about the two mechanisms via two actual application cases.

8.1 Pipe Mechanism

In order to protect the process and complete interprocess communication without crossing the process boundaries, Linux 0.11 bypasses the boundary protection of the process and designs the pipe mechanism. Each pipe allows two processes to interact data. One process inputs the data into the pipe; another one outputs the data from the pipe. Thus it completes interprocess communication and does not need to cross the boundary of process illegally (Figure 8.1).

The operating system provides a page of memory for each pipe. It gives the file attribute to the page of the memory (the reason for giving the file attribute will be explained

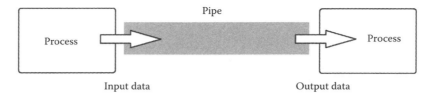

Pipe

Input data   Output data

Figure 8.1 Principle of pipe operation.

in Chapter 9). This page in the main memory is shared by two processes, but it will not be assigned to any of the processes and is controlled only by the kernel.

The pipe operation is divided into two parts. One part is to create the pipe; another part is the read-write operation of the pipe. Here we will introduce these two parts by example 1. The code of example 1 is as follows.

```c
#include <stdio.h>
#include <unistd.h>
int main()
{
    int         n, fd[2];
    pid_t       pid;
int i,j;
char str1[] = "ABCDEABCDEABCDEABCDEABCDEABCDEABCDEABCDEABCDEABCDE
ABCDEABCDEABCDEABCDEABCDEABCDEABCDEABCDEABCDEABCDE
ABCDEABCDEABCDEABCDEABCDEABCDEABCDEABCDEABCDEABCDE
ABCDEABCDEABCDEABCDEABCDEABCDEABCDEABCDEABCDEABCDE
ABCDEABCDEABCDEABCDEABCDEABCDEABCDEABCDEABCDEABCDE
ABCDEABCDEABCDEABCDEABCDEABCDEABCDEABCDEABCDEABCDE
ABCDEABCDEABCDEABCDEABCDEABCDEABCDEABCDEABCDEABCDE
ABCDEABCDEABCDEABCDEABCDEABCDEABCDEABCDEABCDEABCDE
ABCDEABCDEABCDEABCDEABCDEABCDEABCDEABCDEABCDEABCDE
ABCDEABCDEABCDEABCDEABCDEABCDEABCDEABCDEABCDEABCDE
ABCDEABCDEABCDEABCDEABCDEABCDEABCDEABCDEABCDEABCDE
ABCDEABCDEABCDEABCDEABCDEABCDEABCDEABCDEABCDEABCDE
ABCDEABCDEABCDEABCDEABCDEABCDEABCDEABCDEABCDEABCDE
ABCDEABCDEABCDEABCDEABCDEABCDEABCDEABCDEABCDEABCDE
ABCDEABCDEABCDEABCDEABCDEABCDEABCDEABCDEABCDEABCDE
ABCDEABCDEABCDEABCDEABCDEABCDEABCDEABCDEABCDEABCDE
ABCDEABCDEABCDEABCDEABCDEABCDEABCDEABCDEABCDEABCDE
ABCDEABCDEABCDEABCDEABCDEABCDEABCDEABCDEABCDEABCDE
ABCDEABCDEABCDEABCDEABCD";

char str2[512];
    if (pipe(fd) < 0){//create pipe
        printf("pipe error\n");
        return -1;
    }
    if ((pid = fork()) < 0){
        printf("fork error\n");
        return -1;
    }
```

```
    else if (pid > 0)//parent process writes data into the pipe
    {
        close(fd[0]);
        for(i = 0;i<10000;i++)
        write(fd[1],str1,strlen(str1));
    }
    else {        //child process reads data from the pipe
        close(fd[1]);
        for(j = 0;j<20000;j++)
        read(fd[0],,str2,strlen(str2));
    }
    return 0;
}
```

Example 1 demonstrates the scene of sharing data between processes. The parent process writes the data in str1 into the pipe, and the child process reads data from the pipe. The character size of str1 is 1024 bytes, which is 1 KB.

8.1.1 The Creation Process of the Pipe

In the technical view, the pipe is a page in memory, but the process should operate it with the form of manipulating files. Thus it requires that the page in the memory has some file attributes, and the page attributes of the page should be reduced.

The file attributes of this page are shown as follows. Creating a pipe is equivalent to creating a file, such as the connection between filp[20] and file_table[64], and creation of the i node and the connection between file_table[64] and the i node need to be done in the process of creating the pipe. Ultimately, it makes the process know that it is operating the files with the form of the pipe without concerning the others.

The reducing of the page attributes is shown as follows. After all, the page of memory should be used as a file. For example, the process could not access the memory as it accesses the data in its own user space and this page could not be mapped to the linear address space of the process. Another example is that there are two processes operating the page; one is reading while another is writing. It could not trigger page fault protection caused by the writing access to the page that will duplicate the page, and it could not share with the pipe. Next we will show the specific process for creating the pipe.

Apply for an free entry in file_table[64] for pipe file. The created files are all used by the current process (one process) while the pipe file is naturally created for the two processes (the read pipe process and the write pipe process). The pipe in example 1 is created by a parent process (the write pipe process). The parent process prepares everything for the child process (the read pipe process) while creating the pipe. Once the child process is created, it naturally has the capability of operating the pipe.

First, the parent process applies for two free entries in file_table[64] and sets the cited number of the two free entries to be 1. It means that they are cited. The parent and child process could use each of them respectively, when operating pipe files. The code is as follows.

```
//code's path:fs/pipe.c:
int sys_pipe(unsigned long * fildes)
{
    struct m_inode * inode;
    struct file * f[2];
    int fd[2];
    int i,j;

    j = 0;
    for(i = 0;j<2 && i<NR_FILE;i++)         //ready to apply for two free entries in file_table[64]
        if (!file_table[i].f_count)         //find out free entries
            (f[j++] = i+file_table)->f_count++; //set every cited number to be 1
    if (j == 1)
        f[0]->f_count = 0;
    if (j<2)
        return -1;
    ......
}
```

The two free entries that are applied in file_table[64] for creating the pipe file are shown in Figure 8.2.

Connect the table entries between filp[20] in the process task_struct and file_table[64]. We apply for two free entries in *filp[20] in the parent process task_struct. The two free entries connect with the two table entries applied for in file_table[64] previousely, respectively. Thus, there are two table entries in *filp[20], the file management structure of the current process, building the relationship with file_table[64]. When it creates a child process as a parent process, the two table entries in *filp[20] are naturally copied to its child process. It naturally makes the table entries build a relationship with the same pipe files in the file_table[64] structure. The specific code is as follows.

```
//code path:fs/pipe.c:
int sys_pipe(unsigned long * fildes)
{
    ......
    if (j == 1)
        f[0]->f_count = 0;
    if (j<2)
        return -1;
    j = 0;
    for(i = 0;j<2 && i<NR_OPEN;i++)         //ready to apply for two free entries in
                                            //filp[20]
        if (!current->filp[i]) {            //find out out free entries
            current->filp[fd[j] = i] = f[j]; //connect with the two free entries applied
                                            //for in file_table[64] respectively
            j++;
        }
    if (j == 1)
        current->filp[fd[0]] = NULL;
    if (j<2) {
        f[0]->f_count = f[1]->f_count = 0;
        return -1;
    }
    ......
}
```

Figure 8.3 shows the effect after setting up the relationship between the current process and pipe files.

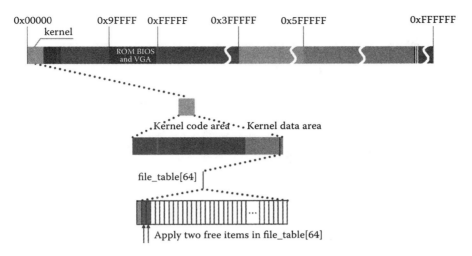

Figure 8.2 Two free entries that are applied for in file_table[64] for creating the pipe file.

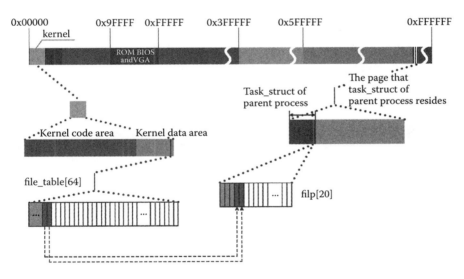

Figure 8.3 Build a relationship between current process and pipe files.

Create i node of the pipe file. The process should build a relationship between i node of the pipe file and file_table[64] if it wants to have the capability of operating the pipe file. To achieve this, we should call function get_pipe_inode() and apply a i node in inode_ table[32] for the pipe file. The specific code is as follows.

```
//code path:fs/pipe.c:
int sys_pipe(unsigned long * fildes)
{
  ......
  if (j = =1)
      current->filp[fd[0]] = NULL;
  if (j<2) {
      f[0]->f_count = f[1]->f_count = 0;
      return -1;
  }
  if (!(inode = get_pipe_inode())) {  //create node i for the pipe
      current->filp[fd[0]] =
          current->filp[fd[1]] = NULL;
      f[0]->f_count = f[1]->f_count = 0;
      return -1;
  }
  ......
}
```

Due to the nature of the pipe being a page of memory, the system applies for an free page of memory and loads the address of the page into i node. It is worth noting that at the moment the field inode->i_size no longer carries the size of the file but the original address of the memory page. The specific code is as follows.

```
//code path:fs/inode.c:
struct m_inode * get_pipe_inode(void)
{
  struct m_inode * inode;

  if (!(inode = get_empty_inode()))
      return NULL;
  if (!(inode->i_size = get_free_page())) {   //apply for the page to
                                              //be the pipe
      inode->i_count = 0;
      return NULL;
  }
  inode->i_count = 2;   /* sum of readers/writers */
  ......
}
```

The pipe file is also a file, so it needs to have a i node. Thus, it should have cited count. Linux 0.11 defaults that it should have two and only two processes to operate the pipe file. One is a read process, and another is a write process. Thus, we set it to be 2 directly.

Then, let both the read pipe pointer and write pipe pointer point to the original position of the pipe (the free page) for the operation of the process of the read and write pipe. Then set the attribute of the i node to be "the type of pipe i node" to identify the particularity of i node. That means actually it is not i node stored in the file in the hard disk; it is only a page of memory. The specific code is as follows.

```
//code path:fs/inode.c:
struct m_inode * get_pipe_inode(void)
{
    ...
    if (!(inode->i_size = get_free_page())) {
            inode->i_count = 0;
            return NULL;
    }
    inode->i_count = 2; /* sum of readers/writers */        //set the cited number to be 2
    PIPE_HEAD(*inode) = PIPE_TAIL(*inode) = 0; //PIPE_HEAD is write pipe pointer,PIPE_TAIL is
                                        //read
                                                            //pipe pointer, set both of them
                                                            //to be 0
    inode->i_pipe = 1;                                      //set up the attribute of the
                                                            //pipe file

    return inode;
}
```

The process of the application for i node for the pipe file and setting process is shown in Figure 8.4.

Build a relationship between i node of the pipe file and file_table[64]. Now, we can build a relationship between i node of the pipe file and file_table[64] because the i node of the pipe file has been set up. The specific operation is shown as follows. Initialize the two free entries in file_table[64] and let them point to the i node of the pipe and let all of the file read and write pointers point to the original position of the pipe. Set the first free entry's mode of file to read and the second to write. Thus, the parent process

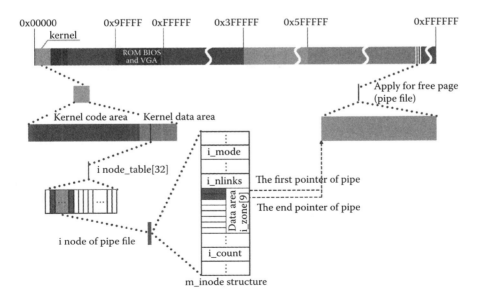

Figure 8.4 Create i node for pipe file.

has got the capability of operating the pipe file. The child process created by the parent process will also get the capability of operating the pipe file naturally. The specific code is as follows.

```
//code path:fs/pipe.c:
int sys_pipe(unsigned long * fildes)
{
    ......
    if (!(inode = get_pipe_inode())) {
            current->filp[fd[0]] =
        current->filp[fd[1]] = NULL;
            f[0]->f_count = f[1]->f_count = 0;
            return -1;
    }
    f[0]->f_inode = f[1]->f_inode = inode;//connect node i and table entry
    f[0]->f_pos = f[1]->f_pos = 0;          //the file pointer return to 0
    f[0]->f_mode = 1;      /* read */       //set it to be read mode
    f[1]->f_mode = 2;      /* write */      //set it to be written mode
    put_fs_long(fd[0],0+fildes);
    put_fs_long(fd[1],1+fildes);
    return 0;
}
```

It is shown in Figure 8.5.

Return the pipe file handle to the user's process. Now return the two handles of the pipe file to the user's process, which is fd[2] in the code of example 1. This array has two entries, and each of them stores a handle. Thus, the child process will inherit the two file handles,

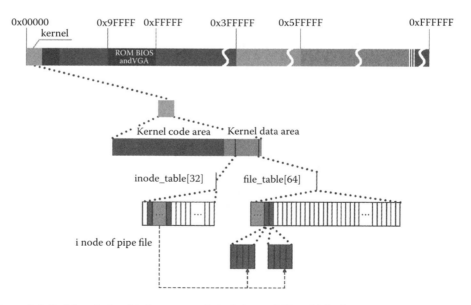

Figure 8.5 Build a relationship between node i of pipe and file_table[64].

and the parent and child processes can operate the pipe file through different file handles.
The specific code is as follows.

```
//code path:fs/pipe.c:
int sys_pipe(unsigned long * fildes)
{
    ......
    f[0]->f_inode = f[1]->f_inode = inode;
    f[0]->f_pos = f[1]->f_pos = 0;
    f[0]->f_mode = 1;          /* read */
    f[1]->f_mode = 2;          /* write */
    put_fs_long(fd[0],0+fildes);        //set the handle of read pipe file
    put_fs_long(fd[1],1+fildes);        //set the handle of write pipe file
    return 0;
}
```

The result of returning the file handle to the user's process is shown in Figure 8.6.

8.1.2 Operation of Pipe

The effect of Linux 0.11 pipe operation is as follows. If there is some unread data in the
pipe during the execution of the read pipe process, the data should be read. If there is not
unread data, the process should be suspend. Thus, the dirty data will not be read. If there
is some excess space in the pipe during the execution of the write pipe process, the data
should be written. And if there is no excess space, the process should be suspended. Thus,
the unread data will not be covered. In addition, the size of the pipe is just one page. So
after the end of the page has been read, the read and write pointer should be able to roll
back to the head of the page in order to continue the operation.

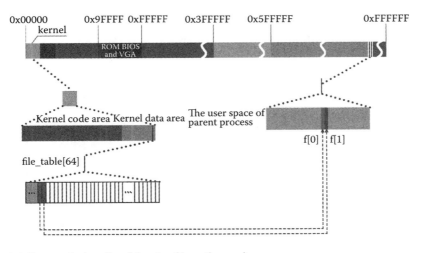

Figure 8.6 Return the handle of the pipe file to the user's process.

The code of rolling back is as follows.

```
//code path:fs/read_write.c:
int sys_read(unsigned int fd,char * buf,int count)//the pointer to read pipe
{
    ......
    while (count>0) {
        ......
        if (chars > size)
            chars = size;
        count - = chars;
        read + = chars;
        size = PIPE_TAIL(*inode);
        PIPE_TAIL(*inode) + = chars;            //the number that the pointer offsets is the
                                                //number which it reads the data when the
        PIPE_TAIL(*inode) & = (PAGE_SIZE-1);    //pointer exceeds one page,(& = )operation
                                                //could achieve automatically rollback
        while (chars- >0)
            put_fs_byte(((char *)inode->i_size)[size++],buf++);
    }
    ......
}


int write_pipe(struct m_inode * inode, char * buf, int count)//write pipe pointer
{
    ......
    while (count>0) {
        ......
        if (chars > size)
            chars = size;
        count - = chars;
        written + = chars;
        size = PIPE_HEAD(*inode);
        PIPE_HEAD(*inode) + = chars;            //the number that the pointer offsets is the
                                                //number which it writes the data when
        PIPE_HEAD(*inode) & = (PAGE_SIZE-1);    //the pointer exceeds one page,(& = )operation
                                                //could achieve automatically rollback
        while (chars- >0)
            ((char *)inode->i_size)[size++] = get_fs_byte(buf++);
    }
    ......
}
```

In the case of rolling back constantly, the code for controlling the write, read, wake up, or hang the process is as follows.

```
//code path:include/linux/fs.h:
......
#define PIPE_HEAD(inode) ((inode).i_zone[0])
#define PIPE_TAIL(inode) ((inode).i_zone[1])
#define PIPE_SIZE(inode) ((PIPE_HEAD(inode)-PIPE_TAIL(inode))&(PAGE_SIZE-1))
......


//code path:fs/read_write.c:
int sys_read(unsigned int fd,char * buf,int count)//the pointer to read the pipe
{
    ......
    while (count>0) {
        while (!(size = PIPE_SIZE(*inode))) {    //when the read pointer and written pointer
                                                 //coincidence, it means the data in the pipe
                                                 //has been read
```

```
                wake_up(&inode->i_wait);                //all the data in the pipe has been read,
                                                        //wake up write pipe process

            if (inode->i_count ! = 2)/* are there any writers? */
                return read;
            sleep_on(&inode->i_wait);                   //there is no data to read, suspend the read
                                                        //pipe process

        }
        chars = PAGE_SIZE-PIPE_TAIL(*inode);
        if (chars > count)
            chars = count;
        if (chars > size)
            chars = size;
        ......
    }
    wake_up(&inode->i_wait);                            //read the data and it means the pipe has
                                                        //excess space, wake up the write pipe
                                                        //process

    return read;
}


int write_pipe(struct m_inode * inode, char * buf, int count)//the pointer to write pipe
{
    ......
    while (count>0) {
        while (!(size = (PAGE_SIZE-1)-PIPE_SIZE(*inode)))    {//written pointer could write at
                                                             //most 4095 bytes
                                                        //of data, then it means the pipe has been
                                                        //fully written

                                                        //(the size of one page is 4096 bytes)
            wake_up(&inode->i_wait);                    //the pipe has been fully written and it has
                                                        //data again, wake up the read pipe process

            if (inode->i_count ! = 2) {/* no readers */
                current->signal | = (1<<(SIGPIPE-1));
                return written?written:-1;
            }
            sleep_on(&inode->i_wait);                   //there is no excess space, suspend the
                                                        //written pipe process

        }
        chars = PAGE_SIZE-PIPE_HEAD(*inode);
        if (chars > count)
            chars = count;
        if (chars > size)
            chars = size;
        ......
    }
    wake_up(&inode->i_wait);                            //it means the pipe has data after writing
                                                        //data into it, wake up read pipe process

    return written;
}
```

When all the writable space has been fully written, the write pipe pointer rolls one circle back. Thus, the write pipe pointer is one byte less than the read pipe pointer. The write pipe process should be suspended then. Linux 0.11 designs function sys_write() as follows. The write pipe process can write 4095 bytes at one time at most.

Now, we will introduce the process of the operation of the pipe through example 1.

Read pipe process begins to operate the pipe file. In example 1, the parent process begins to create the child process that is the read pipe process after creating the pipe. When the process has been created, we may assume that there are only two processes, that is, the read pipe process and the write pipe process, being in the ready state in the system. The read pipe process will execute first, and it will execute the source code "read (fd[0],,str2,strlen(str2))" in example 1. The read() function is mapped to the system call function sys_read() and executed. Ultimately, it will execute into the read_pipe() function. Because there is not any data in the pipe at the moment, the system will suspend the read pipe process and then switch to the write pipe process to execute. The specific code is as follows.

```
//code path:fs/read_write.c:
int sys_read(unsigned int fd,char * buf,int count)
{
    ......
    verify_area(buf,count);
    inode = file->f_inode;
    if (inode->i_pipe)
        return (file->f_mode&1)?read_pipe(inode,buf,count):-EIO;      //call read pipe
                                                                      //function
    if (S_ISCHR(inode->i_mode))
        return rw_char(READ,inode->i_zone[0],buf,count,&file->f_pos);
    ......
}


//code path:fs/pipe.c:
int read_pipe(struct m_inode * inode, char * buf, int count)         //read pipe function
{
int chars, size, read = 0;
while (count>0) {
        while (!(size = PIPE_SIZE(*inode))) {     //there is no data in the pipe, enter into
                                                  //this loop and execute
        wake_up(&inode->i_wait);
        if (inode->i_count != 2)/* are there any writers? */
                    return read;
                    sleep_on(&inode->i_wait);     //suspend the read pipe process and switch
                                                  //to the read pipe process(assume that only
                                                  //two processes in the operation pipe is in
                                                  //the ready state already)
        }
        chars = PAGE_SIZE-PIPE_TAIL(*inode);
        if (chars > count)
                    chars = count;
    ......
    }
    ......
}
```

There is not any data in the pipe at the moment; the read pipe process is suspended. The state of the process is shown in Figure 8.7.

Write pipe process writes data into the pipe. The write pipe process begins to execute, and it will write the specified 1024 bytes of data in the str1 array of example 1 into the pipe cyclically. The process is executing the source code "write(fd[1],str1,strlen(str1))." The write() function will be mapped to the system call function sys_write() to execute, and ultimately, it will be executed to the write_pipe() function. After the writing, the pipe has got the data that can be read out. Then wake up the read pipe process (that the read pipe process has been woken up does not mean the read pipe process will execute immediately).

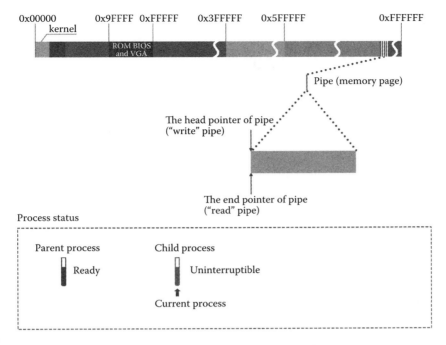

Figure 8.7 The process begins to operate the pipe; suspend the read process.

Thus the execution for the operation of the write pipe completes. The specific code is as follows.

```
//code path:fs/read_write.c:
int sys_write(unsigned int fd,char * buf,int count)
{
    ......
    if (!count)
        return 0;
    inode = file->f_inode;
    if (inode->i_pipe)
        return (file->f_mode&2)?write_pipe(inode,buf,count):-EIO;    //call the write pipe
                                                                      //function
    if (S_ISCHR(inode->i_mode))
        return rw_char(WRITE,inode->i_zone[0],buf,count,&file->f_pos);
    ......
}


//code path:fs/pipe.c:
int write_pipe(struct m_inode * inode, char * buf, int count)        //read pipe function
{
int chars, size, written = 0;
while (count>0) {
        ......
        size = PIPE_HEAD(*inode);
        PIPE_HEAD(*inode) + = chars;
        PIPE_HEAD(*inode) & = (PAGE_SIZE-1);
        while (chars- >0)
                ((char *)inode->i_size)[size++] = get_fs_byte(buf++); //write data into the
                                                                      //pipe
}
wake_up(&inode->i_wait);                                              //wake up the read pipe
                                                                      //process
}
```

The process in which the write pipe process writes data into the pipe is shown in Figure 8.8.

Write pipe process keeps on writing data into the pipe. The current process is write pipe process. After writing data into the pipe, it will return to the user space. We know that the writing process should be operated for 10,000 times while the time slice of the write pipe process has not been used up according to the code "for(i = 0;i<10000;i++)" in example 1. Thus it will keep on executing the writing operation.

The process of writing data into the pipe constantly is shown in Figure 8.9.

The pipe space has been filled up by the write pipe process. Assume that the timer interrupt occurs during the process of the write pipe process works. The time slice has been decreased. As long as the time slice has not reduced to 0, it will keep on executing. The corresponding code is as follows.

```
//code path:kernel/sched.c:
void do_timer(long cpl)                          //timer interrupt processing function
{
    ......
  if (next_timer) {
     next_timer->jiffies- ;
     while (next_timer && next_timer->jiffies < = 0) {
         void (*fn)(void);

         fn = next_timer->fn;
         next_timer->fn = NULL;
         next_timer = next_timer->next;
         (fn)();
     }
  }
  if (current_DOR & 0xf0)
      do_floppy_timer();
  if ((- current->counter)>0) return;            //time slice is not 0, return back
                                                 //dirrectly
  current->counter = 0;
  if (!cpl) return;
  schedule();
}
```

The bottom of Figure 8.10 shows the effect on the write pipe process after the occurrence of the timer interrupt.

During the writing process, the write pipe pointer always points to the position that the data is written in and moves to the end of the pipe continuously until the pipe is fully filled (4095 bytes can be regarded as fully filled).

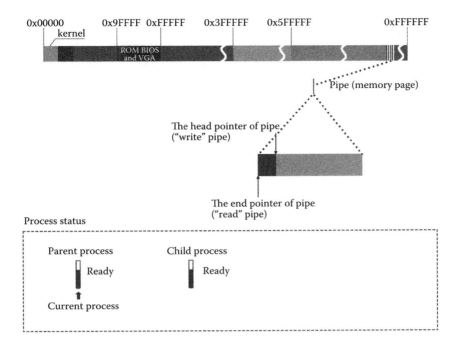

Figure 8.8 Write pipe process writes data into the pipe.

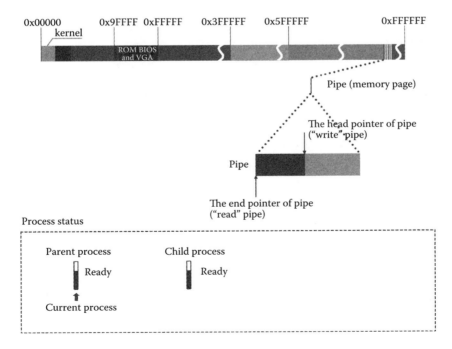

Figure 8.9 Write pipe process writes data into the pipe constantly.

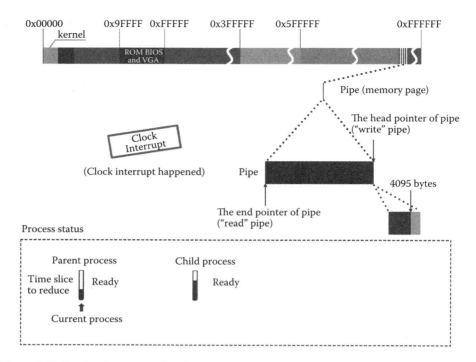

Figure 8.10 During the process that the writing process executes, the timer interrupt occurs.

Suspend the write pipe process. After the pipe is fully filled by written, the system will suspend the write pipe process and switch to the read pipe process to execute. The specific code is as follows.

```
//code path:fs/pipe.c:
int write_pipe(struct m_inode * inode, char * buf, int count)
{
    int chars, size, written = 0;
    while (count>0) {
        while (!(size = (PAGE_SIZE-1)-PIPE_SIZE(*inode))) {   //writing 4095 bytes can be
                                                               //regarded as fully
                                                               //filled, the condition is true
                                                               //and then enter
                                                               //while to execute

            wake_up(&inode->i_wait);
            if (inode->i_count != 2) {/* no readers */
                    current->signal |= (1<<(SIGPIPE-1));
                    return written?written:-1;
            }
            sleep_on(&inode->i_wait);                          //hang the write pipe process and
                                                               //switch to
                                                               //the read pipe process to
                                                               //execute

        }
        ......
    }
    ......
}
```

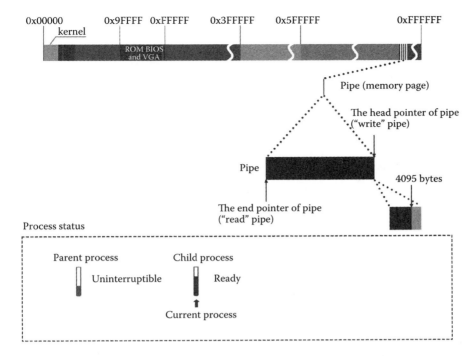

Figure 8.11 Suspend the write pipe process and wake up the read pipe process.

The process of suspending the write pipe process and switching to the read pipe process is shown in Figure 8.11.

Read pipe process reads data from the pipe. The read pipe process will continue to execute in the read_pipe() function. According to the code of example 1, the execution would read 512 bytes of data in the pipe into the user's space of the read pipe process. The specific code is as follows.

```
//code patrh:fs/pipe.c:
int read_pipe(struct m_inode * inode, char * buf, int count)
{
    ......
    while (count>0) {                                              //read 512 bytes of data
        ......
        chars = PAGE_SIZE-PIPE_TAIL(*inode);
        if (chars > count)
                chars = count;
        if (chars > size)
                chars = size;
        count - = chars;
        read + = chars;
        size = PIPE_TAIL(*inode);
        PIPE_TAIL(*inode) + = chars;                               //the number that the
                                                                   //pointer moves is the
                                                                   //number that it
                                                                   //reads

        PIPE_TAIL(*inode) & = (PAGE_SIZE-1);
        while (chars-- >0)
            put_fs_byte(((char *)inode->i_size)[size++],buf++);    //the code of reading
                                                                   //data

    }
    ......
}
```

Reading out data means that the pipe has excess space. Now the system wakes up the write pipe process. The specific code is as follows.

```
//code path:fs/pipe.c:
int read_pipe(struct m_inode * inode, char * buf, int count)
{
    ......
    while (count>0){
        ......
        size = PIPE_TAIL(*inode);
        PIPE_TAIL(*inode) + = chars;
        PIPE_TAIL(*inode) & = (PAGE_SIZE-1);
        while (chars-- >0)
                put_fs_byte(((char *)inode->i_size)[size++],buf++);
    }
    wake_up(&inode->i_wait);          //wake up the write pipe process
}
```

The procedure of the read pipe process reading data from the pipe is shown in Figure 8.12.

Read pipe process continues to execute and keeps on reading data from the pipe. The current process is the read pipe process. After reading data from the pipe once, it will return to the user's space. According to the code "for(j = 0;j<20000;j++)" in example 1, read pipe should be operated 20,000 times while the time slice of the read pipe process has

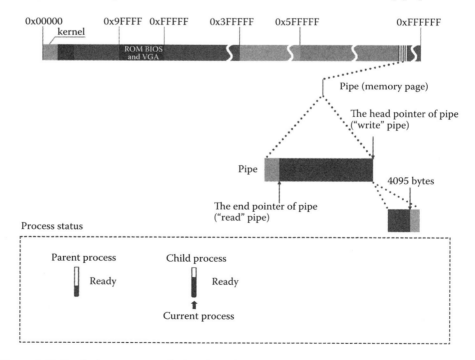

Figure 8.12 Read pipe process reads data from the pipe.

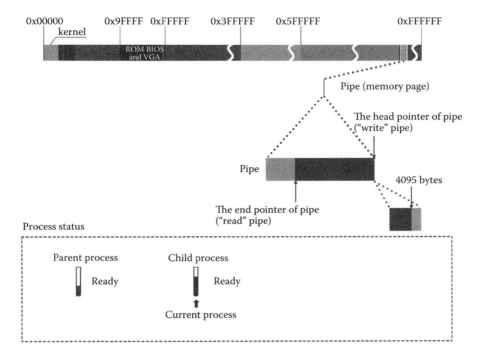

Figure 8.13 Read pipe process reads data from the pipe constantly.

not been used up. Thus the reading process should be operated continually. The process that the read pipe process reads data from the pipe constantly is shown in Figure 8.13.

Timer interrupt occurs during the execution of the read pipe process. Assume that timer interrupt occurs during the execution, and time slice is cut down. As long as it has not reduced to 0, it will continue to execute. The specific code is as follows.

```
//code path:kernel/schde.c:
void do_timer(long cpl)
{
    .....
    if (next_timer) {
        next_timer->jiffies-- ;
        while (next_timer && next_timer->jiffies < = 0) {
            void (*fn)(void);

            fn = next_timer->fn;
            next_timer->fn = NULL;
            next_timer = next_timer->next;
            (fn)();
        }
    }
    if (current_DOR & 0xf0)
        do_floppy_timer();
    if ((-- current->counter)>0) return;        //time slice is not 0, return back directly
    current->counter = 0;
    if (!cpl) return;
    schedule();
}
```

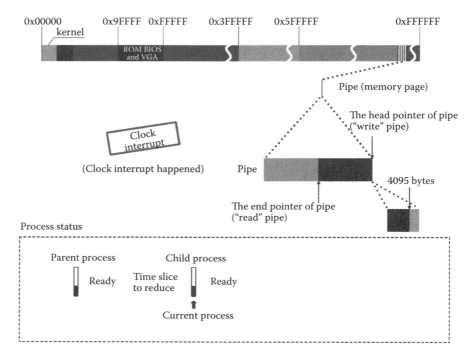

Figure 8.14 Timer interrupt occurs during the execution of the read pipe process.

The processing method for the occurrence of timer interrupt during the execution of the read pipe process is shown in Figure 8.14. Pay attention to the process bar of the read pipe process in the figure; its time slice has been cut down.

Timer interrupt occurs again during the execution of the read pipe process. Timer interrupt occurs again during the execution of the read pipe process, and the time slice of the read pipe process is 0. The read pipe process will be suspended and switched to the write pipe process to execute. The specific code is as follows.

```
//code path:kernel/schde.c:
void do_timer(long cpl)
{
    ......
if (current_DOR & 0xf0)
        do_floppy_timer();
    if ((-- current->counter)>0) return;        //time slice becomes 0
    current->counter = 0;
    if (!cpl) return;
    schedule();                                 //process switch
}
```

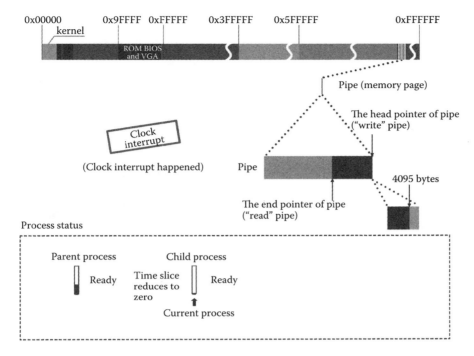

Figure 8.15 Timer interrupt occurs during the execution of the read pipe process.

The process for timer interruption is shown in Figure 8.15. The time slice of the process bar that represents the read pipe process has reduced to 0.

It is worth noticing that the twice timer interrupts cannot affect writing in or reading out the data from pipe. The fundamental reason is that writing or reading the data executed in the kernel code with the 0 privilege level and is completely controlled by the system. It will only cut down the time slice without affecting the execution of the data operation.

Switch read pipe process to the write pipe process to execute. The pointer of pipe operation has been moved to the head of the pipe before the write pipe process is suspended. Then the write pipe process will keep on writing data into the pipe from the head of the pipe until the pipe has no excess space again. The process is shown in Figure 8.16.

Suspending the write pipe process and switch to execute the reading pipe process. The pipe is fully filled again, and the system will suspend the write pipe process. Then it will switch to the read pipe process to execute. The principle of the Linux 0.11 reallocation time slice is that when all the processing time slices in the ready state become 0, then assign a time slice. Because the read pipe process is the only process in the ready state, and its time

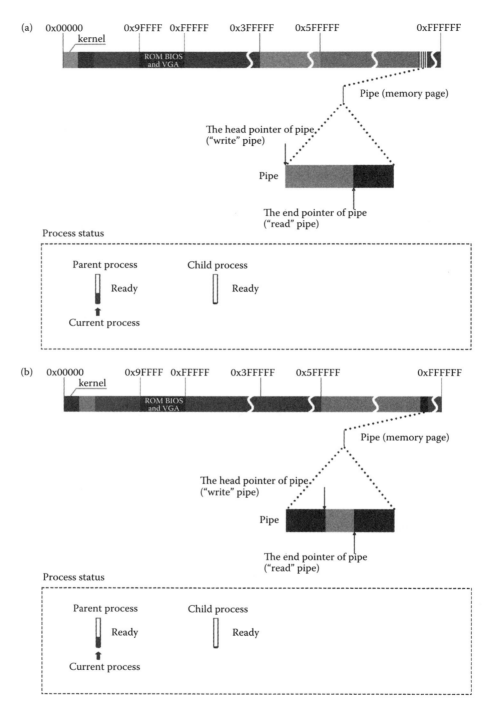

Figure 8.16 Write pipe process continues to write data.

slice has been used up, the system will assign a time slice to them again. The specific code is as follows.

```
//code path:kernel/schde.c:
void schedule(void)
{
    ......
    while (1) {
        c = -1;
        next = 0;
        i = NR_TASKS;
        p = &task[NR_TASKS];
        while (-- i) {
            if (!*-- p)
                continue;
            if ((*p)->state = = TASK_RUNNING && (*p)->counter > c)
                c = (*p)->counter, next = i;
        }
        if (c) break;
        for(p = &LAST_TASK ; p > &FIRST_TASK ;-- p)        //assign time slice
            if (*p)
                (*p)->counter = ((*p)->counter >> 1) +
                                (*p)->priority;
    }
    switch_to(next);
}
```

Then the read pipe process continues to execute. The process of reading a part of data is shown in Figure 8.17.

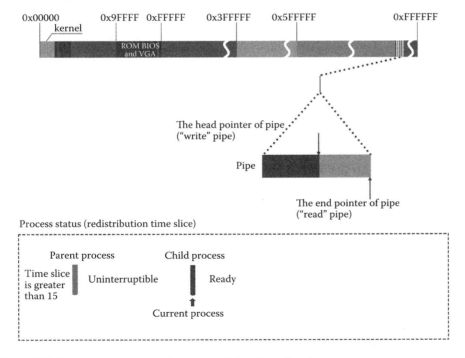

Figure 8.17 Read pipe process continues to read data from the pipe.

The read pipe process continues to execute until it finishes reading data from the pipe. After the beginning of the execution of the read pipe process, it will continue to read data from the pipe. When it operates at the end of the pipe it will move the read pipe pointer from the end of the pipe to the head of the pipe. Then it will continue to read data from the head of the pipe until the data is completely read out. Then the two pointers will coincide. The specific code is as follows.

```
//code path:fs/pipe.c:
int read_pipe(struct m_inode * inode, char * buf, int count)
{
    ......
    while (count>0) {
        while (!(size = PIPE_SIZE(*inode))) {        //the pointers coincide, it means that the
                                                      //data has been read out
            wake_up(&inode->i_wait);                 //wake up the write pipe process
            if (inode->i_count != 2)/* are there any writers? */
                return read;
            sleep_on(&inode->i_wait);                //suspend the read pipe process and switch
                                                      //to the write pipe process to execute
        }
        chars = PAGE_SIZE-PIPE_TAIL(*inode);
        if (chars > count)
            chars = count;
        if (chars > size)
            chars = size;
        count - = chars;
        read + = chars;
        size = PIPE_TAIL(*inode);
        PIPE_TAIL(*inode) + = chars;
        PIPE_TAIL(*inode) & = (PAGE_SIZE-1);
        while (chars-- >0)
            put_fs_byte(((char *)inode->i_size)[size++],buf++);//read data
    }
    ......
}
```

The procedure is shown in Figure 8.18.

According to the previous introduction of the pipe operation, two processes share the same pipe if two processes in file_table[64] occupy the file item of one pipe file, respectively, it can operate the pipe.

If process A creates two pipes and process B, process A and B could conduct reversed communication of data by the two pipes. The procedure is shown in Figure 8.19.

If process A creates six pipes and creates processes B and C, it could conduct reversed communication of data between any two of them through the six pipes. The procedure is shown in Figure 8.20.

As long as the total number of the processes is no more than 64 and the number of file items that the processes occupy does not exceed the carrying capacity of file_table[64], we can build an arbitrarily complex operation structure of pipe combinations.

■ 8.2 Signal Mechanism

A signal mechanism is a "partial similar interrupt mechanism" provided to the process by Linux 0.11. During the process of the execution, if the system finds out that a process receives a signal, it will interrupt the execution of the process temporarily and turn to execute the signal processing handler of the process. After the processing, it will continue to execute from where the process was interrupted.

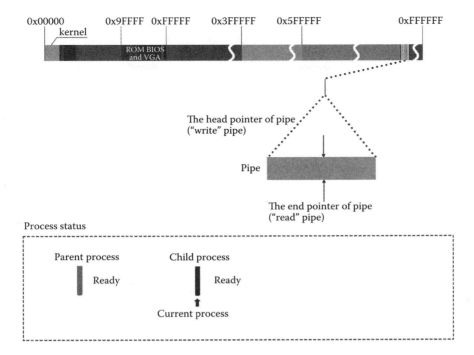

Figure 8.18 Read pipe process reads data from the pipe completely.

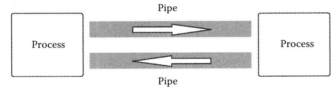

Figure 8.19 Two processes use the pipe to transfer data respectively.

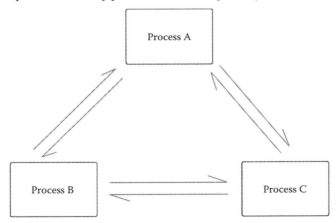

Figure 8.20 Three processes use a pipe to transfer data between any two processes.

This section contains two parts to give a detailed description about signal mechanism.

The first part gives a detailed description about the procedure that the system and the process handle the signal through the process of execution in example 2.

In the second part, the system changes the execution state of the process through the analysis of the signal.

First, here we will introduce the first part: example 2.

This is an example about sending, receiving, and processing the signal. We will introduce the procedure that the system and the process handle the signal by the example.

There are two user processes. One of them is used for receiving and processing the signal. This process is called *processsig*. Its corresponding code is as follows.

```
#include <stdio.h>
    #include <signal.h>

    void sig_usr(int signo)                    //the function for handling signal
    {
        if (signo = = SIGUSR1)
            printf ("received SIGUSR1\n");
        else
            printf ("received%d\n", signo);
        signal (SIGUSR1, sig_usr);             //reset the pointer of the signal
                                               //processing function of processsig
                                               //process for the next use

    }
    int main(int argc, char **argv)
    {
        signal (SIGUSR1, sig_usr);             //connect the pointer of the signal
                                               //processing function of processsig
                                               //process

        for (;;)
        pause();
        return 0;
}
```

Another one is used for sending the signal. This process is called *sendsig*. Its corresponding code is as follows.

```
#include <stdio.h>
    int main(int argc, char **argv)
    {
        int pid, ret, signo;
        int i;

        if (argc ! = 3)
        {
            printf ("Usage: sensig <signo> <pid>\n");
            return -1;
        }
        signo = atoi(argv[1]);
        pid = atoi(argv[2]);

        ret = kill(pid, signo);             //send signal here
        for (i = 0;i<1000000;i++)

        if (ret ! = 0)
            printf("send signal error\n");

        return 0;
}
```

　　　　　　　　　　　　　　　　　　　　　　　　8. Inter-Process Communication

The system needs to have the following three functions to support the signal mechanism.

1. The system needs to support the process to send and receive the signal.

    The system sets the field "signal" (signal bitmap) for receiving the signal in task_struct of every process. The signal that every process receives is stored in this data structure bit by bit. The system supports two ways of sending the signal to the process. One way is that a process sends the signal to another process by calling specific library functions. Another way is that users generate keyboard interrupt by inputting keyboard information, and the interrupt service routine sends the signal to the process. The principals of these two ways to send a signal are the same. They are all achieved by setting the bits of the signal in the signal bitmap.

    The example will be combined with the first way that one process sends a signal to another one to show how the system sends and receives a signal.

2. The system should be able to detect the signal that the process has received in time.

    The system detects whether the process has received the signal by two ways. One way is to detect whether the current process has received the signal before the system call returns. Another way is that after the occurrence of the timer interrupt, the system detects whether the current process has received the signal before the execution of the interrupt service routine ends.

    The two ways of signal detection are similar. The example will be combined with the first way to show how the system detects the signal it receives.

3. The system needs to support the process to handle the signal.

    The system should guarantee that when the user process need not to process the signal, the signal processing function does not participate in the execution of the user process completely, and when the user process needs to handle the signal, the program of the process will stop executing temporarily and switch to executing the signal processing function. When the signal processing function finishes executing, the program of the process will continue to execute from where the pause happened.

    The example will show how the system is achieved these through three aspects. They are "bind the user-defined signal processing function with the process," "the pretreatment that the system does to the signal," and "restore the site of process after the processing of the signal."

Here we will introduce how the two processes begin to run. The user is in the shell interface now.

Step 1: Input the command below and run the program of processsig process.

```
[/usr/root]#./processsig &
<160>              //here we know that the pid of processsig is 160
[/usr/root]#
```

Step 2: Input the command below and run the program of sendsig process. Send SIGUSR1 signal to processsig process.

```
[/usr/root]#./sendsig 10 160            //10 represents signal SIGUSR1, 160
                                        //is the pid of processsig

received SIGUSR1
[/usr/root]#
```

Now we will introduce the execution of the two processes. The processsig process executes first, so first we will introduce its execution.

8.2.1 Use of Signal

Processsig process begins to execute. The processsig process begins to execute and prepares to receive the signal. The specific performance is that specify what kind of signal should be handle. After entering the main() function, we should combine a user-defined signal processing handler with the processsig process. The user program achieves the bind by calling the signal() function. This function is a library function. It will generate soft interrupt int0x80 after the execution and be mapped to the system call function sys_signal() to execute. Its function is to combine the user-defined signal processing handler sig_usr() with the processsig process. It means that as long as the processsig process receives signal SIGUSR1, it will call the sig_usr() function to process the signal. The bind work is done by the function.

After entering the sys_signal() function, the system will detect whether the signal that the user specifies meets the regulation before the combination. Because Linux 0.11 processes only 32 kinds of signals and ignores SIGKILL signal by default, as long as the signal that the user specifies does not meet these requirements, the system will not be able to process it.

```
//code path:kernel/signal.c:
int sys_signal(int signum, long handler, long restorer)
{
        struct sigaction tmp;
        if (signum<1 || signum>32 || signum = =SIGKILL)   //after detecting we know that
                                                          //the signal meets the provision
        return -1;
......
}
```

When the detection is completed, it begins to conduct setting sigaction[32] in task_ struct of processsig process. This structure has 32 members, and it just corresponds to the default 32 kinds of signal. Each member in sigaction[32] will provide a set of services for the process of each kind of signal.

The specific code is as follows.

```
//code path:kernel/signal.c:
int sys_signal(int signum, long handler, long restorer)
{
......
    if (signum<1 || signum>32 || signum = =SIGKILL)
        return -1;
tmp.sa_handler = (void (*)(int)) handler;   //at the moment handler parameter is
                                            //the address of sig_usr()
                                            //function in the code
                                            //"signal(SIGUSR1, sig_usr)" in the
                                            //programme of processsig process.
                                            //The combination makes that as
                                            //long as the process receives signal
                                            //in the future, the signal will
                                            //be processed by sig_usr function.
        tmp.sa_mask = 0;
        tmp.sa_flags = SA_ONESHOT | SA_NOMASK;
        tmp.sa_restorer = (void (*)(void)) restorer;   //here combines
                                                       //the restorer function
        handler = (long) current->sigaction[signum-1].sa_handler;
        current->sigaction[signum-1] = tmp;        //sigaction[signum-1] provides
                                                   //service for SIGUSR1 signal
        return handler;
}
```

The setting is shown in Figure 8.21.

Please note that restorer() is also combined in the sys_signal() function. The function of this function is also very important. We will introduce it in detail later.

The state of the processsig process and the condition of the code in the memory is shown in Figure 8.22. The processsig process is in the ready state at the moment.

Processsig process enter the interruptible state. In the program of the processsig process, we call pause() function specially in order to reflect the signal's effect on the state of the process's execution. The function will eventually lead the process to be set to

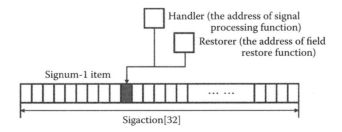

Figure 8.21 Set the address of the user process signal processing function.

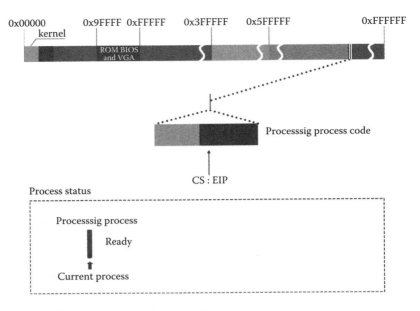

Figure 8.22 Condition of the two processes in the memory.

"interruptible state." When the process has received the signal, its state will switch from "interruptible state" to "ready state."

After the execution of signal(), it will return to the user's space of the processsig process and continue to execute. Then it calls the pause() function, and the function will be mapped into the system call function sys_pause(). The specific code is as follows.

```
//code path:kernel/sched.c:
int sys_pause(void)
{
        current->state = TASK_INTERRUPTIBLE;       //set processsig process to
                                                    //interruptible state
        schedule();                                 //switch process
        return 0;
}
```

The processsig process will be set to interruptible state. It is shown in Figure 8.23.

Sendsig process begins to execute and sends signal to processsig process. The processsig process is suspended temporarily while the sendsig process is executing. The sendsig process will send a signal to the processsig process and then switch to the processsig process to execute.

The sendsig process executes "ret = kill(pid, signo)" first. kill() is a library function, and it will eventually be mapped to the sys_kill() function to execute. In addition, it will

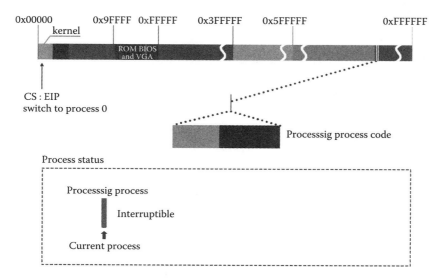

Figure 8.23 Processsig process in interruptible state.

send a SIGUSR1 signal to the processsig process referring to the parameters "10" and "160." The specific code is as follows.

```
//code path:kernel/exit.c:
int sys_kill(int pid,int sig)
{
    ......
    if (!pid) while (-- p > &FIRST_TASK) {
        if (*p && (*p)->pgrp = = current->pid)
        if (err = send_sig(sig,*p,1))
            retval = err;
    }else if (pid>0) while (-- p > &FIRST_TASK) {
        if (*p && (*p)->pid = = pid)           //find out processsig process
            if (err = send_sig(sig,*p,0))      //the function is in charge of specific
                                                //sending work
                retval = err;
    } else if (pid = = -1) while (-- p > &FIRST_TASK)
        if (err = send_sig(sig,*p,0))
            retval = err;
    ......
}



//code path:kernel/exit.c:
static inline int send_sig(long sig,struct task_struct * p,int priv)
{
    if (!p || sig<1 || sig>32)
        return -EINVAL;
    if (priv || (current->euid = =p->euid) || suser())
        p->signal | = (1<<(sig-1));            //find out the corresponding location of
                                                //SIGUSR1 signal in signal bitmap
                                                //signal of processsig process, and then set
                                                //it to 1.
        else
            return -EPERM;
        return 0;
}
```

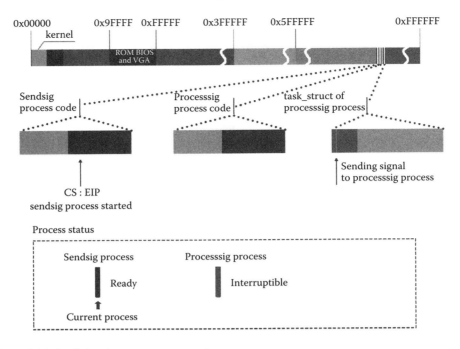

0x00000 0x9FFFF 0xFFFFF 0x3FFFFF 0x5FFFFF 0xFFFFFF

kernel

ROM BIOS
and VGA

Sendsig
process code

Processsig
process code

task_struct of
processsig process

CS : EIP
sendsig process started

Sending signal
to processsig process

Process status

Sendsig process

Ready

Processsig process

Interruptible

Current process

Figure 8.24 Send signal to process processsig.

The procedure of sending the SIGUSR1 signal to the processsig process and the procedure's influence on the corresponding field of the management structure of the processsig process are shown in Figure 8.24.

Later it will return to the user's space of process sendsig and continue to execute. With the occurrence of timer interrupt, the time slice of process sendsig will be cut down to 0. Thus, it leads the process to be switched. The schedule() function begins to execute. The corresponding code is as follows.

```
//code path:kernel/sched.c:
void schedule(void)
{
    ……
    for(p = &LAST_TASK ; p > &FIRST_TASK ;-- p)
        if (*p) {
            if ((*p)->alarm && (*p)->alarm < jiffies) {
                    (*p)->signal | = (1<<(SIGALRM-1));
                    (*p)->alarm = 0;
            }
            if (((*p)->signal & ~(_BLOCKABLE & (*p)->blocked))&& //after traversing processsig
                                                                 //process, the
                                                                 //signal it receives has been
                                                                 //detected
            (*p)->state = =TASK_INTERRUPTIBLE)                   //processsig process is still in
                                                                 //interruptible state
                    (*p)->state = TASK_RUNNING;                  //set it to ready state
        }
    ……
}
```

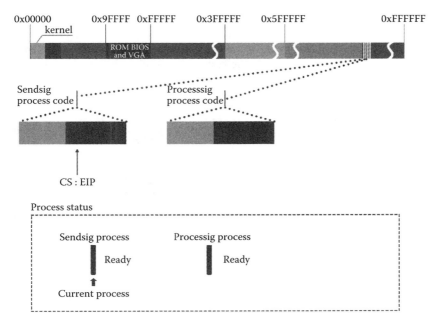

Figure 8.25 Because the processsig process has received a signal, it should be set to be in ready state.

The procedure is shown in Figure 8.25.

It will be switched to the processsig process to execute during the second traverse. The specific code is as follows.

```
//code path:kernel/sched.c:
void schedule(void)
{
......
while (1) {
        c = -1;
        next = 0;
        i = NR_TASKS;
        p = &task[NR_TASKS];
        while (-- i) {
                if (!*-- p)
                    continue;
                if ((*p)->state = = TASK_RUNNING && (*p)->counter > c)
                    c = (*p)->counter, next = i;    //processsig process is
                                                    //already ready
        }
        if (c) break;
        for(p = &LAST_TASK ; p > &FIRST_TASK ;- p)
                if (*p)
                    (*p)->counter = ((*p)->counter >> 1) +
                            (*p)->priority;
        }
        switch_to(next);                            //switch to processsig
                                                    //process to execute
    }
}
```

The system detects the signal that the current process receives and prepares to process. When the processsig process begins to execute, it will continue to execute the pause() function in the loop. Because the function will eventually be mapped to the system calling function sys_pause() to execute, when the system call returns, it must be able to execute at the label of ret_from_sys_call: and call the do_signal() function eventually. Then it will begin to process the signal of the processsig process. The specific code is as follows.

```
//code path:kernel/system_call.s:
......
ret_from_sys_call:
        movl _current,%eax              # task[0] cannot have signals
        cmpl _task,%eax
        je 3f
        cmpw $0x0f,CS(%esp)             # was old code segment supervisor ?
        jne 3f
        cmpw $0x17,OLDSS(%esp)          # was stack segment = 0x17 ?
        jne 3f
        movl signal(%eax),%ebx
        movl blocked(%eax),%ecx
        notl%ecx
        andl%ebx,%ecx
        bsfl%ecx,%ecx
        je 3f
        btrl%ecx,%ebx
        movl%ebx,signal(%eax)
        incl%ecx
        pushl%ecx
        call _do_signal        //prepare to process the signal
......
```

The system detects whether the binding of the pointer of the signal processing handler is regular. Here, we start to introduce the preparation before processing the signal.

After entering the do_signal() function, the signal processing handler of the process processsig should be judged first. As we have introduced earlier in this section, the pointer of the signal processing handler of the process processsig is loaded into the sigaction[32] structure in the task_struct of process. It is shown in Figure 8.26.

Now it begins to play a role in the procedure. If the pointer is null, the process is likely to quit. Of course, the pointer cannot be null in this case. The pointer points to the signal processing handler sig_usr() of the process processsig. The corresponding detection code is as follows.

```
//code path:kernel/signal.c:
        void do_signal(long signr,long eax, long ebx, long ecx, long edx,
        long fs, long es, long ds,
        long eip, long cs, long eflags,
        unsigned long * esp, long ss)
        {
            ......
            struct sigaction * sa = current->sigaction + signr - 1;
            ......
            sa_handler = (unsigned long) sa->sa_handler;
            if (sa_handler = =1)
                return;
            if (!sa_handler) {             //if the pointer of the function is null
                if (signr = =SIGCHLD)      //if it is signal SIGCHLD, then return dirrectly
                    return;
                else
                    do_exit(1<<(signr-1)); //otherwise the current process quits
            }
            ......
        }
```

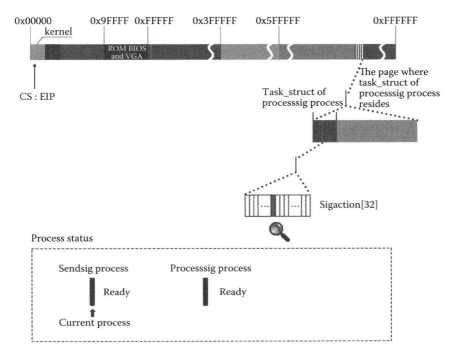

Figure 8.26 Location of the signal processing handler in sigaction structure.

Adjust the kernel stack of the process processsig in order to execute the signal processing handler first after system call return. The core purpose of the preparation we have done is to adjust the data in the user stack, making the "signal processing handler" of process processsig be "first" executed after the system call return and then continue to execute from the user process "interrupt position." As introduced before, when pause() executes, it will trigger int 0x80 soft interrupt, and the next instruction close to the "int 0x80" is the user process "interrupt position" (of course, if the process does not need to deal with signals, it can return to the "interrupt position" place directly, but now we must process the signal problem first, and then go to the "interrupt position").

After the soft interrupt was generated, the CPU automatically saves the "instruction and data" in the kernel stack of current process. The "instruction and data" include the value in EIP, CS, EFlags, ESP, SS registers, and so on. As long as the system call returns, these value in the "kernel stack" will be popped to the corresponding register, so the process will be continued from the user space "interrupt position" place.

Due to this kind of situation, Linux 0.11 will back up these register value, which are saved in the "kernel stack," to the current process' "user stack" first before the system call return (the kernel has the ability to visit all physical memory, so it's no problem), and then change these original register value in the "kernel stack." So after the system call function return, the execution will jump to the signal processing handler place in user space first, according to the latest changed data in the "kernel stack." When the process enters the user space, the "user stack" will play the role. After the signal processing, the execution will return to the "interrupt position" through "instruction and data" backup in the user space before.

This is the strategy of signal processing. Then let's see the concrete implementation code:

```
//code source:kernel/signal.c:
void do_signal(long signr,long eax, long ebx, long ecx, long edx,
        long fs, long es, long ds,
        long eip, long cs, long eflags,
        unsigned long * esp, long ss)
        {
        ......
        if (sa->sa_flags & SA_ONESHOT)
        sa->sa_handler = NULL;
        *(&eip) = sa_handler;          //adjust eip's position in kernel stack,
                                       //making it point processing process' signal process
                                       //function sig_usr()
        longs = (sa->sa_flags & SA_NOMASK)?7:8;
        *(&esp) - = longs;             //adjust the top of stack pointer esp in "user stack"
                                       //space, making the top of stack pointer move the
                                       //inverse direction of the bottom of stack,
                                       //in order to back up data in user stack space next
        tmp_esp = esp;                 //the following is to write the data, which is used
                                       //to restore, to the user stack space
        put_fs_long((long) sa->sa_restorer,tmp_esp++);
        put_fs_long(signr,tmp_esp++);
        if (!(sa->sa_flags & SA_NOMASK))
                put_fs_long(current->blocked,tmp_esp++);
        put_fs_long(eax,tmp_esp++);
        put_fs_long(ecx,tmp_esp++);
        put_fs_long(edx,tmp_esp++);
        put_fs_long(eflags,tmp_esp++);
        put_fs_long(old_eip,tmp_esp++);
        current->blocked | = sa->sa_mask;
}
```

The procedure of modifying the kernel stack and the user stack and the change of user stack space and kernel stack space's data adjustment are shown in Figures 8.27 and 8.28.

The signal preprocessing work has been completed until here, so let's see how these data will be used after the system call return and will influence the "signal processing function execution" and "the process protection site recovery after execute."

We have bound the signal processing handler sig_usr with the process processsig before, so when the system call return, it will execute from the sig_usr() function place in the process processsig, which will processes signal. After the function is executed, it will execute the "ret" instruction. The essence of ret is to use the EIP value that is stored in the stack at that time to restore the EIP register, making the execution jump to the address position EIP pointing. So, at this time, the function address value that "sa - > sa_restorer" in the stack top represents will play a role. At this time, the execution will jump to the position of the function address value that "sa - > sa_restorer" represents.

It has been said in this section previously that we have also bound the function address called restorer with the sigaction[32] structure. Restorer is a library function address. It is an actual parameter passed down by signal(). This library function will restore the "instruction and data" executed by the user process after the signal processing work and finally jump to the user program "interrupt position" to execute.

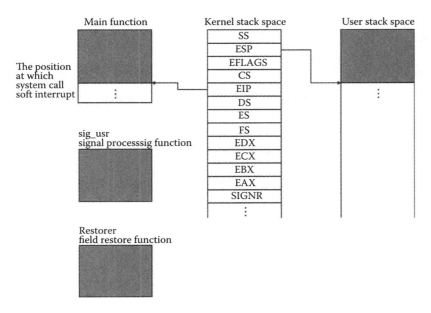

Figure 8.27 Protection site data in the kernel stack before adjusting for its significance.

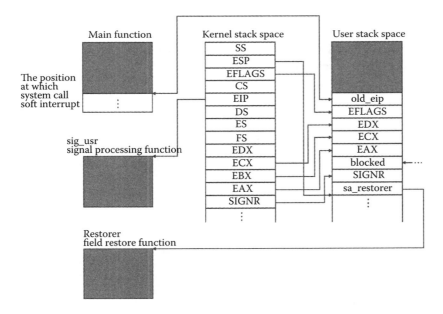

Figure 8.28 Protection site data in the kernel stack after adjusting for its significance.

Now the signal processing has been done, and the restorer function starts to work. Let's take a look at this function code first:

```
.globl ____sig_restore
.globl ____masksig_restore
____sig_restore:
addl $4,%esp
popl%eax          //the content that do_signal () function finally set in
                  //user stack before is just used to popl here to restore
                  //the register value

popl%ecx
popl%edx
popfl
ret

____masksig_restore:
addl $4,%esp
call ____ssetmask
addl $4,%esp
popl%eax          //the content that do_signal () function finally set in
                  //user stack before is just used to popl here to restore
                  //the register value

popl%ecx
popl%edx
popfl
ret
```

We have introduced that the do_signal() function adjusts value in the stack space in front. It will play a role here. Let's review the code shown below:

```
//code source:kernel/signal.c:
void do_signal(long signr,long eax, long ebx, long ecx, long edx,
        long fs, long es, long ds,
        long eip, long cs, long eflags,
        unsigned long * esp, long ss)
        {
        ......
        put_fs_long((long) sa->sa_restorer,tmp_esp++);
        put_fs_long(signr,tmp_esp++);
        if (!(sa->sa_flags & SA_NOMASK))
                put_fs_long(current->blocked,tmp_esp++);
        put_fs_long(eax,tmp_esp++);
        put_fs_long(ecx,tmp_esp++);
        put_fs_long(edx,tmp_esp++);
        put_fs_long(eflags,tmp_esp++);
        put_fs_long(old_eip,tmp_esp++);
        current->blocked | = sa->sa_mask;
}
```

After the protection site has been recovered, the process will continue to execute.

Pay attention to the assemble function "ret" at the last line of the restorer function. Due to the nature of ret being to use the current top of stack value to set EIP and make the program jump to the position of the EIP pointing to execute, obviously, after a series of clear stack operations, the top of the stack value is set by "put_fs_long (old_eip, tmp_esp + +)" this line of code. This old_EIP is the next instruction of soft interrupt int0x80, which was produced when the pause() function tried to map to the sys_pause() function. It's the "interrupt position" of the process processsig. So, after ret was executed, the signal processing was over, and the execution eventually went back to pause() to continue.

This is all the process of Linux 0.11 signal processing.

8.2.2 The Influence of Signal on the Process Execution State

Next we will introduce the second part of this section. It will reflect the different influences of the signal on the execution state of the process by comparing two processes with "interruptible state" and "uninterruptible state" respectively.

The case with interruptible state as follows:

```
#include <stdio.h>
main()
{
    exit();
}
```

After the process shell creates this user process (this process will naturally become the child of the process shell), then it is set to the interruptible state. Now, the user process will exit, so we use that as an example to introduce the influence of signal to the process execution state.

User process exits and sends signals to the process shell.

The user process calls the exit() function to deal with some affairs first before exiting, including releasing the memory page that its own program occupied, removing the relationship between the process and the file on which the process operates, and so on. Then send the "child processes exit" signal to the process shell, informing the process shell that you are going to exit, and set yourself to zombie state and call the schedule() function finally, preparing the process switching. The corresponding code is as follows:

```
//code source:kernel/exit.c:
int do_exit(long code)      //child processes exit
{
    ......
    if (current->leader)
        kill_session();
    current->state = TASK_ZOMBIE;
    current->exit_code = code;
    tell_father(current->father); //send signal to father process
    schedule();                    //process switching
    return (-1);                   /* just to suppress warnings */
}
```

```
static void tell_father(int pid)
{
    int i;
    if (pid)
        for (i = 0;i<NR_TASKS;i++) {        //seek father process, that's,
                                            //process shell

        if (!task[i])
            continue;
        if (task[i]->pid ! = pid)
            continue;
        task[i]->signal | = (1<<(SIGCHLD-1)); //send "child processes exit"
                                              //signal to process shell

        return;
        }

    ......
}
```

The procedure of sending signals in the user's exit process and setting itself to zombie state are shown in Figure 8.29.

Process shell is waken up and switching to execute. After entering the schedule() function, traversal all processes for the first time first. If there is a process that has received specific signals and the process is in the interruptible state, set the process to the ready state. The system can get that process shell to comply with this condition through traversalling, and the process shell is set to the ready state. It is shown in Figure 8.30.

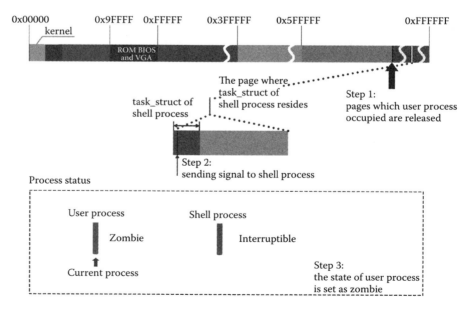

Figure 8.29 User process sends signals to the process shell.

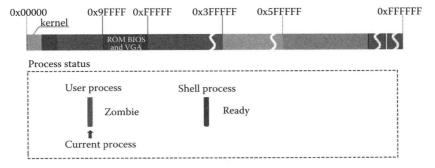

Figure 8.30 Process shell is set to ready state.

The corresponding code is shown as follows:

```
//code source:kernel/sched.c:
void schedule(void)
{
    ......
    for(p = &LAST_TASK ; p > &FIRST_TASK ;-- p)
        if (*p) {
            if ((*p)->alarm && (*p)->alarm < jiffies) {
                (*p)->signal |= (1<<(SIGALRM-1));
                (*p)->alarm = 0;
            }
            if (((*p)->signal & ~(_BLOCKABLE & (*p)->blocked)) &&    //Check whether the process
                                                                     //received signal
                (*p)->state = =TASK_INTERRUPTIBLE)                   //Check whether the process is
                                                                     //can interrupt wait state
                (*p)->state = TASK_RUNNING;                          //If the conditions are
                                                                     //satisfied at the same
                                                                     //time, set the process
                                                                     //to ready state
        }
    ......
}
```

Then, traversal all processes for the second time. There is only the process shell in the ready state, so we switch to the process shell to execute. The execution code is shown as follows:

```
//code source:kernel/sched.c:
void schedule(void)
{
    ......
    while (1) {
        c = -1;
        next = 0;
        i = NR_TASKS;
        p = &task[NR_TASKS];
        while (-- i) {
            if (!*-- p)
                continue;
            if ((*p)->state = = TASK_RUNNING && (*p)->counter > c)
                c = (*p)->counter, next = i;
        }
        if (c) break;
        for(p = &LAST_TASK ; p > &FIRST_TASK ;-- p)
            if (*p)
                (*p)->counter = ((*p)->counter >> 1) +
                        (*p)->priority;
    }
    switch_to(next);      //switch to process shell to execute
}
```

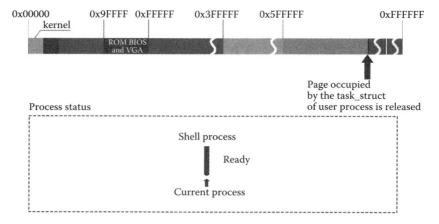

Figure 8.31 Process shell handling the rehabilitation work after user process exit.

Process shell execute, final processing for the exit of child process. After the process shell start, call the wait() function for the child process exit, including releasing the page that the task_struct of child process occupied, etc. It is shown in Figure 8.31.

The code is as follows:

```
//code source:kernel/exit.c:
int sys_waitpid(pid_t pid,unsigned long * stat_addr, int options)
{
    ......
repeat:
    switch ((*p)->state) {
            case TASK_STOPPED:
                    if (!(options & WUNTRACED))
                            continue;
                    put_fs_long(0x7f,stat_addr);
                    return (*p)->pid;
            case TASK_ZOMBIE:                           //detect the child processes is
                                                        //zombie state, do as follows
                    current->cutime + = (*p)->utime;
                    current->cstime + = (*p)->stime;
                    flag = (*p)->pid;
                    code = (*p)->exit_code;
                    release(*p);
                    put_fs_long(code,stat_addr);
                    return flag;
            default:
                    flag = 1;
                    continue;
            }
if (flag) {
        if (options & WNOHANG)
                return 0;
        current->state = TASK_INTERRUPTIBLE;
        schedule();
        if (!(current->signal & = ~(1<<(SIGCHLD-1))))   //get that the signal received is
                                                        //child processes exit signal
                goto repeat;
        else
                    return -EINTR;
        }
        return -ECHILD;
}
```

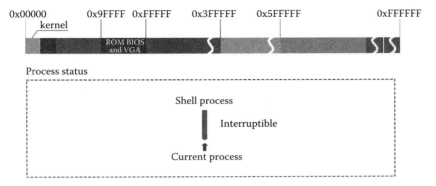

Figure 8.32 Process shell gets into interruptible state again.

Process shell is suspended again. Then the process shell continues executing, reading data from the terminal device file tty0. We assume that the user doesn't input any information through the keyboard at this time, so the process shell doesn't read any data, and so the process shell will be set to the interruptible state, waiting for the next waken up. It is shown in Figure 8.32.

Thus, to the process with interruptible state, if sends signal to it, when the schedule() function executes, the signal it received and its state will be detected, and its state will be changed to the ready state and then wake up the process.

Next, we will introduce the uninterruptible state of the process. We assume that a system has three user processes now, and they are, respectively, process A, process B, and process C, and they are in ready state now. Process B is the child process of process A, and process A is running. We take this scene as an example to introduce the influence of the signal to the state of process execution.

Process A and process B case program:

```
main()
{
    char buffer[12000];
    int pid,i;
    int fd = open("/mnt/user/hello.txt", O_RDWR,0644));
    read(fd,buffer,sizeof(buffer));    //read file
    if (!(pid = fork())) {
        exit();                        //code of process B(child process)
    }
    if (pid>0)
        while (pid ! = wait(&i)        //wait for the child process exit
    close(fd);
    return;
}
```

Process C case program:

```
main()
{
    int i,j;
    for(i = 0;i<1000000;i++)
        for(i = 0;i<1000000;i++)
}
```

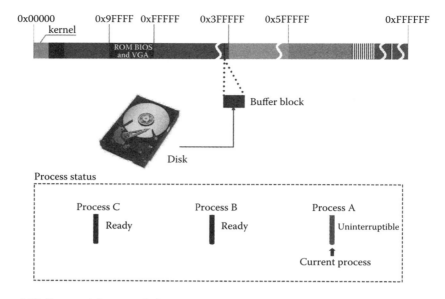

0x00000　　0x9FFFF　0xFFFFF　　0x3FFFFF　　0x5FFFFF　　　　　0xFFFFFF

kernel

ROM BIOS
and VGA

Buffer block

Disk

Process status

Process C　　　　Process B　　　　Process A

Ready　　　　Ready　　　　Uninterruptible

Current process

Figure 8.33 Process A is suspended.

Process A is suspended due to the wait for read disk. Process A needs to read data from hard disk. So it calls the read() function to trigger a soft interrupt, and finally map to the sys_read() function to execute. After a series of function calls, send the read disk command. After it returns, process A is set to the uninterruptible state. This is because the next execution of process A needs the support of the data read out from the disk. Before the data was read, no matter what signal this process has received, it cannot be waken up. If it was waken up, it will operate the data in the buffer, but at this time, the data in the buffer has not been read from the hard disk, so this will cause data chaos. It is shown in Figure 8.33.

Process A executed and was finally suspended. The corresponding code is shown below:

```
//code source:fs/buffer.c:
struct buffer_head * bread(int dev,int block)
{
    ……
    if (bh->b_uptodate)
        return bh;
    ll_rw_block(READ,bh);
    wait_on_buffer(bh);                     //Test whether need to wait until buffer
                                            //block unlock
    if (bh->b_uptodate)
        return bh;
    ……
}
static inline void wait_on_buffer(struct buffer_head * bh)
{
    cli();
    while (bh->b_lock)
        sleep_on(&bh->b_wait);              //Buffer block has really been lock
    sti();                                  //Have to suspend process A
}
```

```
//code source:kernel/sched.c:
void sleep_on(struct task_struct **p)
{
    ......
    tmp = *p;
    *p = current;
    current->state = TASK_UNINTERRUPTIBLE;       //set process A to uninterruptible state
    schedule();
    if (tmp)
        tmp->state = 0;
}
```

Switch process A to process B to execute. It also needs to call schedule() later, and finally switches to the other process to execute. Assume that switch to the child process of process A, namely process B, to execute. Process B was executed and ready to exit, so process B is set to zombie state and then sends a signal to process A, informing process A that it would exit and finally call the schedule() function, preparing process switching. It is shown in Figure 8.34.

Execution code is as follows:

```
//code source:kernel/exit.c:
int do_exit(long code)                           //process B exit
{
    ......
    if (current->leader)
        kill_session();
    current->state = TASK_ZOMBIE;
    current->exit_code = code;
```

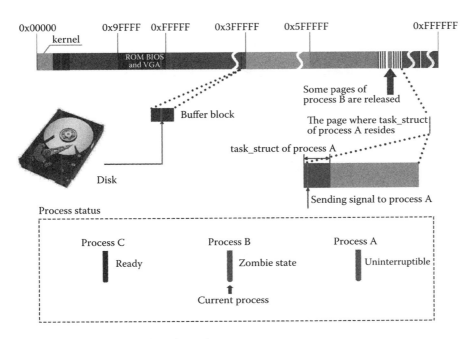

Figure 8.34 Process B exit and send signal to process A.

```
        tell_father(current->father);              //send signal to parent process
        schedule();                                //process switch
        return (-1);                               /* just to suppress warnings */
}
static void tell_father(int pid)
{
    int i;
        if (pid)
            for (i = 0;i<NR_TASKS;i++) {            //seek parent process, namely, process A
        if (!task[i])
            continue;
        if (task[i]->pid ! = pid)
            continue;
        task[i]->signal | = (1<<(SIGCHLD-1));   //send process A "child process exit" signal
        return;
    }
    ......
}
```

Although a signal has been received by process A, it can't be waken up. After entering the schedule() function, traversal all processes for the first time. Although process A has received a signal at this time, because it was uninterruptible state, it would not be set to ready state, and we have to switch to process C to execute (Figure 8.35).

Execution code is shown below:

```
//code source:kernel/sched.c:
void schedule(void)
{
    ......
    for(p = &LAST_TASK ; p > &FIRST_TASK ;-- p)
        if (*p) {
            if ((*p)->alarm && (*p)->alarm < jiffies) {
```

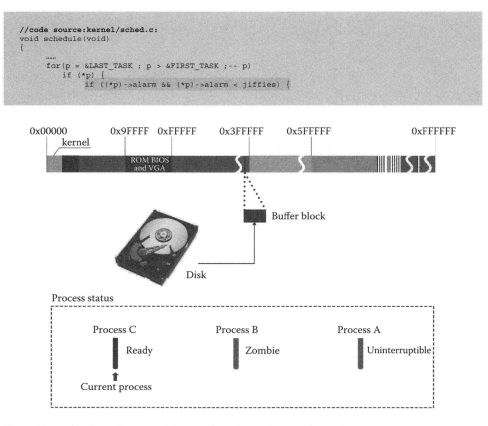

Figure 8.35 For the uninterruptible state, it can't use the signal to wake up.

```
                (*p)->signal | = (1<<(SIGALRM-1));
                (*p)->alarm = 0;
            }
        if ((((*p)->signal & ~(_BLOCKABLE & (*p)->blocked)) &&  //detect process A has
                                                        //really received the signal
            (*p)->state = =TASK_INTERRUPTIBLE)  //process A is uninterruptible state
                (*p)->state = TASK_RUNNING;     //won't execute here
    }
    ……
}
```

Because peripheral data has been read completely, process A was waken up. After process C executes for a period of time, the data process A specified has been read from the hard disk, so the hard disk interrupt service routine will set process A to the ready state forcibly. (This is also the only way to set the process in the uninterruptible state to the ready state.) It is shown in the bottom right of Figure 8.36, and the execution code is shown below:

```
//code path:kernel/blk_dev/blk.h:
extern inline void end_request(int uptodate)
{
    DEVICE_OFF(CURRENT->dev);
    if (CURRENT->bh) {
        CURRENT->bh->b_uptodate = uptodate;
        unlock_buffer(CURRENT->bh);             //buffer block release
    }
    if (!uptodate) {
        printk(DEVICE_NAME " I/O error\n\r");
        printk("dev%04x, block%d\n\r",CURRENT->dev,
            CURRENT->bh->b_blocknr);
    }
    ……
}
extern inline void unlock_buffer(struct buffer_head * bh)
{
    if (!bh->b_lock)
        printk(DEVICE_NAME ": free buffer being unlocked\n");
    bh->b_lock = 0;
    wake_up(&bh->b_wait);                       //waken up the process that wait buffer block
                                                //release, namely, waken up process A
}
```

So process A has executive ability, but this is not equal to process A executing immediately. After the hard disk interrupt routine return, it is still process C to continue executing as shown in the left bottom of Figure 8.36.

Switch to process A to execute and process the signal. The time slice of process C was used up and switched the process. After entering into the schedule() function here, it is found that only process A is in ready state, so switch to process A to execute. As process A was started, process the data that was read out from the hard disk just now first; thus, the sys_read() execution has completed. At this time, soft interrupt is ready to return, and before it returns, it will check whether process A received any signal first. Sure enough, it has detected that process A received a signal, so process the entry address of the processing signal service handler, so that once the soft interrupt returns, the signal processing handler will process the signal as shown in Figure 8.37.

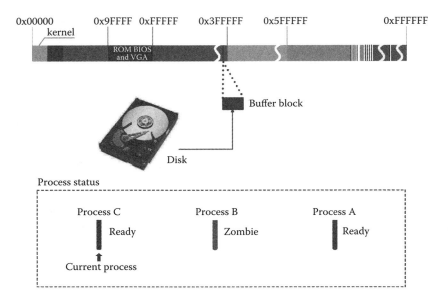

Figure 8.36 Process A is waken up.

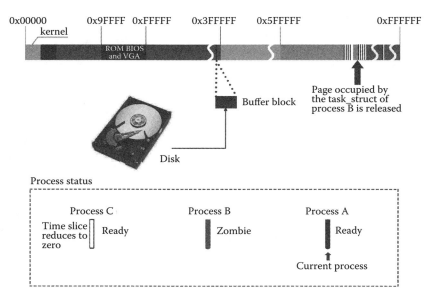

Figure 8.37 Process A execute and process the signal.

Thus it can be seen that for the process in the uninterruptible state, unless it is set to ready state directly, there is no other way to change its state to a ready state, and whether it has received a signal is meaningless.

∎ 8.3 Summary

This chapter takes "processes operating pipe" and "interprocess send signal" as examples to explain the interprocess communication.

In the "processes operating pipe" cases, the operating system allocates a pipe file first in file_table[64] and inode_table[32] and applies for a page as a pipe in memory. After the establishment of the pipe, the two processes begin to exchange data; one reads data from the pipe; the other writes data to the pipe. Even if a clock interrupt interrupts the execution of processes, the data also won't get chaotic.

In the "interprocess send signal" cases, before the completion of the system call, it will process the signal of the current process. If the signal is received, the system does some set preparation. When the system call returns, the signal processing function will be executed immediately, and the process produce system calls soft interrupt will be executed. In addition, for each operating system process scheduling, it will check all processes. If the process is in interruptible wait state and has received the signal, it will be set to task ready. If the signal is in uninterruptible wait state, even if it has received the signal, the state will not be changed.

9 Operating System's Design Guidelines

Kings have long arms; all within the boundaries, has the kings' servants

—The book of *Lesser Odes*

The former eight chapters have analyzed and explained the operation principle and working mechanism of the Linux operating system in great detail, and this chapter will try to explore the operating system design guidelines from the designer's view.

9.1 Run a Simple Program to See What the Operating System Has Done

The most effective way to understand the operating system clearly is to see what the operating system has done when a simple program is executed on a computer.

We take a "hello world" of C language version as example:

```
#include <stdio.h>
void main()
{
        printf("hello world\n");
}
```

After this program is compiled and linked, an executable file will be generated. We run this program on Linux, and eventually the system will display "hello world" on the screen. Intuitively, "hello world" displayed on the screen is all because of the programs we have written, but in fact, the program we have written only plays a small role. Obviously, the program calls the printf library function of C language because the theme of this book is the operating system, so we won't discuss library function.

Let's briefly investigate what the Linux 0.11 operating system has done for running the hello program. The following small words are summary descriptions of the operating system work, involving more than 10,000 lines. Except for interprocess communication, it touches on almost all aspects of the operating system. We want readers have an intuitive understanding of what Linux has done when the simplest program is running.

Case description: There is an executable file named hello in hard disk, and the source program of the file is as front:

Now the system has been in the idle state, the user prepares to make the program of the file in the hard disk load and execute through typing a command, "/hello", and eventually to make the hello world string display.

The first step: The user inputs command, and shell process is waken up to analyze the order.

To achieve this step, the system will do at least the following preparations:

(1) The user stroke, and the information typed in is recorded in terminal equipment file tty0.

If the system operates the terminal equipment in the form of file, it needs to construct a set of file systems first, and then load the file system, so as to operate the files on this basis. The file system includes "super block," "logic block bitmap," "i node bitmap," "file i node," "block," etc. Second, classify the data according to the different function of files, including regular file, device file, directory file, etc. tty0 belongs to device files. It is likely to operate terminal device file tty0 with these preparations.

(2) After stroke, it also produces the keyboard interrupt, and the system will be able to process the keyboard interrupt.

First of all, the interrupt will transmit to programmable interrupt controller 8259A, so we need to set the interrupt controller 8259A. Then, the interrupt will be communicated with the CPU, and the CPU will find the interrupt descriptor table in memory through the interrupt descriptor table register IDTR and then find the keyboard interrupt handler through searching the interrupt descriptor table and execute the program. In order to realize these operations, it needs to construct a set of interrupt service systems, including the interrupt descriptor table register IDTR setting, and establishing an interrupt descriptor table to link the interrupt service routine. Then it also needs to program the interrupt service routine to be able to serve for the specific interrupt. In addition, it also needs to link the interrupt service routine with the interrupt descriptor table.

(3) The interrupt service routine starts to execute and wakes up process shell. After that, switch process 0 to process shell to execute through the process scheduling mechanism.

It needs the system to establish a set of process management mechanisms. For shell, it needs to create process and load process shell, so that we can establish the human-machine interactive interface. At the same time, it also needs to create a process 0 and switch to process 0 to execute when other processes are not in ready state, and once there is a process that has been waken up, switch to the process to execute immediately. This mechanism is applicable to all processes of the operating system. Before supporting multi-processes execution, we need to design a set of process schedule mechanisms, which produce timer interrupt, leading to process switching. There are a lot of problems that need to be considered in this mechanism, such as designing timer interrupt service handler and 8253 timer setting, etc.

(4) Process shell reads the command information that the user has typed from the terminal device file tty0 through the execution of its own program and then analyzes the command and prepares to execute the corresponding treatment. Of course, this command cannot be input by knocking the keyboard only once. Each stroke can repeat the action above, and then process shell sleeps again and waits for the next keyboard interrupt.

So far, the system is only responding to the command the user typed, and the official processing hasn't started yet. These preparations introduced above are the simplest introduction of the specific steps, and behind these preparations, there is more preparation work. Strictly speaking, to carry out this first step, the preparation introduced in the first chapter and second chapter of this book is almost all useful.

The second step: After process shell analyzes the user command, call fork() creates a user process, so that we can control the program of the "hello world" file.

The system needs to create at least a set of process management structures for user process here, and each process will have such a structure in order to control the future loading program. This structure is very complicated, including time slice, priority, process status, the corresponding files of the process, the task state descriptor table TSS of the process, and the local descriptor table LDT of the process, etc. Each of these fields has a strong relationship with the operation of the system. Take TSS as example, it contains all the data in the register for the current running process, and once there is process switching, the system will store the value of each current register in the TSS while, at the same time, using the data in the TSS to set the value of each registers of the process which will switch to and finally switch. Visibly, the data in TSS is the fundamental guarantee for process switching. For another example, LDT contains the code segment descriptor and data segment descriptor for the current process, and the two descriptors both control the program controlled by process directly, and the fundamental purpose of process operation is to execute the user program.

In addition, each process has TSS and LDT. To facilitate the management, it also needs to design a set of data structures, which is a global descriptor table GDT, and the TSS of all process and LDT indices are both stored in the GDT. In order to facilitate the operation of GDT and further operation of LDT and TSS, the system also needs to set the special registers of these three tables in CPU, which are global descriptor table register (GDTR), local descriptor table register (LDTR), and task register (TR).

But only these are far from enough, the beginning of the BOOT is the real mode, and the value in each segment register is the actual address value. The data in the segment register becomes the segment selector until the system gets into protected mode, so that the GDT table can participate in the application, so the system should do a full range of preparations in order to converse from the real mode to protected mode.

These above are only expansion analysis for TSS and LDT, the other fields in the process management structure also have a close relationship with the system; for example, the most basic way of process scheduling is through the time slice rotary, and the most important reference of time slice rotary is the time slice of the current process. For another instance, only process is able to operate files, so the process will build comprehensive relationships with the files, including file i nodes, the item in file management table, and the file management pointer table of process itself, and so on.

To create process, we must create a process management structure, with all fields of process management structure, and all of these fields should all be created and set. In addition to process management structure, when creating process, it also needs to duplicate a pages table and create a page directory entry for the new process, and all of these have a direct relationship with the application of the memory page, and the strategy of the memory application is one of the most complex application strategies in the whole operation system.

Step 3: After creating a new process, load the corresponding program of file hello world.

To complete this step, process will do comprehensive preparation in two aspects: One is files, and the other is memory. The program "hello world" must be stored in the executable file in the hard disk, so it must check whether the files are available before loading the file. It mainly displays in the file i node detection and the file header testing. I node is the file management information; as long as the i node is involved, it can't get away from the i node search, so we should analyze the file path, operate directory file and directory entry, operate i node table, and so on, no one less. File header is stored in the data block and can't manipulate the data block without the support of logical block bitmap, so we will use the whole content involved in the entire file system.

With the file loading conditions, we will load file "hello world" into memory, so the system will solve all issues related to memory, including removing the relationship with the original process shared page. This involves the page reference count, page management mechanism with three level (page directory table, page table, page), page data (read-only/can read write), and a series of problems, and the system will have to establish page write protection mechanisms for this to solve these problems.

But only solving these problems is far from enough; the program's loading is also a very exquisite strategy, of which the most important is page fault interrupt mechanism; namely it must analyze whether it needs to apply for a new page to load the content of the program according to the need. For this reason, it needs to judge much related data so as to determine the necessity of loading, such as whether the corresponding physical address of linear address have been mapped into the linear address space, etc., which requires a physical address to linear address mapping scheme. In addition, the design of the page fault interrupt mechanism is also very exquisite. Page fault is not equal to must loading in the peripherals program. For example, a page fault exeception as the result of pushing stack also needs to apply for a new page to load data, but this has no relationship with peripherals. These are all problems that the designing of the page fault interrupt mechanism needs to be comprehensively considered.

In short, the load of program "hello world" almost involves all aspects of file management and memory management. Moreover, the above is just the most basic introduction of loading process "hello world". Linux supports the execution of the processes, and each process is likely to load its own programs, furthermore, files and memory are the resources all processes share, thus there still exists a more complex management relationship between them. For example, when two processes load the same file "hello world", whether to share, how to share, how to calculate the count of page reference after share, how to determine the attribute of reading and writing, etc., are all problems.

Step 4: Program "hello world" starts to execute, making string "hello world" display on the screen.

Program "hello world" will start to execute after loading into memory. The program is simple, and it is to let the string "hello world" display on the screen. But, even so, the system will have to do a lot of work for this, of which the most important is the aspects about display, such as how to determine the video card attributes, display card is monochrome or color; how to determine the video memory location; how to determine the position displaying on the screen; if there are too many characters; whether rolling show is needed and how to display, etc. These problems will be all done by the operating system, and it directly interacts with the bottom hardware of the display.

From above description, we can easily find that the operating system does a lot of work even to run a simple program. We may conclude that if we think in the contrary way: Without the operating system, we have to write all these complex programs with the function of an operating system even to print a message "hello world" on the screen. No doubt that without the operating system we can hardly load computer with programs and not even get the results.

So what does the operating system do to run the application on earth?

Through comprehensive analysis, we get some conclusions here: OS is supposed to provide applications of the basic programs for the use of hard disks, monitors, and keyboards. In other words, the operating system provides supports to peripherals for the running of an application. If the operating system doesn't write these supporting programs, the application has to write them, and the contents of these programs that all the applications have to write are just alike. So the operating system can be seen as the part that is shared by all the applications.

Modern operating systems like Linux not only provide support to peripherals for applications, but also support the running of several programs at the same time. It means that the operating system not only supports peripherals, but also makes efficient organization management and coordination for many programs that are running, in order to avoid any program obtains the whole resources of CPU, RAM and peripherals, making the other programs unable to work normally. Besides, it has to prevent mutual reading, writing, and covering among running programs to make sure all the programs work normally. The key is that the operating system can't be read or written directly by applications, or covered by applications.

■ 9.2 Thoughts on the Design of the Operating System: Master–Slave Mechanism

These requirements, which seem to be reasonable, hide a problem behind them: An application is a program, and an operating system is also a program, so then how can the operating system organize, manage and coordinate the applications without suffering hurt from the applications?

We think it can be solved by privilege mechanism. To make sure that the operating system is capable of organizing, managing, and coordinating applications, escaping from their hurts at the same time, the most efficient way is to separate the operating system from the applications and to separate applications from applications to make sure that the operating system can't visit applications arbitrarily, applications can't visit the operating system, and there is no mutual visit between applications.

It means that the operating system has to make sure it can do the things listed below: If it wants some application to run in some places of the RAM, this application will follow its order to run there. It should allocate RAM for applications that have their own clear boundaries, so that applications can't reach out. It determines the time during which an application occupies CPU, and the application can only run within this limited time, after which the application has to return the right of CPU use to the operating system without detaining the right of CPU use privately. If some application wants to use peripherals, it can't directly ask for peripherals; it has to ask the operating system for rights. If the operating system thinks the applications can use peripherals, then it lets them use them. If the operating system doesn't think so, then it denies its request.

Under this privilege mechanism, the relationship between operating system and application becomes a master–slave relationship. In order to remember it easily, we call this privilege mechanism the **master–slave mechanism**.

9.2.1 Process and Its Creation Mechanism in the Master–Slave Mechanism

9.2.1.1 Program Boundary and Process

To realize the master–slave mechanism, first of all, we should establish effective boundaries between kernel programs and applications and between applications and applications.

Most objects in real life have natural boundaries, such as houses, desks, and benches around us and ourselves. We have skin, which is our natural boundary. These natural boundaries can effectively prevent fusion between person and person, between object and object, and between person and object, which keeps an independent and integral body and the characteristics of independence and integrity. But there are some objects in real life that don't have natural definite boundaries, such as gasses, liquids, and so on. Because gas doesn't have a boundary, different gases can mix easily, after which they can never be separated. If we want to hold water, the most effective way is to use containers with boundaries, such as cups and bottles.

Program codes in the computer are the same as in the cases of gasses and liquids. They don't have natural and definite boundaries. The operating system is required to determine boundaries artificially, which will play the role of containers that can separate and hold. Therefore designers of modern operating systems put forward the concept of process, using a "task_struct" structure to divide boundaries definitely. "Task_struct" is the main symbol of process. In terms of the operating system, process is a running program that accepts organization management and coordination of the operating system.

9.2.1.2 Process Creation

Technically, there are many ways to create process. Process creation in the Linux uses the mode of object creation. Object creation is using objects that already exist to create a new object and to use a process that already exists to create a new process, which is called the mechanism of parent and child process creation. Essentially, the most important thing when creating a process is to create "task_struct."

It's very easy to deduce in a contrary way in logic that the creation mechanism of a parent and child process means the initial parent process must exist independently, which is process 0. It's easy to understand that process 0 cannot be created by the creation mechanism of parent and child, so the operating system designers have to compile the "task_struct" of process 0 manually. When the process was created, the creation mechanism of parent and child can use process 0 as a parent process to create a child process.

When we have a process, we get the object of organization management and coordination of the master–slave mechanism.

9.2.2 How Does the Designing of Operating System Display the Master–Slave Mechanism?

The relationship between the operating system kernel and user process should be designed as a master–slave relationship in order to realize the master–slave mechanism. The operating system can work stably only if the master–slave mechanism has been realized.

The designer of an operating system uses a full set of design schemes to implement the master–slave mechanism. In terms of an operating system designer, we will analyze how the thoughts of operating system design display the master–slave mechanism in three aspects below. In the first aspect, process scheduling reflects the master–slave mechanism; in the second aspect, RAM management reflects the master–slave mechanism; and in the third aspect, the file system reflects the master–slave mechanism.

9.2.2.1 Master–Slave Mechanism That the Operating System Reflects in Process Scheduling

When the operating system is conducting process scheduling, the ways to treat the kernel and process are entirely different. Precisely, process scheduling is operated by the kernel.

When a timer interrupt occurs, the scheduler will be triggered and will judge whether the time slice of the running process has been used up. If it has been used up, the operating system begins to schedule, and the running process is suspended at once no matter whether this process has been finished, and then the operating system will schedule other processes. If it's the kernel, the scheduler returns after judging and ensuring, and the kernel will go on running until the task is finished. No matter how long the kernel occupies the CPU, it's always so, and all user processes will halt and keep waiting for the end of the kernel running. Thus, it can be seen that when the operating system gained the right of process scheduling, this right only works for its slave, process, and not for its master, kernel.

The run time that is assigned to process by Linux each time is actually several time slices. How much time assigned is determined by the operating system. And there is even no chance for process to increase the time slice. The right to use the CPU will be returned to the kernel once the time slice is used up. It's worth noting that this return is not done in the way of negotiation or by turns, but forcibly withdrawn. If the process is finished, the operating system will withdraw the right to use CPU and not wait even though there are some time slices remaining.

If we don't adopt a master–slave mechanism, the process schedule will be designed to hand in execute permissions to the operating system proactively and consciously. And then whether and when to hand in the right to use CPU directly depend on the design of the program of process, and the operating system can hardly control it. What is more horrible is that if the process is a malware program or a program with frequently exception zombie happens, the operating system will probably never withdraw the right to use CPU, which will lead to paralysis of the entire system.

The design of the master–slave mechanism ensures that the situation in which an application occupies the resources of the CPU will, at most, have a influence on the time slices assigned to it by the operating system. When these time slices are used up, execute permission will be returned to the operating system naturally, after which the operating system can deal with process and forcibly turn off a process that has failed.

Specific details of technique have been introduced in Chapter 6.

9.2.2.2 Master–Slave Mechanism That the Operating System Adopts in Memory Management

As was said previously, the most important symbol of process is the "task_struct" data structure. In a "task_struct" data structure, the boundary of process is definitely defined, and any action to cross a border that has not been permitted will be deterred. The distinct boundaries ensure that process cannot cross a border directly to visit the operating system kernel, and processes cannot visit each other directly. That is the embodiment of the master–slave mechanism.

The kernel and the user process of Linux 0.11 adopt a paging mechanism, respectively, but there are two sets of management data adopted: one set works for the kernel, and its range is the whole memory space of 0–16 M; the other sets works for the user process, and its range is limited to the space from 1 M to 16 M (space size below 1 M is for the kernel), which is shown in Figure 9.1.

It can be clearly seen from Figure 9.1 that if the system kernel code is in the kernel's private space, process can never reach it, and the range of space that the kernel can visit includes the whole memory space. You can't reach the place that is occupied by me, and

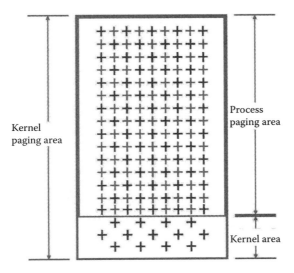

Figure 9.1 Kernel and user process paging sketch.

I can reach the place that is yours because your place is my place. It is "all over the world belongs to the king," which inevitably results in "all the ones with land are the king's servants!"

Besides, the user process can only deal with logic address and can't directly use physical address. When it needs to use RAM and is transformed to an actual physical address by the operating system kernel according to the second set 1–16 M management data scheme, the kernel divides the whole memory into memory blocks with same volume, namely page. When a process is running, the operating system will assign it several pages. If the operating system assigns it more than two pages, these pages will not have to be adjacent, and in fact, they are always nonadjacent. The process doesn't know where these pages have been assigned and how many pages. To be precise, the process doesn't even have the feeling of paging. In the eyes of the process, it uses a continuous logic address in memory.

The process doesn't know where it is, not to mention that it will know where other processes are, so mutual visits between processes will never happen. The kernel code is surely placed in the kernel area. From Figure 9.1, we can easily find that the kernel area is beyond the reach of process; therefore, the process can never visit the kernel. The process storage area is within the reach of the kernel; therefore the kernel can visit the memory space of the process at will. This is the typical master–slave relationship.

Specific details of technique have been introduced in Chapters 3 and 6.

9.2.2.3 Master–Slave Mechanism Is Reflected by OS File System

Applying for disk space when writing files is taken as an example here. When the user wants to write files into disks, first, it needs to apply to the kernel and describe which process it is, the volume of resource it needs, and the right for reading and writing resource. When the kernel receives the application, it will decide whether to fulfill the application at once according to the resource occupied in disks now and the actual situation of buffer area. If there are several processes applying for resources, the kernel will decide which process will gain resources first and make other processes keep waiting. The kernel will manage the sequence of the waiting queue to reach a standard that the kernel thinks to be best. If the current resource can't fulfill the requirement, the kernel will refuse the application. It also reflects the master–slave mechanism between the kernel and the user process. Once the work of the user process reaches the basement, it needs to apply or report to the kernel in advance because it doesn't have the right to apply for resources directly. The kernel handles all sorts of hardware resources and takes charge of organization management and coordination of many processes that apply for resources.

Specific details of technique have been introduced in Chapter 5.

■ 9.3 Three Key Techniques in Realizing the Master–Slave Mechanism

We analyze the thought of the design of the master–slave mechanism reflected in the operating system in detail from three aspects above. We will explain what the designer of the operating system takes to realize the master–slave mechanism below. We think it takes three key techniques: protection and paging, privilege level, and interruption. Relying on the hardware mechanism provided by the CPU is a characteristic shared by the three techniques.

9.3.1 Protection and Paging

As was introduced in Chapter 1, Linux 0.11 opens PE and PG, which means it opens protected mode and paging mechanism. When protected mode is opened, substantial changes occur to the addressing mode of the CPU. Take code addressing for example; it's CS:IP in real mode; IP changes to EIP when in protected mode, and the more important change is that CS changes from a direct code segment base address to a code segment selector. The assigned code segment descriptor in GDT will be gained through analyzing the code segment selector and the code segment base address can be gained through further analysis.

There are two more changes that are profound: One is segment limitation, and the other is privilege level.

Although CS is the segment base address of the code segment under real mode, CS is just in charge of guarding the starting position of the code segment, and Intel CPU doesn't design the segment ending register to guard the ending address of the code segment. Although the segment length is 64 KB, it has to allow the cover of other segments because the case in which code segment is far smaller than 64 KB always occurs in actual use. It has to allow covering in order not to be wasting memory.

Besides the segment base address in real mode, there still is segment limitation, which not only makes it compatible that there is only one segment register in real mode, but also adds a segment ending register in effect, which prevents the covering to code segment and access to code segment out of bounds, which apparently enhances the protective effects.

It is the privilege level that has a great influence on the master–slave mechanism. Starting from Chapter 1, we have mentioned many times that the last two bits of CS are privilege level. On the hardware, Intel forbids codes in a code segment with a low privilege level to use some important instructions, such as LGDT, LLDT, LTR, and LIDT. Besides, Intel also provides some chances to allow the designer of the operating system to forbid the user process to use some important instructions that are of great importance in controlling a situation, such as cli, sti, and so on through some setting to privilege.

On the basis of this hardware, the operating system can design the kernel with the highest privilege level and the user process with the lowest privilege level. Thus, the operating system designer can make sure that the operating system kernel can execute all instructions and do whatever it wants. The operating system can visit GDT, LDT, TR, and GDT, and LDT is the key to the transformation from logic address to linear address, which means the operating system can control the linear address, and the user process cannot do it. The user process can only use the logic address, and the logic process of the user process must transform to a linear address by the kernel, furthermore, the physical address is transformed from the linear address by the kernel, and we won't know the physical address if we don't know the linear address, which also means the operating system can actually reach any physical address. Thus, for the user process, it can feel that it is visiting the memory space of a logic address, just the same as visiting the "real memory space." The mapping from the actual logic address to the physical address is arranged by operating system. The operating system places the memory user process that wants to visit in memory at will, and the user process does not even know where the actually visited physical address is.

The design scheme of the linear address space of the user process in the Linux 0.11 operating system is to divide the 4 GB linear address space into 64 identical parts, and each process has one part, and the logic address space of each process is 64 MB. In other words, from the aspects of the user process, there are 64 MB memory for using, thus 64 MB × 64 = 4 GB. Because the space that the user process can visit cannot go beyond 64 MB, the linear address space of each process will never overlap. Thus theoretically speaking, on the level of linear address space, the direct mutual addressing and visiting among user processes are not available, which means it's more impossible for the user process to visit the operating system kernel.

Thus, protected mode provides the operating system designers the chance to make it possible that the user process can't visit the operating system kernel and can't visit each other, but the operating system kernel can actually visit any user process, which is a reflection of the master–slave mechanism.

The precondition for paging is protected mode, which means PE and PG must open at the same time, and PG without PE will not exist. We can probably say that paging and protection units to be one. The paging mechanism depends on the hardware of the CPU; as well, it not only improves the efficiency of memory space use, but it also makes it possible for operating system designers to realize that there is no mutual visiting among user processes and no access to the kernel, but the kernel can actually visit any user process.

Under the paging mechanism, there is only one paging method to make the linear address equal to the physical address in theory. We will talk about the theory and operation of this method in detail below.

We use a simple linear equation to show the relationship between the linear address and the physical address:

$$y = kx + b,$$

where x represents the linear address, and y represents the physical address. k is the scaling relationship between the linear address and the physical address because the unit of the linear address and the physical address is a byte, and if the growth directions are the same, the scaling relationship between linear address and physical address is 1, which also means

$$k = 1.$$

Thus,

$$y = kx + b$$

becomes

$$y = x + b.$$

It's easy to find out that

$$y = x,$$

which will become true as long as

$$b = 0,$$

which also means the physical address equals the linear address.

If the operating system kernel wants to realize under the paging mechanism that the linear address equals the physical address, it must put the starting position of the paging of the operating system kernel in the starting position of the physical address, which is the key!!!

After recalling Figure 1.23 in and the content of Section 6.2, you can truly understand the profound significance of kernel paging starting from the starting position of memory. Its effect is to make sure that $b = 0$, which means the linear address equals the physical address!

For the kernel, its task is to face physical memory directly, and the most direct way is to realize a one-to-one relationship between the linear address and the physical address. When the kernel wants to visit memory, it can directly visit physical memory and doesn't look like the process that was dragged around by the operating system and doesn't even know the specific position it is in in the physical memory.

To meet this demand under the precondition of the paging mechanism, the operating system has particularly designed a set of page tables for the kernel to use exclusively. The value of this set of page tables can just realize the identity mapping between the value of the linear address and the value of the physical address, and the range of mapping is not limited to the 1 M space of the kernel itself but includes the whole 16 M space, which also means the kernel can actually visit the memory space of any process. The technique details of this specific scheme have been introduced in Figures 1.38 to 1.40 and Section 6.2 in detail.

The user process can only face one logic address, and when it needs to use memory, this logic address first will be transformed into a linear address and transformed into the real address later by MMU according to the paging scheme designed exclusively for the process provided by the kernel. The transformation of the linear address and the physical address is in a contrary way to direct mapping.

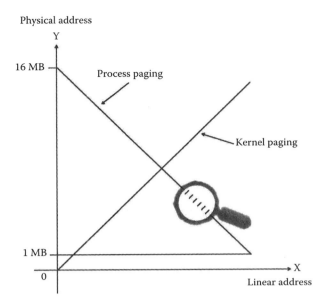

Figure 9.2 Kernel paging and user process paging.

First of all, the distribution of the memory page of the user process begins from high-end of the physical address and moves toward the low address along with the running of programs. It can be roughly believed that the distribution of the page is in the direction contrary to the linear address, and $k = -1$, so b can't be zero naturally. The operating system assigns a process page temporarily, totally depending on the demands of multiprocess when it is actually running, and the page is assigned in the physical memory and is not known beforehand, or precisely speaking, even the operating system kernel can't predict, and it looks like the random distribution of pages. It results in the complete insulation between the logic address of the user process and the real physical memory, which makes it easier for the kernel to manage memory. It fully shows that the kernel as a master directly manipulates and manages memory, has the right to use and manage the whole memory, and knows the exact place that the real memory of each process has been put in. In the mean time, it also shows the user process as the slave who does not know the actual position of memory it uses doesn't have the right to visit the space of other processes. The kernel code and distribution of physical memory of all processes are entirely under the control of the kernel, which realizes the master–slave mechanism.

Specific details of technique have been introduced in Sections 6.3 and 6.4 in detail.

Figure 9.2 shows the principles of kernel paging and user process paging.

9.3.2 Privilege Level

Privilege mainly depends on the protected mode the CPU hardware provides and focuses on "segment." The last two bits of all segment selectors identify privilege levels and will finally influence the segments decided by the segment selectors. These segment selectors include CS, SS, DS, ES, FS, and GS. The key point is that the range influenced by privilege level is the "segment."

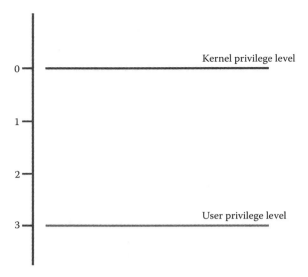

Figure 9.3 Kernel and user privilege level.

For the Linux operating system, the so-called kernel mode and user mode use the exact statement of which is some code segment, data segment or stack segment. The present privilege level is either 0 level, which is the kernel privilege level, or 3 level, which is the user privilege level.

The kernel privilege level can execute all instructions on any condition, and the operating system can make sure that the user privilege level cannot execute instructions that may destroy the kernel privilege level. As for the CPU hardware, it can not only make all the codes stay in the kernel privilege level, but it can also make them stay in the user privilege level, which is shown in Figure 9.3.

But once all the codes in the computer stay in the user privilege level, instructions on the high privilege level will never be used, which is exactly the original intention of the privilege level designer. Besides, if all the codes are on the same privilege level, the chaos phenomena of mutual visiting and covering will easily occur and will be extremely hard to deal with once these situation occur.

The operating system designers are wise and will not do such stupid things. They will design the kernel code of the operating system into a high privilege level and design the code of the user process into a low privilege level. Thus the kernel can execute all the instructions, and the user process cannot do it, which shows again the master–slave mechanism.

9.3.3 Interrupt

After the running of the operating system and user programs, the code and data of the user privilege level and the kernel privilege level in the computer appear alternately because of the transformation of the privilege levels. The Intel CPU provides several ways for transforming, and the main method Linux 0.11 uses is interrupt. Through interrupt and return from interrupt, Linux 0.11 realizes the transformation among privilege levels. Figure 9.4 vividly shows the overturn of the privilege level caused by interrupt.

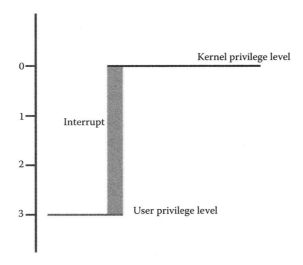

Figure 9.4 Interrupt leading to overturn of privilege level.

We will talk about why the interrupt technique can realize the transformation of the privilege level in detail below.

In our view, the three most important things in the computer are execution sequence, being identifiable, and being predictable.

We will begin to analyze from the execution sequence. Figure 9.5 shows the classification of the computer program execution sequence.

First of all, there are two sorts of execution sequences in the computer: sequence and branch. The realization of sequential execution depends on automatically accumulating the program counter PC in the CPU. Each time an instruction is executed, PC will accumulate automatically. PC unites with the instruction pointer IP or EIP and forms the execution sequence of the sequence. Besides there is branch, which can be divided into two parts: branch with return and branch without return. Branch without return is jump. Jump can happen in some conditions, after which there will be no return. The other sort is return after jumping, which means calling the function and interrupt or, more generally speaking, calling subroutines. Under this condition, after finishing executing subroutines, we have to return to the next line of calling instruction to go on executing.

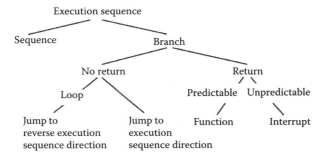

Figure 9.5 Program execution sequence.

The precondition to return to the next line of call instruction is to make sure that "it can return to the next line of calling instruction." So it needs to save the state of the execution of call instruction, which is the so-called site protection and which, in essence, is to protect the values of relative registers, which are the flags of the running state of the CPU and memory. When the call is over and site is restored, the next line of call instruction will be returned to go on running. In this view, there are many parts alike between interrupt and function. But for program designers, the difference between them is whether it is predictable or not, which leads to the huge difference in playing.

Call instructions of function are written by program designers, and they are predictable to program designers and protection actions of function calls. The interrupt technique was originally invented to solve IO problems of peripheral hardware, and later the software interrupt occurred, which imitated the interrupt of the hardware and used similar methods. In short, interrupt is unpredictable to the operating system, and there may be a new event cutting in that disturbs the original execution sequence at any time under the condition that the original execution sequence is unpredictable; therefore, it's called "interrupt."

As the appearance of interrupt is unpredictable, the task of protecting the site can't be finished by programmers and can only be finished by the CPU hardware, which, in fact, equals "call by hardware." Recall the codes talked about in Chapter 2 below:

```
//directory of code:kernel/fork.c
int copy_process(int nr,long ebp,long edi,long esi,long gs,long none,
            long ebx,long ecx,long edx,
            long fs,long es,long ds,
            long eip,long cs,long eflags,long esp,long ss)
```

Parameters in the last line "long eip, long cs, long eflags, long esp, and long ss" can't find parameter passing before calling. It can't find the code of parameter passing and doesn't see any action of pushing or turning other data into stack whether it's original code or disassembling code, but it can work properly, which is indeed puzzling. Because the call of copy process comes from interrupt 0x80, and the five parameters are pushed by the CPU hardware. Attention, the sequence of the five parameters is the same as the sequence of the push of the CPU hardware introduced in the manual of Intel IA-32. This is the characteristic of interrupt. After the interrupt service routine is finished, what will be done is "hardware's ret," iret.

I just want to mention that there is another characteristic hidden in the process of interrupt execution we talked about previously, which is the great difference between interrupt call and ordinary call. It seems that the ordinary call slips smoothly down to the called position along the memory address, which is not right for interrupt. Interrupt seems to be independent of memory. It flips to another position of the interrupt service routine in memory through the CPU hardware.

This characteristic of ordinary call is no problem to the common program but is fatal to the writing operating system, which is the underlying system software. When the user wants to use the code of the kernel's system call, the ordinary call could be used to realize it, which means the user program can visit the operating system kernel at will and may modify and even cover it if the call can visit, which will severely betray the master–slave mechanism and will lead to the chaos of the whole system.

The characteristic of which the interrupt "flips" to the interrupt service routine through the CPU hardware has caught the attention of the operating system designers. When interrupt "flips" through the CPU hardware, the designers of the CPU hardware take this opportunity to make the CPU flip the privilege level of all segments, which makes interrupt become the ladder of the flips between the user privilege level and the kernel privilege level. Besides, the interrupt technique has another important characteristic, which lets the hardware signal cut in directly. From the view of schedule of OS, the most important is timer interrupt.

Reliable process scheduling will be unimaginable if there is no timer interrupt. If so, the operating system could only be designed to consult the right of using the CPU with the user process, wait for the user process to return the right to use the CPU voluntarily.

It is completely different with the timer interrupt in the hardware. Timer interrupt is just like a scepter in the hand of the operating system kernel, which is the symbol of royalty and will never consult with process. It will forcibly chop off the process execution sequence, recapture the right to use the CPU, and perform the master privilege once time is up, which reflects the master–slave mechanism.

9.4 Decisive Factor in Establishing the Master–Slave Mechanism: The Initiative

So far, the master–slave mechanism seems to have been well expressed, and there is a problem that remains unexplained. For the same CPU and instruction set, both the user program and the operating system are programs, but why are the instructions that the operating system kernel program uses not available for the user program? The answer may be that the privilege level of the kernel is higher than the user program's. If further asked, why can the kernel program obtain the high privilege level but the user program can't?

We think that the key point is the initiative!

When the computer boot starts up, the mode is real, and it doesn't have the concept of privilege level. When the operating system kernel starts loading, under normal circumstances, at this time, there is no other programs except BIOS and OS. When the start-up procedures of the operating system opens PE, the privilege level must be the highest privilege level. Otherwise, some parts of the instructions can never be used forever.

This is a very important moment! The operating system designer is to make use of the most favorable time, trade time for privilege, forcibly occupy all the privilege, make full use of the privilege, and create processes. Because all the processes are created by the operating system directly or indirectly, the operating system has the sufficient conditions and chances to lower the privilege level of user process. Once the privilege level of the process has been lowered, it couldn't turn over unless the design of the operating system program code has some mistakes, which raise the privilege level of the process. Obviously, the designer of OS will carefully examine these mistakes and seriously test, finally, avoid any these mistakes. If the code of the operating system has no mistake like this, once process is created, it will never obtain the kernel privilege level and be the slave all its life long. Thus, it can be seen that controlling the initiative makes a decisive role in the master–slave mechanism of the operating system.

Conversely, some malicious programs whose time is later in entering the computer than the operating system will try to use all the available bugs in the operating system design, regain the initiative, and grab the initiative. And once they grasp the opportunities, immediately these malicious programs can obtain the highest privilege level and do whatever they want. There is a certain type of virus program, which uses an operating system bug and tries to stay to the system boot sector of the hard disk, even the BIOS, through this point. According to the principle the front part of the book explains, you can understand that BIOS and the hard disk system boot sector program are prior to the operating system in getting into the memory, so this type of virus program is prior to the operating system in getting into the memory. And once they grab the initiative, they will obtain the highest privilege level, and the operating system will have trouble.

9.5 Relationship between Software and Hardware

A computer can be divided into the host, which includes the CPU, memory, bus, and the peripherals, which include the hard disk, floppy drive, CD-ROM, display, and network card except the host. Because the software programming cannot control the bus directly, we can only pay attention to the CPU and memory in the host.

The host's work is an arithmetic operation, and the peripherals' are data inputting and outputting, data saving during power-off.

Fundamentally, the aim of using a computer is to solve the user's operation problems, whose direct embodiment is the user application. From the view of the operating system, the running user application is the user process. It can be said that the user process represents the user's arithmetic operation.

The user operation needs the support of the peripherals. First, the application and the data to be dealt with need to be input into the host by the peripherals, such as the keyboard, the hard disk, and the network, and go on to the arithmetic operation. The results of the operation need to be output by the display, the printer, and the other peripherals, furthermore, saving and transferring of data during power-off by hard disk, etc. Take the hard disk as an example; as we all know, the data stored on it can be mapped to the files by the operating system. We can expand the concept of the files further from the data on the peripheral extended to the peripheral itself, such as the keyboard, the display, which can also be expanded to the character device file. The files, in this view, embody using the peripherals by user.

We first explain the process in detail, then the file.

9.5.1 Nonuser Process: Process 0, Process 1, Shell Process

First, we can think about a problem, that is, the operating system should have the user interface, namely the so-called shell. For Linux 0.11, the function of shell undertakes by the shell process but not the operating system kernel itself. Obviously, shell is one of the operation system functions. But why is it undertaken by the process and not by the kernel?

After thinking about it carefully, we can find that, if the Linux operating system is only used for a personal computer, the shell can be undertaken by the kernel seemingly. Considering Linux's huge development space in the server field, the server operating system has more demands for multishell; thus, it is better for the process to undertake the shell than the kernel.

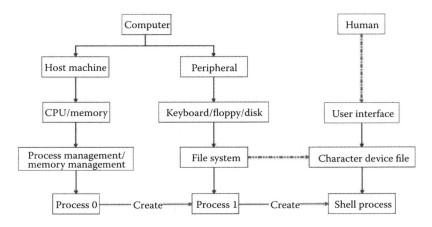

Figure 9.6 Diagram of the relationship between process and hardware.

However, the process of undertaking the shell cannot be the normal user, obviously. For example, if the shell is undertaken by a "Go program", obviously this is not appropriate. The "Go program" itself is an application and needs to be loaded by the shell. If the "Go program" itself becomes the shell, it would be strange that there is a "Go program" that can't quit in the operating system all the time. It will be more terrible if the "Go program" can quit because once the "Go program" ends up and exits, the operating system will have no shell. The operating system without the shell will be useless, and then what's the value of the operating system?

Thus, it can be seen that the shell must be a special process correspondingly designed for the operating system, which can't quit from the beginning of accepting the user's using to shutdown.

The essence of the shell is the user interface program controlling the display, the keyboard, etc., which are all peripherals. The mechanism of creating processes in a Linux operating system is that the parent process creates the child processes, from which we can infer a conclusion that the father process of the shell must have the ability to use peripherals and the available peripheral environment, and the father process is the process like process 1. Peripherals must be controlled by the host, so all processes must have the ability to work in the host. From this, we can infer the father process of the process 1 should be like process 0.

Now, we can see more clearly that the creation of the process 0, process 1, shell process explained in Chapters 2, 3, 4, which embodies the host, peripherals, and special peripherals, the user interface. The three parts are also exactly three components of the computer macroscopic constitution. Thus, it can be seen that the partition of the three processes has a profound meaning. If the three processes merge into one, the structure cannot be indicated clearly. Figure 9.6 expresses the corresponding hardware of process 0, process 1, and process shell.

9.5.2 Storage of File and Data

From the content of the front chapters, it is not difficult to find that although the quantity of the code the file system involves is the biggest and almost accounts for half of the total;

the file system is the easiest to understand relatively. Take the hard disk as an example, the file maps the data stored on the disk whose storage space is very large and much bigger than the memory's. But in the final analysis, the file is also the data storage, and the hard disk can be seen as the computer's data storehouse. Although the steps of storage work are multifarious, they can be much easier than the operation work. And the reason why they are complex is mainly that the hard disk storage space is very large and "the fragment mapping into the fragment." If we use the simple management method, the quantity of data that needs to be managed is very large, and the data in this part not only occupies the space of the hard disk but also doesn't belong to the user data. In order to decrease the amount of the data like this in the space of the hard disk and manage the biggest amount of user data with the least amount of management data, the designers of the operating system put forward a set of management structures with super block, i node, logic block bitmap, i node bitmap, etc. And the structure also involves the process, which makes the file system become very complex. But, in general, the file represents the stored data (and also the equipment), which is more simple than the arithmetic operation.

9.5.2.1 Memory, Hard Disk, Buffer: Computing Storage, Storing Storage, Transition State Storage

The memory is in the host while the hard disk is in the peripheral. On the surface, the function of them is stored, but why are they divided by the host and the peripheral? It is often said that the memory with the fast speed, high price, the small capacity and cannot store the data once power-off while the hard disk and the memory are complementary.

We can further ask that, if the only difference is the function of data storage without power, why do we use two modes that are completely different from each other to manage them? The operating system manages the memory with process, page, privilege level, table, etc. (a lot of complex data structure), and the hard disk is managed with file, i node, bitmap, block, etc., which has a big difference.

The CPU is completely different from the memory in its appearance. In fact, they must be united to complete the most important job, computing, in the computer. That is, computing happens between the CPU and the memory, which means that computing happens in the host and can't be completed only with the CPU. Both the CPU computing instructions and the computing results are stored in the memory. Not only that, but complex computing work can't be finished by one instruction and needs a complex algorithm arranged in the memory. For example, we can transfer a complicated arithmetic operation to a reverse-polish notation and get the algorithm in the memory by the stack operation. Thus, the CPU and the memory operate together and get the computing results finally. In this process, it is hard to deny that the memory is also involved in the "calculation." The memory, which has not only the storing function but also the computing function, is computing level storage. Now look at the hard disk. Although it also has the storing function, little signs of computing can be seen. So it is a very pure storage device and the storage level storage.

Computing level storage has the computing function, which the storing level storage doesn't have. Because computing is more complex than storing, computing level storage has more management information naturally. For example, to the file management and the i node, the file management information in the memory has more fields than the file management information in the hard disk. The file management information in the hard disk is used for storing, and only need to ensure find the correct result without error. But the file management information in the memory is very different. Besides these requirements, it has to execute the search operation, which is computing itself, so the file management information in the memory has the "computing" meaning. While the file management information in the hard disk is really a simple kind of data "accounting library." The hard disk doesn't execute the search computing, which happens in the host, so the hard disk doesn't need extra computing management information.

Let us see the computing by standing higher. It can be seen that the computing, which discussed here, can be classified in two classes: One is the user process computing, namely the user program computing, and another is the kernel computing for running the file system, which has no direct relationship with the user process computing. In order to see clearly, we call the memory participating in the user process as the full-computing storage, the memory participating in computing the kernel for running the file system as semi-computing storage, and the memory, which completely simulates the peripheral and has no computing operation as the noncomputing storage.

When we have the concept of full-computing storage, semi-computing storage, and noncomputing storage, we can understand another concept: the buffer.

The buffer in the memory is a kind of transition state between the full-computing storage and noncomputing storage. And in the operation process of files, for example, the operations of searching for an item in the directory file is finished in the buffer. Because its specific operation is the string-comparison, the process must be the computing process. However, these operations are obviously not the user program operation, so the buffer belongs to the semicomputing storage.

Examining the memory by this view, we can find the file system management structure in the memory, such as "super block management table," "i node management table" (which are residents in the kernel data area in the memory), "logical block bitmap," "i node bitmap," (which are residents in the buffer) etc., which serves the semicomputing obviously, in the memory. We can call the memory space (in the kernel data area or buffer) the management structure occupies as a joint name: the special file system buffer. Compared with the normal buffer, we can clearly know that the two buffers are controlled and operated by the kernel. The buffer is normally aimed at the process while the special file system buffer is aimed at the file system.

Conversely, if the two buffers do not exist, the data in the peripherals data will interact with the memory directly, and the operating system would have to do computing operations such as searching for the file system in the full-computing storage space in which the user process itself should compute. Stirring the full-computing with the semicomputing together is really in chaos. What's worse, the full-computing of the user process is based on the code of the user program, and the semicomputing of the operating system is based on the code of the operating system kernel. The processing data that the kernel code and the user code operated is in the memory space belongs to the user process, which goes against the master–slave mechanism.

Moreover, another function of the buffer is sharing. If a file has been read into buffer by one process and other processes need to read the same file, the file in the buffer can be shared. If there is no buffer existing, every process can only read its files, which may generate multiple copies of the same file in the memory. That is to say, there is only one copy in the memory shared by the buffer.

Examining the Ramdisk with the concept, we can easily find that the Ramdisk is the simple simulating peripheral in the memory. The characteristic of the memory space is noncomputing, which maps the peripherals, such as the floppy disk, not the file. No matter how much the data stored in the floppy disk, even 1k, the whole floppy disk should be mapped, which wastes the memory space obviously. And because the Ramdisk is noncomputing storage, it has to be transferred through the semicomputing when it is used by the user process. Thus, we should avoid the noncomputing memory.

9.5.2.2 Guiding Ideology of Designing Buffer

When designs the operating system buffer, you should ensure the correctness of multiple processes read/write and that the efficiency is as high as possible. The speed of data interaction in the memory is approximately two to three orders of magnitude faster than the speed of data interaction between the memory and the hard disk. The buffer is in the memory, and from the perspective of data flow, the buffer is between the process and the hard disk. In order to meet the requirements of correctness and efficiency, the guiding ideology of the designing buffer is to 1) make the data read/write in order, and 2) make the data stay in the buffer as long as possible and try to use the data that can be used in the buffer. If the buffer really doesn't have the data the user process needs, then the data should be read from the hard disk to the buffer. The design related to the buffer in the operating system reflects the guiding ideology directly or indirectly.

In order to realize the guiding ideology of designing, Linux 0.11 designed a set of data that includes hash_table, b_count, b_lock, b_dirt, *b_data, b_dev, b_blocknr, b_uptodate, b_wait, etc. and relevant functions.

The *b_data is used to point to the buffer block, which has data interaction with the process, and b_dev and b_blocknr are respectively used to assign the device id and the block id ("hard disk block" for short) of a data block. This coupling of buffer block and hard disk block are linked to hash_table, forming the binding relationship, and so on; hash_table would bind all the hard disk block and corresponding buffer block that need read/write, forming the management relationship showed in Figure 9.7.

When the user process reads/writes files, it does not necessarily read/write all the data in the file. The operating system decides which hard disk block to operate through the analysis of files and identifies it with b_dev and b_blocknr. In order to maximize the

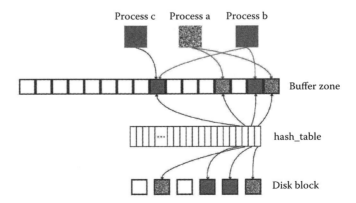

Figure 9.7 Corresponding image of management relationship of buffer, hash table, hard disk data block.

reusability of the buffer block data, after the tasks of files reading/writing are completed, the data in the buffer block corresponding to the hard disk will not be cleared immediately. Thus, when executing the new read/write task, the operating system will search it in the hash_table with buffer management structure first, and compare the recording of the hard disk block of buffer block with the hard disk in the operating system needing, to check whether they are same. As long as they are same, it turns out that the hard disk data that need to be operated do not need to read the disk in all likelihood. According to the guiding ideology that tries to use the data in the buffer as much as possible, use the existing data as much as possible.

However, the two fields, b_dev and b_blocknr, matching with each other can only show that the buffer includes the buffer block corresponding to the hard disk block that the operating system needs to operate, and it does not mean that the data in the buffer block can be used because the data in the buffer block may be invalid. For example, the content of a file has been deleted, and the data in the file's "surviving" buffer block remains, but it can't be reused.

To solve the problem, the operating system sets up b_uptodate. If the value of b_uptodate is 1, this shows the data in the buffer block is valid, and the disk doesn't need to be read. And if the value is 0, the data is invalid and cannot be used directly. The new data has to be read from the hard disk block, and then the buffer block can be used. B_uptodate is important for the read operation. When the data in the hard disk block is read to the buffer block, the interrupt service handler of the operating system sets b_uptodate as 1, which indicates the data in the buffer block is valid now. When a new buffer block is applied, b_uptodate is set as 0, indicating the data in the buffer block is invalid.

In the view of the operating system, the user process writing the data to the disk is really that the operating system writes the data of the user process to the buffer. And the operating system decides when the data in the buffer really writes to the hard disk. That is to say, the user process writing data to the disk contains two steps: first, the operating system writes the user data to the buffer, and the data stays in it as long as possible to be reused. Second, the operating system writes to the disk at the right moment. Usually, the two steps are not continuously executed and may have a pause. In order to make the data in the buffer synchronize efficiently when the operating system pauses and avoid the unnecessary synchronization, b_dirt, whose function is to identify the changed data when the operating system writes the user process data to the buffer block previously, is designed. It sets its value to 1, indicating that the data that is managed in the buffer block needs to be synchronous with the data on the hard disk. After all the data in the buffer block is consistent with the data in the hard disk, the field is set to 0.

Please notice that the write operation is different from the read operation. If the operation is read and the buffer block has no ready-made data, then the data should be read from the hard disk block and be read immediately because the user is still waiting for the use of the data. And the write operation is different. The user process does not know that the so-called writing disk is just writing the data to the buffer block, and the operating system decides when the data synchronizes with the data in the hard disk discretionarily. Before the synchronization work, even if the value of b_dirt is 1, going on writing the data to the buffer block is also feasible. In the future, the operating system only makes the final data synchronous, which reflects the guiding ideology of the designing buffer.

In order to ensure the correctness of the reading/writing data, it must ensure that the data is read in order. For example, the new data can't be written to the buffer block while the data is synchronizing between the buffer block and the hard disk. B_lock has the identification function. Before the data in the buffer is synchronized, the buffer block must be locked; namely b_lock is equal to 1. When the operating system kernel sees the identification, it will not write the data from the process to the buffer block. So in the synchronization procedure, the data in the buffer block will not be changed, ensuring the data consistency between the buffer block and the hard disk before the synchronization operation is done. That is to say, reading/writing the buffer block and the data synchronization operation can't be done at the same time. When b_lock is set to 0, only the data interaction between process and the buffer block is permitted by operating system. And when b_lock is set to 1, only the data interaction between the buffer block and the hard disk is permitted. So the simultaneous operations can be avoided.

When the buffer block is locked, it is possible that other processes need to do data interaction with the locked buffer block. Because the operating system prohibits data interactions between any process and the locked buffer block, the operating system can only suspend the process, switch to another process, and use *b_wait to point at the suspended process in order to wake up the suspended process after the buffer block is unlocked. When the number of the processes that need data interactions with the locked buffer block is more than one, *b_wait points at the last process applying for the data interaction with the locked buffer block and the other processes form an implicit queue, which is shown in Figure 9.8. And the waiting queue is shown on the top left corner.

When a process needs data interaction with the hard disk, the operating system first goes through the management structure hash table of the buffer. And if it finds the ready-made buffer block from the hash table, even if it is being used by another process, then using the ready-made comes first so long as the data is valid. Using the ready-made is more convenient than operating the hard disk because data does not need to be read from the hard disk block. If the ready-made can't be found, then applying for a free buffer block is needed. B_count is the identification of whether the buffer block is free. Actually, several

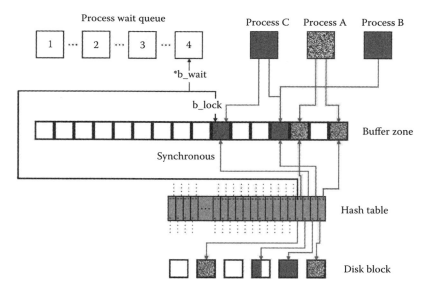

Figure 9.8 State diagram of the multiprocesses accessing the device.

processes may put forward applications and need to exchange data with the same buffer block. And when a process putting forward application is added, b_count adds 1, conversely sub 1. If the result is reduced to 0, which shows that the buffer block has not been referenced, then the buffer block is free.

With these measures, the data consistency between the user process and the hard disk can be ensured in system, and efficiency as high as possible can be realized.

Below we will explain another connection between the file system and the process: pipe.

9.5.2.3 Use the File System to Implement Interprocess Communication: Pipe

Pipe, which is for interprocess communication and remains in the memory, should follow the policy of memory management. It is strange that the pipe's management style is not the memory's but the file system's. Why?

The guiding ideology of designing the process management is to make the processes fully independent and isolated with each other. The design of protected mode is based on this idea. Interprocess communication means the data needs to flow across the process border. And if the way of direct interaction is adopted, it will violate the design guiding ideology obviously. What can we do to make the data flow across the process border reasonably and realize the interprocess communication without damaging the protection from the operating system for processes.

After careful analysis, we can find that, for processes, file is a kind of resource every process can access. That is to say, the file can be shared by the processes. If the data needs to be transmitted between the processes, take the files as its transfer station, and multiple processes access one file at the same time. Some of the processes write the data, and some read the data, realizing the interprocess data transmission. This not only satisfies the ideology of the independence and isolation but also realizes the function of the communication between processes. However, file represents peripheral and the speed of communication between the CPU and peripheral is two or three magnitudes slower than the speed between the CPU and memory. Because the operating system can virtualize a floppy disk in the memory, it can also virtualize the file. In the memory a file is virtualized for interprocess communication, and this is the pipe. Because the operating system has the pipe, which not only gets the file as the interprocess communication transfer station, but it also gets the speed of memory level. Because the pipe derives from the file, its management style is like the file's. This is the reason why the pipe is managed by the file system.

▌ 9.6 Parent and Child Processes Sharing Page

When the parent process creates the child process, the operating system first copies all the management data structure of the parent to the child. Before the child loads its code, it shares the parent's code. And the child cuts off the sharing relationship with the parent's code after it loads its own code. Why doesn't the child cut off the relationship at the moment of its being created?

Because the child, at this time, does not have any code itself, and the work of loading its own code also needs code that only the parent has according to the Linux rules. So if the child could not share the parent's code, it would not finish the work of loading its own code.

The mechanism of sharing the parent's code provides conveniences to many server programs. Because the parent code sharing is permitted, the child should be permitted to execute the parent code completely, thus, it must face the situation that the parent and child use the same code and data and result in data corruption possibly. To avoid the situation, the page write protected mechanism, whose technical details are explained in Section 6.4.2. The design guiding ideology of the page write protected mechanism is to avoid the data corruption that multiple processes accessing the sharing data brings. And so on, for all the data corruption introduced by accessing the sharing data (including the memory's and the peripheral's); the basic ideas of solving problems like this are similar.

■ 9.7 Operating System's Global Interrupt and the Process's Local Interrupt: Signal

Previously, we mentioned interrupt many times. For the operating system, the importance of interrupt cannot be overemphasized. Below, we continue extending along the interrupt's technology route and analyze the relationship between interrupt and TASK_INTERRUPTIBLE, TASK_UNINTERRUPTIBLE.

In Chapter 1 of this book, use the "cli" instruction to disable interrupt has been mentioned. We know that cli can prevent the operating system receiving the interrupt signal, which is equal to disable the interrupt of the whole system.

Even though TASK_INTERRUPTIBLE and TASK_UNINTERRUPTIBLE contain the characters of interrupt, the relationship between them and interrupt in normal sense can't be seen.

Through following the track of using TASK_INTERRUPTIBLE and TASK_UNINTERRUPTIBLE, we can find that signal is closely related to them. Why do the parameters related to signal have a name related to interrupt?

From reviewing the interrupt technology, we can know that the initial motivation of interrupt technology invention is to avoid the operating system's active polling to the IO states of the peripherals and wasting of host resources. Interrupt technology changes the operating system's active polling to passive response, reducing the cost of host resources greatly and improving the operating efficiency.

Comparing and analyzing interrupt and signal, it can be seen that signal obviously imitates the technology route of interrupt. Changing active polling to passive response between processes reduces the operating system cost of communication between processes and enhances the whole running efficiency. For example, the shell process creates a child process, and if the child process exits, theoretically, the management structure of the child process should be released by shell, which is the subsequent work for the exiting of the child. The problem is how shell knows the child process wants to exit? It is easy to think about a method that is to inquire the child process if it wants to exit. If shell has created dozens of child processes, according to this method, it has to periodically poll every process to know whether the child wants to exit. And no matter how many child processes are wanting to exit, even zero, shell has to poll the child processes frequently for dealing with the exiting of the child processes in a timely manner. This is very like the situation in which the host frequently polls the peripheral IO before interrupt technology is invented. The designer of the operating system designs the signal simulating interrupt by referring

Interrupt	Signal
cli	TASK_UNINTERRUPTIBLE
sti	TASK_INTERRUPTIBLE
IDT, interrupt vector	Sigaction
Interrupt service routine	Signal service handler
......	......

Figure 9.9 Diagram of comparing interrupt with signal.

to the interrupt technology route. We can easily find that the technology routes of them are very similar by comparing them. Their relationship is shown in Figure 9.9.

It can be found that symmetry is obvious, and they are highly comparable. The difference is that interrupt is aimed at the operating system while the signal is aimed at the process. We can even consider the normal interrupt as a "global interrupt" and the signal as a "local interrupt," which you can see the essence of it clearly. The reader can understand and master signal, TASK_UNINTERRUPTIBLE, TASK_INTERRUPTIBLE by using comparison.

9.8 Summary

So far, we have already seen the content of the operating system design guiding ideology in this chapter. However, an operating system is very complex, and only depending on the content of this chapter is not enough to design an operating system that can be used. But the content of this chapter is enough to help readers fully understand and master the operating system in the perspective of the designer of the operating system.

Conclusion

Now it is the end of this book; glad to see you here. According to our many years of teaching experience, seeing you here shows that your knowledge of the operating system will not be looked down upon because the operating system is too complex for most readers to stick it out. If you are still feeling fully enjoyable, return to the start, and read it again!

Index

Page numbers followed by f indicate figures.